MOVIE
facts and feats
A GUINNESS RECORD BOOK

MOVIE
facts and feats

A GUINNESS RECORD BOOK

Patrick Robertson

Sterling Publishing Co., Inc. New York

GUINNESS FAMILY OF BOOKS

Air Facts and Feats
Animal Facts and Feats
Antique Firearms
Antiques
Art Facts and Feats
Astronomy Facts and Feats
Bicycling
Boating Facts and Feats
Car Facts and Feats
English Furniture 1760-1900
English Pottery and Porcelain
Equestrianism
Golf Facts and Feats
Grand Prix Motor Racing
History of Air Warfare
History of Land Warfare
History of Sea Warfare
Motorboating Facts and Feats
Motorcycling
Motorcycling Facts and Feats
Mountains and Mountaineering Facts and Feats
Movie Facts and Feats
Music Facts and Feats
Rail Facts and Feats
Soccer Facts and Feats
Steeplechasing
Tank Facts and Feats
Towers, Bridges and Other Structures
Weather Facts and Feats

CONTENTS

ACKNOWLEDGEMENTS

The author gratefully acknowledges the help he has received from the following individuals and organisations:

The American Society of Cinematographers; Archiva Naţionalǎ de Filme, Bucharest; Al Archive al Kawmy Lil-Film, Cairo; The Barnes Museum of Cinematography, St Ives; John Baxter; Lord Bernstein; Blackburn District Central Library; Stephen Bottomley; British Board of Film Censors; British Film Institute; Brooklyn Public Library; Bundesstaatliche Hauptstelle für Lichtbild und Bildungsfilm, Vienna; Canadian National Film Archives; Centre Algerien de la Cinématographie; Centre National de la Cinématographie, Paris; Československy Filmový Archiv; Cheshire Libraries and Museums Department; Cinema Papers (Australia); The Cinema Organ Society; Cinemateca de Cuba; Cinemateca Nacional Venezuela; Cinemateca Uruguaya; Cinema Theatre Association; Cinema Veterans (1903); Cineplex Corporation, Toronto; Colne Library & Museum; Columbus Public Library; Compania Cinematografica Nacionale, Chile; Geoff R. Crambie; Edward Craig ('Edward Carrick'); Det Danske Filmmuseum; Deutsches Institut für Filmkunde; Deutsches Museum, Munich; B.V. Dharap, Humberto Didonet; Motion Picture Enterprises, Poona; Eastman Kodak Co.; Monday Ellis; Embrafilme; Patricia Erens; Michel do Espírito Santo; Filmmuseum Amsterdam; Filmoteca Nacional de España; Filmoteca Polska; Ford Archives, Dearborn; Fundacao Cinemateca Braileira; Fundacion Cinemateca Argentina; G.C.C. Theatres Inc.; General State Establishment for Cinema & Theatre, Iraq; Ghana Film Industry Corporation; Denis Gifford; Gosfilmokond, Moscow; Harvard Lampoon; Edith Head; Hungarofilm; Ilford Ltd; Imax Systems Corporation, Ontario; Instituto Nacional do Cinema, Brazil; Instituto Português de Cinema; Islington Central Library; Japan Film Library Council; Lionel Jones; Det Kongelige Bibliotek, Copenhagen; Miles Monroe Kreuger; Liam O'Leary Film Archives, Dublin; Locare Motion Picture Research Group; Christopher Lowder; Macau Centro de Informacâo; Magyar Filmtudományi Intézetés Filmarchivum; Hameeduddin Mahmood; Movietone; Museo Nazionale del Cinema, Turin; National Association of Theatre Owners, New York; National Diet Library, Tokyo; National Film Archive, Australia; National Film Development Corporation, Pakistan; National Film Library, New Zealand; Nelson District Central Library; Dido Nicholson; Kemp R. Niver; Nordisk Films Kompagni; Norsk Filminstitutt; Osterreichisches Filmarchiv; Osterreichisches Filmmuseum; Osterreichisches Kulturinstitut, London; Araken Campos Pereira Jr; Andrew Pike; Polish Cultural Institute, London; Pusat Perfilman H. Usmar Ismail, Indonesia; Quigley Publications; Radio City Music Hall; Mrs Eric Reade; T.K.H. Robertson; David Robinson; Kevin Rockett; The Royal Film Archive of Belgium; Dr Barry Salt; Silvana Sammassimo; Caio Scheiby; Sinema-TV Enstitüsü, Istanbul; Singapore Board of Film Censors; Société Anonyme Tunisiènne de Production et d'Expansion Cinematographique; The Society of Motion Picture & Television Engineers; South African National Film Archives; Clive Sowry; Staatliches Filmarchiv der Deutsches Demokratischen Republik; Statisches Budesamt, Wiesbaden; Stiftung Deutsche Kinemathek, Berlin; Stratford Shakespearean Festival Foundation of Canada; Sri Lanka State Film Corporation; Suomen Elokuvasäätiö; Svenska Filminstitutet; Technicolor Inc.; Thai Motion Picture Producers Association; Bruce T. Torrence; Twentieth Century-Fox International Corporation; United Artists; United Methodist Church, Nashville, Te; U.S. Department of Commerce; Universal City Studios; University of Iowa; Variety; Vereniging der Kinemabestuurders van Belgie VKBB v.z.w.; Walter N. Vernon; Alex Viany; Dr Hans Vogt; Mrs Audrey Wadowska; Wakaaladda Filimmada Soomaaliyeed; Walt Disney Productions; Herman Weinberg; Western Costume Co., Los Angeles; The White House, Washington; Will Rogers Memorial, Claremore, Okla.

In addition to the acknowledgement above, I wish to record special thanks to the Librarian and staff of the British Film Institute Information Department, who have put both their resources and their uncommon expertise at my disposal, and have provided a large number of illustrations for the book. While many national archives throughout the world have been forthcoming with information, I would like to pay special tribute to two other film institutes which have particularly impressed me with their efficiency and commitment – those of Hungary and Indonesia.

I would also like to express gratitude for his fine work to my researcher, Stephen Bottomore; and to my wife Karla for her enthusiasm and forbearance during the four years it took to compile this book.

Most books on films are concerned about quality – the cinema as art. This book is unashamedly about *quantity* – together with 'firsts', records, oddities, remarkable achievements, historic landmarks and the wilder extravagances of the motion picture business during the eighty years of its colourful history.

This is not the place to seek potted biographies of favourite stars or great directors, but it does offer a gamut of film facts, ranging from the significant to the absurd, many of which have never appeared in any film book before. For the historically minded there are old orthodoxies explored and often rejected – Who really 'invented' the close-up? What was the first western? Where did full-length feature films begin? Hollywood receives due attention, of course, as the centre of world film production, but many other countries – no less than 80 in all – have been approached for information. There is something about each of them, including a chart which records, for the first time, the number of features made each year by every film producing nation since the earliest days (pp. 26–9).

Devotees of Dracula will find a complete filmography; Shakespeare buffs a listing of all 39 versions of Hamlet, including the four in which the Prince was played by a woman; film fans may read about other film fans, including Queen Victoria, Hitler and James Earl Carter. (And if you want to know who has played Carter in a movie – that's here too, together with all the other portrayals of US Presidents.) Records range from the largest and smallest cinema theatres, the longest career in movies, the biggest cast (187000) and the most remakes to the heaviest actress, the last silent picture and the longest and shortest film titles. And the poor relations of cinema are not neglected either – did you know that both home movies and advertising films were already in existence in the 1890s?

Wherever I have provided lists – for example, all the people who have played themselves in movies, or stars who finished their careers as extras, or movies that last longer than *Gone With the Wind* – I have tried to make them complete. That is, of course, a challenge to readers to prove that they are *not* complete. Supplementary information will be very gratefully received and considered for future editions. Notable facts absent from this edition (because after five years' research I have been unable to track them down) are: the first 'coming next week' film trailer; the director who has directed the most movies; and the oldest cinema theatre in the world. Somebody out there must know the answers. Could it be you?

CHAPTER 1

FADE IN

The first motion picture films were taken with a camera patented in Britain by French-born Louis Aimé Augustin Le Prince (1842–90?) in November 1888. Two fragments survive: one taken at a speed of 10–12 frames per second early in October 1888 in the garden of his father-in-law, Mr Joseph Whitley, at Roundhay, Leeds; the other taken at 20 frames per second later in the month and showing traffic crossing Leeds Bridge. According to Le Prince's mechanic, James Longley, the latter film was shown on a projector incorporating a Maltese cross for intermittent picture shift. He claimed that the image obtained was sufficiently clear for smoke to be visible rising from the pipe of a lounger on the bridge. Both films were made on sensitised paper rolls $2\frac{1}{8}$ in wide and it was not until a year later that Le Prince was able to obtain Eastman celluloid roll film, which had just been introduced into Britain. This provided a far more suitable support material and it seems likely that the inventor was able to start the commercial development of his motion picture process by the beginning of 1890. A new projector was built so that a demonstration could be given before M. Mobisson, the Secretary of the Paris Opera. On 16 September 1890 Le Prince boarded a train at Dijon bound for Paris with his apparatus and films. He never arrived. No trace of his body or his equipment was ever found and after exhaustive enquiries the police were unable to offer any rational explanation of his disappearance. The mystery has never been solved.

The first commercially developed motion picture process was instigated by Thomas Alva Edison (1847–1931), American electrical engineer. His initial attempt to produce an illusion of movement, by means of an apparatus called the 'optical phonograph', resulted in failure, and in January 1889 Edison assigned William Kennedy

The Le Prince camera of 1888

Laurie Dickson (1860–1935), an assistant at his laboratories in West Orange, NJ, to work on the development of what was to become the Kinetoscope, a film-viewing machine designed for use in amusement arcades. Dickson, the French-born son of English parents, had early training as a photographer and was better suited to this kind of research than his mentor, who knew little of optics. Abandoning the use of rectangular sheets of celluloid for camera work, he substituted 50 ft lengths of celluloid film produced by the firm of Merwin Hulbert. These long rolls were first purchased on 18 March 1891, which is the earliest date at which it seems likely that Dickson could have made successful films for viewing in the peep-show Kinetoscope apparatus.

The first public demonstration of motion pictures took place at the Edison Laboratories at West Orange, NJ, on 22 May 1891, when 147 representatives of the National Federation of Women's Clubs, having lunched with Mrs Edison at Glenmont, were taken over her husband's workshops and allowed to view the new Kinetoscope. The New York *Sun* reported:

The surprised and pleased clubwomen saw a small pine box standing on the floor. There were some wheels and belts near the box, and a workman who had them in charge. In the top of the box was a hole perhaps an inch in diameter. As they looked through the hole they saw the picture of a man. It was a most marvellous picture. It bowed and smiled and waved its hands and took off its hat with the most perfect naturalness and grace. Every motion was perfect...

The film used for this demonstration appears to have been taken with a horizontal-feed camera without sprockets. This would have been an imperfect apparatus at best, and not until October 1892 is there evidence that William Dickson had built an effective vertical-feed camera using perforated film. In that month the *Phonogram* published an illustration showing sequences from four films evidently taken with such a device. These included pictures of Dickson himself, together with his helper, William Heise, and also shots of wrestling and fencing. By this date, then, it can be positively asserted that Dickson had overcome all the

The earliest known motion picture film —
Traffic Crossing Leeds Bridge (GB 88)

obstacles that had stood in the way of making films suitable for commercial exhibition. He was to receive little thanks for his work. After Dickson left West Orange in 1895, following a dispute with his employer, Edison steadfastly refused to concede that anyone but himself was responsible for bringing the invention to fruition. Most historians were content to accept Edison's own version of events until the appearance in 1961 of a painstaking work of scholarship titled *The Edison Motion Picture Myth*. The author, Gordon Hendricks, demonstrates by reference to hitherto unpublished papers in the Edison archives that all the experimental work on the Kinetoscope was conducted by Dickson, or under his direction, and that Edison himself can be credited with little more than instigating the research programme and providing facilities for carrying it out.

The practical development of motion pictures in Britain can be dated from the construction of a camera by Birt Acres (1854–1918) and R.W. Paul (1869–1943) at the latter's optical instrument works in Saffron Hill. Paul's interest in films had been aroused the previous October, when he was approached by a Greek showman, George Trajedis, with a request to manufacture some Edison Kinetoscopes. This Paul agreed to do on learning that Edison had omitted to patent the machine in Britain. Since Edison's agents understandably refused to sell films for the pirated machines, Paul approached Acres with the suggestion that they should construct a camera together (later each claimed to have been the only begetter of the apparatus) so that they could make their own Kinetoscope subjects, Acres to be the cameraman. Using film obtained from the American Celluloid Co. of Newark, NJ, Acres tried out the camera for the first time with a scene of a cricketer (his assistant Henry Short) coming out of Acres' home in Barnet, Clovelly Cottage. This was followed by what Paul described as 'our first saleable film', *The Oxford and Cambridge University Boat Race*, which was premièred in a Kinetoscope at the India Exhibition, Earl's Court on 27 May 1896. This film, together with *The Derby* and *The Opening of the Kiel Canal* (cf. News Film), formed the first programme presented on screen in Britain since Le Prince's experiments, when Acres gave a private show with his Kineopticon

Clovelly Cottage, Barnet 1895

projector in a coach-house at Wrotham Cottage, Barnet in August 1895. Acres was also the first to give a public screening (*see* below), while Paul became the first manufacturer of projectors (q.v.) and Britain's pioneer film producer.

The first commercial presentation of motion pictures took place at Holland Bros' Kinetoscope Parlor, 1155 Broadway, New York, which opened for business on 14 April 1894. The Kinetoscopes were arranged in two rows of five, and for 25c viewers were allowed to watch five films – to see the whole programme they had to pay double entrance money. The first day's take of $120 suggests that this first 'cinema audience' totalled nearly 500. The films, made in the Edison 'Black Maria' (*see* Film Studio, p. 151) at West Orange, were titled: *Sandow, Bertholdi (mouth support), Horse Shoeing, Bertholdi (table contortion), Barber Shop, Blacksmiths, Cock Fight, Highland Dance, Wrestling, Trapeze.*

The first commercial presentation of films in Britain took place at the kinetoscope parlour opened by the Continental Commerce Co. of New York at 70 Oxford Street, London, on 18 October 1894. The twelve machines offered such titillating delights as *Carmencita* (a buxom vaudeville artiste) and *Annabelle Serpentine*

Dance, as well as more prosaic fare like *Blacksmith Shop*, *Wrestling Match* and *The Bar Room*.

The first film presented publicly on screen was *La Sortie des Ouvriers de l'Usine Lumière* (Fr 94) which was shown before members of the Société d'Encouragement a l'Industrie Nationale by Auguste and Louis Lumière at 44 rue de Rennes, Paris, on 22 March 1895. Believed to have been taken in August or September 1894, the film showed workers leaving the Lumière photographic factory at Lyons for their dinner-hour.

The first public screening in Britain was given by Birt Acres at the London headquarters of the Royal Photographic Society, 14 Hanover Square, on 14 January 1896. The programme, comprised of films taken by Acres himself, consisted of *The Opening of the Kiel Canal*, *The Derby*, *Boxers*, *Three Skirt Dancers* and *Rough Seas at Dover*.

The first film to be screened before a paying audience was a four-minute boxing subject, *Young Griffo* v *Battling Charles Barnett*, presented by Major Woodville Latham of the Lamda Co. at 153 Broadway, New York, on 20 May 1895. The projector was a primitive and imperfect machine called the Eidoloscope, designed for the Lamda Co. (the first film company established as such) by former Edison employee Eugene Lauste. Although some authorities have cast doubt on the Eidoloscope's ability to create an illusion of movement on a screen, it must have achieved a sufficient level of technical acceptability, however jerky and inadequate the picture, for Latham to have attracted paying customers. Another commercial show was given by C. Francis Jenkins and Thomas Armat, using a projector they had designed themselves, at a purpose-built temporary cinema at the Cotton States Exposition at Atlanta, Ga., in September 1895. After making various improvements to the machine, Armat came to an arrangement with Thomas Edison, who had failed to produce a workable projector himself, by which the celebrated inventor would be allowed to exploit it as his own. As the Edison Vitascope, the improved machine was debuted at Koster and Bial's Music Hall on Broadway on 23 April 1896, an occasion which has often and erroneously been heralded as the first time that motion pictures were presented on a screen to a paying audience.

The first screening before a paying audience in Europe was given by Max and Emil Skladanowski with a projector of their own invention at the Berlin Wintergarten on 1 November 1895. The films were made up of endless loops and the action lasted only a few seconds before it was repeated. Taken at the rate of eight pictures a second, the films were flickering and jerky, but the fact that there was movement on the screen at all was sufficient for the Nazis to claim, some 40 years later, that Germany was the cradle of the cinema industry. In fact neither the work of Lauste and Latham in America, nor that of the Skladanowskis in Germany, was destined to have any lasting effect on the development of the cinema. It is generally agreed that the première of the Lumière brothers' show, before a paying audience at the Grand Café, 14 Boulevard des Capucines, Paris, on 28 December 1895, marks the debut of the motion picture as a regular entertainment medium. Their projector was the first to advance beyond the experimental stage and the first to be offered for sale.

The first screening before a paying audience in Britain took place at the Regent Street Polytechnic on 20 February 1896, when the French magician Felicien Trewey exhibited the Lumière Cinématographe with accompanying commentary by M. Francis Pochet. Admission was 1s and the engagement lasted three weeks, hours 2–4 p.m. The opening programme included the Lumière films *Arrival of a Train at a Station*, *The Baby and the Goldfish*, *The Family Tea Table* and *M. Trewey: Prestigidateur*. The first commercial show outside London was presented by Birt Acres at Cardiff Town Hall on 5 May 1896.

HOW THE CINEMA SPREAD ROUND THE WORLD

Few inventions have spread more rapidly than cinematography. By the end of 1896, a mere twelve months after the real start of commercial cinema in France, nearly all the major countries of the western world had witnessed their first demonstration of the new art. It is clear from the following chronology that the Lumière Brothers of Lyon were the most positive force in introducing motion pictures to the world. (The designation 'Lumière' below signifies that the programme was made up of Lumière films.) The presentations listed were public shows before a paying audience unless otherwise indicated.

1895

22 March
France: *La Sortie des Ouvriers des l'Usine Lumière* (Fr 94), presented by Louis and Auguste Lumière before the Société d'Encouragement pour l'Industrie Nationale at 44 rue de Rennes, Paris. (see p. 12.)

20 May
United States: *Young Griffo* v *Battling Charles Barnett* (US 95) presented before paying audience at 153 Broadway, New York. (see p. 12.)

1 November
Germany: Eight short films (for subjects, *see* Production: firsts by countries, p. 12) presented by Max and Emil Skladanowski at Berlin Wintergarten.

10 November
Belgium: Lumière programme before invited audience of scientists, etc., in Brussels. First before paying audience at 7 de la Galerie du Roi, Brussels, 1 Mar 1896.

1896

14 January
United Kingdom: Programme (subjects *see* p. 12) presented by Birt Acres before Royal Photographic Society, London. First before paying audience: Lumière programme by F. Trewey at Regent Street Polytechnic, London, 20 Feb 1896.

?? February
Italy: Lumière presented by Vittorio Calcina at the Ospedale di Carita, Turin.

19 March
Austria: Lumière presented by E.J. Dupont at the Graphic Arts Teaching & Research Centre, Vienna.

6 April
Norway: Skladanowski programme presented at Circus Variété, Oslo.

20 April
Ireland: Unidentified programme presented at Star of Erin Variety Theatre, Dublin.

4 May
Russia: Lumière presented by Francis Doublier at Aquarium Theatre, St Petersburg.

9 May
South Africa: R.W. Paul's Theatrograph programme – *Highland Dancers* (GB 96), *Street Scenes in London* (GB 96), *Trilby Dance* (GB 96), *A Military Parade* (GB 96), *The Soldier's Courtship* (GB 96) – presented at Empire Theatre of Varieties, Johannesburg.

10 May
Hungary: Lumière presented at Royal Hotel, Budapest. Included street scenes taken in front of Opera House and Chain Bridge, Budapest, and Hungarian Millenary Procession.

15 May
Spain: Lumière presented by M. Promio at 34 Carrera de San Jeronimo, Madrid.

The movies reach Tokyo – 1897

27 May
Romania: Lumière presented at Salon l'Independenta Romana, Bucharest.

7 June
Yugoslavia (Serbia): Lumière presented at Kod Zlatnog Krsta Café, Belgrade.

7 June
Denmark: Lumière presented by Vilhelm Pacht in Raadhuspladsen, Copenhagen.

9 June
Netherlands: Lumière presented at the Kurhaus, Scheveningen.

18 June
Portugal: Lumière (?) presented by Erwin Rousby at Real Coliseu, Rua da Palma, Lisbon.

28 June
Sweden: Lumière presented by C.V. Roikjer at the Industrial Exhibition, Malmö.

28 June
Finland: Lumière presented at the Societetshuset, Helsinki.

7 July
India: Lumière presented at Watson's Hotel, Bombay.

15 July
Czechoslovakia: Lumière presented at the Lázeňský dům, Karoly Vary.

21 July
Canada: Edison Vitascope programme presented at West End Park, Ottawa.

28 July
Argentina: Lumière presented by Francisco Pastos and Eustaquio Pellier at Colón Theatre, Buenos Aires.

?? July
Brazil: 'Omniographo' presented at 57 Rua do Ouvidor, Rio de Janiero.

11 August
China: French programme (negative evidence suggests *not* Lumière) presented as act of variety show at Hsu Gardens, Shanghai.

15 August
Mexico: Lumière presented by engineering student Salvador Toscano Barragan at 17 Calle de Jesus, Mexico City.

22 August
Australia: R.W. Paul programme presented by conjurer Carl Hertz at Melbourne Opera House.

13 October
New Zealand: R.W. Paul (?) programme of English films presented by Profs Hausmann and Gow at Auckland Opera House.

?? October
Poland: Edison programme presented at Lvov.

Date unknown
Egypt: unidentified programme at Zavani Café, Alexandria.

1897

24 January
Cuba: Lumière presented by Gabriel Veyre at Teatro Tacón, Havana.

28 January
Venezuela: Edison presented by Manuel Trujillo at Teatro Baralt, Maracaibo.

?? June
Japan: Lumière presented by Katsutaro Inahata at Osaka.

25 December
Uruguay: Lumière at Montevideo.

Date unknown
Tunisia: Lumière at store show established by Albert Samama on rue Es-Sadika, Tunis.

1898

Spring
Greece: Lumière at Place Kolokotronis, Athens.

Date unknown
Bulgaria: unidentified programme presented by Frencz Echer in Sofia.

1899

Date unknown
Turkey: unidentified programme presented privately before Sultan by Spaniard Don Ramirez and then publicly at his *Electric Circus*, Constantinople.

1900

30 (?) November
Indonesia: Nederlandsche Bioscope Maatschappij presented at Batavia.

Date unknown
Korea: free film show sponsored by Anglo-American Tobacco Co. of Shanghai. Admission in exchange for cigarette coupons.

Date unknown
Senegal: Lumière presented at Dakar.

Date unknown
Iran: unidentified programme presented before Shah by Mirza Ebrahim Khan at Royal Palace, Teheran. First public show opened in Avenue Cheraq Gaz, Teheran, by Sahâf Bâshi in 1905.

CHAPTER 2

THE INDUSTRY

FEATURE FILMS

The first feature film, according with the Cinématheque Française definition of a feature being a commercially made film of over one hour duration, was Charles Tait's *The Story of the Kelly Gang* (Aus 06), which was 4000 ft (1219 m) long and had a running time of 60–70 min. A biopic of Victoria's notorious bushranger Ned Kelly (1855–80), the film was produced by the theatrical company J. & N. Tait of Melbourne, Victoria, and shot on location over a period of about six months at Whitehorse Road, Mitcham (Glenrowan Hotel scenes, including the last stand of the Kelly Gang); at Rosanna (railway scenes); and on Charles Tait's property at Heidelberg, Vic. (all other scenes). The actual armour which had belonged to Ned Kelly – a bullet-proof helmet and jerkin fashioned from ploughshares – was borrowed from the Victorian Museum and worn by the actor playing the role, an unidentified Canadian from the Bland Holt touring company who disappeared before the film was finished. It had to be completed with an extra standing in as Ned, all these scenes being taken in long shot. Elizabeth Veitch played Kate Kelly, and others in the cast included Ollie Wilson, Frank Mills, Bella Cole and Vera Linden.

Made on a budget of £450, *The Story of the Kelly Gang* was premièred at the Athenaeum Hall, Melbourne, on 24 December 1906 and recovered its cost within a week, eventually grossing some £25000, including receipts from the English release. No complete print survives, but stills from the film were issued as picture postcards and give the impression of a vigorous, all-action drama made with imaginative use of outdoor locations – a significant advance on the studio-bound one-reelers being turned out in Europe and America at this period. It was long believed that the film had been totally lost, but recently a 210ft (64m) long fragment was discovered in Melbourne. Other versions of the Ned Kelly story survive. There were remakes in 1910, 1917, 1920, 1923, 1934, 1951 and 1970, all of them Australian productions except the last, a British film with Mick Jagger in the title role.

Australia was the only country in the world to have established regular production of feature-length films prior to 1911. For figures on early output, see Production: World Output (p. 26).

The first feature-length film made in Europe was Michel Carré's 90-minute long production *L'Enfant prodigue* (Fr 07), premièred at the Théâtre des Variétés in the Boulevard Montmartre, Paris, on 20 June 1907. This was a straightforward screen representation of a stage play, with little or no attempt at adaptation.

The first European feature film scripted for the screen was a four-reel version of *Les Misérables* (Fr 09), produced by Pathé from the novel by Victor Hugo.

The first feature film exhibited in the United Kingdom was Charles Tait's *The Story of the Kelly Gang* (Aus 06), which had its British

première at the Assembly Rooms, Bath, in January 1908. The film was released by the Colonial Picture Combine.

The first feature film produced in the United Kingdom was Thomas Bentley's *Oliver Twist* (GB 12), a Hepworth production in four reels starring ex-beauty queen Ivy Millais as Oliver Twist, Alma Taylor as Nancy and John McMahon as Fagin. It was released in August 1912, two months after Vitagraph's version in America (*see* below).

The first feature film produced in the United States was Vitagraph's four-reel production of *Les Misérables* (US 09), released in separate one-reel parts between 18 September and 27 November 1909. Charles Kent's Vitagraph production of *The Life of Moses* (US 09), in five reels, was also released in separate parts (4 December 1909–19 February 1910) because the producers did not consider that the American public were prepared to sit through a film that lasted over an hour. The first feature film to be released in its entirety in the USA was *Dante's Inferno* (It 11) in August 1911. *Queen Elizabeth* (Fr 12), which is nearly always cited as the first feature film shown in America, was in fact the third, because in the meantime the first domestic feature-length production to be shown whole had been released. This was *Oliver Twist* (US 12), produced by H.A. Spanuth and starring Nat C. Goodwin and Winnie Burns, which was premièred on 1 June 1912, nearly six weeks before *Queen Elizabeth* (12 July 1912). However, the prejudice against long films was so insistent in America (at least amongst producers and distributors) that even in 1913 the major European success of that year, August Blom's feature *Atlantis* (Den 13), had to be compressed into a half-length version for US release. Domestic production was a modest two in 1912 and 12 in 1913, the real watershed being in 1914, when no less than 212 features were produced. The delay in going over to feature-film making suggests that the impact of *Queen Elizabeth's* successful exploitation by Adolph Zukor in 1912 may not have been so influential as his-

Left: The world's first feature film – *The Story of the Kelly Gang* (Aus 06)

torians of the cinema have generally believed. Competition from the major European film-producing nations, most of whom had a two-year lead on America in feature production (*see* below), may in fact have been the deciding factor.

THE FIRST 12 FEATURE FILMS PRODUCED IN THE USA

Release Date	Title	Length (reels)	Production Co.
June 1912	*Oliver Twist*	5	H. A. Spanuth
Dec 1912	*The Beloved Vagabond*	6	Gold Rooster
Jan 1913	*Cleopatra*	6	United States Film Co.
Jan 1913	*From the Manger to the Cross*	6	Kalem
Aug 1913	*Moths*	5	Thanhouser
Aug 1913	*Arizona*	6	All Star Feature Corp.
Oct 1913	*In the Bishop's Carriage*	5	Famous Players
Nov 1913	*The Count of Monte Cristo*	5	Famous Players
Nov 1913	*Traffic in Souls*	6	Imp
Dec 1913	*The Sea-Wolf*	7	Bosworth
Dec 1913	*Ten Nights in a Bar-room*	5	Photo Drama
Dec 1913	*Hoodman Blind*	5	Pilot

It is worthy of note that neither Cecil B. De Mille's *The Squaw Man* (US 14) nor D.W. Griffith's *Judith of Bethulia* (US 14), each of which has been cited as the first feature-length film produced in the US, appears in the above list.

THE FIRST 12 FEATURE FILMS PRODUCED IN THE UK

Release Date	Title	Length (reels)	Production Co.
Aug 1912	*Oliver Twist*	4	Hepworth
Dec 1912	*Lorna Doone*	5	Clarendon
May 1913	*East Lynne*	6	Barker
July 1913	*The Battle of Waterloo*	5	British & Colonial
July 1913	*Ivanhoe*	6	Zenith Films
July 1913	*A Message from Mars*	4	United Kingdom Films
Aug 1913	*David Copperfield*	8	Hepworth
Sept 1913	*King Charles*	4	Clarendon
Sept 1913	*A Cigarette-Maker's Romance*	4	Hepworth
Sept 1913	*The House of Temperley*	5	London Films
Oct 1913	*The Grip*	4	Britannic Films
Oct 1913	*Hamlet*	6	Hepworth

Countries producing feature films by 1914: By the outbreak of World War I, the following countries had commenced feature-film production (alphabetically by year of first feature production). For the title of the first feature-length movie produced in each country, *see* under Production: Film Producing Nations, pp. 18–25.

1906: Australia
1909: France

Mary Pickford was the first major star to appear in feature-length productions. *In the Bishop's Carriage* (US 13) marked her feature debut

1911: Denmark, Germany, Italy, Poland, Russia, Spain
1912: Austria, Greece, Hungary, Japan, Norway, Romania, United Kingdom, United States
1913: Brazil, Finland, India, Sweden, Venezuela
1914: Canada

PRODUCTION

Film Producing Nations

The following list chronicles, wherever known, the first motion picture production, the first dramatised (ie acted) production, the first feature film (over one hour duration) and the first talkie feature of each of the film-producing countries of the world, signified by the abbreviations Film, Drama, Feature, Talkie. The first feature film in natural colour is included for

Cecil Mannering as Steerforth and Amy Verity as Little Emily in *David Copperfield* (GB 13). It was Britain's first eight-reeler, running for nearly two hours

major film-producing nations. The first motion picture production means a film made by a native or permanent resident of the country, as opposed to a visiting cameraman or non-resident producer. Where a category has been omitted no information is available. Drama/Feature and Feature/Talkie signify respectively that the first feature-length film was also the first dramatic production of any length and that the first talkie was also the first feature-length production.

Other abbreviations: doc. = documentary; f. = filmed; d. = directed; pr. = première; prod. = produced.

ALGERIA
Film: *La Prière du muezzin* (1906), d. Felix Mesguich. Drama: *Ali Bouf a l'huile* (1907), d. Felix Mesguich. Feature/Talkie: *Peuple en marche* (1963), d. Ahmed Rachedi and René Vautier.

ANGOLA
Film: *Monangambé* (1968), d. Sarah Maldoror. Feature/Talkie: *Des fusils pour Banta* (1970), d. Sarah Maldoror.

ARGENTINA
Film: *La Bandera Argentina* (1897), d. Eugenio Py. Drama: *El Fusilamiento de Dorrego* (1908), d. Mario Gallo and Salvador Rosich. Feature: *Nobleza Gaucha* (1915), d. Humberto Cairo. Talkie: *Muñequitas porteñas* (1931), with Maria Turguenova – Vitaphone system.

AUSTRALIA
Film: *The Melbourne Cup* (3 Nov 1896), d. Marius Sestier. Drama: *Soldiers of the Cross* (pr. 13 Sept 1900), d. Herbert Booth of the Salvation Army. Feature: *The Story of the Kelly Gang* (pr. 26 Dec 1906), d. Charles Tait. (NB: **First feature film** (q.v.) **in world**.) Talkie: *Fellers* (press shown 23 May 1930), d. Arthur Higgins and Austin Fay, prod. Artaus Films, starring Arthur Tauchert.

AUSTRIA
Drama: *Ein Walzertraum* (scene from opera) f. 2 Mar 1907. Feature: *Zweierlei Blut* (1912), starring Luise Kohn and Jakob Fleck. Talkie: *G'schichten aus der Steiermark* (pr. 23 Aug 1929), d. Hans Otto Löwenstein, prod. Eagle Film and Ottoton Film, starring Hilde Maria and Anny Burg.

BANGLADESH
Feature/Talkie: *Mukh O Mukhosh* (1956), d. Jabbar Khan.

BELGIUM
Film: *Le Marché aux poissons de Bruxelles* (1897) and other actualities, d. M. Alexandre. Drama: *'chand d'habits* (1897), d. M. Alexandre. Feature: *Belgique meurtrie* (1920), d. Paul Flon. Talkie: *La Famille Klepkens* (1930), d. Gaston Schoukens and Paul Flon.

BOLIVIA
Film: actualities by Luis Castillo, 1913. Feature: *La Profecia del Lago* (1923), d. José Maria Velasco Maidana (film banned). Talkie: *La Guerra del Chaco* (1936), d. José Luis Bazoberry.

BRAZIL
Film: *View of Guanabara Bay* (f. 19 July 1898), d. Alfonso Segreto. Drama: *Os Estranguladores* (1906) – crime film based on true story in police files, d. Isaac Sandenberg. Feature: *O Crime dos Banhados* (1913), d. Francisco Santos, prod. Guarany Film. Talkie: *Acabaram-se os Otarios* (1930), country comedy d. Luis de Barros, starring Genésio Arruda and Tom Bill.

BULGARIA
Film: actuality about Bulgarian army, 1910. Drama: *Such is the War* (1914). Feature: *The Bulgar is a Gentleman* (1915), satire about Sofia snobbery, d. Vassil Guendov, starring ditto and Mara Lipina. Talkie: *A Song of the Balkan Mountains* (1934), d. Peter Stoychev.

BURMA
Feature: *Dana Pratap* (1925), prod. London Art Photo Co. of Rangoon. Talkie: *Nihon no Musume* (1935).

CAMEROON
Film: *L'Aventure en France* (1962), d. Jean-Paul N'Gassa. Feature/Talkie (doc.): *Une Nation est née* (1972). Feature/Talkie (drama): *Pousse-pousse* (1975), d. Daniel Karawa.

CANADA
Film: actualities of life on the prairies made by James Freer of Brandon, Manitoba, 1897. Drama: *The Great Unknown* (1913), d. Oscar Lund, starring Barbara

Canada's first full-length feature film – *Evangeline* (Can 14)

Tennent and Fred Truesdell. Feature: *Evangeline* (1914), d. E.P. Sullivan and W.H. Cavanaugh, prod. Canadian Bioscope Co., starring Laura Lyman and John F. Carleton. Talkie (English): *North of '49* (1929), d. Neal Hart, prod. British Canadian Pictures. Talkie (French): *A la croisée des chemins* (1943), d. and starring Paul Guévrement. Colour: *Talbot of Canada* (1938), Kodachrome.

CHILE
Feature: *La Baraja de la muerte* (1916), d. Salvador Giambastiane. Talkie: *Norte y Sur* (1934), d. Jorge Délano.

CHINA
Film/Drama: *Tingchun Mountain* (1908), d. Lin Ten-lun of the Feng Tai Photo Shop, Peking, starring Tan Hsin-pei. Feature: *Yen Rei-sun* (1921), about embezzler who murders prostitute, d. Ren Pun-yen, prod. China Film Research Society, starring Chun Tso-Tze and Wang Tsai-yun. Talkie: *Singsong Girl Red Peony* (1930), d. Chang Shih-chuan, prod. Star Film Co., starring Butterfly Wu.

COLOMBIA
Film/Drama: *The Life of General Rafael Uribe* (1914), d. brothers Di Domenico. Feature: *La Maria* (1922), d. Alfredo Del Diestro. Talkie: *Flowers of the Valley* (1939), d. Pedro Moreno Garzón.

CONGO
Film: *Kayako* (c.1967), d. Sébastien Kamba. Feature/Talkie: *La Rançon d'une alliance* (1973), d. Sébastien Kamba.

CUBA
El Brujo desapareciendo (1898), d. José E. Casasús. Drama: *El Cabildo de ña Romualda* (1908), d. Enrique Diaz Quesada, prod. Metropolitan Films. Feature: *El Rey de los campos de Cuba* (1913), d. Enrique Diaz Quesada, starring Gerardo Artecona and Evangelina Adams. Talkie: *El Caballero de Max* (1930), d. Jaime San-Andrews, starring Nancy Norton and Wilfredo Genier – Vitaphone. (The Cuban government had made a sound-on-film documentary by the Phonofilm process in 1926.)

CZECHOSLOVAKIA
Film/Drama: *Vystavni Parkar a Lepic Plakatu* (1898), *Dostavenicko Ve Mlynici* (1898), *Pláč a Smich* (1898), etc., actualities and short comedies featuring Bohemian cabaret artiste Josef Šváb-Malostranský, d. Prague student Jan Kříženecký. Feature: *Pražští Adamité* (1917), d. Antonin Fencl, prod. Lucemafilm, starring Josef Vošalik. Talkie (Czech): *Tonka of the Gallows* (1930), d. Karel Anton. *Talkie* (Slovak): *The Singing Land* (1932), d. Karel Plicka. Colour: *Jan Roháč of Duba* (1947), d. Vladamir Borský.

DAHOMEY (BENIN)
Film: *Ganvié, mon village* (1966), d. Pascal Abikanlou.

Feature/Talkie: *Sous le signe du Vaudoun* (1974), d. Pascal Abikanlou.

DENMARK
Film: *Kørsel med grønlandske Hunde* (1896), d. Peter Elfelt. Drama: *Henrettelsen* (1903), d. Peter Elfelt, starring Francesca Nathansen and Victor Betzonich. Feature: *Den sorte Drøm* (pr. 4 Sept 1911), circus drama d. Urban Gad, starring Valdemar Psilander and Asta Nielsen. Talkie: *Eskimo* (pr. 9 Oct 1930), d. G. Schneevogt, starring Mona Martenson and Paul Richter. Colour: *Tricks* (pr. 7 May 1956), d. Erik Balling.

ECUADOR
Feature/Talkie: *Se Conocieron en Guayaquil* (1949), d. Alberto Sanatana, prod. Ecuador Sono Films.

EGYPT
Film: *Dans les rues d'Alexandrie* (1912), d. M. de Lagarne. Drama: *Sharaf el Badawi* (1918), prod. Italo-Egyptian Cinematographic Co. Feature: *Koubla Fil Sahara'a* (1927), d. Ibrahim Lama, prod. Condor Film. (NB: Shooting on *Laila* (1927), generally credited as first Egyptian feature, started earlier, but the film was released later.) Talkie: *Onchoudet el Fouad* (pr. 14 Apr 1932), d. Mario Volpi.

FINLAND
Film: *Pupils of Nikolai Street School during Break* (1904). Drama: *Salaviinanpolttajat* (1907), d. Louis Sparre, starring Teuvo Puro and Jussi Snellman. Feature: *Kun Onni Pettää* (pr. 23 Nov 1913), d. Konrad Tallroth, starring Axel Precht and Sigrid Precht. Talkie: *The Log-Driver's Bride* (1931), d. Erkki Karu.

FRANCE
Film: *La Sortie des Usines* (1894), d. Louis Lumière. Drama: *L'Arroseur arrosé* (1895), d. Louis Lumière, starring Lumière's gardener M. Clerc and apprentice boy Duval. Feature: *L'Enfant prodigue* (pr. 20 June 1907), d. Michel Carré. Talkie: *Les Trois masques* (1929), d. André Hugon, prod. Pathé-Natan, starring Renée Heribel and Marcel Vibert. Colour: *L'Eternal amour* (1921), d. Gaston Colombani in Héraute Colour.

GABON
Film: *M'Bolo Gabon* (1967). Feature/Talkie: *Où vas-tu Koumba* (1971), d. Alain Ferrari and Simon Auré.

GERMANY
Films: Italian Dance, Kangaroo Boxer, Juggler, Acrobats, Russian Dance, Serpentine Dance, *Lutte, Apothéose* (all pr. 1 Nov 1895), d. Max and Emil Skladanowsky. Feature: *In dem grossen Augenblick* (pr. 11 Aug 1911), d. Urban Gad, prod. Deutsche Bioscop GmbH, starring Asta Nielsen and Hugo Hink. Talkie: *Melodie der Welt* (pr. 12 Mar 1929), d. Walter

A scene from Czechoslovakia's first feature film, *Prăzští Adamité* (1917)

Ruttman, starring J. Kowal Samborsky and Renée Stobrawa.

GHANA
Drama: Amenu's Child (1949), d. Sean Graham. Feature/Talkie: *Boy Kumasenu* (1951), d. Sean Graham.

GREECE
Film: Olympic Games actuality (1906). Drama: *Quo Vadis Spiridion* (1911), comedy d. Spiros Dimitracopoulos, prod. Athina Films. Feature: *Golfo* (1912), d. Costas Bahatoris from Spiros Peressiadis' folk-story play. Talkie: *Les Apaches d'Athenes* (1930), musical d. D. Gaziadis, prod. Dag Films, starring Mary Sayannou and Petros Epitropakis.

GUATEMALA
Feature/Talkie: *El Sombreron* (1950).

GUINEA
Film: *Mouramani Mamadou Touré* (1953). Feature/Talkie: *Sergent Bakary Woolén* (1966), d. Lamine Akin.

GUYANA
Feature/Talkie: *Aggro Seizeman* (1975), d. James Mannas and Brian Stuart-Young, starring Gordon Case and Martha Gonsalves.

HONG KONG
Dramas: *The Widowed Empress, The Unfilial Son, Revealed by the Pot, Stealing the Cooked Ducks* (all 1909), d. Benjamin Polaski, prod. Asia Film Co.

HUNGARY
Film: *The Emperor Franz Josef opening the Millenial Exhibition* (1896), d. Arnold Sziklay. Drama: *Siófoki kaland* (pr. 29 Apr 1898) – shown as sequence in stage production *Mozgáfényképek/Moving Pictures*. Feature: *Ma és holnap* (1912), d. Mihály Kertész (Michael Curtiz). Talkie: *A Kék Bálvány* (pr. 25 Sept 1931), d. Lajos Lázár, starring Pál Jávor. Colour: *Ludas Matyi* (1949), d. K. Nádasdy.

ICELAND
Feature/Talkie: *Milli fjalls og fjöru* (1948), d. Loftur Gudmundsson.

INDIA
Film: *Cocoanut Fair* (1897), maker unknown, probably English. First by Indian: *The Wrestlers* (f. Nov 1899),

d. Harishchandra S. Bhatvadekar of Bombay. Drama: *Pundalik* (pr. 18 May 1912), d. R.G. Torney. Feature: *Raja Harischandra* (pr. 17 May 1913), d. D.G. Phalke of Bombay. Talkie (Hindi): *Alam Ara* (pr. 14 Mar 1931), d. A.M. Irani, prod. Imperial Film Co., starring Master Vithal and Zubeida. Talkie (Bengali): *Jamai Sasthi* (1931), prod. Madan Theatres. Colour: *Kisan Kanya* (1937), d. Moti B. Gidwani, prod. Imperial Film Co. – Cinecolor.

INDONESIA
Feature: *Loetoeng Kasaroeng* (1927), d. G. Kruger at Bandung. Talkie: *Njai Dasima* (1931), d. Lie Tek Soi and Bakhtiar Effendi, prod. Tan's Film.

IRAN
Film: Scenes of religious procession and of Shah's private zoo, d. Mirza Ebrahim Khan (Court Photographer to Shah Mozaffareddin) 1900. Drama/Feature: *Abi and Rabi* (1932), comedy d. Ohanian. Talkie: *Dokhta Lor* (1934), d. Abdol Hoseyn Sepenta.

IRAQ
Drama/Feature/Talkie: *Leila in Iraq* (1949).

IRELAND
Drama: *Fun at Finglas Fair* (1915), d. F.J. McCormick. Never released, as all prints destroyed in Easter Rising. Feature: *Knocknagow* (1918), d. Fred O'Donovan, prod. Film Co. of Ireland, starring Fred O'Donovan and Kathleen Murphy, featuring Master Cyril Cusack in screen debut. Talkie (English): *The Voice of Ireland* (1932), d. Col Victor Haddick. Talkie (Irish): *see* Languages: Irish Gaelic (p. 170).

ISRAEL
Feature: *Oded Hanoded* (1933), d. Nathan Axelrod. Talkie: *Me'al Hekhoravot* (1936), d. Nathan Axelrod.

ITALY
Film: *Arrivo del treno stazione di Milano* (1896), d. Italo Pacchioni. Drama: *La Presa di Roma* (1905), d. Filoteo Albernini, starring Carlo Rosaspina. Feature: *La Portatrice di pane* (1911), d. S. De Montépin, prod. Vesuvio Films, Naples. Talkie: *La Canzone dell' amore* (1930), d. Genarro Righelli. Colour: *Toto a colori* (1952) – Ferraniacolor.

IVORY COAST
Film: *Sur la dune de la solitude* (1964), d. Timité Bassori. Feature/Talkie: *Korogo* (1964), d. Georges Keita.

JAMAICA
Feature/Talkie: *The Harder They Come* (1972), d. Perry Henzell, starring Jimmy Cliff and Janet Bartley.

JAPAN
Film: Street scenes in Tokyo's Ginza and shots of geisha from Shimbasi and Gion districts, d. Tsunekichi Shibata of the Mitsukoshi Department Store's photo dept., 1897. Drama: *Momiji-gari* (1897), Noh drama d. Tsunekichi Shibata, starring Kikugoro V and Danjuro IX. Feature: *The Life Story of Tasuke Shiobara* (1912). Talkie: *Taii no Musume* (1929), prod. Nikkatsu Co. Colour: *Karumen Kokyo ni Kaeru* (1951).

JORDAN
Feature/Talkie: *Watani Habibi* (1964).

KOREA
Drama: *The Righteous Revenge* (1919), d. Kim Do-san. Feature: *A Pledge in the Moonlight* (1923), morality tale about importance of keeping money in banks, d. Yun Paek-nam. Talkie: *Chun Hyang-jon* (1939), d. Yi Pil-u and Yi Myong-u.

KUWAIT
Feature/Talkie: *Bas Ya Bahar* (1972), d. Khaled el Seddik, starring Mohamad Monsour and Amal Baker.

LEBANON
Drama/Feature: *The Adventures of Elias Mabrouk* (1929), comedy about Lebanese emigrant returning from USA, d. Jordano Pidutti. Talkie: *In the Ruins of Ba'albak* (1936), d. George Costi, prod. Lumnar Film Co.

LIBYA
Feature/Talkie: *Lorsque le destin s'acharne* (1972), d. A. Zarrouk.

MADAGASCAR
Film: Centenary celebrations of martyrdom of Malagasy hero Rasalama, d. M. Raberono 1937. Feature/Talkie: *Le Retour* (1973), d. Randrasana Ignace Solo.

MALAYSIA (Malaya)
Talkie: *Chandu* (1939), prod. Malayan Films Inc.

MALI
Feature/Talkie: *Les Wandyalankas* (1973), d. Alkaly Kaba.

MALTA
Feature/Talkie: *Katarin* (1977), d. Cecil Satariano, starring Anna Stafrace.

MAURITANIA
Feature/Talkie: *Soleil O* (1971), d. Med Hondo.

MEXICO
Drama: *Don Juan Tenorio* (1898), d. Salvador Toxano Barragan. Feature: *Fatal Orgullo* (1916), prod. México Lux. Talkie: *Más fuerte que el deber* (1930), d. Raphael J. Sevilla. Colour: *Novillero* (1936), d. Boris Maicon – Cine-color.

MOROCCO
Feature/Talkie: *Itto* (1934), d. Jean Benoit-Levy.

NEPAL
Feature/Talkie: *Harischandra* (1951).

NETHERLANDS
Drama: *The Misadventures of a Small French Gentleman without Trousers in Zandvoort* (1902), d. Albert and Willy Mullens. Talkie: *Vader des Vaderlands* (1933), d. G.J. Teunissen.

NEW ZEALAND
Film: *Opening of the Auckland Exhibition* (f. 1 Dec 1898), d. A.E. Whitehouse. Drama: *A Message from Mars* (1903), d. W.F. Brown. Feature: *The Test* (1916), d. and starring Rawdon Blandford. Talkie: *Down on the Farm* (1935), d. Lee Hill and Stuart Pitt, prod. Sound Film Productions Ltd.

NIGER
Film: *Aouré* (1962), d. Mustapha Allasane. Feature/Talkie: *FVVA* (1971), d. Mustapha Allasane.

NIGERIA
Drama: *My Father's Burden* (1961), d. Segun Olusola. Feature/Talkie: *Two Men and a Goat* (1966), d. Edward Jones Horatio.

NORWAY
Film: Reception of the newly-elected King Haakon VII in Oslo, 1905. Drama: *The Dangerous Life of a Fisherman* (1907), prod. Norsk Kinematograf A/S, starring Alma Lund. Feature: *Anny – Story of a Prostitute* (1912), d. Adam Eriksen, starring Julie Jansen. Talkie: *The Great Christening* (pr. 26 Dec 1931).

OUTER MONGOLIA
Feature/Talkie: *At the Frontier* (1937).

PAKISTAN
Feature/Talkie: *Teri Yaad* (1948), prod. Dewan Pictures, d. Dawood Chand, starring Asha Posley and Nasir Khan. Urdu.

PERU
Film: *Peruvian Centaurs* (1908), actuality of cavalry manoeuvres.

PHILIPPINES
Film: *El Fusilamiento de Rizal*. Feature: *Dalagang Bukid* (1919), d. Jose Nepomuceno. Talkie: *Punyal na Ginto*.

POLAND
Film: actualities made by Kazimierz Proszynski with a camera of his own invention – the 'pleograph' – 1894. Drama: *His First Visit to Warsaw* (1908), comedy starring Antoni Fertner. Feature: *Dzieje Grzechu* (pr. 26 Aug 1911), d. Antoni Bednarczyk, starring Maria Mirska and Teodor Roland. Talkie: *The Morals of Madame Dulska* (1930), d. B. Newolyn.

PORTUGAL
Film: *Leaving the Factory* (1896), d. Aurelio Da Paz Dos Reis. Drama: *Rapto duma Actriz* (1907), d. Lino Ferreira, starring Carlos Leal and Luz Velozo. Feature: *A Rosa do Adro* (1919). Talkie: *A Severa* (pr 17 June 1931), d. Jose Leitao de Barros, prod. Super-Filmes, starring Dina Teresa and Conde Marialava.

ROMANIA
Film: actuality 10 May 1897 by Paul Menu. Drama: *Amor fatal* (pr. 26 Sept 1911), d. Grigore Brezeanu, starring Lucia Sturdza and Tony Bulandra. Feature: *Războiul Independentei* (pr. 1 Sept 1912), d. Grigore Brezeanu, starring C. Nottra and Ar. Demetriade. Talkie: *Ciuleandra* (pr. 30 Oct 1930), d. Martin Berger, starring Jeana Popovici-Voinea.

SENEGAL
Film: *C'était il y a 4 ans* (1955), d. Paulin Vieyra. Feature/Talkie: *La Noire de . . .* (1967), d. Ousmane Sembène.

SINGAPORE
Feature/Talkie: *White Golden Dragon* (1936).

SOMALIA
Film/Drama: *The Love that Knows no Barrier* (1961), d. Hossein Manrok. Feature/Talkie: *Town and Village* (1968), d. El Hadji Mohamed Giumale.

SOUTH AFRICA
Film: Scene taken from front of tram travelling down Commissioner Street, Johannesburg, d. Edgar Hyman, 1896. Drama: *The Star of the South* (1911), about theft of diamond found on banks of Vaal by a Hottentot, prod. Springbok Film Co. Feature: *De Voortrekkers* (pr. 16 Dec 1916), d. Harold Shaw, prod. African Film Productions Ltd, starring Dick Cruickshanks and Zulu actor Goba as Dingaan. Claimed (in S. Africa) that *The Covered Wagon* (US 23) was inspired by this film. Talkie (Afrikaans): *Mocdertjie* (1931), d. Joseph Albrecht, starring Carl Ricjter and Joan du Toit. Talkie (English): *They Built a Nation* (1938), d. Joseph Albrecht, prod. African Film Productions Ltd.

SPAIN
Film: *Salida de misa de doce en la Iglesia del Pilar en Zaragoza* (1896), d. Eduardo Jimeno. Drama: *Riña en un Café* (1897), d. Fructuoso Gelabert. Feature: *Lucha por la herencia* (1911), d. Otto Mulhauser, prod. Alhambra Films. Talkie: *Yo quiero que me lleven a Hollywood* (pr. 20 June 1932), d. Edgar Neville. Colour: *En un rincon de España* (1949), d. Jerónimo Mihura.

SRI LANKA
Feature/Talkie: *Banda Nagarayata Pemineema* (1953).

SUDAN
Feature/Talkie: *Hopes and Dreams* (1969), d. Al Rachid Mehdi.

SURINAM
Feature/Talkie: *Wan Pipel* (1976), d. Pim de la Parra, starring Borger Breeveld and Diana Gangaram.

SWEDEN
Film/Drama: *Slagsmål i Gamla Stockholm* (pr. 3 July 1897), two 17th-century cavaliers fighting over a girl, d. Ernest Florman, prod. Numa Handels & Fabriks AB. Feature: *Blodets Röst* (pr. 20 Oct 1913), d. Victor Sjöström, prod. Svenska Biografteatern, starring Victor Sjöström and Ragna Wettergreen. Talkie: *Konstgjorda Svensson* (pr. 14 Oct 1929), d. Gustaf Edgren, prod. Film AB Minerva, starring Fridolf Rhudin and Brita Apelgren.

SWITZERLAND

Films: *Zurcher Sechseläuten-Umzag* (*c.* 1901) and *Montreux Fête des Narcisses* (*c.* 1901), d. Georges Hipleh-Walt. Feature: *Der Bergführer* (1917), d. Eduard Bienz, prod. La Société bâloise EOS. Talkie: *Bünzli's Grosstadtabenteuer* (1930), d. Robert Wohlmut, starring Freddy Scheim.

SYRIA

Drama/Feature: *Al Moutaham al Bari* (1928), gangster movie, d. and starring Ayoub Badri, prod. Hermon Film. Talkie: *Leila Al-Amira* (1947), d. Niazi Mustafa.

TAIWAN

Drama: *The Orphan who Saved his Grandfather* (1922).

THAILAND

Drama/Feature: *Miss Suwan* (1922), d. and prod. Henry McRay and the Wasuvati family. Performers were 'noble families and high-ranking government officials'.

TRINIDAD

Drama: *Callaloo* (1937), starring Ursula Johnson. Feature/Talkie: *The Right and Wrong* (1970), d. Harbance Kumar, prod. De Luxe Films, starring Ralph Maharaj and Jesse Macdonald.

TUNISIA

Drama: *Ain el Ghezal* (1924), d. Haydée Samama-Chikly, starring Si Haj Hadi Djeheli. Feature: *The Secret of Fatouma* (1928), d. Dedoncloit, starring Véra de Yourgaince. Talkie: *Majnunal Kairouan* (1937), d. J.A. Creuzi, starring Fliza Chamia and Habib el Manaa.

TURKEY

Film: *Collapse of the Russian Monument in Ayestafanos* (1914), d. Fuat Uzkinay. Drama: *The Wedding of Himmet Aga* (1916). Feature: *Pençe* (1917), d. Sedat

Simavi. Talkie: *Istanbul Sokaklarinda* (1931), d. Muhsin Ertugrul, prod. Ipek Film.

UK

Film: *Traffic Crossing Leeds Bridge* (1888), d. Louis Aimé Augustin Le Prince. Drama: *The Soldier's Courtship* (f. Apr 1896), d. Robert Paul, starring Fred Storey. Feature: *Oliver Twist* (1912), d. Thomas Bentley, prod. Hepworth, starring Ivy Millais and Alma Taylor. Colour feature: *The World, the Flesh and the Devil* (1914), d. F. Martin Thornton, prod. Union Jack Photoplays and Natural Colour Kinematograph Co., starring Frank Esmond. Talkie: *Blackmail* (pr. 21 June 1929), d. Alfred Hitchcock, prod. British International Pictures, starring Anny Ondra and John Longden.

USA

Film: Actualities of fencers and wrestlers etc., d. W.K.L. Dickson, prod. Edison Co., 1892. Drama: *The Execution of Mary Queen of Scots* (f. 28 Aug 1895), d. Alfred Clark, prod. Raff & Gammon and Edison Co., starring Mr R.L. Thomas (as Mary!). Feature: *Oliver Twist* (pr. 1 June 1912), prod. H.A. Spanuth, starring Nat C. Goodwin and Winnie Burns. Colour Feature: *The Gulf Between* (pr. 21 Sept 1917), prod. Technicolor Motion Picture Corp., starring Grace Darmond and Niles Welch. Talkie: *The Jazz Singer* (pr. 6 Oct 1927), d. Alan Crosland, prod. Warner Bros, starring Al Jolson.

USSR

Film: *Cossack Trick Riders* (f. 29 Sept 1896), d. amateur cinematographer A.P. Fedetsky at Kharkov. Drama: *Boris Gudonov* (1907), d. A.O. Drankov, starring F.G. Martini and Z. Lopanskaya. Feature: *Story of Sin* (pr. 15 Nov 1911), d. unknown, prod. S. Mintus of Riga, starring M. Mirskaya and S. Zheromsky. Soviet Feature: *Signal* (1918), d. Alexander Arkatov, prod. Moscow Cinema Committee, starring Grabevetskaya. Talkie: *The Earth Thirsts* (1930), d. Yuli Raizman. Colour: *Nightingale, Little Nightingale* (1936), d. Nikolai Ekk.

UPPER VOLTA

Film: *A Minuit . . . l'Independence* (1960). Feature/Talkie: *Le Sang des parias* (1973), d. Mamadou Djim Kolla.

URUGUAY

Film: *Una Carrera de Ciclismo en el Velodrome de Arroyo Seco* (1898), d. Felix Oliver. Drama: *Oliver, Juncal 108* (1900), d. and starring Felix Oliver. Feature: *Del Pingo al Volante* (1928), d. Roberto Kouri, prod. Bonne Garde. Talkie: *Dos Destinos* (1936), d. Juan Etchebchere, prod. Estudios Ciclolux, starring Pepe Corbi.

VENEZUELA

Film: *Muchachas bañádose en el Lago* (1897) and *Un gran especialista sacando muelas en el Hotel Europa*

Sweden's first talkie – *Konstgjorda Svensson* (Sw 29). It contained an unusual number of outdoor scenes for an early talking picture (*Svenska Filminstitutet*)

(1897), d. Manuel Trujillo Durán at Maracaibo. Drama: *Carnival in Caracas* (1909), d. Augusto Gonzalez Vidal and M.A. Gonham. Feature: *The Lady of Cayenas* (1913), parody of *Camille*, d. E. Zimmerman. Talkie: *El Rompimiento* (1938), d. Antonio Delgado Gomez, starring Rafael Guinard.

VIETNAM

Drama: *Vie du Detham* (1910), biopic of guerilla leader, d. Rene Batisson. Talkie: *Canh dong ma* (1940).

YUGOSLAVIA

Film: *Odhod od mase v Ljutomeru* (1905), made in 17·5mm by Ljutomer lawyer Karl Grossman. Drama/ Feature: *Zivot i Dela Besmrtnog Vožda Karadjordje* (pr. 17 Nov 1911), biopic of 'Immortal Leader Karadjordje', d. I. Stojadinović, starring M. Petrović. Talkie: *Nevinost Bez Zastite* (1942), d. D. Aleksić.

ZAIRE

Feature/Talkie: *La Nièce captive* (1969), d. Luc Michez.

PRODUCTION OUTPUT

Total world output of feature films is nearly 4000 annually. Asian countries (including Australasia) account for approx. 50 per cent of output, European countries (including USSR) for approx. 33 per cent, the Middle East and Africa for approx. 5·5 per cent, North America for approx. 6 per cent, and Latin America for approx. 5·5 per cent.

The country with the largest production output in the world is India, with an estimated 714 full-length feature releases in 1979 and an annual average of 498 during the 1970s.

The twelve major film-producing countries of the 1970s in terms of output were the following (average annual output 1970–79 in brackets): India (495); Japan (367); Italy (204); Turkey (202); France (191); USA (189); Philippines (166); USSR (141); Hong Kong (approx 130); Spain (98); Thailand (98); Pakistan (92).

The following countries have held the production record since the inception of feature films:

1906–11	Australia	1936–38	Japan
1912	Hungary	1939	USA
1913	Germany	1940	Japan
1914–22	USA	1941–53	USA
1922–32	Japan	1954–70	Japan
1933–35	USA	1971–	India

The best year for UK film production was 1936, with 192 features released. The most productive year of the silent era was 1920, with 155 features.

The worst years for UK film production (since 1914) were 1925 and 1926, in each of which only 33 features were released. The worst year of sound pictures was 1979, with 38 releases. On two occasions in the past 60 years, feature-film production in Britain has come to a total halt. There were no films being made during November 1924 and the studios were also empty for a three-week period in 1975.

The best year for US film production was 1921 with 854 feature releases.

The worst year for US film production (since 1913) was 1963 with 121 feature releases.

The highest output of any Hollywood studio was 101 features from Paramount in 1921; highest of the sound era was 68 by Paramount in 1936 and the same number from Warner Bros in 1937.

WORLDWIDE PRODUCTION OF FEATURE FILMS 1906–79

The figures given in the chart on pp. 26–29 refer to feature films of an hour or more in length, including co-productions and feature-length documentaries. TVM's are excluded unless they have had a theatrical release. Production is attributed to the country in which the production company is registered. The figure quoted for any year represents the number of features completed and released.

In addition to the 67 countries listed in the chart, the following have a significant annual output but were excluded because of insufficient data: Burma (approx. 70 p.a.); Iran (pre-revolution 75–100 p.a.); Malaysia (approx. 12 p.a.); Mongolia (approx. 10 p.a.); Taiwan (80–90 p.a.).

Countries with an output of under ten films a year include Afghanistan, Angola, Bolivia, Brunei, Cameroun, Chile, Colombia, Congo, Cyprus, Ecuador, Gabon, Ghana, Guatemala, Guinea, Guyana, Ivory Coast, Jamaica, Jordan, Kuwait, Lebanon, Libya, Mali, Mauritania, Morocco, Niger, Nigeria, Peru, Senegal, Somalia, Surinam, Tanzania, Trinidad, Upper Volta, Sudan, Vietnam. Cambodia had a flourishing film industry until 1975, when the Communist take-over brought production to a halt.

	1906	1907	1908	1909	1910	1911	1912	1913	1914	1915	1916	1917	1918	1919	1920	1921
Algeria	0	0	0	0	0	0	0	0	0	0	0	0	0	0	0	0
Albania	0	0	0	0	0	0	0	0	0	0	0	0	0	0	0	0
Argentina	0	0	0	0	0	0	0	0	0	4	12	16	2	15	5	11
Australia	1	2	0	0	3	16	8	4	3	8	15	6	13	16	10	15
Austria	0	0	0	0	0	0	1	6	9	10	7	9	40	56	48	47
Bangladesh	0	0	0	0	0	0	0	0	0	0	0	0	0	0	0	0
Belgium	0	0	0	0	0	0	0	3	0	0	0	0	0	1	1	7
Brazil	0	0	0	0	0	0	0	2	–	3	6	4	2	6	6	2
Bulgaria	0	0	0	0	0	0	0	0	0	1	0	2	0	0	0	3
Canada[1]	0	0	0	0	0	0	0	0	1	0	3	2	2	2	2	1
China	0	0	0	0	0	0	0	0	0	0	0	0	0	0	0	–
Cuba	0	0	0	0	0	0	0	1	1	1	1	3	1	2	5	8
Czechoslovakia	0	0	0	0	0	0	0	0	0	0	0	1	13	23	17	25
Denmark	0	0	0	0	0	1	2	13	16	24	34	40	21	20	8	10
Egypt	0	0	0	0	0	0	0	0	0	0	0	0	0	0	0	0
Eire	0	0	0	0	0	0	0	0	0	0	0	1	0	0	3	0
Finland	0	0	0	0	0	0	0	1	1	0	1	0	0	0	1	2
France	0	1	0	1	–	–	–	–	–	–	–	–	–	–	–	–
Germany (and W. Ger)	0	0	0	0	0	1	3	49	29	60	107	117	211	345	485	646
Germany East																
Greece	0	0	0	0	0	0	1	0	0	0	1	0	1	0	0	0
Hong Kong	–	–	–	–	–	–	–	–	–	–	–	–	–	–	–	–
Hungary	0	0	0	0	0	0	14	11	19	27	52	77	107	48	54	25
India	0	0	0	0	0	0	0	3	1	0	0	3	7	8	27	44
Indonesia[2]	0	0	0	0	0	0	0	0	0	0	0	0	0	0	0	0
Iraq	0	0	0	0	0	0	0	0	0	0	0	0	0	0	0	0
Israel	0	0	0	0	0	0	0	0	0	0	0	0	0	0	0	0
Italy	0	0	0	0	0	2	5	29	16	39	57	37	46	151	152	56
Japan	0	0	0	0	0	0	2	0	5	3	–	–	–	–	–	–
Korea, South	0	0	0	0	0	0	0	0	0	0	0	0	0	0	0	0
Malaysia	0	0	0	0	0	0	0	0	0	0	0	0	0	0	0	0
Mexico	0	0	0	0	0	0	0	0	0	0	1	11	6	13	7	8
Netherlands	0	0	0	0	0	0	–	–	–	–	–	–	–	1	–	–
New Zealand	0	0	0	0	0	0	0	0	0	0	1	0	0	0	0	0
Norway	0	0	0	0	0	0	1	0	0	0	2	3	3	2	2	3
Pakistan																
Philippines	0	0	0	0	0	0	0	0	0	0	0	–	–	–	–	–
Poland	0	0	0	0	0	3	2	5	5	3	5	7	6	7	8	17
Portugal	0	0	0	0	0	0	0	0	0	0	0	0	0	4	2	3
Romania	0	0	0	0	0	0	1	10	0	0	0	0	0	0	2	1
Singapore	0	0	0	0	0	0	0	0	0	0	0	0	0	0	0	0
South Africa	0	0	0	0	0	0	0	0	0	0	14	7	5	6	4	2
Spain	0	0	0	0	0	–	–	–	–	–	–	–	–	17	12	8
Sri Lanka	0	0	0	0	0	0	0	0	0	0	0	0	0	0	0	0
Sweden	0	0	0	0	0	0	0	4	5	2	4	7	6	11	20	7
Switzerland	0	0	0	0	0	0	0	0	0	0	0	0	–	–	–	–
Thailand	0	0	0	0	0	0	0	0	0	0	0	0	0	0	0	0
Tunisia	0	0	0	0	0	0	0	0	0	0	0	0	0	0	0	1
Turkey[3]	0	0	0	0	0	0	0	0	0	0	0	2	1	3	0	3
United Kingdom	0	0	0	0	0	0	2	18	15	73	107	66	76	122	155	137
United States	0	0	0	0	0	0	2	12	212	419	677	687	841	646	797	854
Uruguay	0	0	0	0	0	0	0	0	0	0	0	0	0	0	1	0
USSR	0	0	0	0	0	1	9	31	17	44	74	57	27	12	8	5
Venezuela	0	0	0	0	0	0	0	1	0	1	0	0	0	0	0	0
Yugoslavia	0	0	0	0	0	1	–	–	–	–	–	–	–	6	–	–

[1] Completions per year   [2] Starts per year   – No data available

1922	1923	1924	1925	1926	1927	1928	1929	1930	1931	1932	1933	1934	1935	1936	1937	1938	1939	1940	1941	1942
0	0	0	0	0	0	0	0	0	0	0	0	0	0	0	0	0	0	0	0	0
0	0	0	0	0	0	0	0	0	0	0	0	0	0	0	0	0	0	0	0	0
10	15	13	15	7	6	6	4	5	4	2	6	6	13	15	28	41	50	49	47	56
7	7	10	9	16	4	13	3	3	6	4	7	9	3	6	5	7	4	3	3	1
64	45	30	24	17	18	19	22	17	9	11	18	17	32	25	18	11	11	10	5	6
0	0	0	0	0	0	0	0	0	0	0	0	0	0	0	0	0	0	0	0	0
8	3	4	10	2	2	1	4	3	3	5	1	6	5	3	7	5	3	2	3	5
4	6	4	12	12	10	10	13	14	4	8	6	2	2	3	0	3	2	7	1	1
3	1	0	1	0	2	2	7	3	2	0	2	2	0	1	1	1	1	2	4	1
10	2	0	0	0	3	4	4	2	1	2	1	2	4	6	4	3	2	0	0	1
–	–	–	–	80	75	50	40	–	–	60	–	69	80	–	75	86	58	–	–	–
5	0	0	1	3	2	1	3	2	0	0	0	0	0	0	1	2	8	2	1	1
30	18	8	17	31	24	16	35	23	23	24	44	34	34	31	49	41	41	31	21	11
8	15	9	8	7	6	4	3	5	4	6	10	8	11	6	13	10	9	12	16	18
0	0	0	0	0	2	3	2	2	4	6	6	7	12	13	17	10	15	12	12	22
3	0	0	2	0	0	0	0	0	0	1	0	0	1	1	0	2	0	0	0	0
3	3	4	2	2	6	3	7	2	7	3	5	4	5	9	12	20	21	22	15	18
–	–	68	73	55	74	94	52	98	157	156	152	119	128	145	124	122	94	40	41	74
474	347	271	228	195	241	226	194	180	199	150	129	142	111	128	108	113	118	89	71	64
3	2	1	2	2	2	2	4	13	6	6	2	1	0	0	1	3	1	0	1	0
–	–	–	–	–	–	–	–	–	–	–	–	–	–	150	55	100	–	–	–	–
6	13	9	3	3	8	2	5	3	3	8	9	12	18	28	36	35	27	39	41	48
64	52	54	86	94	90	109	140	194	228	148	144	171	233	217	179	172	165	170	167	173
0	0	0	0	1	1	2	5	7	5	5	1	3	3	2	3	4	4	13	31	1
0	0	0	0	0	0	0	0	0	0	0	0	0	0	0	0	0	0	0	0	0
0	0	0	0	0	0	0	0	0	0	0	1	–	–	–	–	–	–	–	–	–
34	38	35	16	10	15	22	10	6	12	20	34	35	21	37	32	68	79	85	89	119
–	–	875	–	–	648	798	850	–	–	498	450	413	470	558	583	554	437	497	232	87
0	–	–	–	–	–	–	–	–	–	–	–	–	–	–	–	5	–	–	–	–
0	0	0	0	0	0	0	0	0	0	0	0	0	0	0	0	0	0	6	0	1
4	3	–	7	4	2	2	2	1	1	6	21	23	22	25	38	57	37	29	37	47
–	–	–	–	–	–	–	–	0	0	1	0	7	–	9	3	2	–	–	–	–
2	0	1	1	0	2	1	0	0	0	0	0	0	1	3	0	0	0	1	1	0
3	1	1	2	5	5	3	2	2	1	5	3	2	1	1	2	5	4	4	4	5
–	–	–	–	3	4	–	–	–	16	20	–	–	–	15	32	55	–	–	–	–
15	11	8	5	8	12	12	16	12	10	14	11	14	14	24	28	21	18	0	0	0
2	7	3	0	1	1	1	1	5	2	0	0	3	1	1	3	4	1	3	2	4
0	1	1	6	4	3	4	5	3	3	1	0	2	0	0	1	0	3	0	0	1
0	0	0	0	0	0	0	0	0	0	0	0	0	0	1	–	–	–	0	0	0
3	1	1	1	0	0	0	0	0	2	0	0	0	0	1	0	1	1	3	0	0
4	8	10	38	39	25	12	21	8	2	9	17	23	44	19	10	4	20	40	33	49
0	0	0	0	0	0	0	0	0	0	0	0	0	0	0	0	0	0	0	0	0
11	23	16	18	18	11	6	6	13	24	22	22	19	20	28	22	27	30	36	34	34
–	–	–	–	–	–	–	–	–	–	–	–	6	–	–	3	1	1	9	11	13
1	1	1	2	3	3	8	–	–	–	–	–	–	–	–	–	10	12	–	–	–
2	0	1	0	0	2	2	1	1	0	0	0	0	2	0	1	1	0	0	0	0
2	3	1	0	0	0	1	1	0	1	1	7	3	0	0	1	1	4	4	1	4
110	68	49	33	33	48	80	81	75	93	110	115	145	165	192	176	134	84	50	46	39
748	576	579	579	740	678	641	562	509	501	489	507	480	525	522	538	455	483	477	492	488
0	1	0	0	0	1	1	0	1	1	0	0	0	0	0	1	0	3	0	0	0
9	12	41	76	77	106	125	103	123	88	67	35	59	34	49	45	41	52	50	50	26
0	0	1	0	1	0	3	1	0	1	1	3	0	0	0	1	0	2	1	1	2
–	–	–	–	–	–	0	–	–	–	4	2	0	0	0	0	0	1	0	0	0

	1943	1944	1945	1946	1947	1948	1949	1950	1951	1952	1953	1954	1955	1956	1957	1958
Algeria	0	0	0	0	0	0	0	0	0	0	0	0	0	0	0	0
Albania	0	0	0	0	0	0	0	0	0	0	0	0	0	0	1	1
Argentina	36	24	23	32	38	41	47	56	53	35	37	45	43	36	15	32
Australia	0	1	1	3	1	1	4	1	3	1	1	2	2	2	3	1
Austria	10	8	1	4	13	25	25	17	28	19	28	22	28	37	26	23
Bangladesh	0	0	0	0	0	0	0	0	0	0	0	0	0	1	0	0
Belgium	1	1	9	8	3	3	1	2	1	2	4	5	5	8	3	12
Brazil	1	7	5	11	9	14	18	30	22	31	31	25	24	21	36	41
Bulgaria	3	1	2	4	3	0	0	1	2	2	1	4	2	9	5	9
Canada[1]	0	1	0	3	0	2	5	3	3	1	2	2	0	2	3	3
China[3]	–	–	–	–	–	–	7	26	–	–	17	–	–	–	–	52
Cuba	3	1	2	1	2	2	4	10	5	5	4	11	7	5	3	6
Czechoslovakia	10	9	3	11	19	17	20	20	8	16	18	14	16	21	25	29
Denmark	18	18	10	13	13	10	8	14	18	12	12	13	13	13	16	16
Egypt	15	23	42	52	55	49	44	48	52	59	62	65	51	39	40	55
Eire	0	0	0	0	0	0	0	0	0	0	0	0	0	0	1	3
Finland	22	16	20	16	15	16	16	14	19	28	25	28	30	18	21	17
France	81	27	50	81	88	84	97	104	109	100	111	98	110	129	142	126
Germany (and W. Ger)	83	75	72	1	6	21	56	61	69	73	103	109	128	122	107	115
Germany East				3	4	7	12	10	8	6	7	9	13	19	22	17
Greece	3	2	5	4	6	6	8	6	12	17	19	19	16	26	28	38
Hong Kong	–	–	–	–	–	–	256	202	192	259	188	167	235	311	223	237
Hungary	53	22	3	2	4	5	7	4	9	5	6	8	10	10	15	13
India	161	127	99	200	281	263	291	241	221	233	260	278	289	295	294	294
Indonesia[2]	0	6	0	0	0	3	8	23	40	42	50	59	64	36	21	19
Iraq	0	0	0	0	2	0	3	0	0	0	0	0	1	1	3	5
Israel	–	–	–	–	–	–	–	–	–	–	–	–	–	–	–	–
Italy	70	19	28	66	69	49	95	74	113	142	170	145	133	114	155	137
Japan	61	46	38	57	97	123	156	215	212	258	302	370	423	514	443	516
Korea, South	–	–	–	–	–	–	–	–	–	–	–	–	26	40	44	80
Malaysia	0	0	0	0	2	3	3	8	11	18	16	11	9	9	16	23
Mexico	70	73	82	72	58	81	108	124	101	99	83	105	84	87	106	92
Netherlands	–	–	2	1	0	2	2	0	1	1	2	0	2	0	3	4
New Zealand	0	0	0	0	0	0	0	0	0	1	0	0	0	0	0	0
Norway	4	3	4	6	1	4	3	2	7	7	6	9	9	8	9	9
Pakistan					0	0	4	15	10	7	10	7	19	31	27	33
Philippines	–	–	–	10	24	–	–	–	–	–	–	–	–	–	–	97
Poland	0	0	0	1	2	2	3	4	2	4	3	10	8	6	16	16
Portugal	4	3	4	6	7	4	7	2	2	8	4	3	0	4	1	4
Romania	2	0	1	4	0	0	1	0	2	1	2	3	4	3	8	4
Singapore	0	0	0	–	–	–	–	–	15	14	21	13	20	12	13	19
South Africa	0	1	0	4	2	1	4	2	5	1	5	5	4	2	2	5
Spain	53	34	33	41	48	44	37	49	41	41	43	69	56	75	72	75
Sri Lanka	0	0	0	0	0	0	0	0	0	0	6	5	7	7	8	9
Sweden	43	43	44	36	43	40	34	25	31	25	31	30	30	34	32	29
Switzerland	5	–	–	0	2	2	1	1	1	4	0	1	3	3	3	3
Thailand	–	–	–	–	–	–	10	–	–	–	–	–	–	–	–	–
Tunisia	0	0	0	0	0	1	0	0	1	0	0	1	0	0	0	1
Turkey	2	2	3	6	12	16	18	21	32	52	50	53	64	52	60	80
United Kingdom	47	35	39	41	58	74	101	81	75	101	102	110	95	91	115	111
United States	397	401	350	378	369	366	356	383	391	324	344	253	254	272	300	241
Uruguay	0	0	0	1	1	1	2	2	1	2	0	0	0	0	1	2
USSR	27	21	20	19	22	22	13	14	10	20	42	35	84	98	144	130
Venezuela	0	0	4	1	0	3	4	4	1	3	1	1	2	3	2	1
Yugoslavia	0	0	0	0	2	4	3	4	6	5	9	7	14	10	15	15

[1] Completions per year   [2] Starts per year   [3] 1949–66: 614; 1967–76 (Cultural Revolution): 103   – No data available

1959	1960	1961	1962	1963	1964	1965	1966	1967	1968	1969	1970	1971	1972	1973	1974	1975	1976	1977	1978	1979
0	0	0	0	1	0	3	1	2	4	2	8	1	9	6	10	3	4	1	5	2
1	1	1	1	1	1	1	2	3	4	–	4	3	4	5	5	7	10	–	12	–
22	31	25	32	27	37	30	34	27	32	29	28	38	32	39	38	33	21	21	22	33
2	2	1	1	0	0	0	3	2	1	6	14	10	7	12	11	24	16	17	10	18*
19	20	23	20	15	19	16	18	12	7	3	7	5	9	6	8	6	5	8	3	9
3	2	5	5	4	17	12	24	22	34	30	41	6	28	31	30	34	44	31	42	–
6	9	9	11	4	2	5	3	31	10	15	12	16	20	27	16	21	11	30	20	10
30	29	36	28	21	23	26	30	41	47	46	70	69	81	58	82	90	78	73	101	93
3	10	9	8	9	10	8	12	15	6	14	25	18	22	18	19	25	20	21	21	22
4	2	5	4	5	14	15	10	11	13	25	46	32	32	43	41	39	30	39	39	70
70	82	85	80	–	–	3	–	2	4	–	1	1	5	6	5	9	13	–	–	12
5	2	2	2	4	6	4	2	3	4	1	0	4	2	3	2	2	5	3	3	5
33	30	39	35	36	38	40	31	40	36	25	38	37	35	36	38	39	46	42	46	46
14	19	22	23	21	19	16	18	20	19	23	28	33	17	12	14	17	20	20	16	11
58	59	52	49	48	45	43	39	33	40	44	48	46	41	43	44	49	47	50	51	39
2	0	1	0	0	0	0	0	0	0	1	0	0	0	1	0	0	0	1	2	0
15	18	18	21	14	6	9	7	3	12	9	13	9	6	8	3	5	9	7	10	9
133	158	167	125	141	148	142	130	120	117	154	138	127	169	200	234	222	214	142	227	234
106	94	80	61	66	77	69	60	96	107	121	113	99	85	98	80	81	61	60	64	66
28	24	27	24	20	16	14	16	20	16	13	–	12	17	16	15	16	17	15	17	17
59	68	56	78	66	94	96	106	76	95	88	86	83	63	63	38	47	38	21	18	–
239	293	303	261	260	235	204	171	169	156	158	138	127	133	201	148	112	–	118	–	144
18	14	19	17	21	18	20	20	22	21	20	20	20	21	18	19	19	17	19	23	25
304	318	298	315	302	310	322	311	329	349	379	398	432	411	448	432	470	507	555	612	714
16	38	37	12	19	19	15	13	13	8	9	21	52	50	58	84	39	58	124	81	51
1	2	0	7	6	3	1	1	4	1	2	2	0	1	0	0	1	0	3	2	3
–	–	3	4	5	6	7	6	10	11	10	9	14	15	14	9	9	11	14	11	13
160	129	200	197	254	245	206	217	280	297	246	228	223	316	207	265	158	223	156	123	141
500	555	537	378	363	346	487	442	410	494	494	423	421	400	405	333	333	356	337	326	335
109	85	91	115	146	148	189	124	155	175	229	224	202	122	–	142	99	86	66	90	80
28	13	19	18	15	13	12	9	10	11	11	9	2	2	3	6	4	4	3	4	5
84	64	49	–	–	–	52	–	48	90	93	–	–	81	48	44	40	43	59	63	85
1	6	1	5	2	3	1	6	7	4	6	3	4	6	11	9	14	8	8	9	14
0	0	0	0	0	1	0	1	0	0	0	0	1	0	1	0	1	0	4	2	3
8	6	6	5	6	6	8	7	6	6	5	11	6	8	12	12	14	12	10	6	10
34	38	34	34	46	67	54	72	66	99	91	85	79	99	93	107	111	109	74	87	80
92	112	108	152	142	161	161	201	180	175	169	194	253	181	146	120	143	174	141	135	170
16	21	23	23	26	25	20	26	21	18	22	25	25	20	25	31	36	28	32	27	30
5	2	2	5	8	8	6	5	7	4	4	4	7	8	6	11	10	18	19	5	6
4	9	10	8	10	11	14	15	14	7	12	8	13	16	16	18	23	22	20	23	28
17	12	19	27	21	19	11	12	10	5	5	4	3	3	4	1	4	2	2	0	0
6	8	19	13	7	8	6	10	9	12	12	17	17	24	22	32	26	18	18	14	11
68	73	91	89	113	123	133	152	138	117	123	105	107	104	112	115	102	90	97	79	73
9	9	8	6	11	15	15	20	21	20	20	17	14	20	18	41	31	30	75	–	29
24	23	18	17	18	24	19	25	27	34	24	20	19	14	18	24	20	16	22	17	18
5	7	9	4	4	4	10	5	4	7	–	7	–	–	18	15	15	10	–	10	–
50	43	35	96	48	44	44	54	51	52	64	73	74	70	81	83	90	130	98	148	150
1	0	1	0	0	0	1	2	7	3	5	4	2	4	2	2	3	1	2	3	2
71	68	116	127	125	178	214	238	206	177	229	225	266	298	208	188	124	164	225	123	195
99	110	109	126	107	75	80	69	89	73	85	103	97	90	80	81	80	64	43	49	38
187	154	131	147	121	141	153	156	178	180	177	231	223	224	201	179	161	188	157	162	167
1	0	0	0	0	0	0	0	0	0	0	0	0	0	0	0	0	0	0	0	1
145	139	137	97	96	108	127	131	136	121	141	130	133	127	150	140	148	149	143	141	151
1	1	0	3	4	9	3	3	2	5	1	4	4	1	5	3	5	13	29	12	
14	14	32	22	18	17	20	21	31	–	35	25	28	21	16	11	19	18	15	16	

* Provisional figure

ACCIDENTS

Worst accident: The largest number of fatalities incurred in the production of a film was 27 when the ship *Viking* blew up off Newfoundland on 15 March 1931 during the shooting of *The Viking* (Can 31), a drama about the seal fishing industry. The producer, Varick Frissell, was amongst those killed.

Reports of prodigious death rolls on Hollywood movies tend to be exaggerated. Neither version of *Ben Hur* (US 25 and US 59) resulted in any deaths, except of horses. **Hollywood's worst accident** took place during production of *Such Men Are Dangerous* (US 30), when two planes collided on the way to shoot a scene. Ten members of the film crew were killed.

Three stuntmen were killed shooting the Cooper River rapids for *The Trail of '98* (US 28); three extras were drowned in the *Noah's Ark* (US 28) flood scenes; three aerial stuntmen were killed on *Hell's Angels* (US 30), though only one of them while actually filming; three horsemen died in the cavalry charge in *They Died with Their Boots On* (US 41). One of the latter was Bill Mead, whose horse tripped as he rode by the side of Errol Flynn. He had the presence of mind to fling his sword forward to avoid falling with it, but by incredible mischance the hilt stuck in the ground and Mead fell on the tip of the blade, impaling himself.

It is rare for scenes of actual deaths during filming to be retained in the completed picture, but one known example is the anti-British propaganda drama *Mein Leben für Irland* (Ger 41). In the final battle scene several extras were killed when one stepped on a live land-mine and the footage was included in the release prints.

ARCHIVES

The first film archive was the Danish Statens Arkiv for historiske Film og Stemmer, which had its origins in the spring of 1910 when Anker Kirkeby of the Copenhagen newspaper *Politiken* approached Ole Olsen of Nordisk Films with the idea of preserving a selection of films likely to be of historic interest in the future. During the ensuing three years a collection of films was assembled, including a number, specially taken for the archive, which showed prominent Danish writers, scientists, politicians, etc., and shots of parts of old Copenhagen due for re-development. The archive was formally established at the Royal Library in Copenhagen on 9 April 1913.

By the outbreak of war in 1914, film collections had been formed at the Louvre in Paris, the National Records Office in Madrid, the New York Public Library, and in Brussels, Rome, Berlin, and the Indian state of Baroda. These pioneer efforts, and those that followed in the 1920s, were generally concerned with the preservation of films as a record of national or civic history. **The first National Film Archive formed as a record of the film industry,** rather than as a retrospective of public events, was the Reichsfilmarchiv established in Germany at the instigation of Arnold Raether on 4 February 1935. The Svenska Filminstituter Archive claims an earlier date of foundation, but it originated with the Filmhistorika Samlingarna, a private collection formed in 1933 by Einar Lauritzen.

Two other major archives were founded in 1935. The British Film Institute (founded 1933) set up the National Film Archive under Ernest Lindgren in May, and in New York Iris Barry and John Abbott established the Museum of Modern Art Film Library. The following year, Henri Langlois formed the Cinémathèque Française from his own private film collection and this rapidly grew into a national institution, though the government support enjoyed since the end of World War II was withdrawn in 1969 when the French government established its own archive. The USSR's giant Gosfilmofond, which occupies a 150-acre site at Bielye Stolbi near Moscow and employs a staff of 600, was not founded until 1948.

The largest collection of films in the world is preserved by the Motion Picture Section of the Library of Congress in Washington, DC, which has 70 000 titles spanning a period of some 85 years. **The oldest film in the collection,** which is also **the oldest American film in existence** anywhere in the world, is catalogued as *Edison Kinetoscopic Record of a Sneeze* (US 94). Produced by Edison's assistant W.K.L. Dickson, the 45 frames of surviving footage show a man called Fred Ott sneezing in close-up. The film was copyrighted on 9 January 1894.

The Library of Congress's Motion Picture Section is a copyright repository rather than a film archive in the conventional sense. **The world's largest service film archive** is the Cinémathèque Française, with 60000 films. The Soviet Union's Gosfilmofond and the DDR's Staatliches Filmarchiv each claim to have over 40000 films, while the British National Film Archive preserves 26000 films and television recordings.

The largest collection of film stills in the world is the three million housed at the Department of Film of the Museum of Modern Art in New York.

CO-PRODUCTIONS

The first co-production was *Das Geheimnis der Lüfte* (Austria/Fr 13), a full-length feature thriller starring Julius Brandt. The Austrian production company was Wiener Autorenfilm; the French company is believed to have been Pathé.

The first Anglo-American co-production was James Whale's *Journey's End* (GB/US 30), from R.C. Sheriff's war drama of the same name, which was made in Hollywood by Gainsborough/Welsh-Pearson of Britain and Tiffany-Stahl of the US. The film had an all-male cast headed by Colin Clive as the alcoholic war hero.

The first Anglo-Soviet co-production is to be a biopic of Constantin Stanislavski (1865–1938), founder of the Moscow Art Theatre and originator of method acting, which was announced by Cupid Productions of London and Sovinfilm of Moscow in September 1979 and scheduled for production in 1980. The director is Nikita Mikhalkov.

The first Sino-American co-production is to be *The Marvellous Mongolian* (US/China i.p.), a Sidney Glazier production about the love of a Mongolian boy and a Welsh girl. The director is James Hill.

The most cosmopolitan co-productions are the seven-nation films *Soldaty svobody* (USSR/Bulg/Hung/DDR/Pol/Rom/Cz 77) and *West Indies Story* (Tunisia/Mali/Ivory Coast/Mauritania/Algeria/Senegal/Fr 79). *Soldaty svobody* involved the most production companies, namely Mosfilm (USSR), Za Ugrakbu Film (Bulg),

Mafilm (Hung), Defa (DDR), PRF EF (Pol), Bukuresti (Rom), Barrandov (Cz) and Koliba (Cz).

Films co-produced by five different countries have included *The Behest of the Inca* (Bulg/W.Ger/It/Sp/Peru 66); *Love at 20* (Fr/It/Jap/Pol/W.Ger 63); *Marco the Magnificent* (Afghanistan/Egypt/Fr/It/Yug 66); *The Call of the Wild* (GB/W.Ger/Sp/It/Fr 72).

HOLLYWOOD

The first European inhabitant of the area now known as Hollywood, then called Nopalera, was Mexican-born Don Tomas Urquidez, who built an adobe dwelling in 1853 at what is now the northwest corner of Franklin and Sycamore Avenues.

The name 'Hollywood' was conferred on her Cahuenga Valley ranch by Mrs Harvey Henderson Wilcox, wife of one of the district's earliest real estate developers, in 1886. The name had nothing to do with holly-bushes imported from England, as some accounts have it. Mrs Wilcox had been travelling by train to her old home in the east when she met a lady with a summer home near Chicago called 'Hollywood'. She was so charmed by the name that she decided to borrow it for her own property. In 1903 the village of Hollywood and its environs were incorporated as a municipality, but in 1910 the citizens voted to become a district of Los Angeles in order to secure water supplies. At that date the population was 5000; by 1919 it was 35000 and by 1925 it had grown to 130000.

Beverly Hills: The exodus of Hollywood's upper crust to Beverly Hills began when Douglas Fairbanks rented sports goods manufacturer Syl Spaulding's 36-room house on Summit Drive in 1919. At that time Beverly Hills was mainly agricultural land given over to the cultivation of beans and there was only one house between Fairbanks' rented property and the sea seven miles away. Early in 1920 he bought a hunting lodge adjacent to the Spaulding mansion and rebuilt it in a style befitting his new bride, Mary Pickford. Named *Pickfair* after the first syllables of their names, Doug's wedding gift to Mary was and remained Beverly Hills' most regal establishment, a magnet that drew the elite of the film colony to what was soon to become America's richest

suburb. In 1980, following the death of Mary Pickford, the 45-room mansion was put up for sale at an asking price of $10 million.

The first dramatic film made in the Los Angeles area was Francis Boggs' *The Count of Monte Cristo* (US 08), a Selig production made partly in Colorado and partly in the Laguna and Venice districts of what is now Greater Los Angeles. The first made wholly in LA was Francis Boggs' *The Power of the Sultan* (US 09), starring Hobart Bosworth, a Broadway actor who had lost his voice through TB and was seeking recuperative sunshine. The movie was shot in three days, 8–10 May 1909, on a rented lot next to a Chinese laundry on Olive and Seventh Streets, Los Angeles. Boggs, who might have become prominent as California's pioneer director, was unfortunately cut down in his prime, murdered by a crazed Japanese studio gardener in 1911.

The first studio in the Los Angeles area was established by the Selig Co. at 1845 Allesandro Street, Edendale. Construction began in August 1909 and enlargements were made in 1910 and again in 1911, so that within two years of opening it was occupying a 230×220ft (70×67m) building.

The first film made in Hollywood was D.W. Griffith's *In Old California* (US 10), a Biograph melodrama about the liaison between a Spanish maiden (Marion Leonard) and a dashing hero, destined to become Governor of California (Frank Grandin), who have an illegitimate wastrel son (Arthur Johnson). It was shot in two days, 2–3 February 1910, and released on 10 March.

The first studio in Hollywood was established there as the result of a toss of a coin. Al Christie, chief director of the Centaur Co., wanted to make westerns in California, since he was tired of having to simulate sagebush country in New

The first film studio in the Los Angeles area – Selig Polyscope at Edendale 1909 *(Bruce Torrence Historical Collection, c/o Pacific Federal Savings)*

Jersey. Centaur's owner, David Horsley, thought that Florida would be better, but agreed to abide by a heads-or-tails decision. Christie tossed and won. After viewing various possible sites in Southern California, he found a derelict roadhouse on Sunset Boulevard which looked suitable and cost only $40 a month to rent. This building was converted into a studio in October 1911. Today the site is occupied by the West Coast headquarters of CBS. By the end of the following year there were 15 film companies operating in Hollywood. Uninterrupted sunshine and a comforting distance from the agents of the Patents Co. were not the only attractions of Southern California as a film-making base. The astonishing range and variety of its scenery enabled locations to be found that could reasonably represent any terrain from Cornwall to the Urals; westerns could be located in the real west rather than New Jersey, South Sea island pictures could be shot on Catalina and neighbouring islands, an oil field in Los Angeles itself served for Texan oilman dramas, Spanish missions set the scene for old Mexico, and there were even sufficient baronial mansions to cater for the needs of pictures playing in Hollywood's England. Only a jungle was missing, but studios like Selig and Universal established their own zoos and built their African locales on the backlot.

The first talking picture made in Hollywood was a Fox Movietone short *They're Coming to Get Me* (US 26), with comedian Chic Sale, released in May 1926.

Above left: Panorama of Hollywood 1905. The movie makers began to arrive five years later *(Bruce Torrence Historical Collection, c/o Pacific Federal Savings)*

Below left: Pickfair from the air 1932. Mary Pickford was chatelaine of Hollywood's most sumptuous mansion for nearly sixty years *(Bruce Torrence Historical Collection, c/o Pacific Federal Savings)*

The celebrated Hollywood sign was erected on Hollywood Hills in 1923 at a cost of $21 000. Originally the sign spelt out the word HOLLY-WOODLAND, in letters 30 ft (9 m) wide and 50 ft (15 m) tall and built up from 3 × 9 ft (1 × 3 m) sheet metal panels attached to a scaffolding frame. Each letter was studded with 20-watt light bulbs at eight-inch intervals. A man called Albert Kothe, who lived on the job – in a hut behind one of the 'L's' – was employed full time to change the bulbs when they burned out. The sign has often been featured in movies as a means of establishing locale, most recently in *The Day of the Locust* (US 75) and *1941* (US 79). It has been put to more macabre use for frequent suicide attempts.

LONGEST FILMS

The longest film ever made was the underground movie titled *The Longest Most Meaningless Movie in the World* (GB 70), produced by Anthony Scott in association with the Swiss Film Centre, London, directed by Vincent

Dedication of the Hollywood sign 1923. Originally it marked a real estate development *(Bruce Torrence Historical Collection, c/o Pacific Federal Savings)*

Patouillard and featuring Hermine Demoriane, Roger Dixon, Graham Stevens, Carla Liss and Martine Meringue. It was premièred in its original 48-hr version at the Cinémathèque de Paris in October 1970.

The longest commercially made film was *The Burning of the Red Lotus Temple* (China 28–31), adapted by the Star Film Co. from a newspaper serial *Strange Tales of the Adventurer in the Wild Country* by Shang K'ai-jan. It was released in 18 feature-length parts over a period of three years. Although never shown publicly in its 27-hr entirety, some cinemas would put on all-day performances of half-a-dozen parts in sequence.

The longest commercially made American movie to be released uncut was Erich von Stroheim's

Foolish Wives (US 22), which was distributed to Latin American countries in its original 6 hr 24 min version. In the United States, however, it was seen only in severely cut form, a 12-reel version for the road show and a 10-reel version for general release.

The 42-reel version of von Stroheim's masterpiece *Greed* (US 24) – Hollywood's longest-ever film in its original form – was shown only once at a 9-hr screening at MGM on 12 January 1924. Idwal Jones, drama critic of the *San Francisco Daily News*, who was present, commented that it had 'every comma of the book put in'. It was subsequently cut to 24 reels by an aggrieved von Stroheim, who had already spent four unpaid months editing the original footage down to 48 reels; then to 18 reels by Rex Ingram, and finally 10 reels by Joe Farnham. The 32 reels of cut negative were melted down by MGM to retrieve the minute quantity of silver nitrate they contained.

The longest commercially-made American movie shown in America was George Stevens' *The Greatest Story Ever Told* (US 65) with Max von Sydow, which was premièred at 4 hr 20 min, but then cut to 3 hr 58 min and cut again to 3 hr 45 min. The only other Hollywood production longer than *Gone with the Wind* (US 39), which ran for 3 hr 40 min, is Bob Dylan's 3 hr 55 min *Renaldo and Clara* (US 77). Otto Preminger's *Exodus* (US 60) was exactly the same length as *Gone with the Wind*. Prior to *Gone with the Wind* the record for the longest Hollywood talkie was held by MGM's *The Great Ziegfeld* (US 36), which ran for 2 hr 59 min.

The longest commercially-made British film was was A.E. Coleby's *The Prodigal Son* (GB 23), a Stoll Film Co. production from the novel by Hall Caine, shot on location in Iceland, and starring Stewart Rome. The 4 hr 40 min picture was released in two parts, one of eight and the other of nine reels. **The longest commercially-made talkie** was David Lean's 3 hr 42 min *Lawrence of Arabia* (GB 62), which was two minutes longer than *Gone with the Wind*.

Films running four hours: The following are films originally shown in public in a version lasting four hours or longer. The list includes films issued in parts, but not serials. The duration of the silent films listed is calculated on the assumption that they were projected at 16 f.p.s.

4 hr	*Chusingura* (Jap 55)
4 hr	*Gosta Berlings Saga* (Sw 24)
4 hr 5 min	*The Keys of Happiness* (Rus 13)
4 hr 5 min	*Siberiade* (USSR 79)
4 hr 12 min	*L'Amour fou* (Fr 68)
4 hr 15 min	*Molière* (Fr 78)
4 hr 15 min	*Out 1: Spectre* (Fr 72)
4 hr 15 min	*Mera Naam Jokar* (India 70)
4 hr 16 min	*Gustaf Wasa* (Sw 28)
4 hr 20 min	*The Greatest Story Ever Told* (US 65)[1]
4 hr 20 min	*Rubens* (Neths 78)
4 hr 30 min	*Imagen de Caracas* (Ven 68)
4 hr 30 min	*The Great Citizen* (USSR 38)
4 hr 30 min	*Le Chagrin et la pitie* (Fr 70)
4 hr 30 min	*La Hora de los hornos* (Arg 68)
4 hr 38 min	*The Memory of Justice* (W.Ger 76)
4 hr 40 min	*The Prodigal Son* (GB 23)
4 hr 45 min	*Rameau's Nephew by Diderot* (Can 74)
4 hr 58 min	*Percal* (Mex 50)
5 hr 2 min	*Winifred Wagner und die Geschichte des Hauses Wahnfried* (W.Ger 75)
5 hr 5 min	*Les Misérables* (Fr 27)
5 hr 6 min	*Petersburgskije truscoby* (Rus 15)
5 hr 20 min	*Vindicta* (Fr 23)
5 hr 20 min	*1900* (It 78)[2]
5 hr 32 min	*Les Misérables* (Fr 33)
5 hr 50 min	*Quiet Flows the Don* (USSR 57–58)
5 hr 54 min	*Soldati Svobodi* (USSR/Bulg/Hung/Cz/DDR/Pol/Rom 77)
6 hr	*Hatya Ek Aakar Ki/The Verdict* aka *Gandhi* (India 69)
6 hr	*Idade de Terra* (Br 79)
6 hr 18 min	*Napoleon vu par Abel Gance* (Fr 27)[3]
6 hr 24 min	*Foolish Wives* (US 22)[4]
6 hr 30 min	*Sleep* (US 63)
6 hr 40 min	*Hitler: a Film from Germany* (W.Ger 77)
7 hr	*Der Hund von Baskerville* (Ger 14–20)
7 hr 45 min	*Français si vous savez* (Fr 73)
7 hr 58 min	*Iskry Plamja* (Rus 25)
8 hr	*Empire* (US 64)
8 hr 27 min	*War and Peace* (USSR 63–67)[5]
8 hr 32 min	*La Roue* (Fr 21)[6]
9 hr 29 min	*The Human Condition* (Jap 58–60)

[1] At première only. Release prints were 3 hr 58 min.
[2] Length of version shown at Cannes Film Festival.
[3] Originally exhibited in 3 × 2 hr parts. Shown complete at Telluride, Colorado, September 1979.
[4] Released at this length in South America only. US general release: 10 reels.
[5] Soviet language version. English language version 6 hr 13 min.
[6] Released in 4 hr version, but VGIK in Moscow has print of 8½ hr original.

12hr 43min	*Comment Yukong deplace les montagnes* (Fr 76)	
13hr	*Noli me Tangerey* (Fr 71)[7]	
24hr	**** (US 67)[8]	
27hr	*The Burning of the Red Lotus Temple* (China 28–31)	
48hr	*The Longest and Most Meaningless Movie in the World* (GB 70)[9]	

[7] Shown only once at this length, then re-edited as $4\frac{1}{4}$ hr *Out 1: Spectre*.
[8] Shown only once, then re-edited as two features of conventional length.
[9] Premièred at this length, then cut to $1\frac{1}{2}$ hr.

The longest British films from 1896: The rate at which films progressed from single-scene subjects lasting about a minute to single reel and then multi-reel subjects may be discerned from the table below which lists all the commercially made British dramatic productions that held the record for length at the time they were made. Silent films and talkies are treated separately. Silents are given in feet, since it is not known at what speed some of the earlier titles were shown. As an approximate guide, 1000ft (305m) lasts about 16min, projected at 16f.p.s.

Silent Films

80ft	*The Soldier's Courtship*	May 1896
150ft	*The Death of Nelson*	Oct 1897
210ft	*Sloper's Visit to Brighton*	July 1898
320ft	*Our New General Servant*	Aug 1898
620ft	*Scrooge; or, Marley's Ghost*	Nov 1901
800ft	*Alice in Wonderland*	May 1903
820ft	*Incidents in the Life of Lord Nelson*	Oct 1905
870ft	*The Life of Charles Peace*	Nov 1905
1000ft	*Dick Turpin's Ride to York*	May 1906
1200ft	*Cinderella*	Dec 1907
1240ft	*Romeo and Juliet*	June 1908
1280ft	*Sexton Blake*	Oct 1909
1630ft	*The Martyrdom of Adolf Beck*	Dec 1909
2000ft	*Henry VIII*	Feb 1911
2500ft	*Rob Roy*	Sept 1911
3700ft	*Oliver Twist*	Sept 1912
4300ft	*Lorna Doone*	Dec 1912
6200ft	*East Lynne*	May 1913
7500ft	*David Copperfield*	Aug 1913
9170ft	*The Christian*	Nov 1915
18454ft	*The Prodigal Son*	Feb 1923

Talkies

1hr 36min	*Blackmail*	June 1929
1hr 40min	*Under the Greenwood Tree*	Sept 1929
2hr	*Journey's End*	April 1930
2hr 16min	*The Robber Symphony*	June 1936
2hr 18min	*Caesar and Cleopatra*	Jan 1946
2hr 35min	*Hamlet*	June 1948
2hr 50min	*Don Giovanni*	June 1955
3hr 12min	*Der Rosenkavalier*	Aug 1962
3hr 42min	*Lawrence of Arabia*	Nov 1962

CINEMA MUSEUMS

The first cinema museum was the Čescoslovenskyé Filmové Museum, founded by Jindřrich Brichta at Prague in 1923.

The first cinema museum in America was the Crocker Museum which Charles Chaplin's assistant Harry Crocker, who had a mania for collecting movie *memorabilia*, established on Sunset Boulevard, Hollywood in 1928. The exhibits consisted of props and costumes from silent movies, including Chaplin's original tramp costume, Harold Lloyd's glasses, William S. Hart's first leather chaps, Keaton's pan-cake boater, Gloria Swanson's 'Sadie Thompson' costume, the cabin that tottered on the brink from *The Gold Rush* (US 24), and the winning chariot from *Ben Hur* (US 26).

The Crocker Museum being long since defunct, there is now no cinema museum in the world's movie capital, Hollywood. (Movieland Wax Museum exists, however, in Buena Park, a suburb of LA.) Continuous attempts have been made since the late 1950s to establish one, all of them foundering on lack of suitable premises at an acceptable price. Meanwhile the City of Los Angeles has custody of the $2 million collection of artefacts accumulated by Sol Lesser for his long-projected 'International Center of the Audio-Visual Arts'. Housed at the abandoned Lincoln Heights gaol, it includes such notable *memorabilia* as two locks of Mary Pickford's golden tresses, the first projector brought to Los Angeles, Valentino's matador jacket from *Blood and Sand* (US 22), Fred Astaire's top-hat and cane, and a twelve-piece dress worn by Debbie Reynolds. Miss Reynolds herself presides over another $1·5 million worth of relics, including the red *Wizard of Oz* (US 39) shoes worn by Judy Garland, which fetched $15000 at the MGM props auction, all of which she wishes to put on permanent display. A third prospective founder of the Hollywood Museum, Douglas Wright, inspiration behind the Hollywood Hall of

Fame, seeks accommodation for his own $250000 collection of movie *memorabilia*.

Cinema museums. The following museums are either wholly devoted to cinema or have substantial cinema collections. Film archives are only included if they also administer a museum.

Argentina	Museo Municipal de Arte Moderno, Mendoza.
Australia	Australian Film Institute Museum, Canberra.
	Movie Museum, Buderim.
Austria	Osterreichisches Filmmuseum, Vienna.
Belgium	Musée du Cinéma, Brussels.
	Musée de la Photographie et du Cinéma, Brussels.
	Provinciaal Museum voor Kunstambachten het Sterckshof, Deurne.
Brazil	Embrafilme Cinema Museum, Rio de Janeiro.
	The Cinema Museum, São Paulo.
Denmark	Det Danske Filmmuseum, Copenhagen.
DDR	Kreismuseum, Bitterfeld.
France	Film Museum, Palais de Chaillot, Paris.
	Musée du Cinéma, Rue de Courcelles, Paris.
	Musée du Cinéma, Lyons (Lumière collection).
Germany	Munich City Museum (Film and Photography Department).
	Deutsches Film Museum, Frankfurt-am-Main.
Great Britain	Kodak Museum, London.
	Barnes Museum of Cinematography, St Ives, Cornwall.
Italy	Museo Nazionale del Cinema, Turin.
Mexico	Cinematica Luis Bunuel, Puebla.
	Cinematica Mexicana, Mexico City.
Netherlands	Stichting Nederlands Filmmuseum, Amsterdam.
Norway	Norsk Filminstitutt, Oslo.
Sweden	Asta Nielsen Filmmuseum, Lund.
USA	Tom Mix Museum, Dewey, Oklahoma.
	Will Rogers Memorial, Claremore, Oklahoma.
	International Museum of Photography, George Eastman House, Rochester, NY
	Museum of Modern Art, New York City.
	Hollywood Stuntmen's Hall of Fame, Mojave, California.
USSR	Ukrainian State Museum of Theatrical, Musical and Cinema Art, Kiev.
Yugoslavia	Muzej Jugoslavenske Kinoteke, Belgrade.

NATIONALISATION

The first cinema industry to be nationalised was that of Hungary by a decree of the Hungarian Councils' Republic dated 12 April 1919 which placed under public ownership 'all film-producing studios, film laboratories, film distributing companies, related factories and picture theatres – regardless of the number of employees – as well as their movables and real estate and all their equipment, and the finance required for carrying on production'. During the four months the Soviet survived, 31 films were completed, including works adapted from Daudet *(Fromont Senior and Risler Junior)*, Dickens *(Oliver Twist)*, Strindberg *(Miss Julie)* and, curiously, the English popular novelist Hall Caine *(The Prodigal Son)*. The administrative board included Bela Balogh and (Sir) Alexander Korda. Bela Lugosi and Michael Curtiz also played an important role in helping to establish a nationalised film industry and had to flee Hungary when the Councils' Republic collapsed. Performers had to be registered before they were allowed to work and then only in their designated category – of the 253 registered artists, 45 were juveniles, 130 were extras, 37 were supporting players (designated 'film actor candidates') and an elite of 41 played all the leads. All casting was handled by a central office. With the overthrow of the Republic, many of those involved in this first experiment in nationalisation dispersed to other parts of Europe and to America; some were imprisoned; and at least one, director Sandor Pallos, met a violent death in police hands, allegedly for making a version of Gorky's *Chelkash* (Hung 19).

The oldest nationalised industry is that of the USSR, which was placed under the control of the People's Commissariat of Education by order of Lenin on 27 August 1919 (though there was a brief interlude of private enterprise during the New Economic Policy period of the early 1920s).

The film industries of Czechoslovakia, Yugoslavia, Poland and the DDR were nationalised in 1945, of Hungary, Romania and Bulgaria in 1948 and China in 1949.

PUBLICITY

The largest publicity budget was $9 million, spent by United Artists on promoting Francis Ford Coppola's *Apocalypse Now* (US 79). Production cost of the movie, excluding promotion and prints, was $31 million.

Publicity slogans extolling movies have tended towards hyperbole ever since impresario George Belmont announced his presentation of the 'Theatrograph' at Sadler's Wells in 1896 with

Perhaps the most famous slogan of all time

'A Giggle Gurgling Gulp of Glee' – every picture had a slogan back in 1924 *(Backnumbers)*

the words: 'A mighty mirror of Promethean Photographs and a superb, brilliant, and electrifying entertainment specially adapted to cheer the toiling millions'.

A travelling bioscope showman encountered by a correspondent of *The Pelican* in a Kentish village in 1908 stretched credulity with a sign proclaiming: 'The most extraordinary invention of modern times, as presented before the Emperor Napoleon!'

Impressive figures have often engaged the attention of publicists. India's first feature film *Raja Harischandra* (India 12) was advertised as 'a performance with 57000 photographs . . . a picture two miles in length . . . all for only three annas!' *After Rain, Clear Sky* (China 31), one of China's earliest all-talkies, was promoted with the information that 'on the 977 occasions for dialogue, 6935 sentences are spoken'. The quantitative attractions of Twentieth Century-Fox's *The Egyptian* (US 54) stimulated a slogan writer to even greater flights of figurative fancy with the claim that it had '10965 pyramids, 5337 dancing girls, one million swaying bulrushes, 802 sacred bulls'.

Promoting a film to the wrong audience may be deliberate, in the case of a weak attraction, or perpetrated through sheer ignorance. In 1918 a Chicago theatre urged: 'Tomorrow – Ibsen's *Doll's House* – Bring the Kiddies!' Equally inappropriate was a Toronto cinema's slogan for David Lean's gentle evocation of middle-aged suburban romance *Brief Encounter* (GB 45): 'Girls who live dangerously'. A cinema on New York's 42nd Street, an area noted for vice, booked a nature film titled *The Love Life of a Gorilla* (US 37) and brought the crowds flocking in with a poster asking the searing question 'Do native women live with apes?' Anyone paying good money to see the film was rewarded with the answer – they don't.

An advertisement for a film showing in Washington in 1977 declared: 'Now, all the SENSUAL and VIOLENT passions *Roots* couldn't show on TV'. The picture was *Uncle Tom's Cabin* (W.Ger/It 69).

Attempts to summarise the story in a phrase could involve criminal assault on the English language. *Bridal Suite* (US 39) was encapsulated: 'Howl Bent for Laugh Heaven, Four Zanies Tangle with Cock-Eyed Love'. Real extravagance of prose style, though, was reserved for the epics. Cecil B. De Mille's *King of Kings* (US 27) was advertised in New York as abounding in 'Dramatic Magnificence, Spectacular Splendor, Riotous Joy, Tigerish Rage, Undying Love, Terrifying Tempests, Appalling Earthquakes'. (Audiences might be forgiven for not recognising this as the story of the Gospels.)

In contrast, publicity could hardly be more downbeat than the announcement on the marquee of a drive-in in Cleveland County, NC in 1960: 'Two Features'. The manager explained that he never advertised the titles of the films because 'the people who patronise this drive-in don't care what's playing'.

Devastating honesty was seldom an attribute of movie publicists, but individual cinema managers would occasionally give a frank opinion of their offerings. In 1947 an exhibitor in Hastings, Neb. announced: 'Double Feature – One Good Show and One Stinker'.

An advertisement in the *Shanghai Shun-Bao* for the first Chinese feature film, *Yen Rei-hsun* (China 21), assured patrons that 'the acting stars all enjoyed a superior education'.

Slogans could be used to take a side-swipe at another star. Fox's advertising to promote George O'Brien in *The Iron Horse* (US 24), which declared 'He's not a Sheik or a Caveman or a Lounge Lizard – He is a Man's Man and An Idol of Women', was clearly meant to draw a denigratory comparison with Latin lover Rudolph Valentino. It was not unknown, however, for one star to laud another in advertising. Al Jolson paid for a full page in *Variety* to extol Charlie Chaplin's *The Circus* (US 28), which he described as 'the greatest comedy ever made. If a greater one is ever made, Chaplin will make it. Dem's my sentiments. Boy, wait till you see it! Signed Al Jolson.'

If the star was not the main attraction, someone else might be. When Oscar, the well-known Negro boot-black on the Paramount lot, played a bit part in *Gambling Ship* (US 33), a coloured-only cinema on Los Angeles' Central Avenue billed the film with the legend: 'Sensational star in *Gambling Ship*, Oscar supported by Cary Grant'. The pictures outside were entirely of Oscar.

Howard Hughes made immediate impact with the posters promoting his controversial picture *The Outlaw* (US 43) when it was briefly released in 1943 before being withdrawn again. The slogan – 'Mean, Moody and Magnificent' – was spread below a picture of a rampant-breasted Jane Russell standing bare-legged bestride a haystack with a pistol in each fist. When re-released in 1946 a far more decorous though equally striking copy-line had taken its place, a quote from Judge Twain Michelsen, who had tried the film for indecency: 'We have seen Jane Russell. She is an attractive specimen of American womanhood. God made her what she is.'

Briefer, but equally apt, was the slogan promoting Tony Richardson's *The Loved One* (US 65): 'The Picture with Something to Offend Everyone'. Briefer still and perhaps even more effective was the slogan accompanying *Baby Doll* (US 56): 'Condemned by Cardinal Spellman'.

Above right: Walt Disney's *Cinderella* (US 50)

Below right: Lotte Reiniger's silhouette *Cindrella* (Ger 28)

REMAKES

The longest interval between remakes with the same actor playing the same role was 34 years in the case of Tito Lusiardo's performances in *El Dia que me Quitas/The Day You Leave Me* (US 35 and Arg 69).

The story which has been remade the most times is *Cinderella*, of which there have been 58 productions since 1898, including cartoon, modern, ballet, operatic, pornographic and parody versions. In the following filmography the player performing the title role precedes the title (if known):

Laura Bayley: *Cinderella and the Fairy Godmother* (GB 98); Jeanne d'Alcy: *Cendrillon* (Fr 99); Dolly Lupone: *Cinderella* (GB 07), *Cendrillon* (Fr 07); *Cenerentola* (It 08); *Cendrillon* (Fr 09); Florence LaBadie: *Cinderella* (US 11); Mabel Taliaferro: *Cinderella* (US 11); Louise Legrange: *Cendrillon ou le pantouffle mysterieuse* (Fr 12); *Cinderella* (GB 12) –

animated toys; Fernanda Negri Pouget: *Cenerentola* (It 13); Lillian Walker: *Cinderella's Slipper* (US 13); Gertie Potter: *Cinderella* (GB 13); *Cinderella and the Boob* (US 13); Daisy Dormer: *Potted Pantomimes* (GB 14); Mary Pickford: *Cinderella* (US 15); *Cinderella and the Magic Slipper* (US 18); Agnes Ayres: *Forbidden Fruit* (US 21) – Cinderella story told in flashback sequence; Helga Thomas: *Der verlorene Schuh* (Ger 23); *Cinderella* (US 25) – Dinkey Doodle cartoon; Betty Bronson: *A Kiss for Cinderella* (US 25) – Cinderella story recalled in dream sequence; *Aschenputtel* (Ger 28) – Lotte Reiniger silhouette film; *Cinderella* (US 30) – Krazy Kat cartoon; *Cinderella* (US 33) – Terry-Toon cartoon; *Poor Cinderella* (US 34); Joan Warner: *Cendrillon* (Fr 37); *The Glass Slipper* (US 38) – Terry-Toon cartoon; Deanna Durbin: *First Love* (US 39) – modern version; *Bright Path* (USSR 40) – Communist interpretation of Cinderella story; Juanita Quigley: *Cinderella's Fella* (US 40); *Cinderella Goes to a Party* (US 42); M. Shapiro: *Cinderella* (USSR 47); Billy Daniels: *Sepia Cinderella* (US 47) – black version; *Erase una Vez* (Sp 50) – cartoon feature; Ilene Woods (voice): *Cinderella* (US 50) – cartoon feature; Leslie Caron: *The Glass Slipper* (US 54); Rita-Maria Nowotny: *Aschenputtel* (W.Ger 55); Renee Stobrawa: *Aschenputtel* (DDR 55);

Cinderella (US 58); Jerry Lewis: *Cinderfella* (US 60) – male parody; Raissa Stroutckova: *The Glass Slipper* (USSR 61) – ballet film; Suzanne Sybele: *SINderella and the Golden Bra* (US 64) – soft porn; Lesley Ann Warren: *Cinderella* (US 65) – Rodgers & Hammerstein TVM musical; *Princess Cinderella* (US *c.* 67); *Cinderella* (GB? 67) – cartoon; *Rindercella* (US 70) – porno movie; Eva Reuber-Staier: *Grimm's Fairy Stories for Adults* (W.Ger 71) – soft porn; *Sinderella* (GB 72) – porno cartoon; *Cinderella* (Sp 76) – feature cartoon; Cheryl Smith: *Cinderella*/GB title *The Other Cinderella* (US 76) – soft porn; Gemma Craven: *The Slipper and the Rose* (GB 76); Catherine Erhardt: *Cinderella 2000* (US 77) – 'musical parody'; *Cinderella* (Iran 77); *A Fairy Story* (GB 78) – 'updated version'; *Cinderella* (DDR/Cz 79); *Cinderella* (GB 79) – puppet film.

The following works have had a dozen or more movies based on them:

Shakespeare's *Hamlet* – 41 + 9 parody versions; *Carmen* (Merimée's story and Bizet's opera) – 43 + 2 parody versions; *Faust* (Marlowe and Goethe) – 43; R.L. Stevenson's

The 35 versions of *La Dame aux camélias* include examples from Denmark, Italy, France, USA, Venezuela, China, Germany, UK, Mexico, Sweden, Spain, Argentina and Chile. These stills show three French versions of the story, made in 1911, 1932 and 1952, with the role of Marguerite played respectively by Sarah Bernhardt, Yvonne Printemps and Micheline Presle

Dr Jekyll and Mr Hyde – 40 (including parodies and variants); Defoe's *Robinson Crusoe* – 36 (inc. 1 porno); Dumas fils' *La Dame aux camelias* – 35; Cervantes' *Don Quixote* – 31; Dumas père's *The Three Musketeers* – 30+10 variants featuring the character d'Artagnan; Shakespeare's *Romeo and Juliet* – 28+4 modern versions+8 parodies; Shakespeare's *Macbeth* – 26+2 modern versions+1 parody; the Hindu epic *Harischandra* – 25 in 9 languages; Hugo's *Les Misérables* – 25; Dumas père's *The Count of Monte Cristo* – 21+13 variants featuring the character Edmond Dantes; Tolstoy's *Resurrection* – 23; Shakespeare's *Julius Caesar* – 18+1 modern version; Dickens' *Oliver Twist* – 18; Dickens' *A Christmas Carol* – 16; *William Tell* (Schiller and legend) – 15; Dostoevsky's *Crime and Punishment* – 14; Tolstoy's *Anna Karenina* – 13; Shakespeare's *Othello* – 13; Tolstoy's *The Living Corpse* – 13; Dumas père's *The Corsican Brothers* – 12; Harriet Beecher Stowe's *Uncle Tom's Cabin* – 12.

For a filmography of *Hamlet* remakes and other Shakespeare films, see Author: Most Filmed (pp. 55–7).

SEQUELS

The longest interval between a sequel and its original was 34 years in the case of *The Maltese Falcon* (US 41) and *The Black Bird* (US 75) and a similar period between *National Velvet* (US 44) and *International Velvet* (GB 78). In *The Black Bird* George Segal played Sam Spade's son, who has inherited Effie (Lee Patrick), the elder Spade's secretary in *The Maltese Falcon*, along with his father's detective agency. Miss Patrick had also played Effie in the 1941 picture. The role of Velvet grown up in *International Velvet* was offered to Elizabeth Taylor, who had played the child Velvet when she was 12 years old, but she turned it down and the role was played with mature dignity and charm by Nanette Newman. The star of the picture was Tatum O'Neal as Velvet's niece from America, who comes to live with her aunt in Britain, becomes a show-jumper, and wins an Olympic Gold Medal.

'Prequels' are sequels that relate the story that *preceded* the original film. *Another Part of the Forest* (US 47) recounted the earlier lives of the Hubbard family portrayed in *The Little Foxes* (US 41); Steve McQueen's title role in *Nevada Smith* (US 66) centred on the earlier life of the character played by Alan Ladd in *The Carpetbaggers* (US 64); Michael Winner's *The Night Comers* (GB 71) told the story of how the ghosts in *The Innocents* (GB 61) – the manservant

Any passing resemblance to Newman and Redford is illusory. Tom Berenger and William Katt played the outlaws in their earlier days in *Butch and Sundance* (US 79)

Quint and the 'former governess' – lost their lives; *Rhapsody* (US 54), from Henry Handel Richardson's novel *Maurice Guest*, was followed 25 years later by the film of the preceding volume of the story, *The Getting of Wisdom* (Aus 79). Richard Lester's *Butch and Sundance – The Early Days* (US 79) recounts the story of how the outlaw pair (Tom Berenger and William Katt) met and teamed up together, while the earlier George Roy Hill picture *Butch Cassidy and the Sundance Kid* (US 69) related the events leading up to the death of Butch and Sundance (Paul Newman and Robert Redford) in a shootout with the Bolivian army. Zoltán Fábri brought Jósef Baláz's novel *Hungarians* (Hung 79) to the screen before embarking on the preceding story of the hero's father in his youth, told in *Bálint Fábián's Encounter with God* (Hung 80). Both Bálint Fábián and his son András were played by the same actor, Gábor Koncz.

CHAPTER 3

BOX OFFICE AND BUDGETS

BOX OFFICE

The film with the highest gross earnings worldwide is George Lucas's *Star Wars* (US 77) which had earned $248 million in rentals by the end of 1979.

Previous box office champions were *Snow White and the Seven Dwarfs* (US 37), which was the first talkie to overtake the record for silent pictures set by *The Big Parade* (US 25) (see below); *Gone with the Wind* (US 39), which held the record from 1940 until overtaken by *The Sound of Music* (US 65) in August 1966 and again in 1971–2 as the result of a reissue; *The Godfather* (US 72), which set a new record the year of its release; and *Jaws* (US 75), also a record-breaker in its first year and box office champion until surpassed by *Star Wars* in 1977.

The top grossing silent film was King Vidor's *The Big Parade* (US 25), with worldwide rentals of $22 million. No exact figure is available for D.W. Griffith's *The Birth of a Nation* (US 15), which was long thought of as the top grossing silent, with estimates of up to $50 million receipts in the domestic market alone. This is now considered to be a wildly exaggerated figure, and *Variety* quotes $5 million as a reasonable 'guestimate'. Griffith himself stated in 1929 that the film had earned $10 million worldwide.

The Twenty-five Top Grossing Films

The list below was published by the American trade paper *Variety* in 1980 and represents the North American (US and Canada) rentals for the 25 top grossing films of all time. As a very approximate guide, films which are successful in the North American market can usually expect to earn about the same in overseas rentals as they do in domestic rentals.

	Title	N. American Rentals ($)
1	*Star Wars* (US 77)	175 849 013
2	*Jaws* (US 75)	133 429 000
3	*Grease* (US 78)	93 292 000
4	*The Exorcist* (US 73)	88 100 000
5	*The Godfather* (US 72)	86 275 000
6	*Superman* (GB 78)	81 000 000
7	*The Sound of Music* (US 65)	79 000 000
8	*The Sting* (US 73)	78 889 000
9	*Close Encounters of the Third Kind* (US 77)	77 000 000
10	*Gone with the Wind* (US 39)	76 700 000
11	*Saturday Night Fever* (US 77)	73 522 000
12	*National Lampoon Animal House* (US 78)	63 471 000
13	*Smokey and the Bandit* (US 77)	61 017 000
14	*One Flew Over the Cuckoo's Nest* (US 75)	59 000 000
15	*American Graffiti* (US 73)	55 886 000
16	*Rocky* (US 76)	54 000 000
17	*Jaws II* (US 78)	50 569 000
18	*Love Story* (US 70)	50 000 000
18	*Towering Inferno* (US 75)	50 000 000
20	*The Graduate* (US 68)	49 078 000
21	*Every Which Way But Loose* (US 78)	48 000 000
22	*Heaven Can Wait* (US 78)	47 552 000
23	*Doctor Zhivago* (US 65)	46 550 000
24	*Butch Cassidy and the Sundance Kid* (US 69)	46 039 000
25	*Airport* (US 70)	45 300 000

Annual Top Moneymaker USA: Prior to 1947 there are no consistent records. Since that date *Variety* has identified the following pictures as top moneymaker of the year in the domestic market (US and Canada). Where the top moneymaker is a non-American production, the top American grosser is listed second.

1947	*The Best Years of Our Lives*
1948	*The Road to Rio*
1949	*Jolson Sings Again*
1950	*Samson and Delilah*
1951	*David and Bathsheba*
1952	*The Greatest Show on Earth*
1953	*The Robe*
1954	*White Christmas*
1955	*Cinerama Holiday*
1956	*Guys and Dolls*
1957	*The Ten Commandments*
1958	*The Bridge on the River Kwai* (GB)
	Peyton Place (US)
1959	*Auntie Mame*
1960	*Ben Hur*
1961	*The Guns of Navarone* (GB)
	The Absent-Minded Professor (US)
1962	*Spartacus*
1963	*Cleopatra*
1964	*The Carpet-Baggers*
1965	*Mary Poppins*
1966	*Thunderball* (GB)
	Doctor Zhivago (US)
1967	*The Dirty Dozen*
1968	*The Graduate*
1969	*The Love Bug*
1970	*Airport*

The Big Parade (US 25) — the most profitable silent film ever made

1971	*Love Story*
1972	*The Godfather*
1973	*The Poseidon Adventure*
1974	*The Sting*
1975	*Jaws*
1976	*One Flew Over the Cuckoo's Nest*
1977	*Star Wars*
1978	*Grease*
1979	*Superman* (GB)
	Every Which Way But Loose (US)

Of the 33 top grossers listed above, 9 were contemporary dramas, 7 were historical epics, 5 were comedies, 5 were musicals, 3 were war films, 2 science-fiction, one was a Bond movie and one a Cinerama travelogue. Only two took crime as a principal theme (*The Godfather* and *The Sting*).

Annual Top Moneymaker GB: The following have been the annual top moneymaking British films in the domestic market since 1936:

1936	*The Ghost Goes West*
1937	*Good Morning Boys*
1938	*A Yank at Oxford*
1939	*Pygmalion*
1940	*Convoy*
1941	*49th Parallel*
1942	*The First of the Few*
1943	*In Which We Serve*
1944	*This Happy Breed*
1945	*The Seventh Veil*
1946	*The Wicked Lady*
1947	*The Courtneys of Curzon Street*
1948	*Spring in Park Lane*
1949	*The Third Man*
1950	*The Blue Lamp*
1951	*Laughter in Paradise*
1952	*Where No Vultures Fly*
1953	*The Cruel Sea*
1954	*Doctor in the House*
1955	*The Dam Busters*
1956	*Reach for the Sky*
1957	*Doctor at Large*
1958	*The Bridge on the River Kwai*
1959	*Carry on Nurse*
1960	*Doctor in Love*
1961	*The Swiss Family Robinson*
1962	*The Young Ones*
1963	*From Russia with Love*
1964	*Goldfinger*
1965	*Help!*
1966	*Thunderball*
1967	*You Only Live Twice*
1968	*Up the Junction*
1969	*Oliver!*
1970	*Battle of Britain*
1971	*On the Buses*
1972	*Diamonds are Forever*

1973	*Live and Let Die*
1974	*Confessions of a Window Cleaner*
1975	*The Man with the Golden Gun*
1976	*The Return of the Pink Panther*
1977	*The Spy Who Loved Me*
1978	*The Revenge of the Pink Panther*
1979	*Moonraker*

Of the 44 films listed, 15 were comedies, 9 were war films, 9 were Bond movies, 7 were contemporary dramas, 2 were historical and 2 were musicals. Significantly only one straight crime drama (*The Blue Lamp*) is included.

The country with the highest box office gross is the USA, whose 1120 million paid admissions in 1979 were worth $2806 million.

The highest worldwide rentals earned by any studio in a single year was $429 890 000 by Paramount in 1978.

BUDGETS

The most expensive film ever made is Sergei Bondarchuk's four part, eight-hour epic *War and Peace* (USSR 63–67), which was reported to have cost in excess of $100 million. It was shot on 168 different locations and employed 120 000 Red Army extras at three roubles (£1·38 or $3·15) per month.

The most expensive silent film was Fred Niblo's *Ben-Hur* (US 25) at $3·9 million.

Prior to *War and Peace*, the record for the most expensive production had been held successively by the films listed below. Figures quoted are those reported at the time the films were produced and in most cases are impossible to verify.

Title	($)
Napoleon (US 08)	30 000
Queen Elizabeth (Fr 12)	47 500
The Prisoner of Zenda (US 13)	50 000
Cabiria (It 14)	210 000
Intolerance (US 16)	575 000
A Daughter of the Gods (US 16)	1 000 000
Foolish Wives (US 22)	1 100 000
When Knighthood Was in Flower (US 22)	1 500 000
The Ten Commandments (US 23)	1 800 000
The Thief of Bagdad (US 24)	2 000 000
Ben-Hur (US 25)	3 900 000
Hell's Angels (US 30)	3 950 000
Wilson (US 44)	5 200 000
Duel in the Sun (US 46)	6 000 000
Quo Vadis (US 51)	8 250 000

Akira Kurosawa's *Rashomon* (Jap 50) cost only $40000 to make, but succeeded in opening world markets to Japanese films

The Ten Commandments (US 56)	13 500 000
Ben Hur (US 59)	15 000 000
Mutiny on the Bounty (US 62)	19 000 000
Cleopatra (US 63)	44 000 000

The only Hollywood movie which may have exceeded *Cleopatra's* cost was *The Deer Hunter* (US 79). According to *Variety* (18.4.79), the picture had run $20 million over budget, eventually totalling $50 million.

The least expensive full-length feature film on record is Victorian Film Productions' part-colour *The Shattered Illusion* (Aus 27), which took twelve months to complete and included spectacular scenes of a ship being overwhelmed by a storm. Total cost of production was £300 ($1460).

The least expensive all-colour talkie was Pat Rocco's 80-minute psychological drama *Someone* (US 68), with Joe Adair and four other paid performers, which was made on an eight-day schedule for $1200 (£500).

Other low budget movies which have achieved box office and/or critical success include Marco Bellocchio's *I Pugni in Tasca* (It 66), which cost $78000; Truffaut's *The Four Hundred Blows* (Fr 59), $65000; *Never on Sunday* (Greece 59), $100000; Nasser Gholam-Rezai's highly acclaimed *How Starry was My Night* (Iran 77), $28000; Philippe Garrel's *La Concentration* (Fr 68), $14000; Celestino Coronado's *Hamlet* (GB 77), $5000; Jon Jost's colour feature *Angel City* (US 77), $6000; Ingmar Bergman's *Prison* (Sw 48), $40000; Ermano Olmi's *Il Posto* (It 61), $15000; Akira Kurosawa's *Rashomon* (Jap 50), $40000; Claude Lelouch's *Smic, Smac, Smoc* (Fr 71), $30000; Wim Verstappen's award winning *Joszef Katus* (Neths 67), $2400; Jon Jost's *Last Chants for a Slow Dance* (US 79), $2000; Josef Rodel's *Albert – Why* (W. Ger 78), winner of the 1979 German Critics' Film Prize, $5000. *The Night of the Living Dead* (US 68) was made for $114000 and brought in $12 million in worldwide rentals; John Waters' *Pink Flamingos* (US 72), billed as 'An Exercise in Poor Taste' and described in one review as 'the sickest movie ever made', cost $12000 to produce and grossed $1250000 in two years; while the notorious *Deep Throat* (US 71), made for $25000, grossed $4·6 million over the same length of time, **a record budget/box office ratio** of 1:184.

Average Hollywood budgets for feature films

1915	$21 800 (5 reels)	1960	$1 000 000
1919	$60 000 (5 reels)	1965	$1 500 000
1924	$300 000	1970	$1 750 000
1932	$153 000	1972	$1 890 000
1935	$209 000	1974	$2 500 000
1940	$314 000	1976	$4 000 000
1941	$400 000	1978	$5 300 000
1948	$1 000 000	1979	$6 700 000 (estimate)
1955	$900 000	1980	$7 500 000 (estimate)

Figures prior to 1972 are quoted from *Motion Picture Almanac*. The decrease in the average budget between 1924 and the early 1930s may be accounted for by the increase in the number of cheap 'B' pictures, economies forced on studios by the depression, and a decline in the general index of prices. Early talkies also tended to have smaller casts and less elaborate sets than the silent features of the 1920s. The apparent stability between 1948 and 1960 is harder to explain, particularly as this period saw a vogue for expensive historical epics, a substantial increase in the use of colour, and the demise of the 'B' picture. It is possible, therefore, that the figures quoted for this decade should be regarded with caution.

CHAPTER 4

STORY AND SCRIPT

AUTHORS

Novels, first to be filmed. Producers began turning to literature for their plots soon after the turn of the century. In 1902 Ferdinand Zecca of Pathé succeeded in compressing Zola's *L'Assommoir* into five minutes of screen time as *Les Victimes de l'Alcolisme* (Fr 02), while Edwin S. Porter of the Edison Co. presented *Uncle Tom's Cabin* (US 02) in 14 'tableaux' lasting some 17 minutes. Probably the first novel to be adapted at sufficient length for an adequate presentation of the story was *Robbery Under Arms*, by Rolf Boldrewood, which was brought to the screen by the Australian producer C. McMahon in a five-reel version premièred at the Athenaeum Theatre, Melbourne, on 2 November 1907. The first in Europe was Viggo Larsen's three-reel version of Guy Boothby's *Dr. Nicola* (Den 09), starring August Blom. In America the same year Vitagraph produced a four-reel version of Dickens' *Oliver Twist* (US 09) and soon found they had set a trend, eight versions of the story appearing in various countries during the following three years. Among them was Britain's first essay at a 'full-length' screen adaptation, Thomas Bentley's *Oliver Twist* (GB 12), with Ivy Millais in the title role.

Film rights: The payment of film rights was first put on an organised basis in France, where the Société Cinématographique des Auteurs et Gens de Lettres was established in 1908 to act as a performing rights society interceding between companies like Film d'Art – who based all their films on works of literature – and the members of the two leading literary associations,

the Société des Auteurs and the Société des Gens de Lettres.

It was only the previous year that the matter of film rights to an author's work had arisen for the first time, when the Kalem Co. produced a one-reel version of *Ben-Hur* (US 07). The publishers of Lew Wallace's novel, Harper's, and the producers of the very successful play based on the book, promptly sued. Kalem defended themselves on the grounds that neither publisher nor author had suffered damage and that the film was a good advertisement for the book and the play. The case lasted four years, Kalem finally conceding defeat and settling for $25000.

In the meantime **the first copyright fee paid in the US for film rights** had been negotiated

---

Rolf Boldrewood's *Robbery Under Arms* was the first novel to be brought to the screen in a feature-length production. The Australians were the pioneers of full-length motion pictures *(The Australian Film Institute)*

Above: There have been 207 full-length animated cartoon features produced up to the end of 1979. Halas & Batchelor produced Britain's first full-length feature cartoon in 1954, a much acclaimed interpretation of George Orwell's parable on Stalinism *Animal Farm*. (See p. 243)

Unusual cinemas abounded in the thirties. This one was flourishing in Havana, Cuba in 1931 *(Backnumbers)*

Above: Talkie superstar – Marlene Dietrich
(Backnumbers)

Right: Silent superstar – Mary Pickford
(Backnumbers)

Indomitable Lillian Gish has had the longest screen career of any Hollywood star. On the right she is seen soon after she made her screen debut under the direction of D.W. Griffith in 1912; on the left as a matriarch in Bob Altman's *The Wedding* (US 78). (See p. 110)

What did the Red Chinese make of a troop of dancing Victorian piglets? *The Tales of Beatrix Potter* (GB 71), based on a series of English nursery stories, was one of the first films from the West admitted behind the bamboo curtain

Best selling thriller writer Mickey Spillane as his own creation Mike Hammer in *The Girl Hunters* (US 63)

between Biograph and Little, Brown & Co., publishers of Helen Hunt Jackson's *Ramona*, a best-selling romance about an Indian maiden, originally published in 1884. The film of *Ramona* (US 10) was directed by D.W. Griffith with Mary Pickford in the title role. The fee was $100 and the authoress received the rare distinction of a credit following the main title.

Film rights were not to remain on this modest level for long. In Italy Gabriele D'Annunzio (1863–1938) signed an historic contract with Ambrosio-Films in May 1911 disposing of rights to six of his works at 40000 lire each, equivalent to $7845 at the then rate of exchange. Ambrosio later bought eight more, but far from delighting in this good fortune D'Annunzio displayed only contempt for the medium which had so wholeheartedly embraced his work. He saw only one of the films, *La Leda senza cigno* (It 12), which he dismissed as 'childish and grotesque'. So far as the 40000 lire fees were concerned, he declared that they were just a means of buying meat for his dogs.

The record fees noted below do not take account of *The Birth of a Nation* (US 15), for which the copyright fee was paid on a royalty basis. The film was based on a disagreeably racist novel called *The Clansman*, for which author Thomas Dixon had demanded an unprecedented (for the US) rights fee of $25000. Producer-director D.W. Griffith was unable to raise such a sum and offered him a $2000 advance against a 25 per cent royalty instead. Dixon ultimately received some $750000, **the highest sum made by the author of any silent film property.**

The highest sum made by any novelist in film history has almost certainly accrued to William Peter Blatty, author of *The Exorcist*. The amount of money involved is indeterminate, since Mr Blatty, as producer of the film, was on 40 per cent of the gross. *The Exorcist* (US 73) has grossed over $88 million in North American rentals alone.

The highest price ever paid for film rights is the $9500000 (£4950000) announced by Columbia on 20 January 1978 for Charles Strouse's Broadway musical *Annie*. **The highest sum for a film which has been made** was the $5500000 (£1964285) paid by Warner Bros for the rights to *My Fair Lady* (US 64), an Alan Jay Lerner musical based on George Bernard Shaw's play *Pygmalion*.

The highest sum paid for rights during the silent era was $600000 (£170000) by the Classical Cinematograph Corporation in 1921 for *Ben-Hur*, the Lew Wallace novel made into a 1925 movie.

The first million dollar property was Garson Kanin's Broadway show *Born Yesterday*. Kanin had instructed his agent to refuse any offers from Columbia owing to a long-standing feud with production chief Harry Cohn. The unprecedented size of the offer undermined Kanin's resolve and Columbia made the picture (US 50) with Judy Holliday and Broderick Crawford.

The highest ratio of rights to budget was 78 per cent in the case of Pathé's *Les Misérables* (Fr 11). The film had a budget of 230000f, of which 180000f was paid to the Victor Hugo estate for the rights.

The highest rights paid for a first novel was a

million dollars by Hollywood producer Dan Melnick for English author and ex-bit part player Stephen Sheppard's best-seller *The Four Hundred*, in 1979.

Starring . . . The Author. Novelists have occasionally appeared in the screen version of their own works. The American black writer Richard Wright played the lead in *Native Son* (Arg 50), a film of his novel about a black youth afflicted by racism in the Chicago ghetto. A young Japanese student called Kunie Iwahashie, who won early renown as a novelist in the Françoise Sagan idiom, starred in the film of her novel *Nissholu no Natsu/Summer in Eclipse* (Jap 57). The film of Sir Compton Mackenzie's best-selling novel *Whisky Galore!* (GB 49) – US title *Tight Little Island* – featured the author in the role of the ship's captain. The role of private eye Mike Hammer was played by his creator Mickey Spillane in *The Girl Hunters* (US 63), and best-selling novelist Peter Benchley played a reporter in his own *Jaws* (US 75). Anne-Cath Vestly starred in *Mormor og de Atte Ungene I Byen* (Nor 76), based on her own short stories, while Amos Kolek, son of the Mayor of Jerusalem, had the satisfaction of playing a character based on himself in the film of his autobiographical novel *Don't Ask Me Why I Love* (Israel 79).

The most filmed author is William Shakespeare (1564–1616), whose plays have been presented in 270 straight or relatively straight film versions, 25 'modern versions' (where the story line has been loosely based on Shakespeare, e.g. *West Side Story*) and innumerable parodies. Not surprisingly *Hamlet* has appealed most to film-makers, with 39 movie versions (*see also* Remakes, p. 43), followed by *Romeo and Juliet*, which has been filmed 28 times, and *Macbeth*, filmed 26 times. The accompanying check-list (see below) is intended to indicate no more than the number of screen versions of each play (including TV productions where

Above left: Anthony and David Meyer played the Prince interchangeably in *Hamlet* (GB 78)

Above right: Laurence Olivier in *Hamlet* (GB 48)

Below: Innokenti Smoktunowski in *Hamlet* (USSR 64)

these have been made available on film), with their dates and countries of origin. Space precludes cast-lists, though in the case of *Hamlet* the actor (or actress) playing the title role has been named where it has been credited. It will be noted that on four occasions Hamlet has been played by a woman, by Sarah Bernhardt in a French synchronised sound short of 1900 (*see also* Sound Film, First, p. 161); by the great Danish star Asta Nielsen in a German version of 1920 where Hamlet is revealed at the end to have been a girl raised as a boy; by Joy Caroline Johnson, who interchanged with male thespian Rick McKenna in the 1971 film version of Toronto's Theatre of God production; and recently by Fatma Girik in the explicitly titled *Female Hamlet* (Turkey 77).

SHAKESPEARE ON FILM

HAMLET

Fr 00 with Sarah Bernhardt; Fr 07 with Georges Méliès; It 08 (Cornerio); It 08 (Milano); It 08 (Cines); Fr 09; It 10 with Dante Capelli; Fr 10 with Jacques Grétillat; Den 10 with Alwin Neuss; GB 12 with Charles Raymond; Fr 13 with Paul Mounet-Sully; GB 13 with Sir Johnston Forbes-Robertson; It 14 with Hamilton A. Revelle; US 14 with James Young; GB 14 with Eric Williams; US 14 with Alla Nazimova (there is some doubt whether this film was ever made, nor is it known whether Nazimova played Hamlet or Ophelia if it was); It 17 with Ruggero Ruggeri; Ger 20 with Asta Nielsen; India 28; US 33 with John Barrymore (test reel of Act I Scene 5 and Act II Scene 2); India 35 with Sohrab Modi; GB 48 with Sir Laurence Olivier; India 54 with Kishore Sahu; US 58 (Baylor Theater production); US 59 (Encyclopaedia Britannica 16mm production); Ger 60 with Maximilian Schell; Pol 60 (short directed by Jerzy Skolimowski); US 64 with Richard Burton; USSR 64 with Innokenti Smoktunowski; *Hamile* aka *The Tongo Hamlet* Ghana 65 with Kofi Middleton-Mends; Hung 65 (animated); GB 69 with Nicol Williamson; US 70 with Richard Chamberlain (TVM); *Heranca* aka *Hamlet* Brazil 70 with David Cardaso; US 71 with David Suchet (16mm); Can 71 (musical) with Rick McKenna and Caroline Johnson; *Un Amleto di meno* It 73 with Carmelo

Bene; *Female Hamlet* Turkey 77 with Fatma Girik; GB 78 with Anthony and David Meyer.

Modern versions: *Der Rest ist Schweigen* Ger 59 with Hardy Kruger; *Ophelia* Fr 61 with André Jocelyn; *Ithele na yini vasilas/He Wanted to be King* Greece 67 with Angelos Theodoropoulos; *Quella sporca storia del West* It 68 with Enio Girolami.

Parodies: GB 15; US 16; US 16; It 16; GB 19; US 19; Den 22; Den 32; US 37; it 52.

ANTONY AND CLEOPATRA
It 08; Fr 10; It 13; GB 51; Swz 65; GB 72.

AS YOU LIKE IT
Seven Ages US 05; US 08; US 12; GB 15; GB 36.

COMEDY OF ERRORS
US 08; W. Ger 64 (TVM).
Modern version: *The Boys from Syracuse* US 40.

CORIOLANUS
Coriolano, Eroe Senza Patria aka *Thunder of Battle* It/Fr 63.

CYMBELINE
US 13.

HENRY IV
GB 61 (16mm); US 17 (16mm). Orson Welles' *Campanadas a Medianoche* Sp/Swz 66 (partly based on).

HENRY V
GB 13 (amateur); *England's Warrior King* GB 15; GB 44; GB 58; GB 61 (16mm). Orson Welles' *Campanadas a Medianoche* Sp/Swz 66 (partly based on).

HENRY VI
GB 61 (16mm).

HENRY VIII
GB 11; *Cardinal Wolsey* US 12.

JULIUS CAESAR
Le rêve de Shakespeare, ou la mort de Jules César Fr 07; US 08 (Lubin); US 08 (Vitagraph); It 09; It 10; GB 10; GB 11; US 13 (Kinetophone talkie); It 13; It 16; GB 18; GB 26; GB 45; US 49 (16mm); GB 51; US 53; GB 53; GB 69.
Modern version: *An Honourable Murder* GB 60.

KING JOHN
GB 99; *Hubert and Arthur* GB 14.

KING LEAR
US 09; It 10; It 12; US 16; Ger 29; GB 57 (16mm); USSR 67; GB 70; US 70 (16mm).
Modern versions: *The Yiddish King Lear* US 35; *Broken Lance* US 54.

MACBETH
US 05; US 08; It 09; Fr 10 (Film d'Art); Fr 10

(Andréani); GB 11; Ger 13; US 16; Fr 16; *Lady Macbeth* It 18; Ger 22; GB 22; India 38; GB 45 (16mm); US 46 (16mm); US 48; US 50; GB 53; US 55 (TVM); *Throne of Blood* Jap 57; US 57 (16mm); GB 61; US 64 (16mm); GB 71; W. Ger 71 (Rosa von Praunheim); W. Ger 71 (Werner Schroeter: opera); *Maxhosa* S. Africa 74 (black version with Xhosa cast).

Modern versions: *Le Rideau Rouge* Fr 52; *Joe Macbeth* US 55.

Parody: *The Real Thing at Last* GB 16.

MEASURE FOR MEASURE
US 09; It 13; *Dente per Dente* It 42; *Zweierlei Mass* W. Ger 63 (TVM).

THE MERCHANT OF VENICE
Une mesaventure de Shylock Fr 01; US 08; It 10; US 12; Fr 13; US 14; GB 16; GB 22; Ger 23; GB 27 (Phonofilm talkie); India 41; It/Fr 52; US 71 (16mm); *A Pound of Flesh* HK 77.

THE MERRY WIVES OF WINDSOR
US 10; *Falstaff* Fr 11; Ger 17 (opera); *John Falstaff* GB 23; Ger 35; DDR 50; Liechtenstein 64. Orson Welles' *Campanadas a Medianoche* Sp/Swz 66 (partly based on).

A MIDSUMMER NIGHT'S DREAM
US 09; Fr 09; It 13; Ger 13; Ger 17; Ger 25; US 29; US 35; GB 53 (16mm); US 54 (16mm); Cz 57 (feature-length puppet version); GB 58 (TVM); US 62; US 66 (ballet); GB 68; US 70 (16mm); GB 78 (Colfox School).

MUCH ADO ABOUT NOTHING
Cz 12; USSR 56; DDR 63; USSR 73.
Modern version: *Wet Paint* US 26.

OTHELLO
Ger 07; It 07; Den 08; US 08; Austria 08 (opera); It 09 (Latium); It 09 (Cines); It 09 (Film d'Art Italiana); Den 12; It 14; Ger 18; Ger 22; US 32 (in Arabic); GB 46; GB 53 (16mm); Morocco 55; USSR 56; USSR 60 (ballet); GB 65; USSR 67 (cartoon version).

Modern versions: *Men Are Not Gods* GB 36; *A Double Life* US 47; *Jubal* US 55; *All Night Long* GB 61; *Catch My Soul* US 73.

Parodies: It 09; US 13; Ger 18; It 20.

RICHARD II
US 55 (TVM); *The Hollow Crown* GB 61 (16mm); *The Dangerous Brother* GB 61 (16mm); *The Boar Hunt* GB 61 (16mm). Orson Welles' *Campanadas a Medianoche* Sp/Swz 66 (partly based on).

RICHARD III
US 08; GB 11; Fr 12; US 13; Fr 14; GB 55; *Essais pour Richard III* Fr 71; Fr 73 (expansion of former); Hung 73.

ROMEO AND JULIET
Fr 00 (opera); US 08 (Vitagraph); US 08 (Thanhouser); It 08; GB 08; Ger 09 (opera); It 11; It 12; Fr 13; Fr 14; US 16 (Metro); US 16 (Fox); US 17 (animated clay models version); US 35; Sp 40; Mex 43; *Shuhuda Al-Gharam* Egypt 45; India 47; It/GB 54; Arg 54; USSR 54 (ballet); Cz 58 (puppet); It/Sp 64 (ballet); GB 65 (RADA); GB 66 (ballet); It 68; US 71 (16mm); GB 77 (amateur dance drama); *The Secret Sex Life of Romeo and Juliet* GB 70 (porno).
Modern versions: *Les Amants de Vérone* Fr 48; *Romanoff and Juliet* US 61; *West Side Story* US 62; *Un Retablo Para Romeo y Julieta* Cuba 71.
Parodies: US 10; US 11; US 14; GB 15; Ger 20; US 20; US 21; US 24.

THE TAMING OF THE SHREW
US 08; It 08; GB 11; Fr 11; It 13; Den 14; GB 15; GB 23; US 29; It 41; Hung 43; *Enamorada* Mex 46; India 55; *El Charro y la dama* Mex 49; *La fierecilla domada* Sp 55; *Ukroscht-schenie Stroptiwoi* USSR 61; US/It 66; US 71 (16mm).
Modern versions: *You Made Me Love You* GB 33; *Kiss Me Kate* US 53; *Mas fuerte que el amor* Mex 59.

THE TEMPEST
GB 05; GB 08; US 11; Fr 12; *Ariel Loquitur* It 67; GB 79.
Modern version: *Forbidden Planet* US 56.

TWELFTH NIGHT
US 10; GB 53 (16mm); USSR 56; W.Ger 62; DDR 63; GB 69 (TVM); US 70 (16mm); GB 74 (TVM).
Modern version: *Noche de reyes* Sp 47.

TWO GENTLEMEN OF VERONA
W. Ger 63 (TVM).

THE WINTER'S TALE
US 10; It 10; It 13; Ger 14; GB 53 (16mm); GB 62 (TVM); GB 66.

Never filmed: *Titus Andronicus; Love's Labour's Lost; All's Well That Ends Well; Timon of Athens; Pericles; The Two Noble Kinsmen.*

Among the more bizarre film versions of Shakespeare's greatest play is one in which the Prince of Denmark has undergone a metamorphosis into a gunslinger in the Wild West – *Quella sporca storia del West* (It 68). Hamlet has yet to meet Frankenstein's Monster, but one fears this is only a matter of time. Even the most well-intentioned treatment of Shakespeare's work can be subject to the grossest liberties. One of the most inexplicable is the translation of the sub-titles on the US/GB release prints of Grigori Kozintsev's *Hamlet* (USSR 64), intended as a word-for-word film version of the play. The title-writer has given a modern English rendering of Boris Pasternak's scrupulous Russian translation of Shakespeare's original text. Other debasements of the bard's work have been more deliberate. We may be thankful that there has been no follow-up to the soft-porn British film *The Secret Sex Life of Romeo and Juliet* (GB 70) and even more so that among the many projected Shakespeare films that have failed to go into production was Joseph Goebbels' viciously anti-semitic version of *The Merchant of Venice*.

The most filmed novelist is Edgar Wallace (1875–1932), whose books and short stories have been made into 132 British, American and German films. In addition there have been 19 films based on Edgar Wallace plays, making him the most filmed 20th-century writer. (The total of 151 films excludes those based on his characters only.) The first movie derived from one of Wallace's works was *The Man who Bought London* (GB 16), from his novel of the same name. Despite the royalties from his prodigious literary output, his film rights (37 of the films were made in his lifetime), and fees for script-writing, directing, and chairing the board of British Lion, Edgar Wallace died owing $315000.

The most filmed American writer is the western novelist Zane Grey (1875–1939), with 103 films of his works, starting with *Riders of the Purple Sage* (US 18) and ending with *The Maverick Queen* (US 56). All but one were American movies (including a Spanish language western), the exception being *Rangle River* (Aus 37). Grey wrote over a hundred novels, not all of which have been filmed, though a number have been made four times. Zane Grey movies nearly always featured on the bottom half of the bill and the finish of Hollywood 'B' movie production in the mid-50s brought an end to the filming of his works.

Since both the Edgar Wallace and Zane Grey literary lodes seem to have been fully worked (the last Wallace was made in 1971), it seems probable that their records will be overtaken within a few years by one of the runners-up, all of them writers of enduring quality. Sandwiched between Wallace and Grey is Alexandre Dumas (père) (1802–70), author of *The Count of Monte Cristo* and *The Three Musketeers*, whose works have been brought to the screen in 118 films, exactly 100 films have been based on the novels of Count Leo Tolstoy (1828–1910) and Charles Dickens (1812–70) will soon reach the century, with 98 films to his credit. Somewhat further behind, but still eminently filmable, is Edgar Allan Poe (1809–49), whose works have directly

The most filmed American writer has been Zane Grey. *The Border Legion* (US 30) was one of 103 films based on his work

contributed to 95 movies (a great number more have invoked his name in their publicity), and the great Russian playwright and short-story writer Anton Chekhov (1860–1904), with 78 films.

SCRIPT

The world's first film scenario was written by the Australian poet Henry Lawson (1867–1922) in 1896 and told the story of a drover and his aboriginal tracker who die of thirst in the desert while the drover's wife and family wait for him at home. After a record delay in production of 77 years it was brought to the screen by Keith Gow as *Where Dead Men Lie* (Aus 73). Lawson was inspired to write the scenario, which he titled *The Australian Kinematograph*, by the introduction of the films of R.W. Paul and the Lumière Bros into Australia that year.

The first scriptwriter was New York journalist Roy McCardell, who was hired in 1900 by Henry Marvin of the American Mutoscope & Biograph Co. to write ten scenarios a week at $15 each. Since most of the films made by Biograph at that time were 50–100 ft in length (about 1½ minutes), McCardell found he was able to complete his first week's assignment in a single afternoon.

The first contract writer (i.e. full-time employee of a studio) was Louis Feuillade, who joined the Gaumont Studios in Paris in 1905.

Britain's first regular scriptwriter was Harold Brett, engaged by H.O. Martinek of the British & Colonial Kinematograph Co., whose earliest known scenario was for a spy picture called *A Soldier's Honour* (GB 11). Previously it had been the custom of British film producers to shoot without a script or write their own screenplays.

The first writer of literary distinction to be engaged to produce a scenario was the French playwright Henri Lavedan, whose *L'Assassination de le Duc de Guise* (Fr 08) was made by Film d'Art.

In the USA the first eminent writer under contract was Emmett Campbell Hall, who was engaged by D.W. Griffith to script the Biograph pictures *His Trust* (US 11) and *His Trust Fulfilled* (US 11), a two-part story of the American Civil War.

The first scriptwriter to 'have his name in lights' – in other words, to be credited on a cinema marquee – was H.H. Van Loon, author and adaptor of *The Virgin of Stamboul* (US 20), who was afforded this tribute by the Strand Theater, San Francisco, in November 1920.

The first scriptwriters to write dialogue for a sound feature film were Joseph Jackson and Edward T. Lowe Jr., who composed the four talking sequences of Warner Bros' crime melodrama *Tenderloin* (US 28). The dialogue was so ludicrous that two of the sequences were cut after the first week of the film's run. (The dialogue sequences in *The Jazz Singer* (US 27) had been *ad libbed* by Al Jolson in the title role.)

The shortest dialogue script since the introduction of talkies was written for Mel Brooks' *Silent Movie* (US 76), which had only one spoken word throughout. The dialogue sequence in the otherwise silent movie occurs when mime artiste Marcel Marceau, having been invited by telephone (silently) to appear in a silent movie, replies (audibly) 'Non!' The person making the call is asked (according to the inter-title) 'What did he say?' Response, also by inter-title: 'I don't know. I don't understand French.'

The only other film with but a single word of dialogue, Paul Fejos's *Marie, A Hungarian Legend* (Hung 32), used a longer word – the name 'Marie'.

The most co-writers credited for any film was 21 in the case of *Forever and a Day* (US 43). They included C.S. Forester, John van Druten, Christopher Isherwood, R.C. Sherriff, James Hilton and Frederick Lonsdale.

A Yank at Oxford (GB 38) credited only eight scriptwriters, but at least 31 are known to have been employed by MGM on the screenplay. Among those uncredited were Herman J. Mankiewicz, John Paddy Carstairs, Hugh Walpole and F. Scott Fitzgerald.

Profanities, obscenities and expletives: It is Hollywood myth that Clark Gable's celebrated closing line in *Gone with the Wind* (US 39) – 'Frankly, my dear, I don't give a damn' – was the first occasion on which the word 'damn' had been spoken on the screen. It was said by both Leslie Howard and Marie Lohr in *Pygmalion*

(GB 38) and had featured in at least two earlier Hollywood pictures. Fred Stone said 'Damn you!' to the heroine's boss (who had wronged her) in *Alice Adams* (US 35) and three years before that Emma Dunn had exclaimed 'Well, I'll be damned' in *Blessed Event* (US 32). After *Gone with the Wind* there was a long interval before 'damn' was uttered again in an American movie, the next occasion being in *Cease Fire* (US 53), which also gave US audiences their first encounter with 'hell!' as an on-screen expletive. Nothing stronger was allowed until the sixties, the obscenities voiced by Mickey Shaughnessy in *Don't Go Near the Water* (US 56) being bleeped out.

British censors had less reserve about the use of realistic language where it was appropriate. 'Bloody' was heard for the first time in *Pygmalion* (GB 38), 'fanny' in *Convoy* (US 41), and 'arse' in *The Guinea Pig* (GB 49). The British also pioneered the on-screen use of 'bugger' in *Poor Cow* (GB 67) and the most over-used four-letter word in *I'll Never Forget Whatshisname* (GB 68), in which Marianne Faithful made a little piece of film history by breaking the ultimate 'word barrier'. (Critic Kenneth Tynan had, however, said it earlier on television.) The Americans were first, however, with 'shit', which was heard in *In Cold Blood* (US 67) a year earlier than its first appearance on a British soundtrack in *Boom!* (GB 68), while the permissive Danes led with the first on-screen use of a four-letter word in reference to female genitalia in *Quiet Days in Clichy* (Den 69).

Most of the above words had been used at one time or other by actors in silent films. When Edmund Lowe and Victor McLaglen indulged in a fine exchange of Billingsgate in *What Price Glory* (US 26), the studio received hundreds of letters of protest from outraged lip-readers. Likewise in *Sadie Thompson* (US 28), lip-readers would be the only ones to appreciate the full rich flavour of Gloria Swanson's language as Sadie – which made no concessions to the censors. The title cards only reproduced what she was *not* saying.

The most hackneyed line in movie scripts is 'Let's get outta here'. A recent survey of 150 American features of the period 1938–74 (revived on British television) showed that it was used at least once in 84 per cent of Holly-wood productions and more than once in 17 per cent.

The longest monologue in a dramatic film is a 20-minute speech by Edwige Feuillère in *L'Aigle à deux têtes/The Eagle has Two Heads* (Fr 48).

The longest monologue in a Hollywood movie is by Lionel Barrymore in *A Free Soul* (US 31). Six cameras were used to film the 14-minute speech in one take, since sound editing had yet to be perfected.

Statesmen as scriptwriters: A number of Statesmen have turned their hands to scriptwriting, including Sir Winston Churchill, who was under contract to London Films from 1934 until the war and worked on such films as *The Twenty Five Year Reign of King George V* (uncompleted) and *Conquest of the Air* (GB 38). He is also said to have contributed a speech to the script of *That Hamilton Woman*/UK: *Lady Hamilton* (US 42). On the other side of the Atlantic, President Roosevelt wrote the original scenario for *The President's Mystery* (US 36), about a lawyer (Henry Wilcoxson) who fakes his own death so that he can right the wrongs he did in the name of big business. Carmine Gallone's vast and sprawling epic *Scipio Africanus* (It 37), a story of Roman victories in Africa intended to parallel Mussolini's contemporary victories in Abyssinia, was alleged to have been written by Il Duce himself. Another dictator with a screenplay to his credit was General Franco who wrote the scenario for *The Spirit of Race* (Sp 41) an adaptation of his own novel, under the pen-name Jaime de Andrade. In more recent times former Philippines Prime Minister Kurkrit Pramoj wrote *Fai Dang/The Red Bamboo* (Ph 79). Field Marshal Idi Amin Dada, before he was deposed as President-for-Life of Uganda, scripted an adulatory biopic of himself, but happily this was never made. India's former premier Moraji Desai is probably the only world leader to have scripted a film while in office. Having committed himself to producer J. G. Mohla before being gaoled under Mrs Gandhi's State of Emergency, and finding himself Prime Minister shortly after his release, he nevertheless felt under an obligation to fulfil his undertaking. Working in the early mornings he completed his English-language script of *Yogeshwar Krishna* (India i.p.), the story of Lord Krishna, a few months later.

CHAPTER 5

CHARACTERS AND THEMES

SCREEN CHARACTERS

The character most often portrayed on screen since the inception of the story film has been Sherlock Holmes, the master detective created by Sir Arthur Conan Doyle (1859–1930), who has been played by 61 actors, including one black (Sam Robinson), in 175 films produced between 1900 and 1980. The only actor to have played both Sherlock Holmes and Dr Watson was Reginald Owen, who was Watson in *Sherlock Holmes* (US 32) and Holmes in *A Study in Scarlet* (US 33). The filmography below includes feature length TVM's, but excludes filmed television series. Where known the actor playing Sherlock Holmes is included.

Sherlock Holmes Baffled (US 00); Maurice Costello: *The Adventures of Sherlock Holmes* (US 03); *Sherlock Holmes Returns* (US? 06?); Bauman Károly: *Sherlock Holmes* (Hung 08); Viggo Larsen: *Sherlock Holmes I Livsfare* (Den 08); Viggo Larsen: *Sherlock Holmes II* (Den 08); Viggo Larsen: *Sherlock Holmes III* (Den 08); *Sherlock Holmes in the Great Murder Mystery* (US 09); Viggo Larsen: *Sangerindens Diamanter* (Den 09); August Blom: *Droske No 519* (Den 09); Viggo Larsen: *Den Graa Dame* (Den 09); *The Latest Triumph of Sherlock Holmes* (Fr 09); *Sherlock Holmes* (It 09?); Viggo Larsen: *Der Alte Sekretar* (Ger 10); Viggo Larsen: *Der Blaue Diamant* (Ger 10); Viggo Larsen: *Die Falschen Rembrandts* (Ger 10); Viggo Larsen: *Die Flucht* (Ger 10); Otto Lagoni: *Sherlock Holmes I Bondefangerklør* (Den 10); Forrect Holger-Madsen (?): *Forklaedte Barnepige* (Den 11); Holger Rasmussen: *Medlem af den Sorte Hand* (Den 11); Alwin Neuss: *Millionobligation* (Den 11); *Hotel Mysterierne* (Den 11); Viggo Larsen: *Arsène Lupins Ende* (Ger 11); Viggo Larsen: *Sherlock Holmes contra Professor Moryarty* (Ger 11); Henri Gouget: *Les Aventures de Sherlock Holmes* (Fr 11); *Schlau, Schlauer, am Schlauesten* (Fr 12) – French title unknown; Georges Treville: *The Speckled Band* (GB 12); Georges Treville: *The Reigate Squires* (GB 12); Georges Treville: *The Beryl Coronet* (GB 12); Georges Treville: *The Adventure of the Copper Beeches* (GB 12); Georges Treville: *A Mystery of Boscombe Vale* (GB 12); Georges Treville: *The Stolen Papers* (GB 12); Georges Treville: *Silver Blaze* (GB 12); Georges Treville: *The Musgrave Ritual* (GB 13); *Verrater Zigarette* (Ger 13); *Schwarze Kappe* (Ger 13); *Gli artigli di griffard* (It 13); *Forte di Sherlock Holmes* (It 13); Harry Benham: *Sherlock Holmes Solves the Sign of Four* (US 13); Ferdinand Bonn: *Sherlock Holmes contra Dr Mors* (Ger 14); *En Raedsom Nat* (Den 14); Em Gregers (?): *Hvem er Hun?* (Den 14); James Bragington: *A Study in Scarlet* (GB 14); Francis Ford: *A Study in Scarlet* (US 14); Alwin Neuss: *Der Hund von Baskerville* (Ger 14); Alwin Neuss: *Der Hund von Baskerville II* (Ger 14); Alwin Neuss: *Der Hund von Baskerville III* (Ger 15); Alwin Neuss: *Der Hund von Baskerville IV* (Ger 15); Eugen Burg: *Der Hund von Baskerville V* (Ger 15); Alwin Neuss: *Ein Schrei in der Nacht* (Ger 15); Bloomer Tricks Sherlock Holmes (It 15); Alwin Neuss: *William Voss* (Ger 15); William Gillette: *Sherlock Holmes* (US 16); H.A. Saintsbury: *The Valley of Fear* (GB 16); Alwin Neuss: *Sherlock Holmes auf Urlaub* (Ger 16); Alwin Neuss: *Sherlock Holmes Nächtliche Begegnung* (Ger 16); Hugo Flink: *Der Erstrommotor* (Ger 17); Hugo Flink: *Die Kasette* (Ger 17); Hugo Flink: *Der Schlangenring* (Ger 17); Hugo Flink: *Die Indische Spinne* (Ger 18); Viggo Larsen: *Rotterdam-Amsterdam* (Ger 18); Ferdinand Bonn: *Was er im Spiegel sar* (Ger 18); Ferdinand Bonn: *Die Giftplombe* (Ger 18); Ferdinand Bonn: *Das Schicksal der Renate Yongk* (Ger 18); Ferdinand Bonn: *Die Dose des Kardinals* (Ger 18); Sam Robinson: *Black Sherlock Holmes* (US 18) – only time Holmes has been played by a black; Viggo Larsen: *Drei Tage Tot* (Ger 19); Kurt Brenkendorff: *Der Mord im Splendid Hotel* (Ger 19); Erich Kaiser-Titz (?): *Dr Macdonald's Sanitorium* (Ger 20); Adolf D'Arnaz (?): *Harry Hill contra Sherlock Holmes* (Ger 20); Lu Jurgens (?): *Das Haus ohne Fenster* (Ger 20); Eille Norwood: *The Dying Detective* (GB 21); Eille Norwood: *The Devil's Foot* (GB 21); Eille Norwood: *A Case of Identity* (GB 21); Eille Norwood: *The Yellow Face* (GB 21); Eille Norwood: *The Red-Headed League* (GB 21); Eille Norwood: *The Resident Patient*: Eille Norwood: *A Scandal in Bohemia* (GB 21); Eille Norwood: *The Man with the Twisted Lip* (GB 21); Eille Norwood: *The Beryl Coronet* (GB 21); Eille Norwood: *The Noble Bachelor* (GB 21); Eille Norwood: *The Copper*

Beeches (GB 21); Eille Norwood: *The Empty House* (GB 21); Eille Norwood: *The Tiger of San Pedro* (GB 21); Eille Norwood: *The Priory School* (GB 21); Eille Norwood: *The Solitary Cyclist* (GB 21); Eille Norwood: *The Hound of the Baskervilles* (GB 21); Eille Norwood: *Charles Augustus Milverton* (GB 22); Eille Norwood: *The Abbey Grange* (GB 22); Eille Norwood: *The Norwood Builder* (GB 22); Eille Norwood: *The Reigate Squires* (GB 22); Eille Norwood; *The Naval Treaty* (GB 22); Eille Norwood: *The Second Stain* (GB 22); Eille Norwood: *The Red Circle* (GB 22); Eille Norwood: *The Six Napoleons* (GB 22); Eille Norwood: *Black Peter* (GB 22); Eille Norwood: *The Bruce-Partington Plans* (GB 22); Eille Norwood: *The Stockbroker's Clerk* (GB 22); Eille Norwood: *The Boscombe Valley Mystery* (GB 22); Eille Norwood: *The Musgrave Ritual* (GB 22); Eille Norwood: *The Golden Pinz-Nez* (GB 22); Eille Norwood: *The Greek Interpreter* (GB 22); John Barrymore: *Sherlock Holmes* (US 22); Eman Fiala: *The Abduction of Banker Fusee* (Cz 23); Eille Norwood: *Silver Blaze* (GB 23); Eille Norwood: *The Speckled Band* (GB 23); Eille Norwood: *The Gloria Scott* (GB 23); Eille Norwood: *The Blue Carbuncle* (GB 23); Eille Norwood: *The Engineer's Thumb* (GB 23); Eille Norwood: *His Last Bow* (GB 23); Eille Norwood: *The Cardboard Box* (GB 23); Eille Norwood: *Lady Frances Carfax* (GB 23); Eille Norwood: *The Three Students* (GB 23); Eille Norwood: *The Missing Three-Quarter* (GB 23); Eille Norwood: *Thor Bridge* (GB 23); Eille Norwood: *The Stone of Mazarin* (GB 23); Eille Norwood: *The Dancing Men* (GB 23); Eille Norwood: *The Crooked Man* (GB 23); Eille Norwood: *The Final Problem* (GB 23); Eille Norwood: *The Sign of Four* (GB 23); Philip Beck: *Kobenhavns Sherlock Holmes* (Den 25); Carlyle Blackwell: *Der Hund von Baskerville* (Ger 29); Clive Brook: *The Return of Sherlock Holmes* (US 29); Clive Brook: *Paramount on Parade* (US 30); Arthur Wontner: *The Sleeping Cardinal* (GB 31); Raymond Massey: *The Speckled Band* (GB 31); Robert Rendel: *The Hound of the Baskervilles* (GB 32); Clive Brook: *Sherlock Holmes* (US 32); Arthur Wontner: *The Sign of Four* (GB 32); Arthur Wontner: *The Missing Rembrandt* (GB 32); Martin Fric: *Lelicek ve Sluzbach Sherlocka Holmese* (Cz 32); Richard Gordon: *The Radio Murder Mystery* (US 33); Reginald Owen: *A Study in Scarlet* (US 33); Arthur Wontner: *The Triumph of Sherlock Holmes* (GB 35); Arthur Wontner: *Silver Blaze* (GB 37); Bruno Güttner: *Der Hund von Baskerville* (Ger 37); Hermann Speelmans: *Die Graue Dame* (Ger 37); Hans Albers: *Der Mann, der Sherlock Holmes war* (Ger 37); Basil Rathbone: *The Hound of the Baskervilles* (US 39); Basil Rathbone: *The Adventures of Sherlock Holmes* (US 39); Basil Rathbone: *Sherlock Holmes and the Voice of Terror* (US 42); Basil Rathbone: *Sherlock Holmes and the Secret Weapon* (US 42); Basil Radford (cameo role):

Left, top to bottom: John Neville in *A Study in Terror* (GB 65)

Raymond Massey in *The Speckled Band* (GB 31)

Viggo Larsen *(right)* in *Sherlock Holmes I Livsfare* (Den 08)

Robert Stephens in *The Private Life of Sherlock Holmes* (GB 70)

Crazy House (US 43); Basil Rathbone: *Sherlock Holmes in Washington* (US 43); Basil Rathbone: *Sherlock Holmes Faces Death* (US 43); Basil Rathbone: *Sherlock Holmes and the Spider Woman* (US 44); Basil Rathbone: *The Scarlet Claw* (US 44); Basil Rathbone: *The Pearl of Death* (US 44); Basil Rathbone: *The House of Fear* (US 45); Basil Rathbone: *The Woman in Green* (US 45); Basil Rathbone: *Pursuit to Algiers* (US 45); Basil Rathbone: *Terror by Night* (US 45); Basil Rathbone: *Dressed to Kill* (US 45); John Longden: *The Man with the Twisted Lip* (GB 51); Peter Cushing: *The Hound of the Baskervilles* (GB 59); Christopher Lee: *Sherlock Holmes und das Halsband des Todes* (W.Ger 62); Jerome Raphel: *The Double-Barrelled Detective Story* (US 65); John Neville: *A Study in Terror* (GB 65); Nando Gazzolo: *La Valle della paura* (It 68, TVM); Nando Gazzolo: *L'Ultimo dei Baskerville* (It 68); Robert Stephens: *The Private Life of Sherlock Holmes* (GB 70); Radovan Lukavsky: *Touha Sherlocka Holmese* (Cz 71); George C. Scott: *They Might Be Giants* (US 72); *The Case of the Metal-Sheathed Elements* (GB 72) – cartoon; Stewart Granger: *The Hound of the Baskervilles* (US 72, TVM); Keith McConnell: *Murder in Northumberland* (GB 74); Rolf Becker: *Monsieur Sherlok Holmes* (Fr 74, TVM); Harry Reems: *Sherlock Holmes* (US 75) – porno; Douglas Wilmer: *The Adventure of Sherlock Holmes' Smarter Brother* (GB 75); Roger Moore: *Sherlock Holmes in New York* (US 76, TVM released theatrically in Europe); Keith McConnell: *Murder by Death* (US 76) – SH role cut in some release prints; Nicol Williamson: *The Seven-Per-Cent Solution* (GB 77); Trevor Ainsley: *The Case of the Mounting Fortune* (GB 78); Peter Cook: *The Hound of the Baskervilles* (GB 78); Christopher Plummer: *Murder by Decree* (GB/Can 79); Jeremy Young: *The Case of the Fantastical Passbook* (GB 79); Aljgis Masjulis: *The Blue Carbuncle* (USSR 80, TVM).

The other fictitious or legendary characters most frequently represented on screen have been Count Dracula – 133 films (see p. 75); Frankenstein's monster – 91 films; Tarzan – 83 films (*see* filmography below); Hopalong Cassidy – 66 films (see p. 117); Zorro – 65 films; Charlie Chan – 49 films; and Robin Hood – 48 films.

Tarzan Filmography

Elmo Lincoln: *Tarzan of the Apes* (US 18); Elmo Lincoln: *The Romance of Tarzan* (US 18); Gene Pollar: *The Revenge of Tarzan* (US 20); P. Dempsey Tabler: *The Son of Tarzan* (US 20); Elmo Lincoln: *The Adventures of Tarzan* (US 21) – serial; James Pierce: *Tarzan and the Golden Lion* (US 27); Frank Merrill: *Tarzan the Mighty* (US 28) – serial; Frank Merrill: *Tarzan the Tiger* (US 29) – serial; Charlie Chase: *Nature in the Wrong* (US 32) – parody; Johnny Weissmuller: *Tarzan the Ape Man* (US 32); Buster Crabbe: *Tarzan the Fearless* (US 33); Johnny Weissmuller: *Tarzan and His Mate* (US 34); Herman Brix: *The New Adventures of Tarzan* (US 35) – serial; Johnny Weissmuller: *Tarzan Escapes* (US 36); John Cavas: *Toofani Tarzan* (India 37); Herman Brix: *Tarzan in Guatemala* (US 38) – feature derived from first half of *The New Adventures of Tarzan* (above); Herman Brix: *Tarzan and the Green Goddess* (US 38) – feature derived from last half of *The New Adventures of Tarzan* (above); Glenn Morris: *Tarzan's Revenge* (US 38);

Manek: *Tarzan Ki Beta* (India 38); Johnny Weissmuller: *Tarzan Finds a Son!* (US 39); Peng Fei: *The Adventures of Chinese Tarzan* Parts 1–3 (Singapore 39–40); Johnny Weissmuller: *Tarzan's Secret Treasure* (US 41); Johnny Weissmuller: *Tarzan's New York Adventure* (US 42); Johnny Weissmuller: *Tarzan Triumphs!* (US 43); Johnny Weissmuller: *Tarzan's Desert Mystery* (US 43); Johnny Weissmuller: *Tarzan and the Amazons* (US 45); Johnny Weissmuller: *Tarzan and the Leopard Women* (US 46); Johnny Weissmuller: *Tarzan and the Huntress* (US 47); Johnny Weissmuller: *Tarzan and the Mermaids* (US 48); Lex Barker: *Tarzan's Magic Fountain* (US 49); Lex Barker: *Tarzan and the Slave Girl* (US 50); Toto: *Toto Tarzan* (It 50) – parody; Lex Barker: *Tarzan's Peril* (US 51); Lex Barker: *Tarzan and the She-Devil* (US 53); Gordon Scott: *Tarzan's Hidden Jungle* (US 55); *Tarzan and Boy* (US c. 55) – porno; Gordon Scott: *Tarzan and the Lost Safari* (GB 57); Gordon Scott: *Tarzan's Fight for Life* (US 58); Manchar: *Thozhan* (India 59) – Tamil; Gordon Scott: *Tarzan's Greatest Adventure* (GB 59); Denny Miller: *Tarzan the Ape Man* (US 59); Gordon Scott: *Tarzan the Magnificent* (GB 60); Azad: *Toofani Tarzan* (India 62); Jock Mahoney: *Tarzan Goes to India* (GB 62); Rudolph Hrušínský: *Tazanova smot/The Death of Tarzan* (Cz 62)*; Azad: *Tarzan aur Gorilla* (India 63); Indrajeet: *Rocket Tarzan* (India 63); Jock Mahoney: *Tarzan's Three Challenges* (US 63); Azad: *Tarzan aur Jadugar* (India 63); Kit Morris: *Tarzan chez les coupeurs de tete* (It 63)*; Joe Robinson: *Tarzan roi de la force brutale* (It 63)*; Vladamir Korenev: *Tarzan des mers* (USSR 63)*; Azad: *Tarzan and Captain Kishore* (India 64); Azad: *Tarzan and Delilah* (India 64); Azad: *Tarzan aur Jalpari* (India 64); Brick Bardo: *Jungle Tales of Tarzan* (W.Ger 64); Don Bragg: *Tarzan and the Jewels of Opar* (Jamaica 64) – uncompleted; Taylor Mead: *Tarzan and Jane Regained Sort Of . . .* (US 64) – Warhol; Dara Singh: *Tarzan and King Kong* (India 65); Dara Singh: *Tarzan Comes to Delhi* (India 65); Azad: *Tarzan and Circus* (India 65); Ralph Hudson: *Tarzak Against the Leopardmen* (It 65); Mike Henry: *Tarzan and the Valley of Gold* (US 66); Hercules: *Tarzan and Hercules* (India 66); Azad: *Tarzan Ki Mehbooba* (India 66); Azad: *Tarzan aur Jadui Chirag* (India 66); Mike Henry: *Tarzan and the Great River* (US 67); *Tarzans Kampf mit dem Gorilla* (W.Ger 68) – short; Mike Henry: *Tarzan and the Jungle Boy* (US 68); Azad: *Tarzan in Fairy Land* (India 68); Ron Ely: *Tarzan's Jungle Rebellion* (US 70) – theatrical release derived from TV series; Ron Ely: *Tarzan's Deadly Silence* (US 70) – theatrical release derived from TV series; Azad: *Tarzan 303* (India 70); *Tarzan the Swinger* (US 70) – underground movie; Johnny Weissmuller Jnr. (voice): *Tarzoon, Shame of the Jungle* (Belg 75) – animated feature; *Tarzan of Bengal* (Bangladesh 76); Karl Blomer: *Jane is Jane Forever* (W.Ger 78); *La Infancia de Tarzan* (Sp 79); Andy Luotto: *Tarzan Andy* (It 80) – parody.

Azad has been listed in a French filmography as starring in *Tarzan's Beloved* (India 64) and *Tarzan and Cleopatra* (India 65), but the release of these titles in India cannot be traced. If the films were made, Azad has played the role 13 times to Johnny Weissmuller's 12. A Hindustani version of *Tarzan Goes to India* (GB 62) was released in 1974 as *Tarzan Mera Sathi*.

* Titles changed after threat of legal action from the Edgar Rice Burroughs Estate.

BALLET

The first ballet films were presented at the Phono-Cinéma-Théâtre at the Paris Exposition on 8 June 1900 and consisted of three single-scene subjects – Rosita Mauri dancing in *Korrigane* and Zambelli in *Le Cid* and *Sylvia* – and a longer film of *The Prodigal Son*, with Felicia Mallet dancing in three scenes from the ballet. All these films had a synchronised musical accompaniment on records.

The first complete ballet to be presented on film was Luigi Manzotti's *Excelsior* (It 14), produced by Comerio Film of Milan as an 'Azione ciné-fono-coreografica' ('Ciné-phono-choreographic Action') with Romualdo Marenco's music on synchronised discs.

The first feature film on a ballet theme was *Roman russkoj baleriny*/*The Romance of a Russian Ballerina* (Rus 13), a five-reel tear-jerker directed by Georg Jacobi and featuring the Imperial Ballet star Smirnova in the title role.

The first British feature on a ballet theme was *Dance Pretty Lady* (GB 32), from Compton Mackenzie's novel *Carnival* about a Cockney ballerina (Ann Casson), which featured the Ballet Rambert in the dance sequences.

The first original full-length film ballet was Sir Frederick Ashton's *The Tales of Beatrix Potter*/US: *Peter Rabbit and Tales of Beatrix Potter* (GB 71), with Sir Frederick himself dancing the role of Mrs Tiggie Winkle the hedgehog. *Don Quixote* (Aus 73), co-directed by Robert Helpmann and Rudolf Nureyev, was also an original ballet for the screen.

BIOPICS

The historical character who has been represented most often on screen is Napoléon Bonaparte (1769–1821), Emperor of the French. The role has been played in at least 163 films. The following filmography records the actor playing Napoleon, where this is known:

Napoléon et la Sentinelle (Fr 97); *Entrevue de Napoléon et du Pape* (Fr 98); *Napoleon Crossing the Alps* (It 04); William Humphrey: *Napoleon* (US 06); *Napoleone I* (It 07); Herbert Darnley: *Napoleon and the English Sailor* (GB 08); *Napoleon – Man of Destiny* (Fr 08); *Napoleon on Elba* (It 08); *Napoleon* (US 08); *Napoléon* (Fr 09); *Napoleon and the Princess Hat-

field* (It 09); *Napoleon Bonaparte and the Empress Josephine of France* (US 09); *Napoleon Outwitted by a Clergyman* (Fr 09); William Humphreys: *Napoleon – The Man of Destiny* (US 09); William Humphrey: *Incidents in the Life of Napoleon and Josephine* (US 09); *Napoleon in Russia* (Rus 09); August Blom: *Madame Sans-Gêne* (Den 09); *Napoleone* (It 09); Viggo Larsen: *Budskab til Napoleon paa Elba* (Den 09); *Napoleone e la Principessa di Katzfeld* (It 09); *Una Congiura sotto Napoleone* (It 09); V. Krivtsov: *Napoleon in Russia* (Rus 10); *Napoléon* (Fr 10); *Il Disertore* (It 10); *Un Ammivatore di Bounaparte* (It 10); *Il Granatiere Rolland* (It 10); *Napoleon og Hans lille Trompetisr* (Den 10); Theo Bouwmeester: *Checkmated – A Story of Napoleon* (GB 10); Henri Etievant: *Napoléon et la sentinelle* (Fr 10); *Annette's Rival or The Emperor Napoleon* (Fr 11); Arrigo Frusta: *Il Granatiere Roland* (It 11); *Un Ammivatore di Bounaparte* (It 11); *Napoleone a Sant' Elena* (It 11); Duquesne: *Madame Sans-Gêne* (Fr 11); *Bonaparte* (Belg 11); *La Bataille de Waterloo* (Belg 11); *Napoleon in 1814* (Fr 11); *Napoleon and his Son* (Fr 11); *The Emperor's Return* (Fr 11); Salustiano: *Salustiano, Napoleon* (It 12); *The Two Grenadiers* (Fr 12); Johnny Butt: *The Emperor's Messenger* (GB 12); P. Knorr: *The Year 1812* (Rus 12); George Hernandez: *The Count of Monte Cristo* (US 12); *Napoléon, Bébé et les Cosaques* (Fr 12); *Mémorial de Saint-Hélène* (Fr 12); Charles Sutton: *The Prisoner of War* (US 12); *Napoleon and the English Sailor* (Fr 12); *Napoleon and the Sentinel* (GB 12); *Josephine Empress and Queen* (Fr 12); *A Bogus Napoleon* (US 12); *Epopea Napoleonica* (It 13); Ernest G. Batley: *The Battle of Waterloo* (GB 13); Fred Evans: *Adventures of Pimple – The Battle of Waterloo* (GB 13); *Episodes de Waterloo* (Fr 13); *Napoleon* (US 13) (Solax); *Napoleon* (US 13) (Vitagraph); Stephan Jaracz: *Bog Wojny* (Pol 14); Carlo Campogalli: *Epopea Napoleonica* (It 14); Albert A. Capozzi: *Napoleone* (It 14); *I Cento giorni di Napoleone* (It 14); *The Hundred Days* (US 14); *Napoléon* (Fr 14); Charles Sutton: *Man of Destiny* (US 14); *War and Peace* (Rus 15); Vladamir Gardin: *War and Peace* (Rus 15) (rival version); *The Fortunes of Fifi* (US 17); *Madame Récamier* (Fr 20); Rudolph Lettinger: *Napoleon und die kleine Wäscherin* (Ger 20); Camillo de Rossi (?): *Madame Sans-Gêne* (It 20); Rainer Simons: *Der Herzog von Reichstadt* (Austria 20); Rudolph Lettinger: *Grafin Walenska* (Ger 20); Karel Faltys: *Cikani* (Cz 21); Emile Drain: *L'Aiglonne* (Fr 21); Karl Etlinger: *Die Schauspieler des Kaisers* (Austria 21); George Campbell: *Monte Cristo* (US 22); Rainer Simons: *Napoleon in Schönbrunn* (Austria 22); Otto Matieson: *Vanity Fair* (US 23); Gwylim Evans: *A Royal Divorce* (GB 23); Charles Barratt: *Madame Récamier* (GB 23); Charles Barratt: *Empress Josephine* (GB 23); Michael Xantho: *Der junge Medardus* (Austria 23); Slavko Vorkapitch: *Scaramouche* (US 24); *Napoleon and Josephine* (US 24); *Destiny* (Fr 25); Emile Drain: *Madame Sans-Gêne* (US 25); Wladamir Roudenko (boy) and Albert Dieudonne (man): *Napoléon vu par Abel Gance* (Fr 26); Max Barwyn: *Fighting Eagle* (US 27); Otto Matieson: *The Lady of Victories* (US 27); Charles Vanel: *Konigen Louise* (Ger 27); Pasquale Amato: *Glorious Betsy* (US 28); Stephan Jaracz: *Pan Tadeusz* (Pol 28); Paul Muni: *Seven Faces* (US 29); Werner Krauss: *Napoléon à Saint-Hélène* (Fr 29); Otto Matieson: *Napoleon's Barber* (US 29); William Humphrey: *Devil-May-Care* (US 29); Paul Muni: *The Valiant* (US 29); Charles Vanel: *Waterloo* (Ger 29); Severin Mars: *L'Agonie des Aigles* (Fr 29); Manuel Paris: *El Barbero de Napoleon* (US 30); Paul Gunther: *Luise,*

Above: Albert Dieudonne on set for Abel Gance's epic *Napoleon* (Fr 26)

Right: Jean-Louis Barrault in *Les Perles de la couronne* (Fr 37)

Below: Emile Drain in *Madame Sans-Gene* (US 25)

Below right: Marlon Brando in *Desirée* (US 54)

Königin von Preussen (Ger 31); Gianfranco Giachetti: *Cento di questi giorni* (It 33); *Not Tonight, Josephine* (US 34); Paul Irving: *The Count of Monte Cristo* (US 34); Esme Percy: *Invitation to the Waltz* (GB 35); Corrada Racca: *Campo di Maggio* (It 35); Werner Krauss: *Hundert Tage* (Ger 35); Claude Rains: *Hearts Divided* (US 36); Rollo Lloyd: *Anthony Adverse* (US 36); Emile Drain and Jean-Louis Barrault: *Les Perles de la couronne* (Fr 37); Victor Varconi: *L'Heroique embuscade* (Fr 37); Charles Boyer: *Conquest*/UK: *Marie Waleska* (US 37); Curt Goetz: *Napoleon ist an allem Schuld* (Ger 38); Pierre Blanchar: *A Royal Divorce* (GB 38); Emile Drain and Jean-Louis Allibert: *Remontons les Champs-Elysées* (Fr 39); Erich Ponto: *Der Feuerteufel* (Ger 40); Albert Dieudonne: *Madame Sans-Gêne* (Fr 41); Herbert Lom: *Young Mr. Pitt* (GB 42); *Hitler's Dream* (USSR 42); Sacha Guitry: *Le destin fabuleux de Desirée Clary* (Fr 42); *Lille Napoleon* (Sw 43); Ruggero Ruggeri: *Sant' Elena piccola Isola* (It 43); Sergei Mezhinsky: *Kutosov in 1812* (USSR 44); Adrián Cúneo (?): *Madame Sans-Gêne* (Arg 45); Emile Drain: *Le Diable Boiteux* (Fr 48); Pedro Elviro: *El Bano de Afrodita* (Mex 49); Arnold Moss: *Reign of Terror* (US 49); Renato Rascel: *Napoleone* (It 51); Gerard Oury: *Sea Devils* (US 52); Marlon Brando: *Desirée* (US 54); Emile Drain: *Versailles m'était conte* (Fr 54); Daniel Gélin and Raymond Pellegrin: *Napoleone Bonaparte* (It/Fr 55); *Napoleon's Return from Elba* (US 55); Robert Cornthwaite: *The Purple Mask* (US 55); Herbert Lom: *War and Peace* (US 56); Dennis Hopper: *The Story of Mankind* (US 57); Rene Deltgen: *Königin Luise* (W.Ger 57); Pierre Mondy: *Napoleon ad Austerlitz* (Fr 60); Julien Bertheau: *Madame Sans-Gêne* (Fr/Sp/It 61); Mario Corotenuto: *Napoleone a Firenze* (It 62); Raymond Pellegrin: *Venere Imperiale* (It 63); *La Malmaison* (Fr 64); Gyula Bodrogi: *Hary Janos* (Hung 65); Janusz Zakrzenski: *Popioly* (Pol 65); Gustav Holoubek: *Maria and Napoleon* (Pol 65); Jock Livingstone: *Zero in the Universe* (US/Neths 66); Vladislav Strzhelchik: *War and Peace* (USSR 63–67); Giani Esposito: *The Sea Pirate* (Fr/Sp/It 67); Harrison Marks: *The Naked World of Harrison Marks* (GB 67); Heinrich Schweiger: *Frau Wirtin hat auch einen Grafen* (Austria/W.Ger/It 68); *Caroline Chérie* (W.Ger 68); Rod Steiger: *Waterloo* (It/USSR 70); Heinrich Schweiger: *Frau Wirtin hat auch eine nichte* (Austria/Hung/W.Ger/It 70); Eli Wallach: *The Adventures of Gerard* (GB/It/Swz 70); *Napoleon: The Making of a Dictator* (US 70); *Napoleon: The End of a Dictator* (US 71); Kenneth Haigh: *Eagle in a Cage* (GB 71); James Tolkan: *Love and Death* (US 75); Aldo Maccione: *The Loves and Times of Scaramouche* (It/Yug 76).

US Presidents: The President of the United States **most often portrayed on film**, as well as **America's most oft portrayed historical character**, is Abraham Lincoln (1809–65). The role has been played in 128 films to date, of which 19 were educational subjects. Those made for commercial release are listed below, together with the other films featuring representations of US presidents. The actor creating the presidential role is given where known, though in some films the actor has been uncredited.

Arthur Dewey as President Washington in *America* (US 24)

The date preceding the presidents' names is the year of inauguration.

1789
GEORGE WASHINGTON (1732–99): *Washington at Valley Forge* (US 08); *Barbara Freitchie* (US 08); Phillips Smalley: *A Heroine of '76* (US 11); *Washington at Valley Forge* (US 14); Charles Ogle: *Molly, the Drummer Boy* (US 14); Joseph Kilgour: *The Battle Cry of Peace* (US 15); Frank Mayo: *Betsy Ross* (US 17); Noah Beery: *The Spirit of '76* (US 17); *Schoolmaster Matsumoto* (Jap 19); Arthur Dewey: *America* (US 24); Joseph Kilgour: *Janice Meredith* (US 24); Francis X. Bushman: *The Flag* (US 27); Edward Hern: *The Winners of the Wilderness* (US 27); Alan Mowbray: *Alexander Hamilton* (US 31); Alan Mowbray: *The Phantom President* (US 32); George Houston: *The Howards of Virginia* (US 40); Montague Love: *Remarkable Andrew* (US 42); Alan Mowbray: *Where Do We Go From Here?* (US 45); Douglass Dumbrille: *Monsieur Beaucaire* (US 46); Robert Barrat: *The Time of their Lives* (US 46); Richard Gaines: *Unconquered* (US 47); John Crawford: *John Paul Jones* (US 59); Howard St John: *Lafayette* (Fr 62); *Washington at Valley Forge* (US 71); Lorne Green: *Washington – The Man* (US c. 75); Patrick O'Neal: *Independence* (US 76).

1797
JOHN ADAMS (1735–1826): *John Paul Jones* (US 59); William Daniels: *1776* (US 72); Pat Hingle: *Independence* (US 76).

1801
THOMAS JEFFERSON (1743–1826): Lionel Adams: *Janice Meredith* (US 24); Frank Walsh: *America* (US 24);

Albert Hart: *The Man without a Country* (US 25); *The Howards of Virginia* (US 40); *Remarkable Andrew* (US 42); Ken Howard: *1776* (US 72); Ken Howard: *Independence* (US 76)

1809
JAMES MADISON (1751–1836): No portrayals on screen.

1817
JAMES MONROE (1758–1831): Emmett King: *The Man without a Country* (US 25).

1825
JOHN QUINCY ADAMS (1767–1848): No portrayals on screen.

1829
ANDREW JACKSON (1767–1845): George Irving: *The Eagle of the Sea* (US 26); Russell Simpson: *The Frontiersman* (US 27); John Barrymore: *The Gorgeous Hussy* (US 36); Hugh Sothern: *The Buccaneer* (US 38); Edward Ellis: *Man of Conquest* (US 39); Brian Donlevy: *The Remarkable Andrew* (US 42); *Der unendliche Weg* (Ger 43); Lionel Barrymore: *Lone Star* (US 52); Charlton Heston: *The President's Lady* (US 53); Basil Ruysdael: *Davy Crockett, King of the Wild Frontier* (US 55); Carl Brenton Reid: *The First Texan* (US 56); Charlton Heston: *The Buccaneer* (US 58).

1837
MARTIN VAN BUREN (1782–1862): Charles Trowbridge: *The Gorgeous Hussy* (US 36).

1841
WILLIAM HENRY HARRISON (1773–1841): Douglass Dumbrille: *Ten Gentlemen from West Point* (US 42).

1841
JOHN TYLER (1790–1862): No portrayals on screen.

1845
JAMES KNOX POLK (1795–1849): Addison Richards: *The Oregon Trail* (US 59).

1849
ZACHARY TAYLOR (1784–1850): *The Fall of Black Hawk* (US 12); Harry Holden: *The Yankee Clipper* (US 27).

1850
MILLARD FILLMORE (1800–74): No portrayals on screen.

1853
FRANKLIN PIERCE (1804–69): Porter Hall: *The Great Moment* (US 44).

1857
JAMES BUCHANAN (1791–1868): No portrayals on screen.

1861
ABRAHAM LINCOLN (1809–65): *Uncle Tom's Cabin* (US 03); *The Blue and the Grey* (US 08); *The Reprieve* (US 08); *Stirring Days in Old Virginia* (US 09); George Stelle: *The Sleeping Sentinel* (US 10); *Abraham Lincoln's Clemency* (US 11); *The Old Man and Jim* (US 11); *The Fortunes of War* (US 11); *Lieutenant Grey* (US 11); Ralph Ince: *Under One Flag* (US 11); Ralph Ince: *The Seventh Son* (US 12); H.G. Lonsdale: *The Fall of Black Hawk* (US 12); Ralph Ince: *Lincoln's Gettysburg Address* (US 12); Ralph Ince: *Songbird of the North* (US 13); Willard Mack: *The Battle of Gettysburg* (US 13); Ralph Ince: *Lincoln the Lover* (US 14); Ralph Ince: *The Man who Knew Lincoln* (US 14); Joseph Henabery: *The Birth of a Nation* (US 15); Francis

Andrew Jackson (Brian Donlevy), President 1829–37, confronts the 20th century in *The Remarkable Andrew* (US 42)

Ford: *The Heart of Lincoln* (US 15); William Ferguson: *The Battle Cry of Peace* (US 15); Frank McGlynn: *The Life of Abraham Lincoln* (US 15); *The Heart of Maryland* (US 15); Samuel Drane: *The Crisis* (US 16); Benjamin Chapin: 10 one-reelers collectively known as *The Lincoln Cycle* (US 17); *Old Abe* (US 17); Ralph Ince: *Battle Hymn of the Republic* (US 17); Rolf Leslie: *Victory and Peace* (GB 18); Benjamin Chapin: *Lincoln's Thanksgiving Story* (US 18); Benjamin Chapin: *Children of Democracy* (US 18); Benjamin Chapin: *Son of Democracy* (US 18); Meyer F. Stroell: *The Copperhead* (US 19); Ralph Ince: *The Highest Law* (US 21); Ellery Paine: *Lincoln's Gettysburg Address* (US 22) – talkie; *Wild Bill Hickock* (US 23); Ellery Paine (?): *An Episode in the Life of Abraham Lincoln* (US 24) – talkie; George A. Billings: *Barbara Freitchie* (US 24); George A. Billings: *The Dramatic Life of Abraham Lincoln* (US 24); Charles E. Bull: *The Iron Horse* (US 24); George A. Billings: *The Man without a Country* (US 25); George A. Billings: *Hands Up* (US 26); Charles E. Bull: *The Heart of Maryland* (US 27); Rev. Lincoln Caswell: *Lincoln's Gettysburg Address* (US 27) – talkie; Frank Austin: *Court Martial* (US 28); Walter Huston: *Two Americans* (US 29); George A. Billings: *Lincoln's Gettysburg Address* (US 30); *Only the Brave* (US 30); Walter Huston: *Abraham Lincoln* (US 30); *Abraham Lincoln* (US 33) – 2 reels, possibly short version of preceding; Frank McGlynn: *The Littlest Rebel* (US 35); Frank McGlynn: *Roaring West* (US 35); Frank McGlynn: *The Prisoner of Shark Island* (US 36); Frank McGlynn: *Hearts in Bondage* (US 36); *Segraren vid Hampton Roads* (Sw c. 36); Bud Buster: *Cavalry* (US 36); Frank McGlynn: *Western Gold* (US 37); Frank McGlynn: *Wells Fargo* (US 37); Frank McGlynn: *The Man without a Country* (US 37);

Frank McGlynn: *The Plainsman* (US 37); Albert Russell: *Courage of the West* (US 37); *Triumph* (GB? 37); Percy Parsons: *Victoria the Great* (GB 37); Frank McGlynn: *The Lone Ranger* (US 37); Frank McGlynn: *The Mad Empress* (Mex 39); Frank McGlynn: *Lincoln in the White House* (US 39); Frank McGlynn and Walter Houston: *Land of Liberty* (US 39) – compilation film; John Carradine: *Of Human Hearts* (US 39); Henry Fonda: *Young Mr Lincoln* (US 39); Raymond Massey: *Abe Lincoln in Illinois* (US 39); Victor Killain: *Virginia City* (US 40); Charles Middleton: *Sante Fe Trail* (US 40); *A Dispatch from Reuters* (US 40); Charles Middleton: *They Died with their Boots On* (US 41); Joel Day: *The Days of Buffalo Bill* (US 46); Jeff Corey: *Rock Island Trail* (US 50); Jeff Corey: *Transcontinent Express* (US 50); Hans Conreid: *New Mexico* (US 51); Leslie Kimmell: *The Tall Target* (US 51); *Suddenly* (US 54); Stanley Hall: *The Prince of Players* (US 55); Merrell Gage: *The Face of Lincoln* (US 55); Tom Tryon: *Springfield Incident* (US 55); *The Abductors* (US 57) – corpse only; Austin Green: *The Story of Mankind* (US 57); Royal Dano: *Lincoln: The Young Years* (US c. 59, TVM); Raymond Massey: *How the West was Won* (US 63); Dennis Weaver: *The Great Man's Whiskers* (US 71); Charlton Heston: *Lincoln's Gettysburg Address* (US 73); William Deprato: *The Faking of the President* (US 76); John Anderson: *The Lincoln Conspiracy* (US 77); Ford Rainey: *Guardian of the Wilderness* (US 77).

1865
ANDREW JOHNSON (1808–75): Van Heflin: *Tennessee Johnson* (US 42).

1869
ULYSSES SIMPSON GRANT (1822–85): *Barbara Freitchie* (US 08); *Grant and Lincoln* (US 11); Donald Crisp: *The Birth of a Nation* (US 15); E. Allyn Warren: *Abraham Lincoln* (US 30); Guy Oliver: *Only the Brave* (US 30); Joseph Crehan: *The Adventures of Mark Twain* (US 42); *Buffalo Bill, l'eroe del Far West* (It/Fr/W.Ger 65); Antonio Albaisin (?): *Ringo e Gringo contro tutti* (It 66).

1877
RUTHERFORD BIRCHARD HAYES (1822–93): No portrayals on screen.

1881
JAMES ABRAM GARFIELD (1831–81): *Night Raiders* (US 39); Lawrence Wolf: *No More Excuses* (US 68); Van Johnson: *Il prezzo del potere* (It/Sp 69).

1881
CHESTER ALAN ARTHUR (1831–86): Larry Gates: *Cattle King* (US 63).

Above left: Percy Parsons in *Victoria the Great* (GB 37)

Centre left: Walter Huston in *Abraham Lincoln* (US 30)

Below left: Charles E. Bull in *The Heart of Maryland* (US 27)

John Alexander *(right)* as Teddy Roosevelt in *Fancy Pants* (US 50)

1885 and **1893**
STEPHEN GROVER CLEVELAND (1837–1908): Topack: *Lively Political Debate* (US 94); William B. Davison: *Lillian Russell* (US 40); Pat McCormick: *Buffalo Bill and the Indians* (US 76).

1889
BENJAMIN HARRISON (1833–1901): – Steele: *Lively Political Debate* (US 94); Roy Gordon: *Stars and Stripes Forever* (US 52).

1897
WILLIAM McKINLEY (1843–1901): Frank Conroy: *This Is my Affair* (US 37).

1901
THEODORE ROOSEVELT (1858–1919): *Terrible Teddy, The Grizzly King* (US 01); *Big Game Hunting in Africa* (US 09) – reconstruction newsfilm with actor portraying T.R.; T.R. as himself in unidentified one-reel comedy starring Matty Roubert (US 14); T.R. himself in *Womanhood, the Glory of a Nation* (US 17); W.E. Whittle: *General Pershing* (US 19); *The Fighting Roosevelts* (US 19); E.J. Radcliffe: *Sundown* (US 24); Buck Black: *Lights of Old Broadway* (US 25); Frank Hopper: *The Rough Riders* (US 27); *The Man who Dared* (US 33); Sidney Blackmer: *This Is My Affair* (US 37); Wallis Clark: *Yankee Doodle Dandy* (US 42); Sidney Blackmer: *In Old Oklahoma* (US 43); Sidney Blackmer: *Buffalo Bill* (US 44); John Alexander: *Arsenic and Old Lace* (US 44); John Morton: *I Wonder Who's Kissing Her Now?* (US 47); Sidney Blackmer: *My Girl Tisa* (US 48); John Alexander: *Fancy Pants* (US 50); Edward Cassidy: *The First Travelling Saleslady* (US 56); Karl Swenson: *Brighty of the Grand Canyon* (US 66); Brian Keith: *The Wind and the Lion* (US 75); James Whitmore: *Bully* (US 78).

1909
WILLIAM HOWARD TAFT (1857–1930): *The Sculptor's Nightmare* (US 08).

1913
THOMAS WOODROW WILSON (1856–1924): himself in introduction to *The Battle Cry of Peace* (US 15); himself in *Womanhood, the Glory of a Nation* (US 17); *The Great Victory* (US 18); *The Kaiser: The Beast of Berlin* (US 18);

R.A. Faulkner: *General Pershing* (US 19); Alexander Knox: *Wilson* (US 44); Earl Lee: *The Story of Will Rogers* (US 52); L. Kovsakov: *The Unforgettable Year 1919* (USSR 52); Frank Forsyth: *Oh! What a Lovely War* (GB 69).

1921
WARREN GAMALIEL HARDING (1865–1923): No portrayals on screen.

1923
JOHN CALVIN COOLIDGE (1872–1933): Ian Wolfe: *The Court Martial of Billy Mitchell* (US 55).

1929
HERBERT CLARK HOOVER (1874–1964): Tom Jensen: *Fires of Youth* (US 31).

1933
FRANKLIN DELANO ROOSEVELT (1882–1945): Capt. Jack Young: *Yankee Doodle Dandy* (US 42); Capt. Jack Young: *This Is the Army* (US 43); *Herr Roosevelt Plaudert* (Ger 43); Godfrey Tearle: *The Beginning or the End* (US 47); Nikolai Cherkasov: *The First Front* (USSR 49); *Secret Mission* (USSR 50); *Beau James* (US 57); Ralph Bellamy: *Sunrise at Campobello* (US 60); Richard Nelson: *The Pigeon that Took Rome* (US 62); Stephen Roberts: *First to Fight* (US 67); Stanislav Jaskevik: *Liberation* (USSR 70–71); Edward Herrman: *Eleanor and Franklin* (US 76); Dan O'Herlihy: *MacArthur – The Rebel General* (US 77); Stephen Roberts: *Ring of Passion* (US 77, TVM); Howard Da Silva: *The Private Files of J. Edgar Hoover* (US 78).

1945
HARRY S. TRUMAN (1884–1972): Art Baker: *The Beginning or the End* (US 47); *Secret Mission* (USSR 50); *Call Me Madam* (US 53); uncredited child: *Alias Jesse James* (US 59); James Whitmore: *Give 'Em Hell, Harry!* (US 75); E.G. Marshall: *Collision Course* (US 76); Ed Flanders: *MacArthur – The Rebel General* (US 77).

1953
DWIGHT DAVID EISENHOWER (1890–1969): Henry Grace: *The Longest Day* (US 72).

It is not always easy to find a professional actor who looks like the President. The casting director of *Fires of Youth* (US 31) chose Los Angeles policeman Tom Jensen to play President Hoover

Left: John Fitzgerald Kennedy as a young PT boat commander during World War II. *Right:* Cliff Robertson as the future President in *PT 109* (US 63)

1961
JOHN FITZGERALD KENNEDY (1917–63): *Kennedy in his True Colours* (China 62); Cliff Robertson: *PT 109* (US 63); William Jordan: *The Private Files of J. Edgar Hoover* (US 77).

1963
LYNDON BAINES JOHNSON (1908–73): Ivan Triesault: *How to Succeed in Business without Really Trying* (US 67); *Colpo di Stato* (It 68); *The Wrecking Crew* (US 69); Andrew Duggan: *The Private Files of J. Edgar Hoover* (US 77).

1969
RICHARD MILHOUS NIXON (1913–): Jean-Pierre Biesse: *Made in USA* (Fr 67); *The Statue* (US 70); *Cold Turkey* (US 70); *Million Dollar Duck* (US 70); Jim Dixon: *Is There Sex After Death?* (US 71); Richard Dixon: *The Faking of the President 1974* (US 76); Richard Dixon: *The Private Files of J. Edgar Hoover* (US 77); Anderson Humphreys: *The Cayman Triangle* (Cayman Is 77); Harry Spillman: *Born Again* (US 78); Richard M. Dixon: *Hopscotch* (US 80).

1974
GERALD RUDOLPH FORD (1913–): Dick Crockett: *The Pink Panther Strikes Again* (GB 76).

1977
JAMES EARL CARTER (1924–): Ed Beheler: *The Cayman Triangle* (Cayman Is 77); *Black Sunday* (US 77).

In addition to those mentioned above **historical characters most often represented on screen** include Jesus Christ, of whom there are 125 recorded film portrayals; Vladymir Ilich Lenin (1870–1924) – 55 film portrayals; Adolf Hitler (1889–1945) – 55 film portrayals; Cleopatra (69–30 BC) – 36 film portrayals; Queen Victoria (1819–1901) – 36 film portrayals; Henry VIII (1491–1547) – 33 film portrayals; Queen Elizabeth I (1533–1603) – 31 film portrayals; Grigori Rasputin (1871?–1916) – 27 film portrayals; Josef Stalin (1879–1953) – 24 film portrayals; St Joan of Arc (*c.* 1412–31) – 23 film portrayals; Pancho Villa (1877–1923) – 19 film portrayals; Sir Winston Churchill (1874–1965) – 15 film portrayals. Chairman Mao Tse-Tung (1893–1976) was portrayed for the first time in *The Great Flowering River* (China 79) and Queen Elizabeth II (1926–) by Jeanette Charles in *Marcia* (GB 77). *See also* Western hero most often portrayed on screen (p. 84).

BLACK FILMS

The first black film was *The Railroad Porter* (US 12), a chase comedy with an all-black cast directed by pioneer black film-maker Bill Foster.

The first black production company was the Lincoln Motion Picture Co., founded in Los Angeles in 1915 by black actors Clarence Brooks and Noble Johnson, a prosperous black druggist called James T. Smith and white cameraman Harry Grant. The company's first release was *The Realisation of a Negro's Ambition* (US 16), with Noble Johnson starring as an oil engineer who makes good.

The first black feature film was the Frederick

Douglass Film Co.'s six-reel *The Coloured American Winning his Suit* (US 16), which was premièred at Jersey City on 14 July 1916. The all-black cast was largely amateur, made up of 'young men and women of the race from . . . the best families in New Jersey'.

The first black talkie was Christie Comedies' two-reel *Melancholy Dame* (US 28), featuring Roberta Hyson and Spencer Williams. The picture was about black 'high society' in Birmingham, Ala.

The first feature-length black talkie was MGM's *Hallelujah!* (US 29), directed by King Vidor and starring Daniel Haynes. **The first made by a black production company** was the Oscar Micheaux Corporation's *The Exile* (US 31), directed by Oscar Micheaux and starring Stanley Murrell.

The first feature-length film produced by blacks in Britain was Horace Ove's *Reggae* (GB 70), a 60-min documentary about the distinctive Jamaican music form. **The first dramatic feature** was Horace Ove's *Pressure*, made on location in the Ladbroke Grove area of London in 1974, but not released until February 1978. Originally commissioned by the BBC, but rejected as 'too heavy', the film told the story of a British-born younger son (Herbert Norville) of an immigrant family from Trinidad who finds himself adrift between two cultures. **The first dramatic feature released** in Britain was *Black Joy* (GB 77), a delightful comedy about an innocent and unsophisticated Guyanan immigrant (Trevor Thomas) exposed to the 'hustlin'' way of life of the Brixton ghetto.

Black films made by the major studios: During the silent period the 'majors' showed little or no interest in black movies and even when black characters were required they were generally played by white actors in black-face. D.W. Griffith's *The Birth of a Nation* (US 15) had a

Hollywood embraces the all-black movie – *Hallelujah!* (US 29)

large cast of black roles, since the controversial plot revolved round the black 'takeover' of the South following the Civil War, yet only one genuine black – the curiously named Madame Sul-Te-Wan – was employed on the film.

The coming of sound altered the picture, since the trend towards greater realism demanded that blacks be played by blacks, though their roles were generally confined to the menial or the comic (usually both combined). At the same time the major studios began to turn out the occasional all-black picture, most of them dependent upon the vocal talents of the black American and aimed principally at white audiences. Those made prior to the sudden explosion of 'superspade' black exploitation pictures in the late sixties were as follows: *Hallelujah!* (MGM 29) with Daniel Haynes; *Hearts in Dixie* (Fox 29) with Clarence Muse; *Green Pastures* (Warner 36) with Rex Ingram; *Stormy Weather* (TCF 43) with Bill Robinson, Lena Horne; *Cabin in the Sky* (MGM 43) with Eddie Anderson, Lena Horne; *Bright Road* (MGM 51) with Dorothy Dandridge; *Carmen Jones* (TCF 54) with Harry Belafonte, Dorothy Dandridge; *Anna Lucasta* (United Artists 58) with Sammy Davis Jr.; *Porgy and Bess* (Goldwyn 59) with Sidney Poitier, Dorothy Dandridge.

No Hollywood films took the subject of contemporary race relations as a main theme until 1949 when three such films came to the screen almost simultaneously, led by *Home of the Brave*, the story of a black veteran undergoing psychiatric treatment following traumatic war experiences. The other two films, *Pinky* and *Lost Boundaries*, dealt with light-skinned blacks passing for white.

The Hays Code ban on miscegenation as a theme was broached by *Island in the Sun* (US 59), which offered twin romances between John Justin and Dorothy Dandridge (who marry in the end) and Harry Belafonte and Joan Fontaine (who part). In Britain the subject had been tackled much earlier in *Pool of London* (GB 50), which depicted the relationship between a Jamaican ship's steward (Earl Cameron) and a white cinema cashier (Susan Shaw).

Production output: A total of 49 all-black silent features are recorded in the US for the period 1917–30; exactly 150 all-black talkies were made in the US 1931–50.

The first black film with an all-African cast was the Stoll Co.'s *Nionga* (GB 25), about a young betrothed couple in Central Africa and the tragic ending to their romance, the man being accidentally killed and the bride burned alive in her hut according to local custom. Such films were rare, the only other pre-war examples on record being *Zeliv* (It 28), a story of tribal life enacted entirely by Zulus, *Samba* (Ger 28) and *Stampede* (GB 30). All these films were aimed at white audiences, a fact made abundantly clear in the sub-titles to *Nionga*, which referred to its protagonists as 'the savages'.

The first feature-length black African movie aimed at African audiences was *Zonk* (S. Africa 50), a 70-min revue produced by African Film Productions Ltd for showing in mining compounds. Another twenty years elapsed before South Africa produced its first dramatic feature for black audiences, a boxing drama set in Soweto called *Knock Out* (S. Africa 70) with Fusizaza Yokwe as hero Joe Thunder. In the meantime Ousmane Sembene had directed **the first African film drama made by a black African,** *La Noire de . . .* (Senegal 67), premièred at the Théâtre Sorano in Dakar on 4 February 1967.

JEWISH FILMS

The first Jewish film with an all-Jewish cast was Stanisław Sebel's screen version of Gordin's *Satan* (Pol 12), produced by Madame Yelizariantz's Sila Co. with a cast drawn from Warsaw's Fishon Theatre. Within a year there were four Polish companies specialising in Jewish films, Sila having been joined by Variag (also run by a woman, Madame Stern), Mintus and Kosmofilm.

The first British example was *The Jewish King Lear* (GB 12), filmed at the Pavilion Theatre and premièred at New King's Hall in the Commercial Road. **America's first Jewish picture** was *A Passover Miracle* (US 14), released by Kalem in two versions, one with English sub-titles, the other with Yiddish.

The first talkie in Yiddish was Sidney M. Goldin's *Style and Class* (US 29), a Judea Films production with Goldie Eisenman and Marty Baratz.

Although no Yiddish films have been produced since 1961, Joseph Green's *Mamele/Little Mother* (Pol *c*. 37) was recently revived in Toronto. Star of the picture Molly Picon *(right)* was present for the opening

Production output: According to Rob Edelman's filmography of feature films in Yiddish (*Films in Review* June/July 1978), there were 53 produced in America 1924–61, 17 in Poland pre-1940, 4 in Russia 1925–33 and solitary examples from West Germany in 1948 and Italy in 1949. Mr Edelman believes there may also have been Romanian and Hungarian Yiddish features. The last Yiddish feature was *Three Daughters* (US 61). Despite the lack of any recent product, a Yiddish Film Festival was held in New York in 1978.

Anti-Semitic films have been rare. In 1935, when Joseph Goebbels ordered a search to be made for foreign anti-Semitic films that could be released in Germany, the only example that could be obtained was a primitive Swedish talkie called *Pettersson and Bendel* (Sw 33). Curiously the Nazi-controlled film industry of the Third Reich made no overtly anti-Semitic pictures until just before the war, when Hans

Heinz Zerlett directed *Robert und Bertram* (Ger 39), a comedy about two German tramps who get the better of a rascally Jew and save the innkeeper's lovely Aryan daughter from the fate of marrying him. The following year cinematic Jew-baiting began in earnest with *Jud Süss* (Ger 40), *Die Rothschilds* (Ger 40) and *Der ewige Jude* (Ger 40), three films whose virulent hatred was a presage of the vengeance to be wreaked on the race they vilified. Of these, *Jud Süss* is undoubtedly the most notorious; it is also the only one to have been released since the war. Dubbed in Arabic, it was distributed in the Arab states in 1955 by the USSR agency Sovexport.

HORROR

The character most frequently portrayed in horror films is Count Dracula, the creation of the Irish writer Bram Stoker (1847–1912), whose novel *Dracula* was published in 1897. Representations of the Count or his immediate descendants on screen outnumber those of his closest rival, Frankenstein's monster, by 133 to 91. The filmography below excludes the frequent appearances that Dracula has made

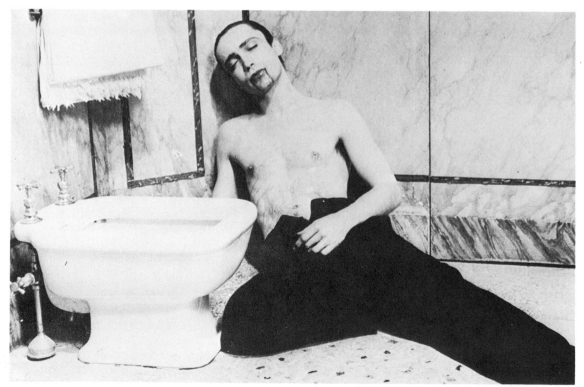

in cartoon films. The name of the artiste portraying the vampire is given before the title where this is known.

Drakula (Hung 21); Max Schreck: *Nosferatu, eine Symphonie des Grauens* (Ger 22); Bela Lugosi: *Dracula* (US 31); Carlos Villarias: *Dracula* (US 31) – Spanish language; Gloria Holden: *Dracula's Daughter* (US 36) – Dracula himself seen as corpse only; Lon Chaney Jnr.: *Son of Dracula* (US 43) – despite title, Chaney plays Dracula himself, there is no son in the picture; John Carradine: *House of Frankenstein* (US 44); John Carradine: *House of Dracula* (US 45); Bela Lugosi *Abbott and Costello Meet Frankenstein* (US 48); Atif Kaptan: *Drakula Istanbula* (Turkey 53); German Robles: *El Fantasma de la operatta* (Arg 55); German Robles: *El Castillo de los monstruos* (Mex 57); Jerry Baline: *Blood of Dracula* (US 57); Victor Fabian: *Frankenstein Meets Dracula* (US 57); Victor Fabian: *Return of the Wolfman* (US 57); Victor Fabian: *Revenge of Dracula* (US 57); *Curse of Dracula** (US 57); Francis Lederer: *The Return of Dracula* (US 58); *Black Inferno** (US 58); Christopher Lee: *Dracula* (GB 58); *Castle of Dracula** (GB 58); *Dracula** (US 59); Gene Gronemeyer: *The Teenage Frankenstein** (US 59); Gene Gronemeyer: *Slave of the Vampire** (US 59); Donald Glut (as Dracula's son): *I Was a Teenage Vampire** (US 59); Richard Christy: *Pawns of Satan** (US 59); Christopher Lee: *Tempi duri per i vampiri* (It 59); Davis Peel: *Brides of Dracula* (GB 60); Chimi Kim: *The Bad Flower* (S. Korea 61); *Frankenstein, el vampiro y cia* (Mex 61); Donald Glut (as Dracula's son): *Monster Rumble** (US 61); Yechoon Lee: *Ahkea Khots* (S. Korea 61); Jeffrey Smithers: *House on Bare Mountain* (US 62); Donald Glut (as Dracula's son): *Dragstrip Dracula** (US 62); *Escala en Hi-Fi* (Sp 63); *Kiss Me Quick!* (US 64); *Sexy Proibitissimo* (It 64); Jack Smith: *Batman Dracula* (US 64); John Carradine: *Billy the Kid versus Dracula* (US 65); *Mga Manugang ni Drakula* (Ph 65); Christopher Lee: *Dracula – Prince of Darkness* (GB 65); Glenn Sherrard: *Horror of Dracula** (US 66); Mitch Evans: *Dr Terror's Gallery of Horrors* (US 66); Pluto Felix: *The Worst Crime of All!* (US 66); Cesar Del Campo (?): *El Imperio de Dracula* (Mex 66); *Chappaqua* (US 66); Cesar Silva: *La Sombra del murcielago* (Mex 66); *Dracula's Wedding Day* (US 67); Harrison Marks: *Vampire* (GB 67); Dante Rivero: *Batman Fights Dracula* (Ph 67); Harrison Marks: *The Naked World of Harrison Marks* (GB 67); Bill Rogers (as descendant of Dracula): *A Taste of Blood* (US 67); John Carradine: *Las Vampiras* (Mex 67); Christopher Lee: *Dracula Has Risen from the Grave* (GB 68); *Santo en el tesoro de Dracula* (Mex 68); *Dracula Meets the Outer Space Chicks* (US 68); *Mondo Keyhole* (US(?) 68); *Isabell, A Dream* (It 68); Vince Kelly (as descendant of Dracula): *Dracula, the Dirty Old Man* (US 69); *Men of Action Meet Women of Dracula* (Ph 69); Christopher Lee:

One More Time (GB 69); Alex d'Arcy: *The Blood of Dracula's Castle* (US 69); Paul Naschy: *Dracula versus Frankenstein/US: Blood of Frankenstein* (Sp.WGer/It 69); *Tales of Blood and Terror* (US/GB 69); Christopher Lee: *The Magic Christian* (GB 69); *Does Dracula Really Suck* (US 69) – homosexual Dracula; Gabby Paul (?): *Il Risveglio di Dracula* (It 69); *Mad Monster Party* (US 69) – puppet feature; Ingrid Pitt: *Countess Dracula* (GB 70); Marty Feldman: *Every Home Should Have One* (GB 70); Des Roberts: *Guess What Happened to Count Dracula?* (US 70); Christopher Lee: *Nachts, wenn Dracula erwacht* (W.Ger/Sp/It 70); Dennis Price: *Vampyros Lesbos/Die Erbin des Dracula* (Sp/W.Ger 70); *Tunnel Under the World* (It 70); Christopher Lee: *Taste the Blood of Dracula* (GB 70); Christopher Lee: *The Scars of Dracula* (GB 70); Eva Renzi (as descendant of Dracula): *Beiss mich Liebling* (W.Ger 70); Des Roberts: *Dracula's lusterne vampire/Dracula's Vampire Lust* (Swz 70); Paul Albert Krumm: *Jonathan, Vampire sterben nicht* (W.Ger 70); Denholm Elliott: *Dracula* (GB 71, TVM); Britt Nichols (as Dracula's daughter): *La Fille de Dracula* (Fr/W.Ger 71); Mori Kishida: *Chi o Su Me/Lake of Dracula* (Jap 71); Paul Naschy: *Hombre que vino de ummo* (Sp./W.Ger 71); Zandor Vorkov: *Dracula versus Frankenstein* aka *Blood of Frankenstein* (US 71); Howard Vernon: *Dracula contra el Dr Frankenstein* (Sp/Fr 71); Jim Parker: *The Mad Lust of a Hot Vampire* (US 71); *The Lust of Dracula* (US 71); *Once Upon a Prime Time* (Can 71); Ferdy Mayne: *Happening der Vampire* (W.Ger 71); Charles McCauley: *Blacula* (US 72); Christopher Lee: *Umbracle* (Sp 72); Dennis Price: *Dracula contra Frankenstein* (Sp 72); Anthony Franciosa: *Schloss des Schreckens* (W.Ger 72); *Dracula, A Family Romance* (US 72); Paul Naschy: *La Messe nere della Contessa Dracula* (It 72); Narcisso Ibañez Menta: *La Saga de los Draculas* (Sp 72); Howard Vernon: *La Hija de Dracula* (Sp 72); Christopher Lee: *Dracula AD 1972* (GB 72); David Azivu (?): *Santo y Blue Demon contra Dracula y el Hombre Lobo* (Mex 72); Christopher Lee: *El Conde Dracula/GB: Bram Stoker's Dracula* (Sp/W.Ger/It 73); *Chabelo y Pepito contra los monstruos* (Mex 73); Paul Naschy: *El Gran amor del Conde Dracula* (Sp 73); Udo Kier: *Blood for Dracula* (It/Fr 73); Christopher Lee: *The Satanic Rites of Dracula* (GB 73); Harry Nillson (as Dracula's son): *Son of Dracula* (GB 73); *The House of Dracula's Daughter* (US 73); Christopher Lee: *Tendre Dracula* (Fr 73); *Shadow of Dracula* (Can 73); Jack Palance: *Dracula* (GB 74, TVM); John Forbes-Robertson: *Legend of the 7 Golden Vampires* (GB/HK 74); David Niven: *Vampira* (GB 74); *Dracula's Blood* (US 74); Hope Stansbury (as Dracula's daughter): *Blood* (US 74); *Dracula Goes to RP* (Ph 74); *Tiempos duros para Drácula* (Arg/Sp 75); Peter Wechsburg (as illegitimate son of Dracula): *Deafula* (US 74); Rossano Brazzi (?): *Il cav. constante nicosia demoniaco ovvero Dracula in Brianza* (It 76); Christopher Lee: *Dracula Père et Fils* (Fr 77); Evelyne Kraft: *Lady Dracula* (W.Ger 77); Louis Jourdan: *Count Dracula* (GB 77, TVM); Michael Pataki (as Dracula's grandson): *Dracula's Dog* (US 78); John Carradine: *Nocturna* (US 78) – 'the first soft-porn-vampire-disco-rock movie'; Christopher Lee: *Count Dracula and His Vampire Bride* (GB 78); Joe Rigoli: *Draculin/US: Dracula and Son* (Sp 78); Stefan Sileanu (as the historical Dracula, Vlad the Impaler): *Vlad Tepes/US: The True Life of Dracula* (Rom 79); George Hamilton: *Love at First Bite* (US 79); *Klaus*

Above left: Jack Palance in *Dracula* (GB 74)

Above right: Christopher Lee menaces Stephanie Beacham in *Dracula AD 1972* (GB 72) (*Copyright Hammer Films*)

Below right: Udo Kier in *Blood for Dracula* (It/Fr 73)

* amateur productions

Kinski: *Nosferatu: Phantom der Nacht* (W.Ger 79); Frank Langella: *Dracula* (US 79); Gianni Garko: *Dracula in Oberbayern* (W.Ger 79); *The Diabolic Loves of Nosferatu* (Sp 79); Peter Lowey: *Dracula Bites the Big Apple* (US 79); Jamie Gillis: *Dracula Sucks* (US 80); Victor Jorge: *Dracula's Last Rites* (US 80).

MUSICALS

The first musical with an original score was MGM's *The Broadway Melody* (US 29), with Bessie Love, Anita Page and Charles King, which was premièred at Grauman's Chinese Theatre in Hollywood on 1 February 1929. The songs were: *Give My Regards to Broadway* (George M. Cohan); *The Wedding Day of the Painted Doll, Love Boat, Broadway Melody, Boy Friend, You Were Meant For Me* (Arthur Freed and Herb Brown); and *Truthful Deacon Brown* (Willard Robison).

The first British musical was BIP's *Raise the Roof* (GB 30), directed by Walter Summers with Betty Balfour as an actress bribed by a rich man to ruin his son's touring review.

The first musical in colour was Warner Bros' *On With the Show*, directed by Alan Crosland in two-colour Technicolor with Betty Compson and Joe E. Brown and premièred in New York on 28 May 1929.

The first British musical in colour was BIP's *Harmony Heaven* (GB 30) with Polly Ward and Stuart Hall.

The musical with the most song numbers was Madan Theatres' *Indra Sabha* (India 32), a Hindi movie with 71 songs.

The Hollywood musical with the most songs was Columbia's *The Jolson Story* (US 46) which had 28 song sequences, one of them a vocal montage of three different numbers.

OPERA

The first operatic films were of an aria from *Romeo and Juliet* sung by Cossira of the Paris Opéra and Victor Maurel singing the title roles from *Don Juan* and *Falstaff*, premièred at the Phono-Cinéma-Théâtre at the Paris Exposition on 8 June 1900.

The first complete opera to be filmed was Gounod's *Faust* (GB 07), directed by Arthur Gilbert in the Gaumont Chronophone sound-on-disc process. **The first in America** was a three-reel version of *Pagliacci* (US 13), produced in the Vi-T-Phone system by the Vi-T-Ascope Co.

The first sound-on-film operatic production was *Rigoletto Act II* (GB 26), presented by the De Forest Phonofilm process. **The first complete sound-on-film opera** was *La Serva Padrona* (It 32), directed by Giogio Mannini for Lirica Film, with Bruna Dragoni, Enrica Mayer and Carlo Lombardi.

SEX

The first nude subject was *Bain de la mondaine* (Fr 95), made by Henri Joly of Paris for presentation in Kinetoscope peep-show machines. **The first actress to appear on screen in the nude** was Jehanne d'Alcy in Georges Méliès' *Aprés le balle tub* (Fr 97). In this 'smoking room' picture, Mlle d'Alcy is seen standing in a shallow bath having soot poured over her for some inexplicable reason. The director fell in love with her naked beauty and eventually married her, though not until 30 years later.

The first star player to appear nude in a feature film was Australian-born Annette Kellerman, whose nymph-like figure was seen undraped in the Fox production *Daughter of the Gods* (US 16). Filmed on location at St Augusta, Jamaica,

Australia's Annette Kellerman became the first star to appear on screen in the nude in *Daughter of the Gods* (US 16)

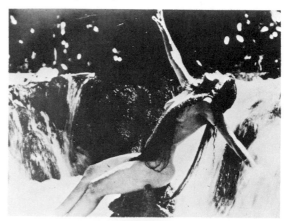

the picture was premièred at the Lyric Theater, New York on 17 October 1916. Miss Kellerman, the Esther Williams of silent movies, was a former professional swimmer who had been the centre of controversy five years earlier when she wore the first one-piece bathing suit. In fact Esther Williams played her in the biopic *Million Dollar Mermaid* (US 52), but by that date the austere provisions of the Hays Code precluded any presentation of the naked human form.

The sensation caused in the 1930s by Hedy Lamarr's nude bathing scenes in *Extase* (Cz 33) has given wide currency to the mistaken idea that Miss Lamarr was the first nude actress on screen. She was not even the first nude in Czech movies, a distinction earned by Ira Rina in Gustav Muchaty's *Eroticon* (Cz 29).

Other nude scenes of the pre-*Extase* period were legion. Celio Film's *Idolo Infranto* (It 13) contained a scene set in an artist's studio with a nude model. 'The Naked Truth' was represented by a nude girl in woman director Lois Weber's *The Hypocrites* (US 15). This Paramount release was banned in Ohio and the Mayor of Boston demanded that clothes be painted onto the image of 'Naked Truth', frame by frame. The nude was uncredited, but has been variously claimed as a Miss Margaret Edwards and Lois Weber herself.

D.W. Griffith hired a number of prostitutes to appear naked in the Belshazar's Feast sequence of *Intolerance* (US 16). Joseph Hanabery, Griffith's assistant, had been ordered to shoot nude scenes, but decided it was more than he could get away with and had his actresses lightly draped for the orgy. Meanwhile Griffith, who was back in New York, did some close shots of nude prostitutes and these were intercut with Hanabery's more discreet scenes. When the film was reissued, in 1942, the New York Censor Board insisted that Griffith's nude inserts be cut.

A nude girl on a crucifix was portrayed in *The Penitentes* (US 16) and a 'Miss Ray' appeared nude in *Le Film du Diable* (Br 17). There were nude bathing scenes in *The Branding Iron* (US 20), *Isle of Love* (US 22) – in the night club scene naked girls threw themselves into a swimming pool as midnight struck – and in Henry Hathaway's *To the Last Man* (US 33),

with Esther Ralston as one of the participants. Clara Bow took to nude bathing in *Hula* (US 27).

Sally Rand performed an alfresco fan dance wearing nothing but a pair of shoes in *Paris at Midnight* (US 26) and a rather more circumspect Elissa Landi played a naked Christian girl bound to the stake in a Roman arena in *The Sign of the Cross* (US 32). Jean Vigo's *A Propos de Nice* (Fr 30) contains a scene of a nude sitting at a cafe table. The 35mm prints of the film imported into Britain had the scene cut, but the sub-standard gauge prints retained it, since 16mm film is not subject to censorship in Britain. A full-length nude is observed in the prison scene in *The Yellow Ticket* (US 31), about prostitution in Czarist Russia. The first nude scene in a Russian film, of a widow hysterically mourning in *Earth* (USSR 30), was cut by order of the authorities before release.

Nude scenes also appeared in *A Man's World* (US 18), *Man, Woman and Marriage* (US 21), *Quo Vadis* (Ger/It 24), *Dante's Inferno* (US 24), *Wege zur Kraft und Schonheit* (Ger 25), *Metropolis* (Ger 26), *Beatrice Cenci* (It 26), *Casanova* (Fr/It 26), *Faust* (Ger 26), *Mandrin* (Fr 28?) and *Secrets of the Orient* (Ger/Fr 28).

Following the introduction of the 1934 Hays Code, nudity disappeared from the Hollywood screen for thirty years. The first picture to bypass the ban was Sidney Lumet's *The Pawnbroker* (US 64), in which a woman was shown naked to the waist. The film was passed uncut by the Production Code Administration on the grounds that the scene was an essential element in the narrative. This decision opened the way for artistically valid scenes of nudity and sexual explicitness; it also hastened the end of the Administration itself, since a more liberal attitude towards sex on screen was difficult to accommodate within a code of prohibitions, and a ratings system was adopted instead.

The cinema of the Eastern world took longer to come to terms with nudity. The same year that *The Pawnbroker* (US 64) was restoring bare bosoms to the American screen, the first Indian films were released in which girls were permitted to be seen in bathing costumes – *April Fool* (India 64) and *Sangam* (India 64). India still bans nudity and has only just allowed kissing (q.v.). In Japan, however, nudity had arrived on screen in the 50s, with a scene in

CARRABASSETT HALL MAY 7

North Anson Mat. & Night, Thursday

THE UNIVERSAL FILM MANUFACTURING CO. Presents

TRAFFIC IN SOULS

6 Parts

700 Scenes

600 Players

The Princess Yang (Jap 55) where the heroine enters the bath. Since the heroine was the distinguished dramatic actress Machiko Kyo, it was unthinkable that she should be seen *in person* in the nude, so a stripper was hired from the Ginza to double for her. Foreign films continued to be subject to strict censorship, though not always simply by cutting. In the Japanese release prints of *A Clockwork Orange* (GB 71) the nude scenes went out of focus, while *Woodstock* (US 69) had the emulsion scraped off the footage containing nudes. Nevertheless, Japan has come a long way since a scene of Cary Grant embracing Sylvia Sidney in *Madame Butterfly* (US 32) was cut by the Japanese censor because Miss Sidney's elbow was exposed.

The first full-frontal male nudes to be seen on screen appeared fleetingly in *Dante's Inferno* (It 12). The first explicit scene revealing male genitalia in a commercial feature was the nude wrestling match between Alan Bates and Oliver Reed in Ken Russell's *Women in Love* (GB 69).

.**Sex on screen** followed rapidly on the emergence of cinema as a public entertainment. The pioneer producer of sex films was Eugène Pirou, beginning with a three minute long production titled *Le Coucher de la mariée* (Fr 96), starring blonde and chubby Louise Willy. Based on an act performed by Mlle Willy at the Olympia music hall in Paris the previous year, the film showed a newly-wed couple preparing for bed. The girl's husband removes her satin slipper and presses it ecstatically to his lips, then she disrobes and puts on her night attire while her husband watches with evident desire. Finally Mlle Willy does a provocative little dance before the couple retire to bed. The film caused a sensation when it was premièred in the basement of the Café de Paris in November 1896 and was soon showing at two other *salles* as well, one in the Boulevard Bonne-Nouvelle and the other at 86 rue de Clichy. Pirou followed this success with other sex subjects, such as *Bain de la Parisienne* (Fr 97), *Lever de la Parisienne* (Fr 97) and *La Puce* (Fr 97), most of them based on strip-tease acts playing in the Paris music halls. *La Puce*, for example, showed a maiden afflicted with a flea

Denmark pioneered the sex film. In this scene from *Den Sorte Drøm* (Den 11), Gunnar Hesengreen is being ungentlemanly with an unresponsive Asta Nielsen. Valdemar Psilander is about to be properly outraged

who removes her garments one by one to locate the offending insect.

Pirou's chief rival in the blue-movie field was Georges Méliès, whose *Les Indiscrets*/*The Peeping Toms* (Fr 96) came out at the end of 1896. Méliès was the man who brought nudity (q.v.) to the screen in *Après le bal* (Fr 97) and won a wide following with such sensational subjects as *En Cabinet particulier*/*A Private Dinner* (Fr 97), *L'Indiscret aux Bains de mer*/*Peeping Tom at the Seaside* (Fr 97) and *La Modèle irascible*/*An Irritable Model* (Fr 97). In England these films were distributed by the Warwick Trading Co., who described them as 'welcome at any smoking concert or stag party'.

The earliest known American film on a sexual theme is American Mutoscope & Biograph's *The Downward Path* (US 02), a five-scene melodrama about a sharecropper's daughter who follows a downward path to prostitution – in one of the scenes she is encountered soliciting in the streets.

While most of the above films were very much of the 'What the Butler Saw' genre, the longer sex drama designed for general release emerged with Fotorama's *The White Slave Traffic* (Den 10), a two-reel shocker of such drawing power at the box office that within a few months Nordisk had produced a rival version with the same name. It was no less sensational. A publicity still shows scenes such as a kidnapped girl being savagely beaten. Ole Olsen of Nordisk

Left: Sex reaches the American screen. The year was 1913

recalled that at the trade show in Berlin, the German cinema managers all clambered onto their seats for a better view. It was the success of these Danish sexploitation films – other titles included *The Last Victim of the White Slave Traffic* (Den 11) and *Dealer in Girls* (Den 12) – that inspired George Loane Tucker to make the first American feature-length sex picture, *Traffic in Souls* (US 13), starring Jane Gail and Matt Moore. Made clandestinely – not because of the subject, but because Universal did not believe that the American public were ready for feature films – Tucker's $5700 movie garnered record earnings of $450000.

The first film made for theatrical release in which the sex act was depicted was *Extase* (Cz 33). The young heroine (Hedwig Kiesler, later known as Hedy Lamarr), who has flown from an impotent husband, runs naked through the woods, bathes, and then has sex with a young engineer in a hut. Curiously *Extase* is celebrated as the first motion picture containing a nude scene, which it was not, rather than the first to show sexual intercourse, which it was.

The first theatrical release to contain a scene of unsimulated sexual intercourse was Jan Lindqvist and Stefan Jarl's *Dom Kallar Oss Mods/ They Call Us Misfits* (Sw 67), starring Kenta Gustafsson and Stoffe Svensson.

The earliest known pornographic film which can definitely be dated is *A l'Ecu d'Or ou la bonne auberge* (Fr 08).

There is no doubt that pornographic filmmaking was well established even by this early date, though for obvious reasons records are sparse. It was in the same year as *A l'Ecu d'Or* was released, 1908, that Russia enacted a law against obscene movies, known there as 'the Paris Genre'. In Moscow the Mephistopholes Kino decided to test its enforcement by presenting a full programme of such films and was promptly closed down.

The earliest known American pornographic film is *A Free Ride* aka *A Grass Sandwich* (US 15).

The first full-length erotic cartoon film was Osamu Tezuka's *A Thousand and One Nights* (Jap 69) – claimed (inaccurately) as 'the first animated film for adults'. David Grant's *Sinderella* (GB 72) was declared obscene by

both Bow Street Magistrates' Court and the High Court of Appeal, but later passed by the British Board of Film Censors with cuts amounting to only 26 seconds.

'Soft porn' for theatrical release started in Japan in 1950 with a wave of teenage sexploitation films with titles like *Teenager's Sex-Manual, Virgin's Clinic, A Virgin's Sex Manual, Bitch* and *Bad Girl*. The title role in the latter was played by the aristocratic Yoshiko Kuga, daughter of a Japanese peer, which gave it an added piquancy for some. The films reflected – and exploited – the revolution in social values of post-war Japan, where a confused generation of teenagers was apt to identify freedom with license. Remarkably the production of these movies began only three years after the first Japanese screen kiss.

The genesis of the American 'skinflick' is generally attributed to ex-Signal Corps cameraman Russ Meyer, who made his soft-porn debut with *The Immoral Mr Teas* (US 59), a comedy about a man with the unusual ability to undress girls mentally. This modest pioneer effort, shot on a budget of $24000 in four days, inspired no less than 150 imitations within a year of its release.

Although sexploitation movies are generally profitable in relation to their modest budgets, the first to achieve an outstanding box office success, even by comparison with major studio productions, was *Emmanuelle* (Fr 74). Of the 607 new films released in Paris in 1974 *Emmanuelle* scored the highest number of admissions (1342921), ahead of such notable box-office draws as *The Sting* (US 73) – 1154952 admissions – and *The Exorcist* (US 73) – 655092 admissions.

The first film about homosexuality was Richard Oswald's *Anders als die Andern* (Ger 19), starring Conrad Veidt, which dared to confront the cinema-going public with a subject still proscribed in literature. Following the resumption of censorship, male homosexuality received no further attention until Gustaf Gründgens' *Zwei Welten* (Ger 40). The story by Felix Lutzkendorff was an innocuous romance about two boys and two girls working together on a farm in the summer holidays. Under the direction of Gründgens it became transformed into an idyll between the two boys.

Elsewhere the theme attracted less sympathetic treatment. During the Japanese occupation of Shanghai, the Japanese made a film in China for native consumption called *Chu Hai-tang* (Jap/China 43), which attempted to propagate the idea of the Chinese as a decadent race with the story of a Chinese General embroiled with a female impersonator from the Peking Opera.

In Britain the subject remained unbroached on screen until Terence Young's *Serious Charge* (GB 59), about a priest (Anthony Quayle) falsely accused by a youth (Andrew Ray) of making homosexual advances. This made relatively little impact, and it was left to Basil Deardon to make a film sufficiently explicit to actually use the word 'homosexual' in the dialogue. The picture was *Victim* (GB 61), in which Dirk Bogarde portrayed a respected barrister who becomes the victim of blackmail as a result of his relationship with a young vagrant (Peter McEnery). In America, the previous year, Joseph Manckiewicz had directed Gore Vidal's screen adaptation of *Suddenly, Last Summer* (US 60), the story of a homosexual poet whose beautiful wife (Elizabeth Taylor) lures Italian beach boys for his delectation. Other British films on homosexual themes followed *Victim* in fairly quick succession, including *A Taste of Honey* (GB 61), *The Leather Boys* (GB 63) and *The Servant* (GB 63), but there was little further development of the theme in the USA between *Suddenly, Last Summer* and John Huston's *Reflections in a Golden Eye* (US 67), again with Elizabeth Taylor, this time as the wife of an army officer (Marlon Brando) infatuated with a young recruit.

Lesbian love was treated with delicacy and discretion in Leontine Sagan's *Mädchen in Uniform* (Ger 31), a tender study of a girl's infatuation for a teacher in a repressive Prussian boarding school. The first explicitly lesbian film from the USA was *The Children's Hour* (US 62), the second film version of Lillian Hellman's play of the same name. Both pictures were directed by William Wyler, but in the earlier version, titled *These Three* (US 36), the original story of two schoolmistresses having an affair was changed to a heterosexual triangle involving two female teachers and a man. Wyler's remake had Shirley Maclaine and Audrey Hepburn

in a sensitively-handled adaptation true to the spirit and the purpose of the play.

SPORT

A Soccer Filmography

Soccer, the most popular spectator sport in the world, is increasingly the subject of feature movies. To date the following have been made:

The Winning Goal (GB 20); *The Ball of Fortune* (GB 26); *Der König der Mittelstürmer* (Ger 28); *Die Elf Teufel* (Ger 28); *The Great Game* (GB 30); *Soccerfans* (Cz 31); *Our Football Eleven* (Cz 36); *Goal!* (Arg 36); *The Goalkeeper* (USSR 36); *The Klapzuba Football Eleven* (Cz 38); *Bola ao Centro* (Port 47); *The Football Parson* (Den 51); *The Merry Duel* (Cz 51); *In the Penalty Area* (Cz 51); *Women Who Have Run Off-Side* (Cz 51); *The Great Game* (GB 53); *Small Town Story* (GB 53); *Plavi 9* (Yug c. 55); *11:1* (DDR 55); *A Football Star* (Hung 56); *Saeta Rubia* (Sp 56); *The Goalkeeper Lives in our Street* (Cz 57); *Favourite No 13* (Bulg 58); *Gambe d'oro* (It 58); *Il Nemico di mia moglie/My Wife's Enemy* (It 59); *Our Lads* (Rom 59); *Los Economicamente debiles* (Sp 60); *Football Fans* (Cz 60); *The Last Goal* (Hung 61); *Comrade President the Centre-Forward* (Yug 62); *Ivana in the Forward Line* (Cz 63); *Pelota de cuero* (Arg 63); *Third Time* (USSR 63); *Fadni odpoledne* (Cz 65); *Let's Go Wakadaisho* (Jap 67); *Somos los mejores!* (Arg 67); *Fish, Football and Girls* (Israel 68); *Volver a vivi* (Sp 68); *Fight for the Glory* (Jap 69); *Aconteceu no Maracanã* (Br 69); *Il Presidente del Borgorosso Football Club* (It 70); *Shoot Paragon!* (Pol 70); *Sekundomer/Stop Watch* (USSR 70); *The Goalkeeper's Fear of the Penalty* (W.Ger/Austria 71); *Bloomfield* (Israel 71); *I Due maghi de pallone* (It 71); *Mother Love* (S. Korea 72); *Willi wird das Kind schon schaukeln* (W.Ger 72); *Tochka, Tochka, Zapiataia/Dot, Dot, a Comma* (USSR 72); *Football of the Good Old Days*

The Klapzuba Football Eleven (Cz 38)

Stubby (Sw 74) was about a six-year-old who becomes a professional soccer star *(Svenska Filminstitutet)*

(Hung 73); *A Goal, Another Goal* (USSR 73); *Stubby* (Sw 74); *Pandhattam/Play Ball* (India 74); *Pirveli Mertskhali/ The First Swallow* (USSR 75); *Furia Española* (Sp 76); *The Memorable Day* (Bulg 76); *Takaya Ona, Igra* (USSR 77); *Trener/The Coach* (Yug 78); *Striker* (India 78); *Yesterday's Hero* (GB 79); *Everything for Football* (Rom 79); *Coup de Tête* (Fr 80).

WESTERNS

The earliest subjects of western interest were *Sioux Indian Ghost Dance, Indian War Council* and *Buffalo Dance,* made by the Edison Co. at West Orange, NJ on 24 September 1894. *Bucking Broncho* followed on 16 October and is notable for the first appearance of a cowboy in a film – Lee Martin of Colorado, who is seen riding *Sunfish* in a corral, while his 'pardner' Frank Hammit stands on the rails and discharges the first of many tens of thousands of pistol shots that were to be seen (and later heard) in almost every western that followed. Annie Oakley, immortalised in *Annie Get Your Gun* (US 50), made her film debut a fortnight later on 1 November 1894.

The first westerns were copyrighted by the American Mutoscope & Biograph Co. on 21 September 1903. One was titled *Kit Carson* (US 03) and related the story of its hero's capture by Indians and subsequent escape through the agency of a beautiful Indian maiden. There were 11 scenes and the film had a running time of 21 minutes, making it the longest dramatic picture (other than Passion Plays) produced in America at that time. The other film, titled *The Pioneers* (US 03), showed the burning of a settler's homestead by Indians, who kill the homesteader and his wife and carry off his daughter. The picture ends with the dramatic rescue of the child by frontiersmen who have found the bodies of her parents. Running time was approximately 15 minutes.

The more celebrated *The Great Train Robbery* (US 03), generally and erroneously described as the first western and often as the first film to tell a story was copyrighted by the Edison Co. some six weeks later, on 1 December 1903.

The first feature-length western was Lawrence B. McGill's *Arizona* (US 13), an All Star Feature Corporation production with Cyril Scott and Gertrude Shipman. It was released in August 1913, six months before Cecil B. DeMille's *The Squaw Man* (US 14), usually credited as the first feature.

The first western in colour was a British production by a Dutch director, Theo Bouwmeester's *Fate* (GB 11), made in Kinemacolor by the Natural Colour Kinematograph Co. Set in Texas, it was about an Englishman who becomes leader of a tribe of renegade Indians. **The first feature-length colour western** was the Famous Players-Lasky production *Wanderer of the Wasteland* (US 24), a Zane Grey horse opera from the novel of the same name. Photographed in two-colour Technicolor by Arthur Ball, it was directed by Irvin Willar, starred Jack Holt, Noah Beery and Billie Dove, and was premièred in Los Angeles on 21 June 1924.

The first western talkie was Fox-Movietone's *In Old Arizona* (US 28), directed by Raoul Walsh and Irving Cummings and starring Edmund Lowe, Warner Baxter and Dorothy Burgess. It was premièred at the Criterion Theater, Los Angeles, on 25 December 1928.

The first western with Indian dialogue was Universal's talkie serial *The Indians Are Coming* (US 31), in which Chief Thunderbird spoke in his native Sioux. In 1970 Dame Judith Anderson, an Australian, successfully coped with all-Sioux dialogue in her role as Buffalo Cow Head in *A Man Called Horse* (US 70).

The first western star was G.M. 'Broncho Billy' Anderson (1881–1971), who was to have been cast as one of the villains for his western debut in *The Great Train Robbery* (US 03), but proved so inept on a horse that he had to be relegated to extra work. Notwithstanding this inauspicious start to a career dedicated to the relationship of man and horse, Anderson starred in *Life of an American Cowboy* (US 06) and then went west with a Selig location crew to make the earliest known western shot in the real west – *The Girl from Montana* (US 07). The following

year he established a West Coast studio for Essany at Niles, California, and decided to embark on a series of one-reelers based on a central character, reasoning that the weakness of the Edison, Selig and Essany westerns he had played in was that they lacked clearly-defined heroes. His original intention had been to find an actor expert in horsemanship whom he could direct, but actors of any kind being in short supply in California, he eventually decided to cast himself in the role. *Broncho Billy and the Baby* (US 10), a sentimental story of a man-gone-wrong who is reformed by the love of a good woman, was the first in a series of nearly 400 Broncho Billy pictures which established Anderson as a major star. A curious feature of the films was their total lack of continuity. If Broncho Billy married in one picture, he would be a bachelor again in the next; he would be reformed inexhaustably by a succession of good women; and death would only interrupt his career in the saddle until the opening scenes of the next one-reeler. He turned to features in 1918, but competition from his successors, Tom Mix and W.S. Hart, was too strong. After a period of producing Stan Laurel comedies for

Joel McCrea in *Buffalo Bill* (US 42)

Metro, he retired in 1923. Nearly half a century after his last silent western role in *The Son of a Gun* (US 18), he made a single excursion into talkies with a guest appearance in *The Bounty Killer* (US 67).

The most popular western star was determined annually with a poll of exhibitors conducted by *Motion Picture Herald* between 1936 and 1954 (when the 'B' western ended). Buck Jones won in 1936, Gene Autry each year from 1937–42, and Roy Rogers from 1943–54 inclusive.

The western hero most often portrayed on screen has been William Frederick Cody (1846–1917), otherwise known as 'Buffalo Bill', a character in 45 dramatic films to date:

Buffalo Bill (Aus 09); Self: *The Life of Buffalo Bill* (US 09); Self: *Buffalo Bill's Far West and Pawnee Bill's Far East* (US 10); Self: *The Indian Wars* (US 13); Self: *Sitting Bull – The Hostile Sioux Indian Chief* (US 14); Self: *Patsy of the Circus* (US 15); Art Acord: *In the Days of Buffalo Bill* (US 22); George Waggner: *The Iron Horse* (US 24); John Fox Jnr.: *The Pony Express* (US 25); Jack Hoxie: *The Last Frontier* (US 26); Roy Stewart: *Buffalo Bill on the UP Trail* (US 26); Wallace MacDonald: *Fighting with Buffalo Bill* (US 26); *Buffalo Bill's Last Fight* (US 26) – MGM colour short; William Fairbanks: *Wyoming* (US 28); Tim McCoy: *The Indians are Coming* (US 30); Tom Tyler: *Battling with Buffalo Bill* (US 31); Douglas Dumbrille: *The World Changes* (US 33); Earl Dwire: *The Miracle Rider* (US 35); Moroni Olsen: *Annie Oakley* (US 35); James Ellison: *The Plainsman* (US 36); Ted Adams: *Custer's Last Stand* (US 36); Carlyle Moore: *Outlaw Express* (US 38); John Rutherford: *Flaming Frontiers* (US 38); George Reeves: *Wild West Days* (US 39); Roy Rogers: *Young Buffalo Bill* (US 40); Joel McCrea: *Buffalo Bill* (US 42); Bob Baker: *Overland Mail* (US 42); Carlos Munos: *El Sobrino de Buffalo Bill* (Mex 44); Richard Arlen: *Buffalo Bill Rides Again* (US 47); Ugo Sasso (?): *Buffalo Bill a Roma* (It 47); Monte Hale: *Law of the Golden West* (US 49); Louis Calhern: *Annie Get Your Gun* (US 50); Dickie Moore: *Cody of the Pony Express* (US 50); Tex Cooper: *King of the Bullwhip* (US 51); Charlton Heston: *Pony Express* (US 52); Clayton Moore: *Buffalo Bill in Tomahawk Territory* (US 53); Marshall Reed: *Riding with Buffalo Bill* (US 54); Malcolm Atterbury: *Badman's Country* (US 58); James McMullan: *The Raiders* (US 64); Rick van Nutter: *Sette ore di fuoco* (It 64); Gordon Scott: *L'Eroe del Far West* (It/Fr/W.Ger 65); Guy Stockwell: *The Plainsman* (US 66); Michel Piccoli: *Touche pas la femme blanche* (Fr 74); Matt Clark: *This is the West that Was* (US 74); Paul Newman: *Buffalo Bill and the Indians* (US 76).

William Bonney (1860–81), alias Billy the Kid, has been portrayed in 44 films; Wild Bill Hickock (1837–76) in 35 films; Jesse James (1847–82) in 32 films; General George Armstrong Custer (1839–76) in 29 films; and Wyatt Earp (1848–1929) in 21 films.

The only western directed by a woman was Ruth Ann Baldwin's curiously titled Universal production '49–'17 (US 17).

Western output: It is estimated that there have been over 3500 multi-reel westerns made since the first two-reeler, the Oklahoma Natural Mutoscene Co.'s *The Bank Robbery* (US 08).

CHAPTER 6

PERFORMERS

The first motion film to employ the use of actors was a brief costume drama titled *The Execution of Mary Queen of Scots* (US 95), which was shot by Alfred Clark of Raff & Gammon, Kinetoscope proprietors, at West Orange, NJ on 28 August 1895. The part of Mary was played by Mr R.L. Thomas, Secretary and Treasurer of the Kinetoscope Co. After approaching the block and laying his head on it, Thomas removed himself, the camera was stopped, and a dummy substituted. The camera was then started again for the decapitation scene. This was **the first use of trick photography or special effect work** in a film.

The first person employed to play a comedy role in a film was M. Clerc, a gardener employed by Mme Lumière at Lyons, France. He was aptly cast in the part of the gardener in the Lumière production *L'Arroseur arrosé* (Fr 95), a film premièred at the Grand Café in Paris on 28 December 1895. Clerc is seen watering flowerbeds with a hose. A mischievous boy, played by a 14-year-old Lumière apprentice called Duval, creeps up behind the gardener and places his foot on the hose to stop the flow of water. As the perplexed gardener holds the nozzle up to his eye to see if there is a blockage, young Duval removes his foot and capers with joy as a burst of water gushes into M. Clerc's face. Clerc and Duval were the first performers to be seen on the screen, since *The Execution of Mary Queen of Scots* had been made for viewing in Edison's 'peep-show' Kinetoscope.

The first professional actors to perform in movies made their screen debuts almost simultaneously on either side of the Atlantic. In America John Rice and May Irwin performed the first screen kiss in *The Widow Jones* aka *May Irwin Kiss* (US 96), which was a scene from the Broadway comedy *The Widow Jones* filmed by Raff and Gammon in April 1896. At about the same time in Britain, Fred Storey played the title role in R.W. Paul's *The Soldier's Courtship* (GB 96), a short comedy made on the roof of the Alhambra Theatre, Leicester Square, and premièred underneath. Storey also got to kiss the heroine, Julie Seale of the Alhambra Ballet. Performers of established reputation rarely appeared in films prior to about 1908 in France and Britain and later elsewhere. There were, however, a few notable exceptions during the primitive period, including Auguste van Biene's role as the cellist in Esme Collings' *The Broken Melody* (GB 96), from the play of the same name; Joseph Jefferson's performance in American Mutoscope & Biograph's *Rip Van Winkle* (US 96); Beerbohm Tree and Julia Neilson in *King John* (GB 99); Sarah Bernhardt in *Hamlet* (Fr 00); Coquelin in *Cyrano de Bergerac* (Fr 00); Marie Tempest and Hayden Coffin in *San Toy* (GB 00); and Marie Tempest, Ben Webster and H.B. Warner in *English Nell* (GB 00). The only one of these to make a career as a screen actor was H.B. Warner (1876–1958), whose most notable performances were in *Kings of Kings* (US 27) as Jesus Christ, *Mr Deeds Goes to Town* (US 36), *Lost Horizon* (US 37) and *Victoria the Great* (GB 37).

The star system emerged in the United States and Europe simultaneously. Previous to 1910 it was the deliberate policy of film-makers not to give their lead players any star billing, lest they should overvalue their services. First to break with this was the American production company Kalem, which in January 1910 began issuing star portraits and posters with the artistes named credited. A few weeks later Carl Laemmle, who had succeeded in luring the still anonymous Florence Lawrence away from Biograph to work for IMP, pulled the kind of outrageous publicity stunt that has enlivened and bedevilled the industry ever since, and in the process created the first real movie star. He began by arranging for a story to break in the St Louis papers that the actress had been killed in a street-car accident. Public interest in the supposed tragedy having been fully aroused, Laemmle placed the following advertisement in the same papers on 10 March 1910: 'The blackest and at the same time the silliest lie yet circulated by the enemies of IMP was the story foisted on the public of St Louis last week to the effect that Miss Lawrence, "The Imp Girl", formerly known as "The Biograph Girl", had been killed by a street car. It was a black lie so cowardly. We now announce our next film *The Broken Path*.' This was followed up with personal appearances by Miss Lawrence and a long interview in the *St Louis Post-Dispatch*; within a year her name was appearing on film posters in larger type than the title.

In Europe the practice of publicising star names began the same year with the outstanding success of two films, one from Denmark, the other from Germany. Asta Nielsen's bravura performance in *The Abyss* (Den 10), one of the first long films to demonstrate a true sense of dramatic construction, brought a hitherto little-known actress almost immediate international recognition and the first of the really prodigious star salaries (cf. Artiste's Earnings, p. 90). Germany's box office success of the year was *Das Liebesglück der Blinden/The Love of the Blind Girl* (Ger 10), starring 'The Messter Girl', a designation that cloaked the identity of Oskar Messter's leading player Henny Porten, who had also scripted the picture. It was received with such acclaim by filmgoers that Messter was persuaded to reveal her name. Once her name

Harlow (US 65) signally failed to catch the style or period atmosphere of early 30s Hollywood, though Carroll Baker might have portrayed a convincing Jean Harlow in a better made picture. (Note the 1965 shoes)

was on the credits, Henny proceeded to justify the producers' worst fears by demanding an increase in salary – from the equivalent of $50 a month to $56. Messter refused and she walked straight out of the studio. Having failed to call what he thought was a bluff, the producer sent his assistant, Kurt Stark, to fetch the girl back with a promise that she could have the raise. Henny returned to the studio, married Stark, and went on to become Germany's idol of the silent screen.

The first wholly fabricated star personality, created by the skill of the publicist rather than through any innate appeal, was Theodosia Goodman, renamed Theda Bara for the screen. As an unknown Shakespearian actress down on her luck, she was cast by director Frank Powell as the exotic femme fatale in *A Fool There Was* (US 15), based on Kipling's poem *The Vampire*.

Fox press agent Johnny Goldfrap, realising that there would be little interest in a middle-class Jewish girl from Cincinnati, gave her a new name, invented a French artist father and an Egyptian mother, and had the fictitious Theda grow up among the nomads of the Sahara Desert. She won instant stardom and the word 'vamp', signifying her particular style of seduction, passed into common use. During the next four years she made some 40 films, developing and refining the vamp roles in which she drove men mad with desire and then sent them to destruction, at the same time leading a quiet and wholly respectable private life, while Goldfrap energetically fostered the legend that her real persona and the torrid screen image were as one.

The first performer to be put under contract by a film company was Florence Turner (1887–1946), who signed with Vitagraph of New York in the spring of 1907. According to Miss Turner, she was encouraged to make the switch from stage work when a fellow artiste on a vaudeville tour remarked: 'You pull such extraordinary faces that you would make your fortune as a motion picture actress'. She made her screen debut in *How to Cure a Cold* (US 07) and went on to become the first major box office draw as 'The Vitagraph Girl'. On leaving Vitagraph in 1913, she went to England to form her own company, appearing in full-length features like *My Old Dutch* (GB 15) and *Far From the Madding Crowd* (GB 16). Her career declined after returning to the USA in 1916, and though she played leading roles in some British films of the early 20s, she never regained her early pre-eminence. By 1937 she was reduced to extra work at MGM and she died at the Motion Picture Country House, a retirement home for ageing film people, in 1946.

Biopics of screen stars are relatively rare and have often concentrated on an aspect of the performer's life other than their screen career. The biopics of Diana Barrymore and Lillian Roth were concerned with their subjects' alcoholism, those of Eddie Cantor and Al Jolson dwelt mainly on their singing careers, and Annette Kellerman's on her swimming exploits, while *The George Raft Story* recounted the star's pre-Hollywood days in the gangster milieu of 20s New York. The following per-

formers have had their life stories, in whole or in part, portrayed in feature movies:

Diana Barrymore (1921–60): *Too Much Too Soon* (US 58) with Dorothy Malone in the story, based on Miss Barrymore's memoirs, of how she went to Hollywood to look after her alcoholic father John Barrymore (Errol Flynn) and herself succumbed to drink.

Humphrey Bogart (1899–1957): *Bogie* (US 80) with Kevin O'Connor, based on Joe Hyams' biography of the same title.

Eddie Cantor (1892–1964): *The Eddie Cantor Story* (US 53) with Keefe Brasselle in the name role. Cantor himself played a bit part and also sang the songs off-screen.

Lon Chaney (1883–1930): *The Man of a Thousand Faces* (US 57) with James Cagney as the character actor and contortionist extraordinary of the silent screen.

Charles Chaplin (1889–1977): *The Life Story of Charles Chaplin* (GB 26) with Chick Wango in a British attempt to cash in on the popularity of the Cockney lad who had made it in Hollywood. The first biopic of a screen star, but never released due to a threat of legal action from its subject.
The Gentleman Tramp (US 75), a documentary feature by Richard Patterson using archive material.

Montgomery Clift (1920–66): Two biopics were announced in 1979, one by Sidney Lumet based on Patricia Bosworth's *Montgomery Clift, A Biography*, the other by Silva Productions based on Robert LaGuardia's *Monty*.

James Dean (1931–55): *The James Dean Story* (US 57), a hasty documentary feature on the moody teenage rebel seemingly designed to fuel the James Dean death cult.

W.C. Fields (1879–1946): *W.C. Fields and Me* (US 76) with Rod Steiger in another study of a star disintegrating from drink. The 'Me' of the title was Fields' mistress Carlotta Monti (Valerie Perrine), who nursed the tyrant comic through his alcoholism to the detriment of her own career.

Clark Gable (1901–60): *Gable and Lombard* (US 76) with James Brolin struggling bravely in a generally misconceived attempt to portray 'the man rather than the star'.

Jean Harlow (1911–37): *Harlow* (US 65) with Carroll Baker in a travesty of the star's life of which the producer, director and screenwriter should be thoroughly ashamed.
Harlow (US 65) with Carol Lynley in a rather better attempt at the subject. Originally made for television, it was released to cinemas in an Electronovision version.

Donald O'Connor as Keaton in *The Buster Keaton Story* (US 57)

Al Jolson (1886–1950): *The Jolson Story* (US 46) and *Jolson Sings Again* (US 49) with Larry Parks in both highly successful films. Jolson himself did the voice-over for the songs and is also seen in long shot during the 'Swanee' sequence of the first picture.

Buster Keaton (1895–1966): *The Buster Keaton Story* (US 57) with Donald O'Connor in what Leslie Halliwell has described as 'a dismal tribute'. Once again the theme is one of drink being the curse of the starring classes.
The Comic (US 69) with Dick Van Dyke as a silent film comedian obviously based on Keaton. Much superior to the above.

Annette Kellerman (1888–1978): *Million Dollar Mermaid* (US 53) with Esther Williams playing the Australian girl who invented the one-piece bathing suit and became the first star actress to appear on the screen in the nude (not depicted in the biopic).

Bruce Lee (1940–73): *The Bruce Lee Story* (US 74) with Hsiao Lung as the Chinese-American actor who achieved international stardom in Hong Kong martial arts movies.

A succession of wholly or semi-fictitious martial arts films followed which purported to portray Bruce Lee: *The Story of the Dragon* (HK 76) with Ho Tsung-tao (Bruce Li); *Bruce Lee – True Story* (HK 76) with Bruce Li; *Bruce Lee and I* (HK 76) with Li Msiu Hsien; *The Dragon Lives* (HK 78) with Bruce Li; *Bruce Lee: the Man, the Myth* (HK 78) with Bruce Li; *Bruce Lee, The Tiger of Manchuria* (HK 78) with Hang Yong Chul; *Young Bruce Lee* (HK 79) with Chuck Norris; *Sexy Isla Meets Bruce Lee in the Devil's Triangle* (Can 7?); *Bruce Lee versus the Gay Power* (Br 7?). *The Death of Bruce Lee* (HK 76) merely invoked the name, not the character.

Carole Lombard (1908–42): *Gable and Lombard* (US 76) with Jill Clayburgh as the love of Gable's life, killed tragically in an aeroplane accident at the age of 34. The film failed to illuminate either the romantic myth of the legendary affair or the earthy reality (Lombard commented to a friend 'He's not what you'd call a helluva great lay'). Though even Hollywood could not bring itself to nominate the film for an Oscar, it did succeed in picking up Harvard Lampoon's 1976 Victor Mature Memorial Award for the most embarrassing line of dialogue. The citation read: '*Gable and Lombard*, for the screen's greatest insouciant comment following the incendiary demise of his beloved in a plane crash, as he gazes fondly over the twisted wreckage: "She should have taken the train".'

Marilyn Monroe (1926–62): *Marilyn* (US 63), compilation feature.
Goodbye, Norma Jean (US/Aus 75) with Misty Rowe, a reasonable look-alike but nothing more, in an exploitation movie that concentrates on Norma Jean Baker's seedy and often degrading existence before her metamorphosis into Marilyn Monroe superstar.
Marilyn (US i.p.) – biopic scheduled for 1981 release.

George Raft (1895–): *The George Raft Story* (US 61) with Ray Danton as the professional athlete, gambler, nightclub dancer and intimate of gangsters who turned it all to good account in Hollywood.

Bill 'Bojangles' Robinson (1878–1949): *Stormy Weather* (US 43) with 'Bojangles' himself in an all-black fictionalised version of his own life story. Also subject of 1979 Broadway musical *Bojangles*.

Above right: Gable and Lombard (US 76). What made the producers think that James Brolin *(right)* could be made to look like Clark Gable *(left)*?

Below right: Australia's Misty Rowe essayed the Marilyn Monroe role in *Goodbye, Norma Jean* (US/Aus 75). Yes, MM did once wear her hair like that

Will Rogers (1879–1935): *The Story of Will Rogers* (US 50) with Will Rogers Jnr. playing his father in a bland homage to the celebrated crackerbarrel philosopher and latecomer movie star.

Lillian Roth (1910–): *I'll Cry Tomorrow* (US 55) with Susan Hayward as the Broadway/Hollywood star of the early thirties whose career became another write-off to alcoholism.

Erich von Stroheim (1885–1957): *The Man You Loved to Hate* (US 79), compilation feature.

Rudolph Valentino (1895–1926): *Valentino* (US 51) with Anthony Dexter in a flat biopic made at a time when Hollywood's attempts to portray the twenties invariably mixed period cliché with blundering anachronisms.
Valentino (GB 77) with Rudolf Nureyev charismatic in Ken Russell's lush and stimulating evocation of man, myth, place and period.

Hansa Wadkar (1920–71): *Bhumika* (India 78) with Smita Patil as the popular Hindi star of the thirties and forties. One of the few foreign-language star biopics.

Pearl White (1889–1938): *The Perils of Pauline* (US 47) with Betty Hutton recreating the career of the silent serial queen in uncompromisingly forties style.

Artiste's earnings, which have now reached as much as $3 million for a single film began at a level commensurate with the penny gaff milieu of early film-making. **The earliest known wage rate** was the gold Louis ($4·30 or 17s) per day paid in the late 1890s by Star Films of Paris, but not all production companies were so generous. Gene Gauntier was offered $3 to play the lead in Biograph's *The Paymaster* (US 06), the story of a mill-girl in love with the manly young paymaster of the mill. Miss Gauntier was required to be thrown into the millstream by the villain, which she allowed him to do, not liking to mention that she was unable to swim. The producer was so pleased with her pluck that the $3 fee was raised to $5. Alma Lund, who played the female lead in the first film drama made in Norway – *Dangerous Life of a Fisherman* (Nor 07) – was paid the equivalent of $1·50 for her part; the boy who played her son got 75c. R.W. Paul paid Britain's first professional film actor, Johnny Butt, a daily wage of 5s ($1·25) in 1899, which was rather better than the 4s ($1) a day accorded to Chrissie White when she joined the Hepworth Co. at Walton-on-Thames in 1908. 'When I really got on', she

The world's first superstar – Denmark's Asta Nielsen

recalled, 'I received 8s a day, and when I was a star they paid me 50 – shillings, not pounds'. Dave Aylott, who joined Cricks & Martin of Mitcham in 1909, remembered that their terms were 7s 6d a day for principal parts, 5s for minor parts, plus 1s 6d travelling expenses to Mitcham and a bread and cheese lunch with beer. In America at this time the $5 a day received by Mary Pickford when she joined Biograph in 1909 seems to have become standard throughout the industry, nothing extra being paid for 'star' roles.

The escalation in salaries, when it came, was rapid and had to do with two factors: the use of major names from the stage, who had to be paid highly to demean themselves in this way; and the introduction of the 'star' system (cf. Artistes: Star System, p. 86) from 1910 onwards. The change began with Film d'Art in Paris, a company established in 1908 to produce prestige films with prestige players. Their leading artistes were paid the equivalent of $40 for each rehearsal and $200 for the actual shoot. Featured players, however, received as little as $2–3 a day for services in a major film like *Germinal* (Fr 13), for which the star, Henry Krauss, was paid $700. In England Will Barker paid Sir Herbert Beerbohm Tree a record £1000 to play Wolsey in *Henry VIII* (GB 11), a two-reeler which was shot in a single day. How far this was from the norm is indicated by the fact that the following year Barker was able to secure the lead player of his *Hamlet* (GB 12), Charles Raymond, for just 10s – which included his services as director of the film!

The first superstar salary was earned not by any of the rising American players, but by Denmark's Asta Nielsen. For her debut in *The Abyss* (Den 10) she was paid a modest 200kr, but the film rocketed her to stardom and by the end of 1912 she was under contract to Berlin producer Paul Davidson with guaranteed annual earnings of $80000. Compared to Asta Nielsen's salary of over $1500 a week, the highest paid stars in America were Gene Gauntier at $200 a week and Florence Lawrence at $250 a week. At this time Mary Pickford, who was soon to eclipse them all, was trailing at $175 a week at Biograph. The following year, however, Adolph Zukor lured her to Famous Players at $500 a week and this was doubled in 1914 and doubled

Marlene Dietrich in *Knight Without Armour* (GB 37) – the highest paid performer in a pre-war British film

again in 1915. Already the highest paid woman in the world, on 24 June 1916 she signed a new contract that put her on a par with the highest paid man in the world – Charles Chaplin, who had contracted with Mutual earlier in the year at a salary of $670000. Miss Pickford's earnings were now half the profits of all her pictures, with a $10000 p.w. minimum, plus a $300000 single payment bonus, plus $150000 p.a. to her mother for 'goodwill', plus $40000 for examining scenarios prior to signing.

In the meantime Francesca Bertini, Italian 'diva', had become Europe's highest paid star in 1915 at $175000 p.a., only slightly behind the $200000 p.a. that Mary Pickford was then earning. European earnings, however, were never to rise above this before World War II, apart from the $450000 that Alexander Korda paid Marlene Dietrich to star in *Knight Without Armour* (GB 37). American earnings continued to spiral upward, but with the three highest paid stars – Mary Pickford, Charlie Chaplin and Douglas Fairbanks – combined together as producers under the distribution banner of United Artists from 1919 onwards, it is hard to assess their new earning power. In that same year Roscoe 'Fatty' Arbuckle had become the first star with a guaranteed minimum of $1 million a year, but his contract with Paramount only lasted until scandal destroyed his career in 1922 and he became the first star to be formally banned.

No other star of the silent era matched Arbuckle's salary, but Nazimova was reported to be the highest salaried woman star in 1920 at $13000 p.w., Tom Mix, the most popular cowboy star of the silents, was earning $17500 p.w. in 1925 and Harold Lloyd's weekly wage was reported to be $40000 p.w. in 1926. Salaries in Britain were a sad contrast. Alma Taylor, the most popular female star of the early 20s, was paid £60 p.w. by the Hepworth Co., but they were less generous with their leading male actor, Stewart Rome, who earned only £10 p.w. Ivor Novello, a matinee idol with a strong stage reputation, could command £3000–£4000 per film at his height in the late 20s, while the highest sum for a silent film was the £10000 paid to music hall artiste Sir Harry Lauder for his role as a retired grocer in George Pearson's *Hunting-tower* (GB 27).

The coming of sound and the depression, almost conterminously, forced most star salaries downward. In 1927 over 40 stars were reputedly earning $5000 or more a week. By 1931 only 23 stars had salaries of $3500 or more. Top earners in that year were Constance Bennett and John Barrymore at $30000 p.w., a sum soon to be matched by Greta Garbo, who earned $250000 for *The Painted Veil* (US 34) and the same for *Anna Karenina* (US 35). Highest earnings of 1935 were the $480833 reported by Mae West to the tax authorities, well in excess of the highest earnings of 1938 – Shirley Temple's $307014, or 1939 – James Cagney's $368333, or even 1946 when Bing Crosby topped both at the box office (rated No. 1 in the Quigley Poll) and at the bank with $325000. During the 40s and 50s top star salaries per film were generally in the $250000–$400000 region, with a new peak of $500000 for a British film – Elizabeth Taylor in *Suddenly Last Summer* (GB 59) – and $750000 for an American production, earned by both John Wayne and William

Holden (plus 20 per cent of the net) on *The Horse Soldiers* (US 59). The 1960s saw the era of the $1 million star salary for single pictures and in the 1970s the multi-million dollar contract. In the mid-1970s Charles Bronson was reported to be earning $20000–$30000, plus $2500 living allowance, per day. However, this was far exceeded by Marlon Brando's reputed $2·5 million for 12 days shooting on *Superman* (GB 78), which works out at $208333 per day. According to a special *Newsweek* report on Hollywood in 1978, the world's highest paid stars were Paul Newman, Robert Redford and Steve McQueen, each commanding some $3 million per picture. By December of the following year McQueen's asking price was way out in front, *Variety* reporting that he required a firm offer of $5 million plus 15 per cent of the gross before he would consent to look at a script. John Travolta and Olivia Newton John are reputed to have earned $10 million each as their percentage of the profits on *Grease* (US 78) and Clint Eastwood's take from *Escape from Alcatraz* (US 79) may exceed this.

The lowest salaries of recent years have seldom fallen below the £1500 that Olivia Hussey claimed she was paid for 11 months work while she was playing the female lead in Zeffirelli's *Romeo and Juliet* (GB 68) – at least in the west. In eastern countries and even Eastern Europe, different standards prevail. Teresa Izewska, star of the award-winning *Kanal* (Pol 57), revealed at the Cannes Film Festival that she earned the equivalent of $12 a month and that the Polish authorities had bought her one dress and one pair of shoes in order to represent them at the Festival. In 1973 *Variety* reported that China's biggest box office star, Shih Chung-chin, drew a salary of $20 a month. She slept in a communal dormitory with other actresses.

The first screen artiste to work on percentage was Nellie Stewart, who was paid £1000 plus a per cent of the gross for her title role in *Sweet Nell of Old Drury* (Aus 11).

The first American artiste to receive a percentage deal was James O'Neill (father of Eugene), who played the wronged Edmond Dantes in Famous Players' maiden production *The Count of Monte Cristo* (US 13). O'Neill had played the part on stage no less than 4000 times over a period of

Australia's Nellie Stewart – the first film star to demand a percentage *(The Australian Film Institute)*

30 years and was both too old (65) and too ham for the screen version, but Daniel Frohman knew that his was the name which would draw theatre-goers to the cinema and he offered the star 20 per cent of the net profits as an inducement. Returns were undermined by a rival Selig version of *The Count of Monte Cristo*, but the Famous Players version eventually grossed $45 539·32, of which O'Neill received $3 813·32.

The lowest paid players in American pictures were found in black movies. White director Edgar G. Ulmer recalls paying the 50 chorus girls in *Moon Over Harlem* (US 39) 25c a day each. The shooting schedule was four days and the girls had to pay their car fares from Harlem to the studio in Jersey out of the $1 they earned for a week's work. A record zero budget for an entire cast was achieved by Action Pictures Co. for their all-black feature *Sugar Hill Baby* (US 38). The casting director announced with disarming frankness that there was no money available for salaries, the only inducement offered being the somewhat doubtful 'chance to

continue to work in future in productions at good salaries'.

Probably the most recent instance of an established star taking a nil salary (and no per cent) was that of Sylvia Kristel who claims that since the success of *Emmanuelle* (Fr 74) she has been the highest paid actress in Europe. She starred in *Pastorale 1943* (Neths 78) for nothing. It was, she explained, a simple matter of tax avoidance.

At the other end of the scale, the most highly-paid stars have always been susceptible to ingenious attempts by the unscrupulous to benefit from their box office drawing power without the formality of payment. In 1917 a film processor in Chicago created his own Chaplin feature film – at a time when Chaplin was the highest paid star in the world – by matching together shots from his old comedies and then interpolating material from Fox's sensational *The Daughter of the Gods* (US 16), in which Australian star Annette Kellerman appeared in the nude. By clever optical work, he succeeded in creating scenes in which Chaplin and the naked Antipodean beauty appeared to be performing together. The film was released to the underground trade under the title *Charlie, Son of the Gods*.

Even more audacious was Soviet director Sergei Komarov's deception that secured him the gratuitous services of not one but two superstars, Mary Pickford and Douglas Fairbanks. During the visit of the couple to Moscow in July 1926, Komarov posed as a newsreel cameraman and followed them round with a camera, shooting enough footage to piece together a full-length comedy feature after their departure. Titled *The Kiss of Mary Pickford* (USSR 26), it was an engaging tale of a film extra who is determined to kiss the 'world's sweetheart' – and succeeds! Most remarkable of all was the climactic sequence of the close embrace between Soviet hero and Hollywood heroine. Although the film has now been shown publicly in the west, no one has been able to offer a convincing explanation of how Komarov managed to contrive this scene.

The first film with a 'cast of thousands' in a literal sense was Luigi Maggi's Napoleonic epic *Il Granatière Rolland* (It 10), for which 2000 extras were employed. A similar number participated in Britain's first extravaganza, Charles Weston's feature-length *The Battle of Waterloo* (GB 13).

The largest number of extras employed on a film was 187 000 in the last Nazi-made motion picture epic *Kolberg* (Ger 45). For this story about Napoleon's siege of Kolberg, whole army divisions were diverted from the front to play Napoleonic soldiers at a time when Germany was facing the prospect of her defeat. The film was started in 1943 and completed at the end of the following year, with drafts of fresh extras continuously replacing those who had to return to more earnest military duties. Released in January 1945, at a time when few Berlin cinemas were still functioning, *Kolberg* was seen by a considerably smaller total audience than the number which had appeared in it.

Other considerable casts include 157 000 for monster movie *Wang Ma Gwi/Monster Wang-magwi* (S. Korea 67), 120 000 for *War and Peace* (USSR 67), 80 000 for *The War of Independence* (Rom 12), 68 894 for *Around the World in 80 Days* (US 56), 60 000 for *Intolerance* (US 16) – publicity for the picture claimed 125 000 – 60 000 for *Dny Zrady* (Cz 72), 50 000 for *Ben Hur* (US 59) and *Exodus* (US 60), 36 000 in *Metropolis* (Ger 26), including 1100 bald men in the Tower of Babel sequence, and 30 000 in *Michael the Brave* (Rom 70).

Extras who became stars: Comparatively few major stars began their film careers as extras, the majority having had stage or, latterly, television experience before entering movies. Those who did do extra work include Theda Bara, Gary Cooper, Marlene Dietrich, Clark Gable, Janet Gaynor, John Gilbert, Paulette Goddard, Stewart Granger, Jean Harlow, Harold Lloyd, Sophia Loren, Marilyn Monroe, David Niven, Ramon Novarro, Merle Oberon, Norma Shearer, Erich von Stroheim, Constance Talmadge, Rudolph Valentino, Michael Wilding and Loretta Young.

Sadly the reverse process could also apply. Leading players who ended their careers as extras were King Baggot, Mae Busch, Ethel Clayton, Grace Cunard, western star Franklyn Farnum, Flora Finch, Francis Ford (brother of John Ford and a leading man in the late teens), John Ince (brother of early mogul Thomas Ince), Douglas Fairbanks' leading

Mickey Rooney began his career in the *Mickey Maguire* series in 1926

lady Julanne Johnston, Alice Lake, original 'Biograph Girl' Florence Lawrence, western star Kermit Maynard, Marshall Neilan, who had once commanded $125 000 per picture, Florence Turner, who was the first star to be put under contract, and 'country boy' hero Charles Ray.

Child stars: Adult stars who succeeded in perpetuating screen careers begun in childhood are few: Sir Stanley Baker (debut aged 14); Cyril Cusack (8); Bebe Daniels (7); Judy Garland (14); Betty Grable (13); Glynis Johns (13); Peter Lawford (7); Roger Livesey (14); Hayley Mills (13); Roddy McDowall (8); Donald O'Connor (11); Mickey Rooney (6); Romy Schneider (14); Anne Shirley (4); Jean Simmons (14); Elizabeth Taylor (10); Anna May Wong (12); Natalie Wood (5). Of these, only Garland, McDowall, Mills, Rooney, Shirley (as Dawn O'Day) and Taylor can be regarded as having been child *stars*.

Peter Lawford made his screen debut at the age of 7 in *Poor Old Bill* (GB 31)

Husky-voiced, perpetually elderly character actor Roger Livesey started on screen as a boy actor. He is seen here at age 15 in *The Four Feathers* (GB 21)

Many child stars became television performers or featured players in movies when they grew up. Those listed below gave up acting in favour of other careers:

Baby Jane: Whatever Happened to Baby Jane? The Real Baby Jane, **Juanita Quigley** (1931–), who was one of Universal's highest paid child stars of the 30s at $1000 p.w., retired from films to become a nun. She took her vows with the Daughters of Mary and Joseph as Sister Quintin Rita.

Baby Le Roy, real name **Le Roy Overacker** (1931–), the infant whose orange juice W.C. Fields is alleged to have laced with gin, attained stardom in 1933 at the age of six months. He became a lifeguard in Southern California.

Baby Peggy, real name **Peggy Montgomery** (1918–), infant star of the silents, failed to make a come-back in talkies but achieved success as a short-story writer instead. Her work appeared in such magazines as *Esquire* and *Saturday Evening Post* under the name Diana Cary.

Freddie Bartholomew (1924–), who won instant star-

Jean Simmons showed early promise of becoming an outstanding beauty when she made her screen debut at 14 in *Give Us the Moon* (GB 43)

dom in *David Copperfield* (US 35), is a New York advertising executive.

Joseph Boudreaux (1935–), who played the boy who sees the coming of the oilmen to the swamplands of Louisiana in *Louisiana Story* (US 48), became an oil driller himself when he grew up.

Jackie Cooper (1921–) became part-owner of a kitchen ventilator company after an unsuccessful attempt at a vaudeville career.

Frankie Darro (1917–), boy hero of Mascot serials of the 30s, became a barman in Long Beach, California.

Bobby Driscoll (1937–68), Jim in *Treasure Island* (GB 50), was an unsuccessful clothing salesman before dying of a heroin overdose aged 31.

Deanna Durbin (1921–), played her last film role in *For the Love of Mary* (US 48) at the age of 27 and then emigrated to France, where she married film director Charles David and settled in a village outside Paris.

Claude Jarman (1934–), who won an Oscar at the age of 11 for his debut in *The Yearling* (US 45), left movies

Baby Peggy – she became a successful writer under the name of Diana Cary

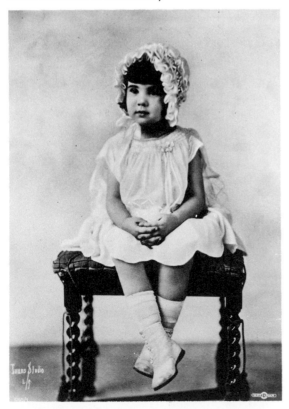

SHIRLEY'S FIRST WRINKLE

Child stars grow up – 9-year-old Shirley Temple was still America's No. 1 box-office star when *Cinema Arts* published this cartoon in 1937 *(Backnumbers)*

after appearing in *The Great Locomotive Chase* (US 56) and became a public relations officer for John Hancock Insurance. He is now manager of San Francisco Opera House.

Gloria Jean (1928–), who received star billing in her first film, *The Under-Pup* (US 39), when she was 12, suffered a declining adult acting career and quit pictures in 1955 to work as a hostess at the Tahitian Restaurant in Encino, California. She married a customer, had a child, divorced, and in 1965 found permanent employment as a receptionist at Redken Laboratories.

The Mauch Twins (1924–), remembered especially for their roles as beggar boy and King in *The Prince and the Pauper* (US 37), stayed in the business but as film editors.

Mandy Miller (1944–) had one great success in the title role of *Mandy*/US: *The Crash of Silence* (GB 52), but continued to act in films until she was 18, when she became a children's nanny in New York. Now Mrs Christopher Davy, she is the wife of an architect and lives in Aberdeenshire.

Colin Petersen (1948–), freckle-faced Australian child star of *Smiley* (GB 57), became a member of the *Bee Gees* pop group in the 1970s.

Sabu (1924–63), young Indian hero of *Elephant Boy* (GB 37) and *The Jungle Book* (US 42), who had been discovered by Robert Flaherty working as a stable boy in Mysore, went into the furniture business after a distinguished war record in the US Army. He continued to make occasional appearances in films, the last *A Tiger Walk* (US 63) in the year of his premature death from a heart attack.

Carl Switzer (1926–59), who played Alfalfa in the *Our Gang* comedies, became a drifter and was killed in 1959 in a fight with a man who owed him $50. Spanky McFarland was a hotdog salesman in later life and Fatty (Joe Cobb) worked in an aircraft factory as a fitter.

Shirley Temple (1928–) made her last movie, *A Kiss for Corliss* (US 49), at the age of 21. As Mrs Shirley Temple Black she entered local politics in California in the 1960s, was appointed Ambassador to Ghana by President Ford, and then served as Head of Protocol at the White House.

Contracts, legal and binding . . . : In the days when studios 'owned' stars, the price of security and gigantic salaries was often freedom of behaviour. All big stars had morality clauses in their contracts (first to sign had been Maryon Aye in 1922), but Joan Crawford's with MGM in 1930 even specified the hour by which she had to be in bed. Mary Miles Minter's contract with the Realart Co. in 1919 was dependent upon her remaining unmarried for $3\frac{1}{2}$ years. Others enjoined to remain single were Clara Bow, at Paramount's insistence, and Alice White, whose contract with First National further obliged her to learn two languages during the course of 1930, preferably French and Spanish. Walter Pidgeon, much in demand for musicals before he became a father figure, was forbidden to sing tenor lest he impair his rich baritone voice. Buster Keaton's famous unsmiling face was a contractual obligation. His contract with MGM in the 20s precluded him from smiling on screen, while Charles Butterworth's with Warner Bros prevented him from smiling in public. Similarly, Roscoe Ates' stutter was legally binding in his contract with RKO. First National demanded of Douglas Fairbanks Jnr. that he never travel in 'planes. Joe E. Brown was forbidden to grow a moustache. A clause in teetotaller Frank McHugh's contract with First National required that he play drunkards whenever required, while Maurice Chevalier's with Paramount, signed as talkies were coming in, insisted that he remain in character – it was rendered invalid if he ever lost his French accent. In 1931 boxing fan Vivienne Segal was directed by her contract with Warner's not to yell at prize fights in case she strained her voice.

Possibly the most difficult contractual obligation to enforce was the one enjoined on Lois Moran not to grow sophisticated for a year after the release of *Stella Dallas* (US 26). Clara Bow was offered a $500000 bonus by Paramount in 1926 provided she kept herself free of scandal during its tenure. She failed to collect. All the cast of Cecil B. DeMille's reverential life of Christ, *King of Kings* (US 27), were bound by contract not to accept any roles without De Mille's consent for ten years after the film's release. Dorothy Cummings, who played the Madonna, was further denied the right to divorce, which she promptly did three months after the première.

Occasionally the stars were able to impose unusual conditions on their masters, the studios. At the Warner studios in the early 30s, George Arliss's contract provided that he did not have to remain on set after 4.30 p.m., while John Barrymore's gave him the privilege of not being on set before 10.30 a.m. Moran and Mack, the Two Black Crows, were the only Paramount stars allowed to drive their car within the studio gates. Garbo's desire to be alone was protected by a clause preventing MGM from demands that she make any public appearances. When stage player Margaret Sullavan was persuaded by director John Stahl to accept the lead in *Only Yesterday* (US 33), she was so reluctant to enter films that she had a clause inserted in her contract to the effect that she could quit after ten days if she disliked Hollywood as much as she anticipated. Although she loathed Tinsel Town, she completed the picture and many others. Joe E. Brown's contract with Warner's demanded that the studio co-operate with him in running a baseball team. Virginal Evelyn Venable's contract with Paramount in 1933 had a clause inserted by her father preventing her from being kissed on screen. The rather less virginal Clara Bow wrote into her contract with

Britain's first black film star – Bermuda born Ernest Trimmingham in *Jack, Sam and Pete* (GB 19)

Paramount that none of the workmen or technicians were to use profane language to her or in her presence.

The most married stars in the Hollywood galaxy are Mickey Rooney (b. 1920), whose eight wives have been Ava Gardner (1942), Betty Jane Rase (1944), Martha Vickers (1949), Elaine Mahnken (1952), Barbara Thomason (1958), Margaret Lane (1966), Carolyn Hackett (1969) and Jan Chamberlain (1975); and Lana Turner (b. 1921), whose eight marriages have been to bandleader Artie Shaw (1940), restauranteur Stephen Crane (twice: 1942 and 1943), baseball team owner Bob Topping (1948), Tarzan player Lex Barker (1953), rancher Fred May (1960), writer Robert Eaton (1965) and hypnotist Ronald Dante (1969 – divorced same year). Elizabeth Taylor has been married seven times, twice to Richard Burton.

The first black actor to play a leading role in a feature film was Sam Lucas, cast in the title role of *Uncle Tom's Cabin* (US 14).

The first black actor to make a career in films was Noble Johnson, who made his debut in a Lubin western in 1914 playing an Indian chief. After arriving in Hollywood in 1915, he graduated from stunt work and bit parts with the formation of the Lincoln Motion Picture Co., an all-black production company specialising in ghetto films, of which he was president as well as leading player. Johnson starred in three Lincoln productions – *The Realisation of a Negro's Ambition* (US 16), *The Trooper of Company K* (US 17) and *The Law of Nature* (US 18) – before leaving the company to concentrate on the Universal serials he had been making between Lincoln pictures.

Britain's first black screen actor was Bermuda-born Ernest Trimmingham, who made his debut in the British & Colonial production *Her Bachelor Guardian* (GB 12). **The first black actor to play a leading role in a British film** was Paul Robeson as Bosambo in Alexander Korda's *Sanders of the River* (GB 35). He also starred in *Song of Freedom* (GB 37), *Big Fella* (GB 37), *King Solomon's Mines* (GB 37) and *Jericho* (GB 37).

Film stars who have played themselves in movies:

Mary Astor: *Hollywood* (US 23). **Anne Bancroft:** *Silent Movie* (US 76). **Tallulah Bankhead:** *Stage Door Canteen* (US 43). **Brigitte Bardot:** *Dear Brigitte* (US 65). **Lionel Barrymore:** *Free and Easy* (US 30). **Noah Beery:** *Hollywood* (US 23). **Dorothy Bellew:** *The Kinema Girl* (GB 14). **William Bendix:** *Variety Girl* (US 47). **Humphrey Bogart:** *The Love Lottery* (US 54). **James Caan:** *Silent Movie* (US 76). **Eddie Cantor:** *The Story of Will Rogers* (US 52). **Charles Chaplin:** *Show People* (US 29). **Julie Christie:** *Nashville* (US 75). **Betty Compson:** *Hollywood* (US 23). **Eddie Constantine:** *Les Septs pêches capitaux* (Fr/It 62); *Warnung vor einer Heiligen Nutte* (W.Ger/It 71). **Jackie Coogan:** *Free and Easy* (US 30). **Gary Cooper:** *Variety Girl* (US 47). **Ricardo Cortez:** *Hollywood* (US 23). **Broderick Crawford:** *A Little Romance* (US 79). **Bing Crosby:** *Variety Girl* (US 47). **Finlay Currie:** *6.5 Special* (GB 58). **Karl Dane:** *Free and Easy* (US 30). **Dolores Del Rio:** *Torero!* (Mex 56). **Douglas Fairbanks:** *The Kiss of Mary Pickford* (USSR 26); *Show People* (US 29). **Marianne Faithful:** *Made in USA* (Fr 67). **Barry Fitzgerald:** *Variety Girl* (US 47). **Cyril Fletcher:** *Yellow Canary* (GB 43). **Henry Fonda:** *Fedora* (W.Ger 78). **Greta Garbo:** *A Man's Man* (US 29). **John Gilbert:** *Married Flirts* (US 24); *A Man's Man* (US 29). **Paulette Goddard:** *Variety Girl* (US 47). **Elliott Gould:** *Nashville* (US 75). **Cary Grant:** *Without Reservations* (US 46). **Greta Gynt:** *I'm a Stranger* (GB 52). **W.S. Hart:** *Hollywood* (US 23); *Show People* (US 29). **Laurence Harvey:** *The Magic Christian* (GB 70) – as self playing Hamlet. **Sessue Hayakawa:** *Night Life in Hollywood* (US 22). **Sterling Hayden:** *Variety Girl* (US 47). **Katherine Hepburn:** *Stage Door Canteen* (US 43). **William Holden:** *Variety Girl* (US 47). **Bob Hope:** *Variety Girl* (US 47); *The Oscar* (US 66). **Sidney James:** *The Beauty Contest* (GB 64). **Al Jolson:** *Hollywood Cavalcade* (US 39). **Buster Keaton:** *Hollywood Cavalcade* (US 39); *Sunset Boulevard* (US 50). **Gene Kelly:** *Love is Better than Ever* (US 52). **George Kennedy:** *The Legend of Lylah Clare* (US 68). **Alan Ladd:** *Variety Girl* (US 47). **Veronica Lake:** *Variety Girl* (US 47). **Dorothy Lamour:** *Variety Girl* (US 47). **Bessie Love:** *Night Life in Hollywood* (US 22); *Mary of the Movies* (US 23). **Linda Lovelace:** *Linda Lovelace for President* (US 75). **Virginia McKenna:** *The Lion at World's End* (GB 71). **George Marshall:** *Variety Girl* (US 47). **Marcello Mastroianni:** *L'Ingorgo/Bottleneck* (It/Fr/Sp/W.Ger 79). **Harpo Marx:** *Stage Door Canteen* (US 43). **Ray Milland:** *Variety Girl* (US 47). **Liza Minnelli:** *Silent Movie* (US 76). **Bull Montana:** *Hollywood* (US 23). **Owen Moore:** *Hollywood* (US 23). **Paul Muni:** *Stage Door Canteen* (US 43). **Mae Murray:** *Married Flirts* (US 24); *Show People* (US 29). **Nita Naldi:** *Hollywood* (US 23). **Pola Negri:** *Hollywood* (US 23). **Paul Newman:** *Silent Movie* (US 76). **Anna Q. Nillson:** *Sunset Boulevard* (US 50). **Merle Oberon:** *Stage Door Canteen* (US 43). **Larry Parks:** *Jolson Sings Again* (US 49) – also played Jolson. **Mary Pickford:** *The Kiss of Mary Pickford* (USSR 26) – made by Sergei Komorov without Miss Pickford being aware of her own participation. **ZaSu Pitts:** *Mary of the Movies* (US 23). **Robert Preston:** *Variety Girl* (US 47). **George Raft:** *Broadway* (US 42); *Stage Door Canteen* (US 43); *Casino Royale* (GB 67);

Sextette (US 78). **Wallace Reid:** *Night Life in Hollywood* (US 22). **Michael Rennie:** *The Body Said No!* (GB 50). **Burt Reynolds:** *Silent Movie* (US 76). **Ralph Richardson:** *The Volunteer* (GB 43). **Patricia Roc:** *Holiday Camp* (GB 47). **Will Rogers:** *Hollywood* (US 23). **Sabrina:** *Just My Luck* (GB 57). **Larry Semon:** *Go Straight* (US 25). **Mack Sennett:** *Abbott and Costello Meet the Keystone Kops* (US 54). **Norma Shearer:** *Married Flirts* (US 24). **Barbara Stanwyck:** *Variety Girl* (US 47). **Tommy Steele:** *Kill Me Tomorrow* (GB 55); *The Tommy Steele Story* (GB 57). **Anita Stewart:** *Mary of the Movies* (US 23); *Hollywood* (US 23); *Go Straight* (US 25). **Gloria Swanson:** *Hollywood* (US 23); *Airport 75* (US 74). **Blanche Sweet:** *Souls for Sale* (US 23). **Constance Talmadge:** *In Hollywood with Potash and Perlmutter* (US 24). **Norma Talmadge:** *In Hollywood with Potash and Perlmutter* (US 24); *Show People* (US 29). **Estelle Taylor:** *Mary of the Movies* (US 23); *Hollywood* (US 23). **Bill Travers:** *The Lion at World's End* (GB 71). **Ben Turpin:** *Hollywood* (US 23). **Liv Ullman:** *Players* (US 79). **Peter Ustinov:** *Players* (US 79). **H.B. Warner:** *Sunset Boulevard* (US 50). **Paul Wegener:** *The Golem and the Dancer* (Ger 14). **Johnny Weissmuller:** *Stage Door Canteen* (US 43). **Natalie Wood:** *The Candidate* (US 72). **Michael York:** *Fedora* (W.Ger 78). **Susannah York:** *Scruggs* (GB 66) – also played heroine; *Long Shot* (GB 78).

Non-actors who have played themselves in films (the list excludes the many bandleaders and vocalists appearing in sound movies):

Princess Aicha Abidir: *Pierrot-le-Feu* (Fr/It 65). **Dragljub Aleksić**, acrobat: *Nevinost bez Zastite** (Yug 68). **Queen Alexandra:** *The Great Love* (US 18); *Women Who Win* (GB 19). **Muhammed Ali**, heavyweight boxing champion: *The Greatest** (US 77). **Mario Andretti**, motor-racing driver: *Speed Fever* (It 78). **Lord Baden-Powell**, defender of Mafeking and founder of the Scout movement: *Boys of the Otter Patrol* (GB 18); *The Man Who Changed His Mind* (GB 28); *The Woodpigeon Patrol* (GB 30). **Admiral Badger:** *Victory* (US 13). **Max Baer**, boxer: *The Prizefighter and the Lady* (US 33). **Joan Bakewell**, TV personality: *The Touchables* (GB 67). **Adolf Beck**, convicted of false murder charge: *The Martyrdom of Adolf Beck** (GB 09). **The Duchess of Bedford:** *The Beauty Contest* (GB 64). **The Duke of Bedford:** *The Iron Maiden* (GB 62). **Alec Bedser**, cricketer: *The Final Test* (GB 53). **Sonny Berger**, Hell's Angels leader: *Hell's Angels* (US 69). **Yogi Berra**, baseball star: *That Touch of Mink* (US 62). **Jasmine Bligh**, TV announcer: *Band Wagon* (GB 40). **Ada Bodart**, assisted Nurse Edith Cavell in establishing her World War I escape organisation: *Dawn* (GB 28). **Lord Boothby**, politician: *Rockets Galore* (GB 58). **Bjorn Borg**, tennis champion: *Racquet* (US 79). **Horatio Bottomley:** politician and financier, three times charged with fraud (convicted 1922): *Was It He?* (GB 14). **Jack Brabham**, motor-racing driver: *The Green Helmet* (GB 61). **RSM Ronald Brittain**, Regimental Sergeant Major of ferocious demeanour: *You Lucky People* (GB 55). **Dr Joyce Brothers**, sexologist: *Embryo* (US 76). **Maurice Buckmaster**, spymaster: *Odette* (GB 50). **Sir Matt Busby**, football manager: *Cup Fever* (GB 65). **José Capablanca**, Chess Grand Master: *Chess Fever* (USSR 25). **Arthur Christiansen**, ex-editor of the Daily Express: *The Day the Earth Caught Fire* (GB 61). **M.E. Clifton-James**, ex-actor who impersonated Mont-

M.E. Clifton-James playing himself impersonating General Montgomery in *I Was Monty's Double* (GB 58)

gomery to deceive Nazi Intelligence: *I Was Monty's Double** (GB 58). **Sir Alan Cobham,** aviator: *The Flight Commander* (GB 27). **William Cody,** Buffalo Bill: *The Life of Buffalo Bill** (US 09); *Buffalo Bill's Far West and Pawnee Bill's Far East* (US 10); *The Indian Wars* (US 13); *Sitting Bull – The Hostile Indian Chief* (US 14); *Patsy of the Circus* (US 15). **Dennis Compton,** cricketer: *The Final Test* (GB 53). **Emmett Dalton,** youngest of the Dalton brothers, notorious desperadoes: *Beyond the Law* (US 18). **Josephus Daniels,** US Secretary of the Navy: *Victory* (US 13). **Moshe Dayan,** Israeli Minister of Defence: *Operation Thunderbolt* (Israel 77). **Cecil B. DeMille,** film producer and director: *Hollywood* (US 23); *Free and Easy* (US 30); *Variety Girl* (US 47); *Sunset Boulevard* (US 50). **Richard Dimbleby,** BBC commentator: *The Twenty Questions Murder* (GB 50); *John and Julie* (GB 55); *Rockets Galore* (GB 58); *Libel* (GB 59). **Georgi Dimitrov,** communist revolutionary tried and acquitted in the 1933 Reichstag Fire trial, Prime Minister of Bulgaria 1946–9: *Kämpfer* (USSR 36). **Sgt Arthur Guy Empsey:** *Over the Top** (US 18). **Godfrey Evans,** cricketer: *The Final Test* (GB 53). **Robert Fabian,** police detective: *Passport to Shame* (GB 59). **Emerson Fittipaldi,** motor-racing driver: *Speed Fever* (It 79). **Michael Foot,** socialist politician: *Rockets Galore* (GB 58). **John Ford,** director: *Big Time* (US 29). **Joe Frazier,** boxer: *Rocky* (US 77). **Samuel Fuller,** director: *Pierrot-le-Feu* (Fr 65). **Frank Gifford,** American footballer: *Paper Lion* (US 68); *Viva Knievel!* (US 77). **Alan Ginsberg,** poet: *Ciao! Manhattan* (US 72). **Raymond Glendenning,** sports commentator: *The Galloping Major* (GB 51); *Make Mine a Million* (GB 59); *The Iron Maiden* (GB 62). **Elinor Glyn,** pioneer of the sex novel: *Show People* (US 29). **Barbara Goalen,** model: *Wonderful Things!* (GB 58). **Pancho Gonzalez,** tennis coach: *Players* (US 79). **John Gorton,** Prime Minister of Australia: *Don's Party* (Aus 76). **Billy Graham,** American evangelist: *Souls in Conflict* (GB 55); *Two a Penny* (GB 67). **Sheila Graham,** journalist and mistress of F. Scott Fitzgerald (played by Deborah Kerr in biopic *Beloved Infidel* (US 59)): *College Confidential* (US 60). **Angèle Grammont,** who escaped from old people's home near Lausanne: *Angèle** (Swz 68). **Earl Haig,** World War I Commander-in-Chief: *Remembrance* (GB 27). **Ernest Haigh,** ex-Chief Inspector of Police: *Leaves From My Life** (GB 21). **Giscele Halimi,** defence counsel in notable 1972 abortion trial: *L'Une

chante, l'autre pas* (Fr/Belg/Curaçao 76). **David Hamilton,** photographer: *Tiffany Jones* (GB 73). **General Sir Ian Hamilton,** leader of the Gallipoli Expedition: *Tell England* (GB 31). **Judge James Hannon,** judge who tried Arlo Guthrie for casting litter: *Alice's Restaurant* (US 69). **Gilbert Harding,** crusty TV personality, famous for rudeness: *Simon and Laura* (GB 55); *As Long as They're Happy* (GB 55); *An Alligator Named Daisy* (GB 55); *My Wife's Family* (GB 56); *Left, Right and Centre* (GB 59); *Expresso Bongo* (GB 59). **Len Harvey,** boxer: *The Bermondsey Kid* (GB 33). **Norman Hartnell,** couturier: *The Beauty Contest* (GB 64). **Edith Head,** Hollywood costume designer: *The Oscar* (US 66). **Hugh Heffner,** founder of Playboy empire: *How Did a Nice Girl Like You Ever Get Into This Business* (W.Ger 70). **Graham Hill,** motor racing driver: *The Fast Lady* (GB 62). **Dennis Hills,** captive of Idi Amin: *The Rise and Fall of Idi Amin* (GB 80). **John Hodge MP,** Minister of Pensions: *Broken in the Wars* (GB 19). **Hedda Hopper,** movie gossip columnist: *Sunset Boulevard* (US 50). **Hubert Humphrey,** US Senator: *The Candidate* (US 72). **James Hunt,** motor-racing driver: *Speed Fever* (It 78). **Len Hutton,** cricketer: *The Final Test* (GB 53). **Father Iliodor,** rascally monk, first protégé, then opponent of Rasputin: *The Fall of the Romanoffs* (US 18). **David Jacobs,** broadcaster: *Otley* (GB 68). **Al Jennings,** convicted bank and train robber: *The Bank Robbery* (US 08); *Beating Back** (US 15). **Amy Johnson,** aviatrix: *Dual Control* (GB 32). **Jack Johnson,** boxer: *Jack Johnson's Adventures in Paris* (Fr 13); *As the World Rolls On* (US 21). **Helen Keller,** deaf-blind scholar:

Wimbledon champion Suzanne Lenglen played herself in *Things Are Looking Up* (GB 35)

Not the real Valentino – Rudolf Nureyev playing the Latin Lover in Ken Russell's *Valentino* (GB 77)

Above: Napoleon Bonaparte has been portrayed on screen more often than any other historical character. Here, Charles Boyer essays the role in *Conquest* (US 37) playing opposite Greta Garbo. (See p. 64)

Not the real W.C. Fields —
the picture is from
W.C. Fields and Me
(US 76) with Rod Steiger
as the tyrant comic

*Deliverance** (US 19). **Evel Knievel,** motorcycle stuntman: *Viva Knievel!* (US 77). **Somchai Koonperm,** village chief: *Kamnan Poh** (Thai 80). **Jim Laker,** cricketer: *The Final Test* (GB 53). **Fritz Lang,** film director (played by Marcel Hillaire in *Take the Money and Run* (US 69)): *Contempt* (Fr 64). **Nikki Lauder,** motor-racing driver: *Speed Fever* (It 78). **Suzanne Lenglen,** Wimbledon tennis champion: *Things Are Looking Up* (GB 35). **Bernard Levin,** journalist: *Nothing But the Best* (GB 63). **Prinz Eduard von und zu Liechtenstein,** of the Royal House of Liechtenstein: *Johann Strauss an der Schönen blauen Donau* (Austria 13). **Vincent Lombardi,** American footballer: *Paper Lion* (US 68). **Joe Louis,** boxer: *The Spirit of Youth** (US 37). **Captain James Lovell,** astronaut: *The Man Who Fell to Earth* (GB 76). **Jem Mace,** boxer: *There's Life in the Old Dog Yet* (GB 08). **Windsor McCay,** cartoonist (*Little Nemo*, etc.) and pioneer film animator: *The Great White Way* (US 24). **John McEnroe,** tennis champion: *Players* (US 79). **George McGovern,** US Senator: *The Candidate* (US 72). **Marshall McLuhan,** Canadian academic, expert on media and communications: *Annie Hall* (US 77). **George McManus,** cartoonist (*Bringing Up Father,* etc.): *The Great White Way* (US 24). **Queen Mary:** *Women Who Win* (GB 19). **Dan Maskell,** tennis player: *Players* (US 79). **Cliff Michelmore,** TV personality: *A Jolly Bad Fellow* (GB 63). **Freddie Mills,** boxer: *6.5 Special* (GB 58). **Leslie Mitchell,** Britain's first TV announcer (1936) and Movietone commentator: *Geneviève* (GB 53). **Jim Mollison,** aviator who made first east-west crossing of N. Atlantic: *Dual Control* (GB 32). **Stirling Moss,** motor-racing driver: *The Beauty Contest* (GB 64). **James Mossman,** broadcaster: *Masquerade* (GB 64). **Malcom Muggeridge,** journalist and pundit: *I'm All Right Jack* (GB 59); *Heavens Above* (GB 63); *Herostratus* (GB 67); *The Naked Bunyip* (Aus 70). **Audie Murphy,** most decorated US Soldier of World War II: *To Hell and Back** (US 55). Subsequently professional actor. **Pete Murray,** disc jockey: *6.5 Special* (GB 58). **Ilie Nastase,** Romanian tennis champion: *Players* (US 79). **Bess Nielsen,** Parisian girl given to amorous adventures: *On n'est pas serieux quand on a 17 ans** (Fr 74). **Officer Obie,** policeman who arrested Arlo Guthrie for casting litter: *Alice's Restaurant* (US 69). **Barney Oldfield,** motor-racing driver: *Barney Oldfield's Race for Life* (US 16). **Ignace Paderewski,** pianist, Prime Minister and later President of Poland: *Moonlight Sonata* (GB 37). **Arnold Palmer,** golfer: *Call Me Bwana* (GB 63). **Huang Pao-Mei,** girl spinner in China's Cotton Mill No 17: *Huang Pao-mei** (China 58). **Michael Parkinson,** TV personality: *Madhouse* (GB 74). **Princess Patricia:** *Women Who Win* (GB 19). **Lieutenant Harold R. Peat:** *Private Peat** (US 18). **Betty Ting Pei,** Bruce Lee's lover: *Bruce Lee and I** (HK 76). **Pablo Picasso,** artist: *Le Testament d'Orphée* (Fr 60). **Luis Procuna,** matador: *Torero!** (Mex 56). **Yizhak Rabin,** Prime Minister of Israel: *Operation Thunderbolt* (Israel 77). **Dame Marie Rambert,** founder of the Ballet Rambert: *The Red Shoes* (GB 48). **Frank Randle,** hypnotist: *When You Come Home* (GB 47). **Carlos Reutemann,** motor-racing driver: *Speed Fever* (It 78). **Robert Ripley,** originator of *Believe It or Not*: *The Great White Way* (US 24). **Charlie Rivel,** circus clown: *Scö-ö-ön** (Ger 43). **Jackie Robinson,** first black to play major league baseball: *The Jackie Robinson Story** (US 50). **Robert Robinson,** broadcaster: *French Dressing* (GB 64). **Sugar Ray Robinson,** boxer: *Paper Lion* (US 68). **Theodore Roosevelt,** ex-President of the USA: *Womanhood, The Glory of a Nation* (US 17). **Lady**

'Bubbles' Rothermere, society hostess: *The Stud* (GB 78). **Damon Runyon,** writer: *The Great White Way* (US 24); *O, Baby* (US 26). **Gunther Sachs,** millionaire industrialist and playboy: *Cardillac* (W.Ger 69). **Joe Schmidt,** American footballer: *Paper Lion* (US 68). **Caporal Sellier,** bugler who sounded the World War I armistice, re-enacted scene in *The Soul of France* (Fr 28). **Ma Sha,** reformed pimp and killer: *The First Error Step** (Singapore 79). **William Shirer,** historian: *The Magic Face* (US 51). **Harry Siegenberg,** bookmaker: *The Stolen Favourite* (S. Africa 19). **George R. Sims,** crusading journalist gaoled in celebrated 1885 *Maiden Tribute of Modern Babylon* case: *The Martyrdom of Adolf Beck* (GB 09). **Anne Sullivan,** who taught blind deaf-mute Helen Keller to speak and read: *Deliverance* (US 19). **Hannen Swaffer,** journalist: *Spellbound* (GB 41). **Crown Princess of Sweden:** *Women Who Win* (GB 19). **Fuji Takeshi,** world junior welterweight boxing champion: *Fuji Takeshi Monogatari** (Jap 68). **Yukio Tani,** martial arts exponent: *Ju-Jitsu to the Rescue* (GB 13). **Alderman C.E. Tatham,** Mayor of Blackpool: *Sing As We Go* (GB 34). **A.J.P. Taylor,** historian: *Rockets Galore* (GB 58). **Evelyn Nesbitt Thaw:** beauty whose husband murdered her lover, architect Stanford White; played by Joan Collins in *The Girl in the Red Velvet Swing* (US 55) and immortalised in E.L. Doctorow's *Ragtime* as the child bride 'habitually whipped' by the sadistic Thaw: *The Great Thaw Trial* (US 07); *Redemption* (US 17). **Wynford Vaughan Thomas,** broadcaster: *John and Julie* (GB 55). **W.M. Tilgham,** Marshal of Cache, Oklahoma: *The Bank Robbery* (US 08). **Mark Twain,** humorous writer: *A Curious Dream* (US 07). **Princess Victoria:** *Women Who Win* (GB 19). **Guillermo Vilas,** tennis player: *Players* (US 79). **The Prince of Wales,** later King Edward VIII: *The Warrior Strain* (GB 19); *The Power of Right* (GB 19); *Remembrance* (GB 27). **Jimmy Walker,** Mayor of New York: *Glorifying the American Girl* (US 29). **Cyril Washbrook,** cricketer: *The Final Test* (GB 53). **Gough Whitlam,** Prime Minister of Australia: *Barry McKenzie Holds His Own* (Aus 74). **Frank Wills,** Watergate security guard who discovered break-in: *All the President's Men* (US 76). **Woodrow Wilson,** President of the USA: *Womanhood, The Glory of a Nation* (US 17). **Walter Winchell,** influential American columnist (played by Lew Ayres in *OKay America!* (US 32)): *The Helen Morgan Story* (US 57); *College Confidential* (US 60). **Godfrey Winn,** journalist: *Billy Liar!* (GB 63). **Maharishi Narish Yogi,** guru: *Candy Baby* (US 69). **Sam Yorty,** Mayor of Los Angeles: *The Candidate* (US 72). **Jimmy Young,** broadcaster: *Otley* (GB 68). **Florenz Ziegfeld,** impresario: *Glorifying the American Girl* (US 29). **Adolf Zukor,** film producer: *Glorifying the American Girl* (US 29).

* Autobiopics

Non-actors in films: Personalities unconnected with stage or screen who have played roles other than themselves (*see also* Personalities playing themselves, p. 99) include:

Horacio Accavallo, world flyweight boxing champion, lead in *Destino para dos* (Arg 67). **Muhammed Ali,** world heavyweight boxing champion, as Gideon Jackson, first black US Senator, in TVM *Freedom Road* (US 79). **Mrs Morgan Belmont,** society leader and member of New York's '400', played the upper crust Diana Tremont in *Way Down East*

(US 20). **Peter Benchley,** author of *Jaws*, played a reporter in *Jaws* (US 75). **Godfrey Binaisa,** President of Uganda, bit parts in *King Solomon's Mines* (US 50) and *The African Queen* (GB 51). **RSM Ronald Brittain,** Regimental Sergeant Major at Sandhurst Military Academy during 1950s, appeared (usually as a Sergeant Major) in *Carrington VC* (GB 54), *The Missing Note* (GB 61), *The Amorous Prawn* (GB 62), *Joey Boy* (GB 65) and *The Spy with a Cold Nose* (GB 66). **Truman Capote,** author, leading role in detective fiction parody *Murder by Death* (US 76). **Primo Carnera,** boxer, played Python Macklin in *A Kid for Two Farthings* (GB 55). **G.K. Chesterton,** author, in *Rosy Rapture – The Pride of the Beauty Chorus* (GB 14). **Daniel Cohn-Bendit,** revolutionary, in Godard's *Vent d'est* (W.Ger/It 70). **James John Corbett,** world heavyweight boxing champion, in *The Midnight Man* (US 19). **Quentin Crisp,** homosexual liberationist, played Polonius in *Hamlet* (GB 76). **Dionne Quins,** world's first surviving quintuplets, in *The Country Doctor* (US 36), *Reunion* (US 36) and *Five of a Kind* (US 38). **Steve Donaghue,** champion jockey, as Steve Baxter, hero of *Riding for a King* (GB 26), *Beating the Book* (GB 26), *The Golden Spurs* (GB 26) and *The Stolen Favourite* (GB 26). **Gertrude Ederle,** first woman to swim the English Channel, in *Swim, Girl, Swim* (US 28). **David Frost,** television commentator, as reporter in *The VIPs* (GB 63). **Althea Gibson,** black tennis star, as maid in John Ford's *The Horse Soldiers* (US 59). **Graham Greene,** author, as the insurance representative in *Day for Night* (Fr 73). **Germaine Greer,** women's liberationist, as Clara Bowden in *Universal Soldier* (GB 71). **Lorenz Hart,** of Rodgers and Hart, played the bank teller in *Hallelujah, I'm a Bum* (US 33). **Len Harvey,** British boxing champion, played a glass collector turned boxer in *Excuse My Glove* (GB 36). **Ernest Hemingway,** author, uncredited bit part in *The Old Man and the Sea* (US 58). **Xaviera Hollander,** prostitute and writer, lead in *My Pleasure is My Business* (Can 74). **Bianca Jagger,** jet-setter, leads in *Flesh Colour* (US 79) and *The Great American Success Company* (US 79). **Jomo Kenyatta,** President of Kenya 1963–78, played an African chief in *Sanders of the River* (GB 35). **Dr Emmanuel Lasker,** world chess champion, played Napoleon's chess partner in Lupu Pick's *Napoléon a Sainte-Hélène* (Fr 29). **John Lindsay,** Mayor of New York, played Senator Donnovan in *Rosebud* (US 75). **Victor Lowndes,** chairman of Playboy UK, as Reeve Passmore in *Fledglings* (GB 65). **Compton MacKenzie,** author, as Sir Robert Dysart in *Chance of a Lifetime* (GB 50). **Yehudi Menuhin,** violinist, in *The Magic Bow* (GB 46). **Freddie Mills,** British champion boxer, in *Fun at St Fanny's* (GB 56), *Breakaway* (GB 56), *Chain of Events* (GB 58), *Carry On Constable* (GB 60), *Carry On Regardless* (GB 61), *The Comedy Man* (GB 63), *Saturday Night Out* (GB 64). **Jóan Miró,** Spanish painter, played the museum curator in *El Umbracle* (Sp 73). **Stirling Moss,** motor-racing driver, in *Casino Royale* (GB 67). **Beverley Nichols,** author, as the Hon. Richard Wells in *Glamour* (GB 31). **Mrs. Richard Nixon,** wife of ex-President Nixon, walk-on parts in *Becky Sharp* (US 36) and *Small Town Girl* (US 37). **Princess Pearl,** daughter of the White Rajah of Sarawak, as Princess Paula in Ruritanian romance *Everything in Rhythm* (GB 36). **Mandy Rice-Davies,** key figure in the Christine Keeler scandal, starred in *Kuni Lemel in Tel Aviv* (Israel 76). **Babe Ruth,** baseball player, subject of *The Babe Ruth Story* (US 48), acted in *Headin' Home* (US 19). **George Bernard Shaw,** playwright, in *Rosy Rapture – The Pride of the Beauty Chorus* (GB 14). **Jean Shrimpton,**

model, leading lady in *Privilege* (GB 67). **Mickey Spillane,** author, played his own creation Mike Hammer in *The Girl Hunters* (US 63). **Jacqueline Susann,** novelist, in *Valley of the Dolls* (US 67). **Leslie 'Squizzy' Taylor,** Melbourne gangster gunned down in 1927, in race-track drama *Bound to Win* (Aus 19). **Leon Trotsky,** revolutionary and founder of the Red Army, played a bit part as a nihilist in Vitagraph's spy drama *My Official Wife* (US 14) and also appeared in *The Battle Cry of Peace* (US 15). **Margaret Trudeau,** estranged wife of Premier of Canada, Pierre Trudeau, starred in *The Guardian Angel* (Can 78) and *Kings and Desperate Men* (Can 79). **Gene Tunney,** heavyweight boxing champion, in Pathé serial *The Fighting Marine* (US 26). **Hugh Walpole,** author, as the vicar in *David Copperfield* (US 35). **Judge Joseph N. Welch,** presiding judge at the McCarthy hearings, played a judge in *Anatomy of a Murder* (US 59). **Bombardier Billy Wells,** British boxing champion, starred as the pilot in *The Silver Lining* (GB 19) and played the hangman in *The Beggar's Opera* (GB 53). **White Man-Runs Him,** last survivor of the Battle of the Little Big Horn (at which Gen. Custer's force was massacred in 1876), played in a Ken Maynard western *The Red Raiders* (US 27). **Godfrey Winn,** journalist, played an announcer in *The Bargee* (GB 64) and Truelove in *The Great St Trinian's Train Robbery* (GB 65). **Yevgeny Yevtushenko,** poet, played leading role as Russian space pioneer Konstantin Tsiolkovsky in *Take-off* (USSR 79).

The performer who played in the most movies was Tom London (1883–1963), who was born in Louisville, Ky., and made the first of his over 2000 appearances on screen in *The Great Train Robbery* (US 03). He was given the role of the locomotive driver, which was also his job in real life. By 1919 he was playing starring roles at Universal under his real name, Leonard Clapham, which he changed to Tom London in 1924. When he became too old for lead roles he receded comfortably into character parts, specialising in sheriffs in 'B' westerns. His last picture was Willard Parker's *The Lone Texan* (US 59).

The performer who has played the most leading roles in feature films is Prem Nazir (*c.* 1930–), superhero of Malayalam language movies, who was cast in his first starring role in 1952 and had appeared in over 300 movies by the end of the 1970s. Of these, 37 were Tamil movies, seven Telegu, two Kannada and the remainder Malayalam. (NB: Press reports in 1979 that Prem Nazir had completed his 500th starring role have now been discounted by the star himself.)

The actress who played the most leading roles was the Japanese star Kinuyo Tanaka (1909–77), who made her debut in a featured role in *Genroku Onna/Woman of Genroku Era* (Jap 24)

PHILATELY HONOURS
FILM MAKERS

1 Georges Méliès (1861–1938); 2 and 4 Auguste Lumière (1862–1954), Louis Lumière (1864–1948) (Insets to 4: Jean Harlow (1911–37), Marilyn Monroe (1926–62); 3 and 14 Charlie Chaplin (1889–1977); 5 Gerard Philipe (1920–59); 6 Raimu (1883–1946); 7 Dadasaheb Phalke (1870–1944); 8, 10 and 15 Will Rogers (1870–1935); 9 Walt Disney (1901–66); 11 D.W. Griffith (1875–1948); 12 Martine Carol (1920–67); 13 Eric Von Stroheim (1885–1957); 16 Marilyn Monroe (1926–62); 17 Serghei Eisenstein (1898–1948)

and performed in a total of 241 movies to *Daichi no Komoriuta/Lullaby Song of the Earth* (Jap 76). Nearly all these roles were leads except for a few at the beginning and end of her career. She also directed six films.

The Hollywood star who played the most leading roles in feature films was John Wayne (1907–79), who appeared in 153 movies from *The Drop Kick* (US 27) to *The Shootist* (US 76). In all except 11 of these films he played leading roles.

Of major international stars still performing, the record for the most screen credits is held by Christopher Lee (1922–), British star of English, French, Spanish, German, Italian and American films. The 143 feature movies and two shorts he played in from *Corridor of Mirrors* (GB 47) to *Bear Island* (US 79) include 15 in which he recreated his most celebrated role, that of Count Dracula.

The most popular actors and actresses

The earliest recorded popularity poll was conducted by a Russian fan magazine in 1911 and was headed by dapper French comedian Max Linder, followed by Denmark's tragic actress Asta Nielsen, with another Danish star, Valdemar Psilander, in third place. America's first poll was staged by *Photoplay* in July 1913 and resulted in J. Warren Kerrigan (1889–1947) being voted most popular male star and the now forgotten Marguerite Snow (1889–1958) most popular actress. By 1915 Mary Pickford had displaced her and for the next ten years 'the girl with the golden curls', otherwise known as 'America's sweetheart', topped virtually every popularity poll held throughout the world, including those conducted in Soviet Russia (where her husband Douglas Fairbanks was voted most popular male star in 1925). The most durable star of talkies would appear to be John Wayne, who featured in the annual 'Ten Top Box Office Stars' Quigley Poll 25 times 1949–74 and headed it in 1950, 1951, 1954 and 1971. For the most popular Hollywood stars of the 1970s, *see* Quigley Poll results.

The first popularity poll confined to British-born stars was conducted by *Pictures and the Picturegoer* in 1915 with the following results: 1 Alma Taylor; 2 Elizabeth Risdon; 3 Charles Chaplin; 4 Stewart Rome; 5 Chrissie White; 6 Fred Evans. Ten years later the *Daily News* poll showed Alma Taylor and Chrissie White, both of whom had joined the Hepworth Co. as child actresses in 1908, still firmly in the public favour: 1 Betty Balfour; 2 Alma Taylor; 3 Gladys Cooper; 4 Violet Hopson; 5 Fay Compton; 6 Chrissie White; 7 Stewart Rome; 8 Matheson Lang; 9 Owen Nares; 10 Ivor Novello.

During the 1930s America's box office was dominated by children, elderly ladies and gentlemen, and a mouse. Marie Dressler topped the Quigley Poll at age 63 in 1932 and again in 1933; Will Rogers came first aged 55 in 1934; then Shirley Temple rose to the top, aged 7, and remained there for the following three years, until 1939, when Mickey Rooney, 18 years old and playing a high school kid in the *Andy Hardy* series, took the lead and held first place for three years. Mickey Mouse was not eligible for the Quigley Poll, but he beat Emil Jannings by 400 000 votes as No. 1 star in a popularity contest held in Australia in 1931, and knocked Wallace Beery into second place in Japan in 1936.

Bridging this period and the John Wayne era were the Bing Crosby-Betty Grable years of the 1940s. Cumulative Quigley Poll results for the 1960s give the following hierarchy of the biggest box-office draws of the decade: 1 John Wayne; 2 Doris Day; 3 Cary Grant, Rock Hudson and Elizabeth Taylor; 4 Jack Lemmon; 5 Julie Andrews; 6 Paul Newman; 7 Sean Connery; 8 Elvis Presley; 9 Sidney Poitier; 10 Lee Marvin. (Of course no such list is definitive. Sophia Loren, who never appeared in the annual Top Ten, was nevertheless voted the most popular star in the world by the US Foreign Press Corps in 1969.) The order for the 1970s: 1 Clint Eastwood; 2 Burt Reynolds; 3 Barbra Streisand; 4 Paul Newman; 5 Robert Redford; 6 Steve McQueen; 7 John Wayne; 8 Woody Allen; 9 Dustin Hoffman; 10 Sylvester Stallone. Results for 1979 had Burt Reynolds leading Clint Eastwood, with Jane Fonda in third place as the female star with the most box office appeal.

QUIGLEY PUBLICATIONS POLL

The annual Quigley Poll is a poll of exhibitors to determine the top ten box-office draws. Listed below are the top male and the top female star for each year – the rating of whichever was not No. 1 is given in brackets after the name.

	Actress	Actor		Actress	Actor
1915	Mary Pickford (2)	William S. Hart	1948	Betty Grable (2)	Bing Crosby
1916	Mary Pickford (2)	William S. Hart	1949	Betty Grable (7)	Bob Hope
1917	Anita Stewart (3)	Douglas Fairbanks	1950	Betty Grable (4)	John Wayne
1918	Mary Pickford (2)	Douglas Fairbanks	1951	Betty Grable (3)	John Wayne
1919	Mary Pickford (3)	Wallace Reid	1952	Doris Day (7)	Dean Martin &
1920	Marguerite Clark (2)	Wallace Reid			Jerry Lewis
1921	Mary Pickford	Douglas Fairbanks (2)	1953	Marilyn Monroe (6)	Gary Cooper
1922	Mary Pickford	Douglas Fairbanks (2)	1954	Marilyn Monroe (5)	John Wayne
1923	Norma Talmadge (2)	Thomas Meighan	1955	Grace Kelly (2)	James Stewart
1924	Norma Talmadge	Rudolph Valentino (3)	1956	Marilyn Monroe (8)	William Holden
1925	Norma Talmadge (2)	Rudolph Valentino	1957	None	Rock Hudson
1926	Colleen Moore	Tom Mix (2)	1958	Elizabeth Taylor (2)	Glenn Ford
1927	Colleen Moore (2)	Tom Mix	1959	Doris Day (4)	Rock Hudson
1928	Clara Bow	Lon Chaney (2)	1960	Doris Day	Rock Hudson (2)
1929	Clara Bow	Lon Chaney (2)	1961	Elizabeth Taylor	Rock Hudson (2)
1930	Joan Crawford	William Haines (2)	1962	Doris Day	Rock Hudson (2)
1931	Janet Gaynor	Charles Farrell (2)	1963	Doris Day	John Wayne (2)
1932	Marie Dressler	Charles Farrell (4)	1964	Doris Day	Jack Lemmon (2)
1933	Marie Dressler	Will Rogers (2)	1965	Doris Day (3)	Sean Connery
1934	Janet Gaynor (3)	Will Rogers	1966	Julie Andrews	Sean Connery (2)
1935	Shirley Temple	Will Rogers (2)	1967	Julie Andrews	Lee Marvin (2)
1936	Shirley Temple	Clark Gable (2)	1968	Julie Andrews (3)	Sidney Poitier
1937	Shirley Temple	Clark Gable (2)	1969	Katharine Hepburn (9)	Paul Newman
1938	Shirley Temple	Clark Gable (2)	1970	Barbra Streisand (9)	Paul Newman
1939	Shirley Temple (5)	Mickey Rooney	1971	Ali MacGraw (8)	John Wayne
1940	Bette Davis (9)	Mickey Rooney	1972	Barbra Streisand (5)	Clint Eastwood
1941	Bette Davis (8)	Mickey Rooney	1973	Barbra Streisand (6)	Clint Eastwood
1942	Betty Grable (8)	Abbott & Costello	1974	Barbra Streisand (4)	Robert Redford
1943	Betty Grable	Bob Hope (2)	1975	Barbra Streisand (2)	Robert Redford
1944	Betty Grable (4)	Bing Crosby	1976	Tatum O'Neal (8)	Robert Redford
1945	Greer Garson (3)	Bing Crosby	1977	Barbra Streisand (2)	Sylvester Stallone
1946	Ingrid Bergman (2)	Bing Crosby	1978	Diane Keaton (7)	Burt Reynolds
1947	Betty Grable (2)	Bing Crosby	1979	Jane Fonda (3)	Burt Reynolds

Handicapped artistes: Crippled with arthritis, Lionel Barrymore played sitting roles, often in a wheelchair, in 35 movies between 1938 and 1953. Susan Peters, who died at the early age of 31 in 1952, also made several films in a wheelchair following a serious accident. Cancer victim Suzan Ball had her leg amputated before starring in *Chief Crazy Horse* (US 54); she died aged 23 soon afterwards. Herbert Marshall, maimed in World War I, already had only one leg when he made his screen debut in 1927, and Donald Gray, who appeared in *The Four Feathers* (GB 39), *Idol of Paris* (GB 48), *Timeslip* (GB 55), etc., had only one arm. Former Al Jolson understudy, Jay C. Flippen, carried on film-making after the amputation of a leg in 1965 until his death in 1971, a week or so after completing *Seven Minutes* (US 71). Sarah Bernhardt was totally immobilised when she took the name part in *Jeanne Doré* (Fr 14). Following the operation in which she lost her leg, Madame Bernhardt had not yet learned to

Blind actor Esmond Knight played a sighted role in
The Silver Fleet (GB 45)

walk on the artificial one and played in over a
hundred scenes either sitting or standing still.
Harold Russell, who had both hands blown off
in World War II, made his screen debut in *The
Diary of a Sergeant* (US 45) and subsequently
won two Oscars for his performance in *The Best
Years of Our Lives* (US 45).

The distinguished deaf and blind American
scholar Helen Keller played herself in *Deliverance* (US 19) and deaf-mute Joe Hermano,
Hollywood juvenile player of the 1930s,
appeared in numerous Richard Dix movies.
Blind actor Esmond Knight played a sighted role
in *The Silver Fleet* (GB 45), while K.C. Dey,
'the blind bard of Bengal', appeared in various
Bombay movies of the 30s. Sightless singer-
guitarist José Feliciano made his screen acting
debut as an airliner pilot in *Airplane* (US i.p.).
Sheldon Lewis became stone deaf shortly after
the introduction of sound and was obliged to
lip read his cues. Throat cancer cost Jack
Hawkins his vocal chords in 1966, but he
taught himself to speak again from the dia-
phragm, appearing in another 11 films in
which his lines were dubbed. Mental defectives
have sometimes been seen as extras in films such
as *One Flew Over the Cuckoo's Nest* (US 75),
but in the recent French film *Un Neveu silencieux*
(Fr 78) the title role was played by real-life
Mongoloid Joel Dupuis.

**The largest number of members of one family to
have appeared in films** is 31 in the case of the
Luevas of Los Angeles, Matriarch Augustina

Lueva (b. La Refugio, Mexico 1852), 18 of her
21 children and 12 of her grandchildren were
reported to be actively employed as film actors
in 1928. Six of the children and four of the
grandchildren appeared together in an unidentified film of that year.

Other films in which families have appeared
together are: *Hearts of the World* (US 18), in
which Bobby Harron played the lead, his
mother played a French woman, her two
daughters Jessie and Mary played her screen
daughters, and Bobby's brother Johnny played
'a boy with a barrel'; *Mr Smith Goes to Washington* (US 39) with brothers and sisters Coy,
Vivian, Gloria, Louise, Harry, Billy, Delmar,
Garry and Bobs Watson playing the Governor
of Montana's children; and *Ein Tag ist Schoener
als der Audere* (W. Ger 70), featuring the seven
von Eichborn children, Clarissa, Justina, Evelyn,
Jacqueline, Wolfram, Holger and Isabella.

The most generations of screen actors in a family
is four in the case of the Redgraves. Roy Redgrave (1872–1922), father of Sir Michael, made
his screen debut in *The Christian* (Aus 11) and
continued to appear in Australian movies until
1920. Sir Michael Redgrave (1908–) married
actress Rachel Kempson (1910–), and their two
daughters Vanessa (1937–) and Lynn (1943–)
and son Corin (1939–) all went into movies.
Vanessa's daughters Natasha and Joely made
their debut in *The Charge of the Light Brigade*
(GB 68) and subsequently appeared in *Dead
Cert* (GB 74) and *Joseph Andrews* (GB 77),
while Corin's daughter Jemima appeared for
the first time in *Joseph Andrews*.

The largest cast of credited performers in a film
was 260 in *Dny Zrady/Days of Treason* (Cz 72),
the story of the betrayal of Czechoslovakia in
1938, including Gunnar Möller as Hitler,
Jaroslav Radimecky as Chamberlain, Alexander
Fred as Goebbels, Rudolf Jurda as Goering
and Vladamir Stach as Mussolini.

Sacha Guitry's *Napoleon* (Fr 54) had 101
credited roles, but was claimed to have 300
speaking parts. MGM claimed 365 speaking
parts (73 credited) for *Ben Hur* (US 59), but this
seems impossible for a 217-minute film unless it
includes groups of people all speaking at once.

Other films with large casts (credited) include
Rottenknechte (DDR 70), with 194; *Baron
Muenchhausen* (Ger 45), with 150; *Sweden for*

the Swedes (Sw 80), with 142; *Around the World in 80 Days* (US 56), with 138; *A Bridge Too Far* (GB 77), with 137; *Oh! What a Lovely War* (GB 69), with 125; and Karl Ritter's *Pour la Merité* (Ger 38), with 102.

For **the largest cast including extras,** see p. 94.

The smallest cast: Excluding movies with an all-animal cast, there has been only one live-action dramatic feature with a cast of none. Kostas Sfikas' *Model* (Greece 74) had no performers, only robots seen in a single set representing a factory yard. The 1 hr 45 min film was intended as a critique of the 'implacable process that transforms mankind into negotiable goods and mere accessories of an industrial machine'.

There have been a number of movies with a cast of one. Olaf Fønns, leading Danish romantic hero of the World War I period, played alone in Fritz Magnussen's *Remorse* (Den 19), made for Dansk Astra Film. The story is of a wealthy man who is ruined and loses his mistress (represented only by a pair of arms), then returns to her in a starving condition, is rejected and kills

Britain's only single role movie was *St Joan* (GB 77) with Monica Buferd

Olaf Fønns achieved the remarkable feat of holding the audience's attention during a full-length *silent* film in which he was the only character – a scene from *Remorse* (Den 19)

her. He restores his fortune but, relentlessly pursued by his own accusing shadow, eventually gives himself up. In addition to its solo performance, the film was distinguished by having no intertitles.

Sunil Dutt's *Yaadein/Recollections* (India 64), in which he starred as well as directed and produced, was a single set, solo movie about a husband deserted by his wife. At the end of the film the woman's shadow seen against a wall indicates that she has returned to him. Robert Carlisle's *Sofi* (US 68), an adaptation of Gogol's *Diary of a Madman*, had Tom Troupe as its only performer. Thierry Zeno's *Vase de noces* (Belg 73) starred Dominique Garny, who does not speak throughout the film. It tells the story of a simple man living alone amongst his poultry and pigs who eventually hangs himself. Danilo-Bata Stojković played alone as a man fleeing from imaginary pursuers in Milos Radivojević's *Testament* (Yug 75), which was also without speech. Jean-Pierre Lefebvre's *L'Amour blessé (Confidences de la nuit)* (Can 75) starred Louise Cuerrier as a lonely woman spending a dull evening in her room listening to a talk show, while Britain's only single artiste film had Monica Buferd in the rather more compelling role of *St Joan* (GB 77). The most recent examples of solo performances are by Anne Flannery in *A State of Siege* (NZ 78), Willeke van Ammelrooy in Frans Zwartje's *It's Me* (Neths 79), and by Alain Cavalier in *Ce repondent ne prend pas de message* (Fr 79).

The longest screen career is that of French character actor Charles Vanel (b. 1892), noted impersonator of Napoleon, who made his screen debut in 1908, aged 16 (in a film whose title he cannot remember), and who declares that he has no intention of retiring. To date he has played in some 200 films.

The actresses with the longest screen careers are Hungary's Margit Makay (b. 1892), who made her debut in *Keserü szerelem/Bitter Love* (Hung 12) and was most recently seen in *Egy erkölcsös éjszaka/A Very Moral Night* (Hung 77); and Lillian Gish (b. 1896), whose debut was in *An Unseen Enemy* (US 12) and who played a major role in Bob Altman's *The Wedding* (US 78).

Considering the lengthy careers of many stage performers, comparatively few of the senior generation of film stars have survived from silent days. In addition to those mentioned above, the following leading players made their screen debut before 1930 and are still active in films:

Bessie Love (b. Midland, Texas 1898): *The Flying Torpedo* (US 15). **Helen Hayes** (b. Washington, DC 1900): *The Weavers of Life* (US 17). **June Havoc** (b. Seattle, Wash. 1916): debut Hal Roach comedies 1918. **Cyril Cusack** (b. Dublin 1910): *Knocknagow* (Ireland 18). **Athene Seyler** (b. London 1889): *The Adventures of Pickwick* (GB 21). **Cathleen Nesbitt** (b. Cheshire 1888): *The Faithful Heart* (GB 22). **Marlene Dietrich** (b. Berlin 1902): *So sind die Männer* (Ger 22). **Joel McCrea** (b. Pasadena, Calif 1905): *Penrod and Sam* (US 23). **Jackie Cooper** (b. Los Angeles 1921): debut in Bobby Clark short 1923. **Sir John Gielgud** (b. London 1904): *Who Is the Man?* (GB 24). **Elizabeth Bergner** (b. Vienna 1900): *Nju* (Ger 24). **Dolores Del Rio** (b. Durango, Mexico 1905): *Joanna* (US 25). **Walter Pidgeon** (b. East St John, New Brunswick 1897): *Mannequin* (US 25). **Gilbert Roland** (b. Chihuahua, Mexico 1905): *The Plastic Age* (US 25). **Mickey Rooney** (b. New York 1920): *Mickey Maguire* short (US 26). **Ray Milland** (b. Neath, Wales 1905): *The Flying Scotsman* (GB 29).

The largest number of roles played by one actor in a single film is not, as generally believed, the eight members of the d'Ascoyne family portrayed by Alec Guinness in *Kind Hearts and Coronets* (GB 49), but the 27 parts taken by Rolf Leslie in Will Barker's life story of Queen Victoria *Sixty Years a Queen* (GB 13). Others who have equalled or exceeded Sir Alec's eight roles are Lupino Lane, who played all 24 parts in *Only Me* (US 29), Joseph Henabery, cast as Abraham Lincoln and 13 other characters in *The Birth of a Nation* (US 15), Robert Hirsch,

seen in 12 roles in *No Questions on Saturday* (US 64), Michael Ripper, with 9 in *What a Crazy World* (GB 63), Flavio Migliaccio, who had 8 parts in *Como Vai, Vai Bem* (Br 69) and Rolv Wesenlund, portraying 8 characters in the comedy *Norske Byggeklosser* (Nor 71). Perhaps the most economically casted film of recent years was *The Great McGonagall* (GB 74) which had 5 actors playing 34 parts between them.

Dual roles are legion, but there has only been one **straight drama in which both hero and heroine have been played by the same performer**. In *Lanka Dahan/The Burning of Lanka* (India 18), A. Salunke was cast as both the lovely Sita, held by a ten-headed monster on the island of Lanka, and her heroic rescuer Rama. At this date no women were permitted to appear in Indian films.

Names: The most usual reasons for actors and actresses changing their names are that those they were born with are too long, too difficult to pronounce, or simply unglamorous. It is not hard to understand why Herbert Charles Angelo Kuchacewich ze Schluderpacheru decided to drop it in favour of Herbert Lom, or why Derek Julius Gaspard Ulric Niven van den Bogaerde thought he would go further with a name like Dirk Bogarde, or why the studios wanted Rodolpho Alfonso Rafaelo Pierre Filibert Guglielmi di Valentina d'Antonguolla to contract his name to something simple like Rudolph Valentino. Equally Larushka Mischa Skikne had good reason to change his to Laurence Harvey and nobody complained when Walter Matasschanskayasky chose to call himself Matthau instead (though he played a character called Walter Matasschanskayasky in *Earthquake* (US 74)).

Briefer names may be just as unacceptable. Sarah Jane Fulks was distasteful to Jane Wyman, as was Alexandra Zuck to Sandra Dee and Diana Fluck to Diana Dors. Olga Kronk preferred Claire Windsor, and not surprisingly Doris Day was as relieved to be free of Doris Kappelhoff as was Cyd Charisse not to have to answer to Tula Finklea. Burl Ivanhoe substituted Ives, while Fabian Forte Bonaparte was satisfied to get along with just his first name. Robert Taylor had rather more appeal for a romantic hero than Spangler Arlington

Brugh and Septimus Ryott was undoubtedly correct in thinking that his female fans would prefer him as Stewart Rome. Austrian actor Jake Kratz doubted he would be able to play hot-blooded Latin lovers with a name like that and changed it to Ricardo Cortez. Many performers born with Latin names preferred something Anglo-Saxon: Dino Crocetti opted for Dean Martin, Margarita Carmen Cansino for Rita Hayworth, Luis Antonio Damaso de Alonso for Gilbert Roland and Anna Maria Luisa Italiano for Anne Bancroft. A few reversed the process, and changed Anglo-Saxon names into something more exotic: Bonar Sullivan became Bonar Colleano, Peggy Middleton assumed the more romantic Yvonne de Carlo and Muriel Harding decided that Olga Petrova held a greater air of mystery for a *femme fatale*.

Some actors chose names that others had discarded. Bernard Schwarz chose Tony Curtis, while the real Tony Curtis had become Italy's best loved comedian Toto. American actor Bud Flanagan changed his name to Dennis O'Keefe, while British actor Robert Winthrop altered his to Bud Flanagan. It was fortunate for James Stewart that his British namesake had already decided to change James Stewart into Stewart Granger before the other James Stewart went into movies.

Alternatively an artiste could sometimes get away with adopting a name which already had cachet. Cambodia's leading female star before the communist take-over, Kim Nova, selected her screen name in unabashed imitation of Kim Novak. In 1974 a Cambodian starlet called herself Kim Novy in imitation of the imitation. Charles Chaplin sued a Mexican comedian called Charles Amador who had changed his name to Charles Aplin, but was unable to do anything about a German comedian who appeared on screen as Charlie Kaplin. Currently Hong Kong's Bruce Li is finding fame and fortune treading in the footsteps of the late Bruce Lee.

It was also perfectly possible to have several actors with a legitimate claim to the same name. There were three Robert Lee's working in Hollywood during the 1920s and four Charles Mack's, two of whom styled themselves Charles E. Mack, and additionally a Mrs Charles Mack, who performed under that name. Some were satisfied simply to change their Christian name: Leslie/Bob Hope; James/David Niven; William/Pat O'Brien; Clarence/Robert Cummings; Hubert/Rudy Vallee; John/Tim McCoy; John/Arthur Kennedy; Julius/Groucho Marx; Virginia/Bebe Daniels; Sari/Zsa Zsa Gabor; Marilyn/Kim Novak; Adolf/Anton Walbrook; Julia/Lana Turner; Ruth/Bette Davis.

Joseph Keaton assumed the first name of 'Buster' at the age of six months when he fell downstairs and Harry Houdini, a family friend, remarked to his father: 'That's some buster your baby took!' Harry Crosby acquired 'Bing' from avid reading of a comic strip called *The Bingville Bugle* when he was at school.

Even simpler was to change a single letter of the name: Conrad Veidt (Weidt); Beulah Bondy (Bondi); George Raft (Ranft); May Robson (Robison); Ronald Squire (Squirl); Gerard Philipe (Philippe); Dorothy Malone (Maloney); Warren Beatty (Beaty); Yul Brynner (Bryner). James Baumgarner was content to drop the 'Baum', Anna Maria Pierangeli split her surname down the middle and eschewed her first names, while Banky Vilma just switched to Vilma Banky.

Choice of a new name is dictated by varied circumstances. Judy Garland (Frances Gumm) took her stage surname from the theatre pages of a Chicago newspaper, whose reviews were written by Robert Garland. It was chosen by George Jessel, to whom the 11-year-old Miss Gumm had appealed for help after being billed as Glumm at the theatre where they were both appearing. Her first name came from a Hoagy Carmichael song *Judy*, of which she was fond. French comedian Fernandel was born Fernand Constandin. His wife called him *Fernand d'elle (her Fernand)*. Luis Alonso selected his new name of Gilbert Roland as a tribute to the two stars he most admired, John Gilbert and Ruth Roland. Stepin Fetchit, the startled black manservant of 20s and 30s Hollywood movies, named himself after a racehorse which had obliged him by winning. Marilyn Monroe's Christian name was selected for her by Fox talent scout Ben Lyon because of his admiration for Marilyn Miller – the Monroe was her mother's maiden name. Bette (Ruth) Davis took her screen Christian name from Balzac's *Cousin Bette*. Gary (Frank J.) Cooper was named after his agent's hometown, Gary,

Indiana. The actor's own hometown would hardly have been appropriate – he came from Helena, Montana. MGM ran a fan contest in 1925 to find a new name for the extravagantly named Lucille Le Sueur. The winner came up with Joan Arden, but as there was already an actress of that name in Hollywood, Miss Le Sueur adopted the name suggested by the runner-up instead – Joan Crawford. Gretchen Young had her first name changed to Loretta by Colleen Moore, who discovered her as a 14-year-old extra in *Her Wild Oat* (US 26). Loretta, said Miss Moore, was the name of 'the most beautiful doll I ever had'. Bela Lugosi, real name Bela Blasko, took his screen surname from his hometown of Lugos in Hungary. Richard Burton, formerly Richard Jenkins, assumed the name of his old teacher in Port Talbot. Gig Young (Byron Barr) took the name of the character he played in *The Gay Sisters* (US 42), Bob Steele (Robert North Bradbury) from his role in *The Mojave Kid* (US 28) and former child star Dawn O'Day switched to Anne Shirley to play the heroine of that name in *Anne of Green Gables* (US 34). The story put about by her studio (and still believed in some quarters) that Theda Bara's name was an anagram of 'Arab Death' was so much hokum: the name was selected by director Frank Powell on learning that she had a relative called Barranger. Equally unromantic was Carole Lombard's (Jane Peters) decision to call herself after the Carroll, Lombardi Pharmacy on Lexington and 65th in New York. Greta Garbo might easily have become Greta Gabor. Long before meeting young Greta Gustafsson, her mentor Mauritz Stiller had cherished the dream of discovering and moulding a great star. He asked his manuscript assistant, Arthur Norden, to select a name. Norden, an historian, chose Gábor, after the Hungarian king, Gábor Bethlen. Stiller wanted something less East European, however, and amended it to Garbo. Another monarch was rather more personally involved in naming Lili Damita (Lilliane Carré). Holidaying at Biarritz in 1921 when she was 17, she attracted the attention of the King of Spain, who enquired after the *damita del maillo rojo (young lady in a red bathing dress)*.

Those who retain their own names may also have cogent reasons for doing so. 'Bradford Dillman', said that actor, 'sounded like a distinguished, phoney, theatrical name – so I kept it.'

The most enduring screen team was that of Indian superstars Prem Nazir and Sheela, who had played opposite each other in 130 movies by 1975.

The Hollywood record pales by comparison. Excluding performers billed together solely in 'series' films, the most enduring screen partners are husband-and-wife team Charles Bronson and Jill Ireland, who have co-starred in twelve films up to and including *Love and Bullets* (US 78). Myrna Loy and William Powell played opposite each other in eleven pictures; Ginger Rogers and Fred Astaire in ten; Katharine Hepburn and Spencer Tracy in nine; and Jeanette MacDonald and Nelson Eddy, Judy Garland and Mickey Rooney, and Greer Garson and Walter Pidgeon were teamed in eight films.

The most extensive screen tests in the history of motion pictures were held for the role of Scarlett O'Hara in *Gone With the Wind* (US 39). MGM shot 149000ft of black-and-white test film and another 13000ft of colour with 60 actresses, none of whom got the part. Having discarded 27 hours of test film, producer David O. Selznick narrowed the choice to three major stars and one unknown – Joan Bennett, Jean Arthur, Paulette Goddard and newcomer Vivien Leigh. The final tests required the four contenders to play the scenes of Scarlett getting into her corset, talking to Ashley in the paddock and drunkenly proposing to Rhett Butler. Miss Leigh's successful test was actually made after shooting of the movie had commenced – perhaps the only instance of a major motion picture going into production before the star role had been cast. Total cost of the 165000ft of tests was $105000 – approximately the budget then of an average second feature.

The longest and most expensive screen test of a single candidate for a role was made by Robert Aldrich at his own expense in 1969 to persuade backers of *The Greatest Mother of Them All* that starlet Alexandra Hay had the potential for the lead. The 30-minute test film, which Miss Hay played opposite Peter Finch, cost Aldrich $125000. Miss Hay was selected for the part, but the film was never completed.

Hollywood's first nude screen tests were held for *Four for Texas* (US 63), which starred Ursula Andress and Anita Ekberg in the *femme* leads. Those actresses who had been unwilling to be tested need not have worried; all nude scenes were cut by the censor.

Stars who failed screen tests: Failing a screen test may not be a passport to stardom, but in some cases it has been no barrier. Bette Davis's first screen test was so appalling that she ran from the Goldwyn projection room screaming. Her next, with Universal, was successful enough for her to be given a job – as a stand-in girl for screen tests of male actors. Clark Gable failed a Warner screen test in 1930 because Jack Warner declared (in Gable's hearing) that he was only 'a big ape'. His next was at MGM, where his prominent ears told against him. Although he failed the test, MGM signed him anyway and he stayed with the studio – contributing significantly to its ascendancy – for 23 years. Another star who failed the rigours of a MGM test was Maurice Chevalier, but he was signed by Paramount in 1928 on the strength of the *same* test.

Shirley Temple, probably the greatest box office attraction of all time, failed a test for the *Our Gang* series. The screen's most prestigious luminary, Laurence Olivier, was turned down for *Queen Christina* (US 33) after testing opposite Greta Garbo, though it is widely held that Garbo deliberately sabotaged the test in order that the role should go to ex-lover John Gilbert, then in decline.

Brigitte Bardot's puppy fat and spots caused her to fail a screen test with Marc Allégret when she was 16. Jane Russell also failed to pass muster. The report on her 1940 test for Fox read 'unphotogenic'. Warner's comments when she tested for them were 'no energy' and 'no spark'. Another star considered physically unsuitable was Robert Taylor. He failed his test for United Artists in 1933 because Sam Goldwyn thought he was too skinny.

Nothing was found wanting in Ava Gardner's physique. After seeing her test for MGM, Louis B. Mayer expostulated: 'She can't talk. She can't act. She's terrific.'

Less enthusiasm was expressed for Fred Astaire in a studio report on his first screen test, even if the words were much the same: 'Can't act. Can't sing. Can dance a little.'

Midgets on the rampage in *Even Dwarfs Started Small* (W. Ger 70)

Not even an established star could afford to be over-confident. According to Hollywood legend, at the height of her screen career Gloria Swanson took a test incognito wearing a blonde wig. She was turned down.

The shortest screen artistes to play leading roles were Daphne Pollard (debut 1928) and Lydia Yeamans Titus (debut 1917), both of whom were 4 ft 9 in. The only major stars under 5 ft were silent-screen heroines Florence Turner and Marguerite Clark, 4 ft 10 in tall. Janet Gaynor and Mary Pickford both stood at 5 ft.

The shortest leading man was French silent-star Max Linder, the impeccable dandy of the Paris boulevards, who was a mere 5 ft 2 in. Hollywood's shortest male stars are Mickey Rooney and Dudley Moore at 5 ft 3 in. Reports that Alan Ladd was only 5 ft tall were quite untrue; he was 5 ft 6 in, which made him an inch taller than Dustin Hoffman and the same height as Al Pacino. Nevertheless, Ladd's lack of inches was proverbial in Hollywood. Sophia Loren has confirmed that he had to stand on a box for his love scenes with her in *Boy on a Dolphin* (US 57) and James Mason, when he was invited to co-star with Ladd in *Botany Bay* (US 54), told the producer that he had no intention of standing in a trench for their scenes together.

Two films have had **all-midget casts**, a western *The Terror of Tiny Town* (US 38) and Werner Herzog's *Even Dwarfs Started Small* (W. Ger 70). *The Little Cigars* (US 73) had a cast of five midgets and one full-sized actress, described as 'a busty blonde'. **The largest cast of dwarves**

Most mountainous movie star — 45-stone Ethel Greer needed some special support in *Hoopla* (US 33)

Above: Richard Kiel, 7 ft 2 in (2·18 m), dwarfs 007 Roger Moore in *The Spy Who Loved Me* (GB 77)

Left: Jimmy Durante was reduced to size by 7 ft 2 in (2·18 m) Johan Aason in *Carnival* (US 35)

and midgets was in *The Wizard of Oz* (US 39), which had 116.

The tallest screen artiste was Clifford Thompson, claimed to be 8 ft 6 in and then the tallest man in the world, who played opposite (and above) ZaSu Pitts in Hal Roach's *Seal Skins* (US 32). No other eight-footers are recorded. Artistes of 7 ft or over include Tex Erikson, 7 ft exactly, who was featured in *Jungle Jim in the Forbidden Land* (US 52); Aason, a 7 ft 2 in character actor who entered Hollywood pictures in 1928; Peter Mayhew, 7 ft 2 in ex-hospital porter, who played a mythical monster in *Sinbad and the Eye of the Tiger* (US 77) and the furry wookie Chewbacca in *Star Wars* (US 77); Richard Kiel, 7 ft 2 in without his size 16 shoes, who played the steel-teethed giant villain in Bond movies *The Spy Who Loved Me* (GB 77) and *Moonraker* (GB/F 79); John Bloom, 7 ft 4 in, who was Franken-stein's monster in *Dracula v Frankenstein* (US 71); and Jack Tarver, 7 ft 10 in, the giant in Fox's feature-length children's picture *Jack and the Beanstalk* (US 17).

The tallest leading men were 6ft 7in James Arness, who starred in *Them* (US 54) and *The First Travelling Saleslady* (US 56), and Bruce Spence, 6ft 7in, in *Stork* (Aus 71), which was scripted by 6ft 7in David Williamson. Christopher Lee is the tallest major star at 6ft 5in.

The heaviest screen artiste was Ethel Greer, who weighed 637lb (45 st 5lb) when she appeared with Clara Bow in *Hoopla* (US 33). Miss Greer's 140lb husband, visiting the set, remarked of the slender 118lb Miss Bow: 'I never could see why some fellows go for these skinny girls'.

The most generously proportioned leading lady of all time was Doris Wishman, the possessor of a 73-in bust, who directed, wrote and starred in *Deadly Weapons* (US 75) under the sobriquet 'Chesty Morgan'.

Statues to stars: Only four stars are known to have been honoured with statues to their memory. Rudolph Valentino (1895–1926) was commemorated with a four-foot high bronze male nude by Roger Burnham representing 'Aspiration', which was unveiled in Hollywood's De Longpre Park on 6 May 1930. *Photoplay* reported that 'not a single great screen figure of Valentino's halcyon days attended'. The statue was generally disliked, both by local residents who objected to nude statuary, and by Valentino fans, who were incensed that their idol had not been represented as they chose to remember him. After years of depradations by vandals, one particularly energetic objector succeeded in flattening the figure with a sledge hammer. Reinforced with steel rods it was replaced, but two years later, in 1952, it was wrested from its base again and a despairing parks department removed it to the safekeeping of a distant warehouse. It was restored to its original pedestal in 1976.

A second statue to the Great Latin Lover was unveiled at his birthplace, the small Italian town of Castellaneta, in 1961. This time Valentino himself was represented, a massive eight-foot figure in the flowing robes of the Sheik, sculpted by Luigi Gheno. The robes were in full colour and for some unexplained reason the face was sky blue.

Dolores Del Rio at the dedication of the Valentino Memorial in De Longpre Park 1930. None of the star's friends or associates were present

Right: Jo Davidson's statue of Will Rogers at Claremore, Oklahoma *(Will Rogers Memorial)*

Another star commemorated with two different statues is the beloved crackerbarrel philosopher Will Rogers (1879–1935). At the Will Rogers Memorial at Claremore, Oklahoma, there is an outdoor equestrian statue as well as an indoor bronze figure by Jo Davidson depicting W.R. in typical pose, standing at his ease in a rumpled suit, hands thrust deep into his pockets. A duplicate of the latter stands in the Capitol at Washington, bearing the same epitaph as the one at Claremore: 'I never met a man I didn't like'.

The most popular star of silent westerns, Tom Mix (1880–1940), is commemorated with a statue of a riderless pony at the spot where he was killed in a car crash at Florence, Arizona. In Nagarcoil, South India, there is a statue to one of India's best loved comedians, N.S. Krishnan (1908–57), who was teamed with comedienne T.A. Mathuram in over a hundred pictures before a tragically early death at the height of his career.

A statue to Brigitte Bardot (1933–) is being erected in the square at St Tropez, where she lives, and the Bristol and West Building Society paid for a larger than lifesize full length bronze effigy of Sir Charles Chaplin (1889–1977), the work of sculptor John Doubleday, to be erected in London's Leicester Square in 1980.

Twins who have played together in movies:

Jennifer and Susan Baker: *Every Day's a Holiday* (GB 65); *No 1 of the Secret Service* (GB 77). The Blackburn Twins: *Her First Affaire* (GB 33). Patrick and Pascal Boitot: *Six chevaux bleus* (Fr 67). Salvatore and Giovanni Borgese: *La Mazzetta* (It 78). Robert and William Bradbury: *The Adventures of Bill and Bob* (US 19), etc. Madeleine and Mary Collinson: *The Love Machine* (GB 71); *Twins of Dracula* (GB 71). Fred and Frank Cox: *Fahrenheit 451* (GB 66). The Crane Twins: *Moulin Rouge* (US 34). The de Briac Twins: *Don't Tell Everything* (US 21); *High Heels* (US 21); *The Bachelor Daddy* (US 22); *Daddies* (US 24). The Dionne Quins: *The Country Doctor* (US 36); *Reunion* (US 36); *Five of a Kind* (US 38). The Dolly Sisters: *The Million Dollar*

Below left: Jutta and Isa Gunther in *Das Doppelte Lottchen* (W.Ger 50)
Emi and Yumi Iro diminished in *Godzilla vs the Thing* (Jap 64)

Below right: The Mawby Triplets in *Baby Cyclone* (US 29)
The Terry Twins in *The Fordington Twins* (GB 20)

Dollies (US 18). Marion and Madeleine Fairbanks: debut as 'The Thanhouser Twins' in Thanhouser shorts 1910; *The Beauty Shop* (US 24); *On with the Show* (US 29). The Forman Twins: *Ecce Homo Homolka* (Cz 69); *Hogo Fogo Homolka* (Cz 70). Jutta and Isa Günther: *Das Doppelte Lottchen* (W.Ger 50) – the original version of *The Parent Trap* (US 61), in which Hayley Mills played both twins; *Die Wirtin vom Worther see* (Austria 52); *Der Zwillinge vom Zillertal* (W.Ger 57). Jane and Jennifer Harris: *The River* (Fr 52). Daisy and Violet Hilton: real-life Siamese twins in *Freaks* (US 32) and *Chained for Life* (US 3?). Lesley Ann and Patricia Ann Hudson: *Three Women* (US 76). Emi and Yumi Iro: *Mothra* (Jap 61); *Double Trouble* (Jap 64); *Godzilla vs the Thing* (Jap 64). Jean-Pierre and Jean-Paul Janssen: *L'Amour a la chaine* (Fr 65). Isabel and Cristina Jardim: *Pour un amour lointain* (Fr 68). Lech and Jaroslaw Kaczynski: *O Dwoch Takich co Ukradli Ksiczyc* (Pol 62). Helen and Elizabeth Keating: *The Mad Parade* (US 31). Alice and Ellen Kessler: *Les Magiciennes* (Fr 60); *La Ruée des Vikings* (Fr/It 61). Ulli and Gaby König: *Ein Zwilling kommt selten allein* (W.Ger 70); *Das haut den Starksten Zwilling um* (W.Ger 71). Ida and Ella Mackenzie: played in early Essany one-reelers. Billy and Bobby Mauch: *The Prince and the Pauper* (US 37); *Penrod and his Twin Brother* (US 38); *Penrod's Double Trouble* (US 38). The Mawby Triplets: *Baby Cyclone* (US 29); *Heavily Married* (GB 35). Anthony and David Meyer: *The Third Walker* (Can 78); *Hamlet* (GB 78). Edna and Alice Nash: billed as 'The Vitagraph Twins' in Vitagraph shorts from 1913. Pili and Mili: *Como dos Gotos de Agua* (Sp 63); *Dos Chicas Locas, Locas* (Sp 65); *Escandalo en la Familia* (Arg 67). Norma and Mimi Pons: *El Bulin* (Arg 67). Simon and Andrew Rankin: *The Third Walker* (Can 78). Teresa and Leslie Scobie: *She Didn't Say No!* (GB 58). Beth and Karen Specht: *Billion Dollar Threat* (US 79). Robert and David Story: *The Ice House* (US 69). The Surtees Twins: *Lord of the Flies* (GB 63). Brent and Stuart Tarleton in *Gone with the Wind* (US 39) – Selznick gave instructions that they were not to be publicised as 'The Tarleton Twins'. The Terry Twins: *The Fordington Twins* (GB 20); *The Foolish Twins* (US 23). Jan and Laura Tiege: *Harper Valley PTA* (US 78). Upendra and Arvind Trivedi: *Verni Vasulaat* (India 78). Leo and Blanche White: *The Damfool Twins*, comedy series (US 20–21). Lee and Lyn Wilde: *Till the Clouds Roll By* (US 46) and Andy Hardy series. Ted and Fred Williams (only black twins in this list): *A Modern Cain* (US 25). Clarice and Ercell Woods: *George White's Scandals* (US 35).

Twins have been played by unrelated actors for laughs in *The Last Remake of Beau Geste* (GB 77), with Michael York and Marty Feldman as the adopted sons of Sir Hector Geste, and straight by Judy Geeson and Martin Potter in *Goodbye Gemini* (GB 70); by Jane Campbell and Tom Bair in *Local Color* (US 77); and by Geoffrey Bowes and Christopher Barry in *Something's Rotten* (Can 79). The only instance in which twins appearing together did not play twins was in Celestino Coronado's *Hamlet* (GB 78), with Anthony and David Meyer acting the title role interchangeably.

Typecasting: The actor who played the same role the most times in feature films was William Boyd (1898–1972), a major star of the 20s whose flagging career was revived in the 30s when Paramount chose him as the gentleman cowboy Hopalong Cassidy. Dressed always in black (usually reserved for villains in 'B' westerns), Boyd rode the range as 'Hoppy' in 66 full-length films, starting with *Hop-a-long Cassidy* aka *Hopalong Cassidy Enters* (US 35) and ending with *Strange Gamble* (US 48). The films were among the first American productions aired on television in the 40s and Boyd then embarked on a long-running Hopalong Cassidy TV series, having already played the character in a network radio series.

A number of actors established a reputation for playing particular historical characters: Charles Vanel as Napoleon, Frank McGlynn as Abraham Lincoln and Robert Watson as Hitler. The most appearances in one historical role was probably by Mikhail Gelovani, who portrayed Stalin in more than 20 Soviet films. The dictator was so gratified by Gelovani's rather wooden projection of him as the wise, all-seeing, noble proletarian that he was never allowed to give the parts any other dimension.

Other actors have found their niche in occupational roles. Arthur Treacher and Charles Coleman seldom played anything but butlers throughout their screen careers, Irish-American actor Tom Dugan played a slow-witted New York cop in over 100 films following his debut in 1926, while Pat O'Brien was cast as a Roman Catholic priest in at least a dozen of his movies. In 1928 Guy Oliver claimed to have been cast as a sheriff in 150 of the 230 westerns he had made and in 1931 Frank Hagney, invariably seen as a boxer, declared ruefully that he had lost the world's heavyweight title no less than 29 times during his career. A number of performers specialised in courtroom dramas, but none with such dedication as Hollywood character actor Richard Tucker, who is known to have played the prosecuting attorney at least 54 times.

Some were cast against type. German-born Peter van Eyck, who became Hollywood's stock Nazi beast, only came to California because as an active anti-Nazi he was forced to flee Hitler's Germany. The ability to play a drunk well is a rare one, which enabled Jack Norton

George Burns left the screen after *Many Happy Returns* (US 39) and made a happy return 37 years later in *The Sunshine Boys* (US 76)

and Arthur Housman to specialise in amiable inebriates, seldom playing anything else. Some special talent must also have inspired producers to cast Carmen Nigro as a gorilla in 32 movies, or 33 if his claim to have played the title role in *King Kong* (US 33) can be sustained (it is generally accepted that all the gorilla scenes were acted with models). He last donned his ape suit for *Gorilla at Large* (US 54).

Versatility is harder to quantify. However, it is doubtful whether any performer ever played with a greater variety of accents than Russian-born Hollywood actor Vladimir Sokoloff, who was cast as 35 nationalities during his career ranging from an Italian physicist in *Cloak and Dagger* (US 46) to a blind Chinese beggar in *Macao* (US 52). The only accent Sokoloff never succeeded in mastering was American.

The most delayed come-back: Of the many stars who have retired from films and made a come-back, the one with the longest interregnum was George Burns, who left the screen after *Many Happy Returns* (US 39) and made a happy return 37 years later in *The Sunshine Boys* (US 76) at the age of 80.

The oldest performer to have played a major role in a feature movie is Estelle Winwood, born Lee, Kent, 24 Jan 1883, who completed her role as Nurse Withers in *Murder by Death* (US 76) on her 93rd birthday. Miss Winwood is currently the oldest member of the Screen Actors Guild. She made her professional debut at the Theatre Royal, Manchester, in 1898 and claims to have been the first woman in America to wear lipstick in public.

Other nonagenarian artistes have been A.E. Matthews (1869–1960) in *Inn for Trouble* (GB 60); John Cromwell (1887–1979) in *The Wedding* (US 78); and Cathleen Nesbitt (1888–) in *The Second Star to the Right* (GB 80).

At least two centenarians were professional extras. William H. 'Dad' Taylor, born Brownsville, Texas, 9 July 1828, appeared in Edwin Carewe's *Evangeline* (US 29) at the age of 101 – a unique instance of a person born during the Georgian era playing in a talkie. The other was Walter 'Cap' Field (1874–1976), who joined the Mexican production company Ammex in 1913 and played his last role in *She's Too Hot to Handle* (US 76) when he was 101. He fondly remembered being 'killed or wounded four or five times' in various small roles in *Gone with the Wind* (US 39). The 'sage' in *The Man Who Would Be King* (US 75) was played by a 102-year-old Moroccan.

The youngest performer in a feature film was Balázs Monori, whose actual birth was shown in *Kilenc Hónap/Nine Months* (Hung 76), the story of a pregnant woman (Lili Monori) torn between two men and striving to improve herself. The director, Márta Meszaros, was reported to be delighted that Balázs's screen debut was so accomplished that no second take was needed.

The youngest performer to receive star billing was Leroy Overacker, known on the screen as Baby Leroy, who was chosen at the age of six months to play the central juvenile role opposite Maurice Chevalier in *Bedtime Story* (US 33). Master Overacker's contract had to be signed by his grandfather, because not only the star but also his 16-year-old mother was under age. The film was about a gay bachelor who becomes encumbered with an abandoned baby whose protruding lower lip matches his own, a circumstance which leads everyone to believe that

Baby Leroy – a star at six months when he played opposite Maurice Chevalier in *Bedtime Story* (US 33)

The oldest working star – Estelle Winwood *(right)* in *Murder by Death* (US 76)

Chevalier is the father of the motherless child. All is unscrambled when it is found that the distinctive facial feature of the baby is accounted for by nothing more reprehensible than a button lodged under his lip.

Insurance of stars' more notable physical accoutrements began when silent screen comedian John Bunny (1863–1915) insured his unlovely face for $100000. Faces were most stars' fortunes and it was an enterprising Los Angeles underwriter, Arthur W. Stebbins, who originated the 'scarred face' policy taken out in the early 1920s by Rudolph Valentino, Douglas Fairbanks and Mary Pickford, the latter for $1 million. Some stars, though, owed their success to individual features, not always facial – Chaplin insured his feet for $150000. Clara Kimball Young (1891–1960), often described as 'the most beautiful woman in films' at the peak of her career, *c.* 1918, insured her large and luminous eyes for the same amount. Cross-eyed Ben Turpin (1874–1940) insured to the tune of $100000 against the possibility of his eyes ever becoming normal again – it would undoubtedly have cost him his career. Suave leading man Edmund Lowe (1890–1971) took

out a $35000 policy on his distinguished nose in the mid-1920s and at about the same time Kathleen Key had her lovely neck underwritten at $25000. A decade later the most famous nose in the business carried a $100000 risk for Jimmy Durante (1893–1980).

Alberta Vaughn took out a $25000 policy in 1925 against the possibility of putting on 20lb weight by 1 June 1927, while Walter Hiers – literally a Hollywood 'heavy' – insured for an equal sum against losing 45lb. RKO insured Roscoe Ates' (1892–1962) inimitable nervous stutter in the early 30s. A year or two earlier, when sound arrived, First National had insured Corinne Griffith (1898–) against loss of voice. Ironically it was her unsuitability for talkies that finished her career. When Anthony Quinn (1915–) had his head shaved for the role of a Greek magician in *The Magus* (GB 68), he insured heavily against the risk of his hair failing to grow again. Fortunately no claim was necessary.

The first actress to insure her legs was Hollywood extra Cecille Evans, whose appendages were underwritten for $100000 in 1921. Miss Evans' speciality was 'doubling' her sensational legs for those of stars less well endowed. The 'Girl with the Million Dollar Legs', Betty Grable (1916–73), actually had them insured for more than that – the sum was $1250000. The legs may have been incomparable, but the policy did not stand comparison with the record risk of $10 million accepted on Cyd Charisse's (1921–) long and lovely limbs. No actor has ever been described as 'The Man with the Million Dollar Legs', but Fred Astaire (1899–) could have claimed the title – his were insured for just that sum.

It is not only performers who have had parts of their bodies insured. In 1939 the Fleischer Studio took out a $185000 policy with Lloyd's of London to cover the hands of the 116 animators working on their first full-length cartoon feature *Mr Bug Goes to Town* (US 41).

The first artiste whose life was insured for the duration of a picture was Lillian Gish (1896–), covered for the sum of $1 million during the film-

Left: Clara Kimball Young's large and luminous eyes were insured for $150000 *(Backnumbers)*

ing of *Way Down East* (US 20). The insurance company turned down director D.W. Griffith's application for insurance on the other principal players on health grounds. Had they known that Miss Gish was to be exposed on an ice floe in sub-zero temperature wearing only a thin frock every day for three weeks, and that she was to be rescued by the hero just before the floe went over the falls without any trick or stunt work, nor any safety precautions in case the rescue failed, doubtless the application on her behalf would have been refused with even greater promptitude.

When seven-year-old Shirley Temple's life (1928–) was insured with Lloyd's, the contract stipulated that no benefit would be paid if the child met death or injury while drunk.

Siobhan McKenna's insurance policy for *Of Human Bondage* (GB 64) forbade her to drive a car while the picture was in production. The first time the Irish actress had taken the wheel she had ended in a ditch, the second time against a wall, the third time up a tree.

The first far eastern country to permit kissing in films was China, the first oriental screen kiss being bestowed on Miss Mamie Lee in *Two Women in the House* (China 26). In Japan, where kissing was considered 'unclean, immodest, indecorous, ungraceful and likely to spread disease' – at least by Tokyo's Prefect of Police – some 800000ft of kissing scenes were cut from American movies that same year. Indians reacted much the same way, though with less rigour about cuts. According to *The Report of the Indian Cinematograph Committee* (1928), during western films 'when a kissing scene is shown, the ladies turn their heads away'.

Japan's first screen kiss was seen in *Hatachi no Seishun/Twenty Year-Old Youth* (Jap 46), directed by Yasushi Sasaki. The honour of directing the inaugural kiss should have gone to Yasuki Chiba, who was planning to introduce the daring innovation in his aptly titled *Aru Yo no Seppun/A Certain Night's Kiss* (Jap 46), but he lost his nerve at the last moment and the big clinch between the two lovers was discreetly obscured by an open umbrella. Only four years later the sex act itself was brought to the Japanese screen in *Yuki Fujin Ezu/Picture of Madame Yuki* (Jap 50).

India's first screen kiss was performed between Zeenat Aman, a former Miss Asia, and the subcontinent's most romantic leading man, Shashi Kapoor, in Raj Kapoor's *Satyam Shivam Sundaram* (India 77), a musical melodrama about a man who falls in love with the compelling voice of an adivasi girl and only learns on their wedding night that half of her face is hideously disfigured by a burn.

The last major film producing country still banning kissing on screen is Turkey.

The longest screen kiss in a commercial feature movie occupied 3 min 5 sec of Regis Toomey's and Jane Wyman's time in *You're in the Army Now* (US 40). Naomi Levine spent the full duration of Andy Warhol's non-commercial 50 min *Kiss* (US 63) kissing Rufus Collins, Gerald Malanga and Ed Saunders.

The most kisses in a single film were the 127 bestowed by John Barrymore on Mary Astor and Estelle Taylor in *Don Juan* (US 26).

The only Hollywood leading lady who never kissed her leading man on screen was the Chinese-American star Anna May Wong (1907–61). She nearly achieved it in *The Road to Dishonour* (GB 29); indeed her kissing scene with John Longden was shot, but cut by the censor on the grounds that inter-racial love would be offensive to some patrons. One other heroine of the American screen also faced a kissing ban: Marguerite Clark (1881–1940), at one time Mary Pickford's chief rival as 'America's Sweetheart'. In this case the ban was imposed by her husband, Harry Palmerson-Williams, whom she married in 1918. Although she made another dozen films, her career was severely damaged by the marital edict and she retired in 1921.

CHAPTER 7

FILM MAKING AND FILM MAKERS

CAMERAS AND CAMERAWORK

The largest number of cameras used for a single scene was 48 for the sea battle in *Ben Hur* (US 25). Another 42 cameras were employed on the chariot-race scene. Concealed in statues, in pits in the ground, and behind soldiers' shields, the 42 operators took 53 000 ft of film – equivalent to seven full-length features – in a single day.

The practice of using more than one camera on a scene was introduced by D.W. Griffith, who used three for the big fight between Dorothy West and Mabel Normand in *The Squaw's Love* (US 14). The three cameramen on this occasion were Billy Bitzer, P. Higginson and Bobby Harron. The use of multiple cameras was not confined to special scenes in Hollywood's silent days. Nearly all feature films were shot with twin cameras, one supplying the master negative from which all release prints for the domestic market were struck, the other the negative for all overseas prints.

The widest aperture lens ever used in production of a feature film was f0.7 by cameraman John Alcott on *Barry Lyndon* (GB 75). Developed for the US space programme, the lens was fitted to a specially modified camera and employed in filming an interior scene lit only by candlelight.

The first motorised camera (professional) in series production was the all-metal Bell & Howell of 1912, manufactured in the USA with the motor as an optional fitment. **The first British motorised camera** was the Aeroscope, invented by Polish cinematographer Kazimierz Prosznski and manufactured in 1913 by Newman & Sinclair. It was used extensively for newsreel work and also by Cherry Kearton for wildlife cinematography.

The first feature film made with a motorised camera was *A Sainted Devil* (US 24) with Rudolph Valentino, which was photographed at Famous Players' Long Island studio by Harry Fishbeck with an electrically-driven camera of unidentified make. Generally cameramen continued to crank by hand throughout the silent era, due to the fact that it enabled action to be speeded up or slowed down at will. The coming of sound rendered hand-cranking impractical, since variations in film speed would have caused a corresponding and unnatural variation in the delivery of synchronised speech.

The earliest known multi-shot scene (different camera positions being used within a single scene) occurs in G.A. Smith's *The Little Doctors* (GB 01), in which there is a cut from a shot of two children administering medicine to a sick kitten to a close-up of the kitten with the spoon in its mouth.

Prior to the recent rediscovery of this film (*see Sight & Sound*, Summer 1978), the innovation had generally been attributed to D.W. Griffith. In *For the Love of Gold* (US 08), Griffith used a medium shot and a three-quarter shot in a card-game scene where he wanted to register the expressions on the gamblers' faces, and this has been credited as the first use of camera movement within a scene. Another recent discovery of the use of close-up (q.v.) shots within a scene in *The Yale Laundry* (US 07), must cast doubt on whether Griffith was the pioneer of the multi-shot scene even as far as the American industry is concerned.

The first panning shots were used by Max Skladanowsky in *Komische Begegnung im Tiergarten zu Stockholm* (Ger 96), a short comedy shot on location in Sweden, and by Lumière representative Eugène Promio in *View of St Mark's Square, Venice* (Fr 96), a panorama of the Square taken from a boat on the Grand Canal.

The earliest known British example appears in a news film of Queen Victoria's Diamond Jubilee Procession shot by R.W. Paul with his 'Kinematograph' camera on 20 June 1897. The camera was mounted on a specially designed tripod with a swivel head. The first in an acted film, a panning shot of Epsom Downs, opens Alfred Collins' *Welshed, a Derby Day Incident* (GB 03).

The first 360° panning shot was made by Edwin S. Porter in *Circular Panorama of the Electric Tower* (US 01), in which the whole of the exhibition grounds of the Pan-American Exposition at Buffalo, NY are seen as the camera slowly revolves. Porter used a geared mounting of his own design for this effect.

No example of a 360° pan is known in any silent feature-film. Its **first use in a full-length dramatic film** was by James Whale in *Frankenstein* (US 31), and the following year Robert Mamoulian employed the technique in *Dr Jekyll and Mr Hyde* (US 32) to give an effect of vertigo during the transformation scene. Other films with 360° pans are *Rain* (US 32), *La Strada* (It 54), *Lola Montes* (Fr/W.Ger 55), *Judgement at Nuremberg* (US 61), *The Manchurian Candidate* (US 62), *Providence* (Fr/Swz 77), *The Swarm* (US 78) and *Eagle's Wing* (GB 79).

The first slow-motion film was made in 1898 by Berlin cinematographer Oskar Messter, using a specially constructed high-speed 60 mm camera of his own design. Among the earliest sequences filmed with this camera was one that showed a cat falling off a wall, with a Hipp millisecond watch inset in one corner to indicate the rate of descent. This was shot at 66 frames a second – over four times normal speed – though the camera was capable of filming at speeds of up to 100 frames a second.

The technique has had its widest application in sports and scientific films. The earliest practical application of slow-motion cinematography was for the purpose of gauging the breaking strain of girders, according to Hopwood's *Living Pictures*, published in 1899.

The time lapse technique was pioneered by Oskar Messter of Berlin, who filmed the blooming and wilting of a flower in 1897. The lapse factor was 1500 frames per 24 hours.

The earliest known American example is a 1902 American Mutoscope & Biograph subject of the demolition of New York's Star Theater.

The earliest known use of a travelling matte is the sequence in *The Great Train Robbery* (US 03) in which the train passes the telegraph office window.

The earliest known wipe appears in G.A. Smith's *Mary Jane's Mishap: or, Don't Fool with the Paraffin* (GB 03), in which Mary Jane does and is blown out of the chimney. A line moving across the screen 'wiped' away the scene of her unfortunate demise and replaced it with one of her forlorn grave. Hitherto the introduction of the wipe has generally been attributed to Georges Méliès in *Le Royaume des fées* (Fr 03), but Dr Barry Salt of the Slade School has established that this is a misconception. What looks like a wipe between scenes is in fact no more than the lifting of a backdrop.

The only full-length feature film to have been made without a camera was Barcelona artist José Antonio Sistiaga's remarkable 75-minute animated, one-man production in Cinemascope *Ere Ereva Baleibu Icik Subua Arvaren/Scope, Colour, Muda* (Sp 70). Completed in 17 months between October 1968 and February 1970, Sistiaga painted each frame of the film separately and single-handed direct on to the film-stock.

The first close-up was a study of a man called Fred Ott sneezing, copyrighted on 7 January 1894 as *Edison Kinetoscopic Record of a Sneeze* (US 94).

The first close-up in a British film was a 50 ft study of a man enjoying a glass of beer, made by G.A. Smith of Brighton and released under the alternative titles of *Comic Face* and *Man Drink-*

ing in September 1897. The man was played by Tom Green. Both the Edison film and Smith's film consisted of a single shot.

The first known film in which close-ups are interpolated with other shots is *Grandma's Reading Glass* (GB 00). A small boy is seen focusing a magnifying glass on various objects, including a watch, a newspaper, canary, kitten and Grandma's eye. These appear in close-up as seen by the boy, probably the earliest use of the subjective camera technique. The identity of the film-maker who pioneered the interpolated close-up is disputed. The film has generally been attributed to G.A. Smith of Brighton (see above), but Mrs Audrey Wadowska claims that it was made by her father, Arthur Melbourne Cooper of St Albans, and that the roles of Grandma and the small boy were played by Miss Bertha Melbourne Cooper and Master Bert Massey.

The earliest known interpolated close-ups in an American film are contained in American Mutoscope and Biograph's *Grandpa's Reading Glass* (US 02), a film so similar to the Smith/Melbourne Cooper subject above that it was almost certainly a plagiarism – common practice in the early days of film-making. The objects viewed by the grandchildren in this film are a bird, a printed page, the eye of a child, the head of an adult woman, the head of an infant, the head of a girl child holding a kitten, and a monkey.

Close-ups of inanimate objects or of hands or feet were not unusual in American films of the early years of the century, particularly in the productions of the American Mutoscope and Biograph Co. (AM & B). Examples include the fire alarm box in Edison's *The Life of an American Fireman* (US 03), a girl's pretty foot in Edison's *The Gay Shoe Clerk* (US 03), the contents of a jewel case in AM & B's *The Great Jewel Mystery* (US 05), gifts in AM & B's *The Silver Wedding* (US 06) and a newspaper article in AM & B's *Trial Marriages* (US 07). Facial close-ups were rarer, though the opening scenes of AM & B's *The Widow and the Only Man* (US 04) introduce the two principal characters with separate close-ups. The persistent claim of D.W. Griffith to have been the only begetter of the close-up – he even went so far as to suggest he could have patented the technique – has now been rejected by most film historians, though many still credit him with having been the first to employ the interpolated facial close-up as a dramatic device to register emotion. Even this had been accomplished a year before Griffith entered the film industry. In the AM & B production *The Yale Laundry* (US 07), a comedy about students at Yale playing a jape on their professors, close-ups are used to show surprise on the faces of the victims. It is precisely this technique of advancing the narrative by means of a close-up shot that Griffith was later to claim as his innovation and his alone. There is a certain irony in the fact that it had been used earlier by an uncredited director of the very company with which Griffith was to establish his reputation. The great director also seems to have overlooked the fact that he himself was the subject of a close-up when he played the part of a clown in *At the French Ball* (US 08), a film made shortly before his directorial debut at Biograph.

Despite the pioneering efforts of the Edison Co., AM & B and 'the Brighton school' (in England), elsewhere the notion that a film should give its audience the same view as a theatre audience received of the stage persisted for many years. As late as 1911 the leading production company in Scandinavia, Nordisk Film, was using a 16 ft long pole attached to the camera as an indication to the actors that they must come no closer. Albert E. Smith recalled that about this period at Vitagraph the actors were always positioned nine yards in front of the camera. Mary Pickford, who claimed that she had been the subject of 'the first close-up' in D.W. Griffith's *Friends* (US 12), said that the 'front office' at Biograph had vigorously protested at the idea on the grounds that audiences were paying to see the whole of the performer, not only the top half.

The first zoom lens was used by cameraman Victor Milner on Rouben Mamoulian's *Love Me Tonight* (US 32). There are two zoom shots in the 'Paris waking' sequence and one in the hunting sequence.

It was many years before zoom lenses became generally available and sometimes considerable ingenuity was exercised to obtain the same effect. Jacques Sigurd wanted the last shot of *Une si jolie petite plage* (Fr 48) to be of the hero and heroine on the beach with the camera tracking away from them until they were merely specks in the distance. He was unable to hire a helicopter and a trolley would have left tracks in the sand. His eventual solution was to have the camera moving forwards, the two performers walking backwards, and the film upside down in the camera.

The longest close-up is to be seen in *Daaera* (India 53) and lasts $6\frac{1}{2}$ minutes.

The first dissolve from one scene to another was used by Georges Méliès in *Cendrillon* (Fr 99).

The earliest known American example is to be seen in the Edison Co.'s *Life Rescue at Long Beach* (US 01), a $2\frac{1}{2}$-minute drama in five scenes about the rescue of a young lady from drowning. The dissolve effects a transition from the fourth scene, in which the lifeguards are reviving the prostrate maiden, to the climax, in which, fully recovered, she embraces her rescuers. The film is believed to have been directed by Edwin S. Porter, better remembered for *The Life of an American Fireman* (US 03) and *The Great Train Robbery* (US 03).

The iris-in, iris-out technique of opening and closing scenes was devised by cameraman Billy Bitzer and used for the first time on D.W. Griffith's *The Battle of Elderbush Gulch* (US 14). The only former use of the iris had been to obtain the effect of a view through a telescope.

The earliest known use of fades at the end of scenes is in James Williamson's *The Old Chorister* (GB 04), about an old man returning to his native village.

The first freeze frame, in which motion is arrested for dramatic effect, was used by David Wark Griffith in *A Corner in Wheat* (US 09). Speculation by Chicago financiers forces up the price of wheat and consequently the price of bread. A scene in a ghetto bakery of poor folk confronted with a notice announcing the price increases is suddenly frozen to emphasise the crowd's inability to resist. Despite the antiquity of the technique, it remained comparatively rare until the 1970s. It was greatly popularised by the telling climax of *Butch Cassidy and the Sundance Kid* (US 69), where the gunning down of the two outlaws by the Bolivian army is frozen at the moment of impact.

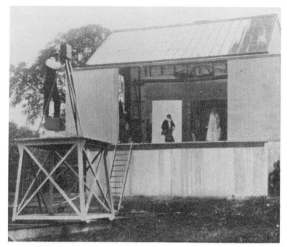

R. W. Paul's camera dolly at his New Southgate studios 1902

The first glass shot was used by Norman Dawn in his *Missions of California* (US 07). Painted on a sheet of glass mounted before the camera was a row of arches beneath a tiled roof. When this was filmed against the ruined stumps of the original arches, the effect was of the mission as it had looked when built.

The first camera dolly was used by British pioneer cinematographer R.W. Paul at the studio he built at New Southgate in 1899. In a lecture he gave before the British Kinematographers' Society in 1936, Paul recalled: 'A trolley mounted on rails carried the camera, which could thus be set at any required distance from the stage, to suit the subject. Sometimes the trolley was run to and from the stage while the picture was being taken, thus giving a gradual enlargement or reduction of the image of the film.' It is not known whether Paul's dolly dates from the opening of the New Southgate studios, but a photograph taken in 1902 shows it in use.

Cecil Hepworth also had a tracked dolly at the Hepworth Studios at Walton-on-Thames in 1905. At the same time Hepworth decided to fit his camera mounting with a panoramic head for panning shots, but both devices had to be abandoned for films he hoped to sell in the American market, since neither tracking nor panning was considered acceptable by American distributors – the camera had to be stationary.

The first use of a camera dolly in a feature film was by Spanish cameraman Segundo de Chomon for Giovanni Pastrone's *Cabiria* (It 14). De Chomon had developed his dolly while working for Pathé in Paris (1906–10) and Pastrone patented it in Italy in 1912.

The dolly arrived in America comparatively late, no examples of its use being known before 1915. Tracking shots were used in two feature films that year, by Alan Dwan on *David Harum* (US 15) to follow the hero as he walks down the street of his small home-town, and by William Bowman in *The Second-in-Command* (US 15). On this film cameraman William F. Alder employed two dollies, one for forward and backward tracking and the other for sideways movement. This was a notable innovation which did not come to its full fruition until Chinese-born James Wong Howe introduced the 'crab dolly' – a dolly that moves in any direction, including sideways and diagonally – on *The Rough Riders* (US 27).

Britain, having pioneered the dolly, then completely forgot about it until the end of the silent era. The first use of 'mobile camera' in a feature film was by Graham Cutts on Gainsborough-Piccadilly's *The Triumph of the Rat* (GB 26), with Ivor Novello.

Camera mobility could be achieved without the use of a dolly. F.W. Murnau overcame the problem of how to depict Emil Jannings' drunken view of the wedding feast in *The Last Laugh* (Ger 25) by mounting his cameraman on roller skates. When Sidney Franklin decided to use a hand-held Bell & Howell Eyemo camera on *Quality Street* (US 27), he emulated Murnau's example, but here the scene was not a drunken one and the camera had to be kept steady. The solution was to have an assistant pushing the roller-skated cameraman from behind. James Wong Howe also found roller-skates the answer for the prize fight scene in *Body and Soul* (US 47), but on *He Ran All the Way* (US 51) he needed higher camera angles. A squatting camera operator could not roller-skate, so Howe found another expedient – the cameraman was pushed in a wheelchair.

The first double exposure was accomplished by Georges Méliès in *La Caverne maudite/The Cave of the Demons* (Fr 98), employing the technique of 'spirit photography'. The evil inhabitants of the cave were first filmed against a black backdrop, so that the background was not exposed, then the film was wound back and the cave setting filmed. The effect was of 'ghost' characters superimposed against a solid background.

An early example of double exposure. In R. W. Paul's *Ora Pro Nobis*, or *The Poor Orphan's Last Prayer* (GB 01), the angel and child were shot against a neutral background and then superimposed over the churchyard scene to achieve the effect on the right

The more normal use of double exposure is to achieve the effect of two characters played by the same performer appearing on screen simultaneously. This is done by 'duplex cinematography', also pioneered by Georges Méliès and at about the same time as the film above. Méliès adapted a technique already well known to still photographers, by which a small frame enclosing two swing doors was mounted in front of the camera lens. When one door was opened, half the scene was exposed on film. The film was then wound back, one door shut and the other opened, and the rest of the scene shot. If the same performer was filmed each time, he or she would appear to be two characters interacting. Méliès' first attempt at this technique was in *Un Homme de tête/The Four Troublesome Heads* (Fr 98), which shows a magician removing his head three times over and in which he used a combination of both spirit photography and duplex photography.

The earliest known British example of double exposure is G. A. Smith's 75 ft version of Dumas' *The Corsican Brothers* (GB 98). One brother returns after death and shows his surviving twin a vision of how he had been killed in a duel.

Double exposure was temporarily abandoned when sound came in, because of the difficulty of post-synching. **The first double exposure with dialogue** was a scene in Fox Movietone's *Masquerade* (US 29) in which Alan Burmingham carried on a conversation with another character also played by Alan Burmingham.

The first triple exposure was achieved by cameraman Al Siegler in Universal's *The Twins' Double* (US 14), in which Grace Cunard played the twin heroines and the villainess, their double – all three characters appearing on the screen at the same time.

In July 1915 it was reported that the Centaur Film Co. had produced an un-named film in which seven characters played by the same person appeared simultaneously – **a septuple exposure**.

Physical contact between two characters played by the same person was first accomplished in *Little Lord Fauntleroy* (US 21), in which Mary Pickford played both the boy and his mother

The first talkie double exposure. Alan Burmingham talks to Alan Burmingham in *Masquerade* (US 29)

'Dearest'. Cameraman Charles Rosher used a 2000 lb camera to achieve absolute steadiness between one take and the next, but the exact details of his extraordinarily advanced technique are still not known. The preparations for each double exposure were amongst the most meticulous and precise in the history of camerawork. It took 15 hours to shoot the scene in which the boy kisses 'Dearest' on the cheek, a take which lasts three seconds on the screen. In another scene they embrace and, in the most spectacular of all, the Little Lord runs and jumps into his mother's arms. The complexity of the operation was enhanced by the fact that Mary Pickford the mother had to be nine inches taller than Mary Pickford the boy. For her adult role in the double exposure scenes she was given platform heels and stood on a concealed ramp, a hazardous operation since she fell off on a number of occasions.

Back projection, the technique by which outdoor scenes can be shot in the studio by placing the actors against a rear projected filmed background, was first employed successfully by director Willis O'Brien for a single scene in *The Lost World* (US 25). The following year back projection was used in the making of

Metropolis (Ger 26), but it was slow to catch on because of the technical difficulties involved. The break-through came with the development of the Teague Back Projector, which was employed for the first time on the Fox production *Just Imagine* (US 30), a science-fiction film set in 1980. Back projection was used to depict a city of the future, with stars Maureen O'Sullivan and John Garrick coasting along in their private aircraft in the foreground.

Back projection in colour was first employed by William Wellman on *Nothing Sacred* (US 37).

The first camera crane was used by cameraman William F. Alder for obtaining elevated shots in Metro's *The Second in Command* (US 15), with Francis X. Bushman. At about the same time Allan Dwan devised a more sophisticated elevator on tracks for use in the Babylonian sequence of D.W. Griffith's *Intolerance* (US 16). The 115ft high structure enabled Griffith to secure a parabolic shot, commencing at the ramparts of the Palace and descending forwards over a sea of extras to ground level and a close shot of the leading players. These early uses of

the crane were exceptional. It was not until F.W. Murnau introduced his 20-ton, 200-hp 'Go-Devil' on *The Four Devils* (US 29), and the appearance of an even larger 28-ton apparatus with a 60ft (18·3m) elevation on the set of *Broadway* (US 29), that the crane came to be regarded as standard studio equipment.

The first woman cameraman was Rosina Cianelli, who made her camera debut with Paolo Benedetti's *Uma transformista original* (Br 09), a Méliès-style trick film made at Barbacena, Brazil, with the Lazzari brothers in the lead roles.

The first American camerawoman was Grace Davison, who joined the Astor Film Corp. at its Long Island studios as an actress in 1915 but was taught to handle a camera by veteran Harry Fishbeck. Miss Davison photographed *The Honeymooners* (US 15), *Spring Onions* (US 15) and other one-reel comedies.

Back projection became a practicable technique with *Just Imagine* (US 30) *(Backnumbers)*

COSTUME

The largest number of costumes in any one film was 32000 for *Quo Vadis* (US 51). *Waterloo* (It/USSR 70) used 29000 costumes and *Cleopatra* (US 63) 26000 costumes.

The largest number of costume changes by one performer was by Elizabeth Taylor in *Cleopatra* (US 63). The 65 costumes designed by Irene Sharaff for Miss Taylor cost $130000. Another 40 costumes and head-dresses designed by Oliver Messel at a cost of $64800 did not appear in the movie as released.

The largest number of costume changes in a silent movie was 50 by Theda Bara in the course of the eleven reels of *Cleopatra* (US 17).

The most expensive costume ever worn in a movie was the barzucine sable coat that enfolded Constance Bennett in *Madame X* (US 65). It was valued at $50000.

Ingrid Bergman's costume in *For Whom the Bell Tolls* (US 43) does not look as if it has been specially designed for her, but the producer insisted

---

Mary Pickford's $32000 costume for *Dorothy Vernon of Haddon Hall* (US 24)

The most expensive costume designed and made specially for a film was Edith Head's mink and sequins dance costume for Ginger Rogers in *Lady in the Dark* (US 44), which cost Paramount $35000. By comparison, Elizabeth Taylor's dress of cloth-of-24-carat-gold in which she made her entry into Rome in *Cleopatra* (US 63) cost a modest $6500. However, the total cost of Miss Taylor's wardrobe, which amounted to $194800, was **the highest sum ever expended on costumes for a single performer in any one film**.

The most expensive single costume of the silent era was made for Mary Pickford to wear in the title role of *Dorothy Vernon of Haddon Hall* (US 24). A sumptuous Elizabethan gown embroidered with real seed pearls, it was designed by Mitchell Leisen at a cost of $32000.

At the other end of the scale, costumes could cost next to nothing even in Hollywood's most extravagant days; except for the studios' insistence that nothing was worthwhile unless it was expensive. When a rough, workaday costume was needed for Ingrid Bergman in *For Whom the Bell Tolls* (US 43), designer Edith Head selected an old pair of men's trousers and a shirt from the extras' wardrobe. Producer David O. Selznick was incensed and demanded that Miss Head should design a new costume. She did so, copying the old garments exactly, then bleaching them and dying them to look as worn as the originals.

The largest costume collection in the world is owned by Western Costume Co. and housed in a six-storey building at 5335 Melrose Avenue, Hollywood, California. The collection consists of approximately one million costumes valued at over $50 million.

Western Costume was established in Los Angeles in 1912. In a curious way its fortune could be said to have been founded on dietary deficiency. Business was slow until a major break came with D.W. Griffith's order for all the Civil War costumes for *The Birth of a Nation* (US 15). Griffith, preoccupied with authenticity, had hoped to use genuine uniforms of the period, but found that progress in nutrition over the intervening 50 years had made the average actor of 1914 too large to fit the average soldier's uniform of the 1860s.

The largest costume collection in Europe is held by Berman and Nathan's of London, who have a stock of over 700 000 costumes.

Chaplin's tramp costume was devised in response to Mack Sennett's request that he 'get into a comedy make-up' for *Kid Auto Races at Venice* (US 14). Chaplin created the costume in a dressing room where Fatty Arbuckle and Chester Conklin were playing pinochle. The moustache was a scrap of crêpe hair borrowed from Mack Swain; the trousers were Fatty Arbuckle's – hence the bagginess – and the Derby came from Minta Durfree's father, Fatty's father-in-law; the cut-away coat belonged to Chester Conklin (or Charlie Avery, according to one account); the size 14 shoes were Ford Sterling's and Chaplin had to wear

Chaplin's first appearance in his tramp costume – in *Kid Auto Races at Venice* (US 14)

them on the wrong feet to keep them on. Only the whangee cane belonged to Charlie himself.

Chaplin gave the original costume to his assistant Harry Crocker in 1928 as a central exhibit in the newly-opened Crocker Museum of props and costumes on Sunset Boulevard.

Fashion and the movies

Movie costumes began to influence fashion as early as 1912, when it was reported that the natives of Tahiti had become so addicted to westerns that they had taken to wearing stetsons. A rather more far reaching fashion was initiated by D.W. Griffith when he invented the first pair of false eyelashes in order to give Seena Owen's eyes an abnormally large and lustrous appearance for her role as Princess Beloved in *Intolerance* (US 16). They were made by a wigmaker who wove human hair through the warp of a 24-inch strip of exceptionally thin gauze. Each day two small pieces were cut from the end of the strip and gummed to Miss Owen's eyelids.

Bessie Barriscale caused a sensation with the backless evening gown she wore in *Josselyn's Wife* (US 19) and soon the middle classes were aping a fashion formerly displayed only by their betters. All classes followed the trend to bobbed hair, which became the style of the 20s after Colleen Moore had created the archetypal flapper role in *Flaming Youth* (US 23). Pola Negri was not only the first to go bare legged and sandalled in summer, but was also the first to paint her toenails. She recalled that when she first did this about 1923, using a bright red polish, a woman glanced down at her feet and shrieked 'She's bleeding'. Nevertheless, within a few weeks, Miss Negri claimed, women everywhere were lacquering their toenails. Joan Crawford was the first to go bare legged with evening clothes in 1926. She stated that she never wore stockings between then and 1930,

Colleen Moore – she created the archetypal twenties style

when long dresses returned to fashion. Bare legs for ordinary 'street wear' were pioneered by blonde starlet Rita Carewe in 1927. To preserve the proprieties, however, Miss Carewe had her legs *polished* to give the impression that she was wearing silk stockings.

Bejeaned teenagers might have made an earlier appearance but for the obduracy of D.W. Griffith. About 1914, 16-year-old Dorothy Gish became the first screen star and one of the first women in America to adopt jeans. She never wore them in films, however, and only once to the studio; a stern message to her mother from Griffith prevented such a solecism from ever being repeated. Another ten years were to pass before a woman wearing trousers as an article of feminine apparel (as opposed to male impersonation costume) appeared on screen in the person of Myrna Loy in *What Price Beauty* (US 24). This seems to have had little impact upon fashion at the time and it was not until Louise Brooks took to wearing silk trousers (indoors only) in 1927 that the practice became accepted amongst the more sophisticated followers of filmdom's fashion decrees. The real breakthrough for emancipated womanhood, though, had to await the release of von Sternberg's *Morocco* (US 30), in which Marlene Dietrich concealed her celebrated legs in slacks. Von Sternberg's purpose was to emphasise the lesbian characterisation of the role, but the innovation was imitated by the women of America to an extent that suggests its implication was wholly lost on them.

Probably the single most influential trend-setter, and the star who made least effort to be one, was Garbo. The enormous fur collars of the 20s owed their genesis to the broad collar designed by Max Ree to conceal her long neck in *The Torrent* (US 26). Garbo's berets, which she wore off-screen, became a universal fashion of the 30s and made a come-back in the 60s after Faye Dunaway had worn one as the 30s woman gangster in *Bonnie and Clyde* (US 67). The diagonally placed Eugénie hat, dipping over one eye, worn by Garbo in *Romance* (US 30), hastened the end of the cloche and introduced the basic configuration that was to dominate hat styles throughout the 30s. Although most fashion design of the period reflected a conscious rejection of the past, Adrian's Eugénie hat was created for a film that was set in the 1850s.

Garbo in *Romance* (US 30), wearing the 1850s
hat which set the headwear style of the 30s

The other major trendsetter of the period was
Joan Crawford, whom women fans watched
spellbound as she suffered in mink. While her
taste in furs was beyond the reach of the majority,
the padded-shoulder costume Adrian designed
for her to wear in *Today We Live* (US 33)
started the vogue for tailored suits that sloped
upwards from the neck. Crawford herself was
so enamoured with the style that she went on
wearing padded shoulders long after they had
gone out of general fashion.

By this time the big studios were co-operating
with the garment trade – most of the moguls
had come from that industry themselves – so
that the costumes designed for the new genre of
'women's pictures' could be in the shops by the
time the film was released. It was another Adrian
creation for Joan Crawford that began this
mass marketing of star costumes, the celebrated
Letty Lynton dress which she wore in the film
of the same name (US 32). Over half a million
copies were sold by Macy's of New York alone.
The success of the venture encouraged its
development. In 1933 a leading department

store in Columbus, Ohio called Morehouse
Martens 'completed an arrangement by which
copies of movie stars' clothes are on sale at the
store prior to or coincident with the opening of
their pictures'. The initial offerings were a
Joan Blondell double-duty dress, a Jean Arthur
frock and Claire Dodd pyjamas. The same year
Bamberger's of Newark, NJ, opened a 'Cinema
Shop' devoted exclusively to copies of the
clothes worn by stars, and their lead was
followed by other major stores from coast to
coast, including such noted names as the Hecht
Co. of Washington, Goldsmith's of Chicago,
Joseph Horne of Pittsburgh ('The Hollywood
Shop') and the May Co. of Los Angeles. The
desire to look like the stars was no less fervent
in Britain, where a magazine devoted to the
subject with the title *Film Fashionland* was
started in 1934.

Generally the adoption of a movie fashion
brought fortunes either to the designer or to
the entrepreneur who succeeded in adapting it
to a mass market. The star who launched the
style seldom derived any direct benefit, with the
notable exception of Shirley Temple. The astute
business sense of Mrs Temple ensured that
when Fox sold the manufacturing rights to
Shirley's party dresses from *Baby Takes a Bow*
(US 35), it was Shirley who garnered the lion's
share of the profits.

What stars did not wear could sometimes
have as much impact on fashion trends as what
they did wear. When Clark Gable opened his
shirt to reveal a bare and matted torso in
It Happened One Night (US 34), men's undershirt
sales took a 40 per cent dive. Mae West also
enjoyed a quite unlooked for effect on fashion, if
the Kansas Restaurant Association is to be
believed. In 1934 the Association publicly
thanked Miss West for stemming the dieting
craze stimulated by the sylph-like figures of
Dietrich, Crawford and Harlow and for restoring well-rounded curves to healthy American
womanhood.

Hollywood also played its part in bringing
an exotic touch to American fashion. When
Dorothy Lamour wore the first of her celebrated
series of sarongs in *Jungle Princess* (US 36), it
generated a demand for tropical fabrics that
lasted for the next ten years. The Latin-American
look that swept the USA in the early 40s was
instigated by Edith Head's costumes for

Barbara Stanwyck in *The Lady Eve* (US 41), and Charles LeMaire's designs for Jennifer Jones in *Love is a Many Splendoured Thing* (US 55) began a trend towards oriental fashion.

The decline of the cinema as a cultural force has reduced its fashion impact in the west, but in the orient, where cinema-going continues to increase, it appears to be breaking down traditional prejudices against western modes of dress. Significant of the trend are recent reports that jeans are now being worn by Indian women since Zeenat Aman, number one at the box office, began appearing in them in public.

DIRECTORS

The first director: The functions of director and producer were first separated for America's earliest 'spectacle' film *The Passion Play* (US 98). Rich G. Hollaman, the producer, engaged a distinguished stage director, L.J. Vincent of Niblo's Garden Theatre in New York, to

Dorothy Lamour's revealing sarong in *Jungle Princess* (US 36) started a fashion for tropical fabrics

direct the picture. Unfortunately, America's first movie director had never seen a movie and nothing could persuade him that the camera was capable of reproducing live action. Convinced that he had been engaged to direct a succession of lantern-slide tableaux, he would rush out onto the set whenever the performance of a scene was progressing favourably and scream 'Hold it!' The film was eventually made by subterfuge. Each afternoon cameraman William Paley would declare that the light was no longer strong enough to continue and as soon as Vincent had departed the actors would reassemble and shoot as much as possible before dark. The two-reel drama was a sensation when it was premièred at the Eden Musée on 30 January 1898, but it is difficult to know whether it would be more accurately described as the first film made by a professional director or the first dramatic film made with no director at all.

The first woman director was Alice Guy (1873–1968), originally secretary to Léon Gaumont, who was given an opportunity to direct after she had complained at the lack of variety in Gaumont productions. She made her debut with *La Fée aux choux*, about a young couple walking in the countryside who encounter a fairy in a cabbage patch and are presented with a child. The film is usually said to date from 1896, but since it is listed No. 370 in the Gaumont catalogue it seems more likely that it was made *c*. 1900. Mlle Guy was Gaumont's sole director of dramatic films until Zecca joined the studios at La Villette in 1905. In 1907 she emigrated to the USA, and founded the Solax Co. on Long Island three years later. Between 1919 and 1922 she directed for Pathé and Metro, then returned to France. Despite her long experience, she was unable to find work as a director in her own country and made a living writing stories based on film scenarios for pulp magazines.

The first feature film directed by a woman was the Rex production of *The Merchant of Venice* (US 14), which had Lois Weber as director. Miss Weber was also **the first American woman director,** starting with Gaumont Talking Pictures in New York in 1907, then working for Reliance in 1908, for Rex 1909–13, for the Bosworth Co. 1914–15 and for Universal 1915–19, after which she went independent. Her best known picture was Universal's highly

The world's first woman director, Alice Guy, on the set of her first movie *La Fée aux choux* (Fr *c*. 1900)

successful *Where Are My Children?* (US 16), a treatise on birth control. As her films became increasingly controversial, she had difficulty in obtaining distribution, and her last picture, *White Heat* (US 34), about miscegenation, was not released.

Sharon Smith, in *Women Who Make Movies* (New York 75), has listed 36 women directors who were active in the United States during the silent era and believes there were others who directed anonymously. The only one to make the transition to sound was Dorothy Arzner, whose *Manhattan Cocktail* (US 28) was **the first talkie directed by a woman**. At the height of her career in the 30s she was listed as one of Hollywood's top ten directors.

The first woman to direct a British production was Jakidawdra Melford, who made her directorial debut with a highwayman picture called *The Inn on the Heath* (GB 14). The first feature by a woman was Dinah Shurey's *Carry On!* (GB 27), a naval war drama, and the first talkie was Elinor Glyn's *Knowing Men* (GB 30).

The first director to direct himself in a full-length feature film was Harold Heath, who

played the lead in Anchor Films' detective thriller *£1000 Reward* (GB 13).

The first black American director to direct a film aimed at multi-racial audiences was Melvin van Peebles, former San Francisco cable-car gripman, who made his directorial debut with *La Permission/The Story of a Three Day Pass* (Fr 67). Based on van Peebles' own novel, *The Pass*, it related the story of a black G.I. on a three-day furlough who has a brief affair with a Parisian shop girl. His first American movie was *The Watermelon Man* (US 70), in which Godfrey Cambridge portrays the white insurance salesman who wakes up one morning to find he has turned black.

The first black American to direct an American film at a major studio was former *Life* photographer Gordon Parks, who directed *The Learning Tree* (US 69) for Warner Bros.

For **the first black director of black films,** see p. 70.

The first black African director was Paulin Soumanou Vieyra, born in Dahomey in 1925, who made his directorial debut with *Afrique sur Seine* (Senegal 55).

The first director to make a film on percentage was D.W. Griffith, who made *The Birth of a Nation* (US 15) while earning his regular $300 a week with Majestic and was offered $37\frac{1}{2}$ per cent of net profits after the film had been completed.

The first director to earn a million dollars for a single picture was Mike Nichols for *The Graduate* (US 67).

The highest return to a director on percentage has been earned by George Lucas, whose contract with Fox gave him 40 per cent of the net profits of *Star Wars* (US 77). Mr Lucas received his first royalties cheque of $40m in October 1978 and it is estimated that his earnings for directing the film will eventually total $80m.

The highest paid director of the silent era was James Cruze (1884–1942), Danish-American film-maker who directed *Dr Jekyll and Mr Hyde* (US 12), *The Covered Wagon* (US 23) and *Merton of the Movies* (US 24). At the end of the silent period (*c*. 1928) he was earning $7000 per week.

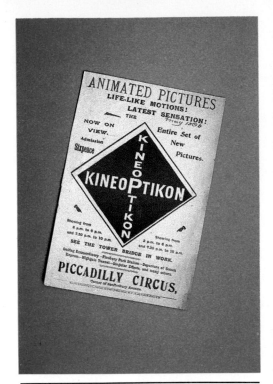

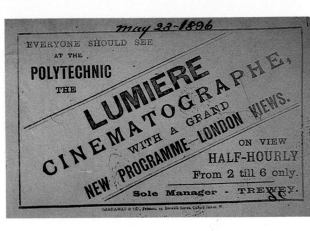

Above: Britain's first attempt at establishing a permanent cinema, March 1896. A fire terminated the enterprise *(Peter Jackson Collection)*

Top right: An early advertisement for Lumière's cinematograph

Right: There was no kissing in Indian talkies until Shashi Kapoor and Zeenat Aman successfully defied the convention in *Satyam Shivam Sundaram* (India 77) (See p. 121)

Below left: A rare colour still showing the effect achieved by two-colour Technicolor. This was a scene from Erich Von Stroheim's *The Wedding March* (US 28)

Below right: A scene from the first live action subject shot in three-colour Technicolor — *La Cucaracha* (US 34). (See p. 160)

CLIVE BROOK.

POLA NEGRI.

BEBE DANIELS.

CLARA BOW.

RICHARD BARTHELMESS.

JOHN GILBERT.

JOAN CRAWFORD

JEAN HARLOW (M-G-M)

CLAUDETTE COLBERT (COLUMBIA)

Stars of the Twenties

The longest directorial career lasted for 60 years in the case of Abel Gance (1889–), beginning with *La Digue* (Fr 11) and culminating in *Napoléon cet Inconnu* (Fr 71). The latter was a reworking of his epic *Napoléon* (Fr 26). His directorial career will extend to 70 years if his projected French-US co-production, *Christopher Columbus,* comes to fruition.

Other **directors with a career spanning half a century** are:

John Ford (1895–1973) – 54 years from *Lucille Love – The Girl of Mystery* (US 14) to *Vietnam, Vietnam* (US 68).
Alfred Hitchcock (1899–1980) – 53 years from *Always Tell Your Wife* (GB 23) to *The Family Plot* (US 76).
George Marshall (1896–1975) – 52 years from Harry Carey westerns and Ruth Roland serials in 1917 to *Hook, Line and Sinker* (US 69).
Louis Buñuel (1900–) – 52 years to date from *Un Chien Andalou* (Fr 28). Still active.
Raoul Walsh (1887–) – 52 years from *The Life of Villa* (US 12) to *A Distant Trumpet* (US 64).
Rudall Hayward (189?–1974) – 51 years from *The Bloke from Freeman's Bay* (NZ 20) to *To Love a Maori* (NZ 71).
Michael Curtiz (1888–1962) – 50 years from *Ma Es Holnap* (Hung 12) to *The Comancheros* (US 62).

Apart from Alfred Hitchcock, most of whose work has been in America, **the most durable British director** was Maurice Elvey (1887–1967), whose directorial career spanned 44 years from *The Fallen Idol* (GB 13) to *Second Fiddle* (GB 57).

The most prolific American directors of feature films were:

William Beaudine (1892–70) – 182 features from *Watch Your Step* (US 22) to *Jesse James Meets Frankenstein's Daughter* (US 66), of which 32 were silents and 144 were talkies. In addition he directed over 120 shorts from 1916.
Richard Thorpe (1896–) – 179 features from *Burn 'em Up Barnes* (US 21) to *The Scorpio Letters* (US 67), of which 63 were silents and 116 were talkies.
Michael Curtiz (1888–1962) – 164 features from *Ma Es Holnap* (Hung 12) to *The Comancheros* (US 62), of which 61 were made in Europe before 1926 and the remainder in Hollywood.

Sam Newfield (1900–64) – 140 talkies.
Allan Dwan (1885–) – 132 features from *Richelieu* (US 14) to *The Most Dangerous Man Alive* (US 61), plus over 200 shorts from *Brandishing a Bad Man* (US 11). Dwan claims to have been involved in the making of 1400 films since 1910 as writer, producer or director.
John Ford (1895–1973) – 132 features from *The Tornado* (US 17) to *Vietnam, Vietnam* (US 68).

Note: It has been claimed that George Marshall (1896–1975) directed 425 features during his career, but only 88 full-length pictures crediting him as director can be traced for the period 1916–69. Ford Beebe (1888–) is said to have directed over 200 westerns, 'B' pictures and serials from 1916, but only 72 known films give him director credit.

The most prolific British director was Darlington-born Maurice Elvey (1887–1967), who directed 149 full-length features from *Her Luck in London* (GB 14) to *Second Fiddle* (GB 57). In addition he directed 41 shorts (mainly two-reelers) from *The Fallen Idol* (GB 13).

The most co-directors on a single film was 16 in the case of *I misteri di Roma* (It 63), an anti-establishment view of 'one day in the life of the city' directed by Gianni Bisiach, Libero Bozzari, Mario Carbone, Angelo D'Alessandro, Nino del Fra, Luigi di Gianni, Giuseppe Ferrara, Ansano Giannarelli, Guilo Macchi, Lori Mazzetti, Massimo Mida, Enzo Mutti, Piero Nelli, Paolo Nuzzi, Dino Partesano and Giovanni Vento.

Deutschland in Herbst (W.Ger 78), *Love for Everyone* (China 42) and *Paramount on Parade* (US 30) each had 11 directors; *Dreams of Thirteen* (W.Ger/Neths 74) had 10; *If I Had a Million* (US 32) and *Forever and a Day* (US 43) had 7. All the foregoing were either non-fiction or episodic fiction films. The most directors on a straight fiction film was seven for *Casino Royale* (GB 67), a Bond movie directed by John Huston, Ken Hughes, Val Guest, Robert Parrish, Joe McGrath, Richard Talmadge and Anthony Squire.

The youngest director of a professionally-made feature film was Lev Kuleshov (1899–1970), who was 17½ when he embarked on his four-reel *Proyekt inzhenera Praita/Engineer Prite's Project* (USSR 18) at the Khanzhonkov Studios in

Moscow. The only other teenage directors have been Japan's Masahiro Makino, who made his directorial debut in 1927 at the age of 18; George Palmer, 17, of Melbourne, Vic., who directed the railroad drama *Northbound Ltd* (Aus 26); and 18 year old Laurent Boutonnat, *enfant terrible* responsible for *La Ballade de la Feconductrice* (Fr 80). Boutannat was just old enough to be allowed to see his own film – it won an adults only rating for its depiction of castration, child slaughter and bestiality.

The most versatile film-maker in terms of the most major functions performed on a single movie was Charles Chaplin, who produced, directed, scripted, composed, edited, choreographed, costume-designed and starred in *Limelight* (US 52).

EDITING

The most edited film in terms of total negative discarded was Howard Hughes' *Hell's Angels* (US 30), which consumed 2 254 750 ft of film during the four years it took to make. If all this footage had been shown unedited, it would have run for 560 hr or 23 days non-stop. The cost of the film stock was $225 475. The final release print was 9045 ft (2 hr 15 min running time), a reduction in the ratio of 249:1. A single scene without actors – a brief close-up of the valves of an aeroplane engine – occupied 20 000 ft of film (the length of four full-length features) before Hughes was satisfied.

Other films with extravagant shooting ratios look modest by comparison: Fritz Lang's *Metropolis* (Ger 26) was reduced from 1 960 000 to 13 165 ft, a ratio of 149:1; Charles Chaplin's *City Lights* (US 31) was reduced from 975 000 to 7784 ft, a ratio of 125:1; *Uncle Tom's Cabin* (US 27) was reduced from 900 000 to 13 000 ft, a ratio of 69:1; Charles Chaplin's *The Kid* (US 20) was reduced from 400 000 to 6000 ft, a ratio of 67:1; Leni Riefenstahl's *Olympische Spiele* (Ger 38) was reduced from 1 300 000 to 20 000 ft, a ratio of 65:1; William Wyler's *Ben Hur* (US 59) was reduced from 1 125 000 to 23 838 ft, a ratio of 47:1; Howard Hughes' *The Outlaw* (US 46) was reduced from 470 000 to 10 451 ft, a ratio of 45:1; Erich von Stroheim's *Foolish Wives* (US 21) was reduced from 360 000 to 10 000 ft, a ratio of 36:1; William Wyler's *The Best Years of Our Lives* (US 46) was reduced from 400 000

to 16 000 ft, a ratio of 25:1; Chuck Wein's *Rainbow Bridge* (US 71) was reduced from 252 000 to 10 300 ft, a ratio of 24:1; three with a ratio of 23:1 were D.W. Griffith's *Intolerance* (US 16), reduced from 300 000 to 13 000 ft, Sergei Eisenstein's *October* (USSR 27), also reduced from 300 000 to 13 000 ft, and *Gone With the Wind* (US 39), reduced from 474 538 to 20 300 ft; and *The Longest Day* (US 72), reduced from 360 000 to 17 000 ft, had a ratio of 21:1, or about twice the average.

The most edited single sequence of a movie was the chariot race scene in *Ben Hur* (US 25), for which editor Lloyd Nosler had to compress 200 000 ft of film into a sparse 750 ft, a ratio of 267:1. Historian Kevin Brownlow has commented: 'Those 750 feet are among the most valuable in motion picture history'.

The least edited films include D.W. Griffith's *Broken Blossoms* (US 19), which was made with no retakes of any scene and had only 200 ft trimmed from its original length of 5500 ft; and William Wellman's *The Public Enemy* (US 31), which was reduced by only 360 ft from its original 8760 ft.

Narrative features which were released unedited include Godard's *One Plus One* aka *Sympathy for the Devil* (GB 68); Andy Warhol's *Chelsea Girls* (US 66); and Laura Mulvey and Peter Wollen's *Penthesilea: Queen of the Amazons* (GB 74). The ultimate was achieved by *The Lacy Rituals* (GB 73), which was unedited to the extent of including shots of the clapper board being clapped and even retained the director's cries of 'cut!' on the soundtrack.

FILM STOCK

Film Stock: Transparent roll film of a kind suitable for motion picture use (though designed for still photography) was first manufactured by the Eastman Dry Plate and Film Co. of Rochester, NY in August 1889. Although Thomas Edison ordered some about this date for experiments in cinematography, it was found unsatisfactory and the first stock used for taking films for the Edison Kinetoscope was supplied by the Merwin Hulbert firm in 50 ft rolls on 18 March 1891. In the meantime, however, Louis Aimé Augustin Le Prince of Leeds, Yorkshire, had succeeded in making experimental cinematograph films on Eastman Kodak stock that he had ordered in the autumn of 1889.

The first commercially-produced films in Britain were made in 1895 by Robert Paul and Birt Acres using stock supplied by the European Blair Camera Co. Ltd of St Mary Cray, Kent. By the end of 1896, film stock specially cut and prepared for motion picture use was being advertised by the Celluloid Co. of New York, Dr J.H. Smith & Co. of Zurich, Switzerland, the Blair Co. of Cambridge, Mass. and London, England, the Eastman Kodak Co. of Rochester, NY and Fitch & Co. of London.

The first perforated film was used by Louis Aimé Augustin Le Prince (1842–90?) in his motion picture experiments conducted at Leeds, Yorkshire, in 1889. The inventor's assistant Longley recalled that 'we had brass eyelets fixed in the band [ie film] similar to the eyelets of boots'. The projector built by Le Prince in 1889 had a wheel with pins 'for gearing into the band of pictures'. Perforated film was not used by Thomas Edison until at least three years later.

Commercially-produced film stock was originally sold unperforated and it was not until 1904 that Eastman Kodak began offering perforation as an optional extra. Even as late as 1922 Richardson's *Handbook of Projection* states 'perforation is usually done by the producer'. Unperforated nitrate stock continued to be available from Eastman Kodak until September 1949.

The first safety film on an acetate base was introduced by Eastman Kodak of Rochester, NY, in the autumn of 1908, but its application was limited due to the fact that it tended to shrink and cockle. The negative safety stock was withdrawn in 1912, though positive safety film continued to be available for use with portable projectors in schools. Little record of production on safety film in the USA survives from this period and the earliest commercially-made movie known to have been released on safety stock, a 345ft drama titled *La Vendetta del Groom* (It 09), was produced by Cines of Rome.

Sub-standard safety film was produced in 28mm gauge by Pathé for use with the K.O.K. home movie projector in France in 1912 and in 22mm gauge by Kodak for use with the Edison Home Kinetoscope the same year.

Safety film continued to be confined to the sub-standard gauges until 1950, when Eastman Kodak reintroduced 35mm uninflammable stock, using a triacetate base immune from shrinkage. The revolution in film stock was total and immediate, so that since 1951 virtually no film has been made on the highly-inflammable nitrate stock previously in use.

Panchromatic film was first used in the production of Gaumont Chronochrome natural colour movies exhibited before the Photographic Society, Paris, on 15 November 1912. The subjects included scenes of the Vilmorin-Andrieux Gardens, butterflies, Deauville beach at the height of the social season, and pastoral views including harvesters at work. The process, involving the exposure of three strips of panchromatic film through colour filters, was too laborious and expensive for commercial exploitation.

In black-and-white cinematography, the use of panchromatic stock, which is sensitive to the light of all colours, was pioneered by Charles Rosher in Hollywood in 1919. The advantage was a much more accurate rendering of tones, since the orthochromatic film then in use was wholly insensitive to red. **The first feature film made on panchromatic stock** was *The Headless Horseman* (US 22), shot by cameraman Ned van Buren. Regular production of negative stock was commenced by Eastman Kodak in 1923, and by 1927 it was in general use in most Hollywood studios.

The first panchromatic stock for amateur use was 16mm Du Pont-Pathé in 1928.

The largest frame format of any film stock was the $2 \cdot 04 \times 2 \cdot 805$ in ($65 \times 71 \cdot 25$ mm) dimension used in the 70mm horizontal feed IMAX system, developed by Multiscreen Corp. of Canada. The first film produced in this $5 \cdot 242$ sq in format, which is nine times the size of the standard 35mm frame, was *Tiger Child* (Can/Jap 70), presented at the Fuji Group's pavilion at Japan's *Expo 70*.

FILM STUDIES

The first course on cinematography was delivered by H. Vodnik at the Slovenija Technical College, Belgrade, Serbia (now Yugoslavia) during the winter semester of 1896–97.

The first in Britain was a course of evening classes commenced under the direction of

The largest frame format – a $5\frac{1}{4}$ sq in Imax frame reproduced actual size

Robert Mitchell at the Regent Street Polytechnic, London, on 1 October 1913.

The first film school was the State School of Cinematography, Moscow (later the Moscow State Film Institute or VGIK), founded on 1 September 1919 with the support of the Moscow Cinema Committee to train directors, actors, cameramen, lighting experts and art directors. Directors did a three-year course, actors a two-year course, and by government decree all studios were required to reserve a certain number of vacancies for the school's graduates each year. The first Principal was pioneer director Vladamir Gardin (1877–1965), who made the earliest version of *War and Peace* (Rus 15), and notable teachers during the school's formative years were Eistenstein, Pudovkin, Kozintsev, Dovzhenko, Yutkevich and Tisse. During the first year of the school's existence, raw film stock was in such short supply that the students 'shot' imaginary films with no film in the camera.

The first privately run film school was established by Gilberto Rossi at São Paulo, Brazil in 1919. Other pioneer film schools were established by Dimos Vratsanos at Athens in 1920 and by Aleksander Vereščagin at Zagreb, Yugoslavia in 1922.

The first film school in Britain was the A.A.T. Film School, established at 14 Soho Square under the auspices of Associated Artist Technicians in 1938. The Director of the school was Edward Carrick (1905–) son of the distinguished stage designer Edward Gordon Craig and grandson of Ellen Terry. Classes were offered in script-writing, editing, sound, special effects, camera work and art direction at a fee of 180 guineas for the full two-year course. The school closed down at the outbreak of war.

University Film Studies: The first course in film studies offered as part of the regular curriculum of a university was instituted at the University of Southern California in 1929. Lecturers included Douglas Fairbanks, Ernst Lubitsch, William de Mille, Clara Beranger and Milton Sills on such topics as 'Photoplay Appreciation', 'Scientific Foundations', 'Growth and Development', 'The Silent Photoplay', 'The Phonophotoplay', 'Principles of Criticism', 'Social Utility of the Photoplay', 'The Actor's Art', etc. By 1932 the university had a fully-fledged Department of Cinematography and offered the first BA degree for students majoring in film studies. Three years later the course was extended to allow a year of graduate study leading to a Master of Arts degree.

In the USA there are over 600 schools and colleges offering nearly 6000 courses in film and TV, of which about 50 award degrees in cinema studies. Full-time film students total 35000.

FLASHBACK

The first flashback was used in *Shin Hototogishu/ The Cuckoo* (Jap 09), directed by Shisebu Iwafuji. **The first in an American production** occurs in *One Night and Then* (US 10), a D.W. Griffith picture about a man with one night to live.

The first sound flashback, in which dialogue and sounds from the past are synchronised with an image of the present in order to conjure up a distant memory, was used by Rouben Mamoulian in *City Streets* (US 31). Dialogue heard earlier in the film was repeated over a huge close-up of Sylvia Sidney's tear-stained face as she recalls the past.

The flashback within a flashback appeared first in Jacques Feyder's *L'Atlantide* (Fr 21); thereafter it was by-passed by film-makers as too confusing until Michael Curtiz challenged the audience's comprehension with a flashback within a flashback within a flashback in *Passage to Marseilles* (US 44). The experiment was repeated in John Brahm's *The Locket* (US 46) and then happily relegated to the limbo of great ideas that do not work.

Unconventional flashbacks include the multiple flashbacks out of sequence employed by William K. Howard in *The Power and the Glory* (US 33) and by Orson Welles in *Citizen Kane* (US 41). Bertolucci's first feature *La Commare secca* (It 62), about the murder of a prostitute in Rome and the subsequent investigation, used the 'against the rules' technique of false flashbacks – deliberately intended to mislead – interspersed with true flashbacks. A charming device was adopted by Keisuke Kinoshita in *Nogiku no gotoku Kimi Nariki/She was like a Wild Chrysanthemum* (Jap 55) – about an old man revisiting his home-town after 60 years and recalling boyhood scenes – when he placed all the flashbacks in an oval-shaped vignette.

GAUGES

The standard gauge of 35mm was adopted by Thomas Alva Edison (1847–1931) of West Orange, NJ, in the spring of 1891 for use with the Kinetoscope peep-show viewing apparatus developed by his assistant W.K.L. Dickson. Edison's choice of four perforations, giving a 4×3 format to the image, was probably dictated by the fact that the film was designed for showing in a viewing machine, not on screen. Had he anticipated that projection would become the normal method of presenting movies, he would doubtless have opted for a wider format, to give an aspect ratio approximating more closely to that of a theatre stage. The Lumière brothers of Lyon, France, who built the first commercially successful projectors, decided to conform to the gauge pioneered by Edison and it was undoubtedly their dominance of the nascent film industry in Europe that established 35mm as the standard gauge. It was officially recognised as such by international agreement in 1907.

The first use of 70mm film was by Birt Acres (1854–1918) of Barnet, Herts, for shooting scenes of Henley Regatta on 7–9 July 1896. He soon abandoned use of wide gauge film because of the high cost.

A 70mm projector was produced by Herman Caster of Canatosta, NY, and introduced into Britain as *The American Biograph* on 17 March 1897 at the Palace Theatre.

The first 70mm feature film was a special widescreen version of *Fox Movietone Follies of 1929*, premièred in the Grandeur process at the Gaiety Theater, New York, on 17 September 1929.

The smallest gauge ever employed for filming was 3mm, developed *c.* 1960 by Eric Berndt and used by NASA in manned space flights in the late 1960s. It had a centre frameline perforation.

The largest gauge ever employed in filming was 73mm, used by the American Mutoscope and Biograph Co. in Britain *c.* 1897.

GAUGES

3mm	NASA, USA *c.* 1968.
4mm	US Air Force 1950s (?).
8mm	Eastman Kodak, USA 1932.
8·75mm	China 1950s (for use in mobile cinemas).
9·5mm	Pathé, France 1922.
11mm	Duplex, USA *c.* 1903.
13mm	GB *c.* 1920; France *c.* 1925.
15mm	Gaumont Pocket-Chrono 1900.
16mm	Eastman Kodak, USA 1923.
17mm	Pathé, Spain *c.* 1920.
17·5mm	Birtac, GB 1898; Biokam, GB 1899; Kino d'Ernemann, Germany 1903, etc.
18mm	USSR *c.* 1925.
20mm	Mirographe, France *c.* 1920.
21mm	Edison, USA *c.* 1905.
22mm	Edison Home Kinetoscope, USA 1912; Cinébloc, France 1921.
24mm	Société d'Exploutations Cinématographiques, France 1925.
26mm	Société Cinelux, France 1920.
30mm	France 1910 (three 10mm frames laterally).
32mm	Vincennes, France 1920 (two 16mm frames laterally).
35mm	Edison, USA 1891; Lumière, France 1894; standard from 1907.
42mm	Tri-Ergon, Germany 1929.
45mm	Claude Autant-Lara, France 1929 (three 15mm frames laterally).
50mm	Le Prince, GB, 1888; Graphophonoscope, France 1899.
51mm	Latham, USA 1895.
55mm	Cinemascope 55, USA 1956.
56mm	Magnifilm, USA 1929.

60 mm	Demeny Chronophotographe, France 1895; Prestwich, GB 1898.
62 mm	American Mutoscope & Biograph Co., USA 1895.
63 mm	Veriscope Co., USA 1897.
65 mm	Warner Bros, USA 1930; Joseph Schenck, USA 1930; Todd-AO, USA 1955.
70 mm	Birt Acres, GB 1896; Herman Caster, USA 1897; Fox Grandeur, USA 1929, etc.
73 mm	American Mutoscope & Biograph, GB c. 1897.

Dual gauge: It is not uncommon for sequences of professional feature films to be shot on 16 mm and then blown up (eg *Doctor Zhivago* (US 65), *Medium Cool* (US 69), *Easy Rider* (US 69), *Downhill Racer* (US 69)), but only one film has been released in a form which switches from one gauge to another. *Une Sale Histoire* (Fr 77) was a featurette of which the first 28 minutes were in 35 mm and the last 22 minutes in 16 mm.

LIGHTING

The first film shot by artificial light was a topical of the Berlin Press Club Ball made by Oskar Messter early in 1897. Illumination for filming was provided by four Körting & Matthiessen 50-amp arc lamps on portable stands. Later the same year Georges Méliès of Paris used electric arcs to shoot *Derrière l'omnibus* (Fr 97), a song-film performed by the popular *chansonnier* Paulus on the stage of the Théâtre Robert-Houdin. (When the film was shown, Paulus would sing from behind the screen.) **The earliest known American film made by artificial light** was an Edison comedy titled *Willie's First Smoke* (US 99).

The earliest use of lighting effects for their aesthetic value is generally attributed to D.W. Griffith, who employed artificial lighting to obtain a 'fireside glow' in *The Drunkard's Reformation* (US 09), for the 'sunlight effect' in *Pippa Passes* (US 09) and the 'dim, religious light' in *Threads of Destiny* (US 10). Griffith had to overcome the resistance of his cameramen Harry Marvin and Billy Bitzer, who regarded shadows as 'amateurish'.

Backlighting by reflectors was introduced by D.W. Griffith's cameraman Billy Bitzer on *Enoch Arden* (US 11), which opens with a superbly backlighted shot of the villagers bidding the sailors goodbye. The technique had been discovered by accident. Normally the camera was never faced directly into the sun, but one day Bitzer turned it playfully onto Mary Pickford and Owen Moore as they sat at a shiny-topped table with the sun behind them. Instead of the couple appearing in silhouette, as he expected, Bitzer found that he had obtained a beautifully lit shot with the two artistes' faces bathed in radiance – suitably, since they were in love – the effect of the sun's light reflected in the table top. Bitzer devised a system whereby one mirror would reflect the sun into another, which could then be beamed to the back of a performer's head.

The first studio built with a 'dark stage' for filming by artificial light was the Ambrosio Studio at Turin, Italy, where production started in 1907. The illumination installed by chief cameraman Carlo Montuori consisted of street lamps. **The first 'dark stage' in Britain** was built in 1914 at the Neptune Studios, Borehamwood to the specification of chief cameraman Alfonso Frenguelli. The lamps were Westminster arcs, some on stands, the others suspended from the roof by pulleys.

The earliest use of incandescent lighting on a feature film has generally been attributed to Erich von Stroheim in *Greed* (US 25). However, Lee Garmes claimed to have used it in a Dorothy Gish movie made in 1919. Garmes did not iden-

Incandescent lighting at the Edison Studios *c*. 1915

On the set of *California* (US 27) with the most powerful lighting unit in the history of motion pictures

tify the film, but he made two pictures with Dorothy Gish in that year – *The Hope Chest* (US 19) and *I'll Get Him* (US 19). **The first feature lighted entirely with incandescent lamps** was *The First Auto* (US 27), a Warner Bros production with Barney Oldfield. Incandescent lighting was particularly suitable with panchromatic film (q.v.). Arcs, because they did not contain all the colours of the spectrum, radiated a 'blue white' illumination, so that colour tones tended to be distorted. The incandescent lamp gave a natural light, enabling cameramen to use faster film and removing the need for the blue and green make-up used formerly to obtain the effect of a natural complexion.

The most powerful lighting used on any film was the 58 000 amps that illuminated the set of *The King and I* (US 56). This is equivalent to the illumination of 258 'brute' arc lights.

The most powerful standard lighting unit currently on sale is the 350-amp Titan Molarc, manufactured by the Mole-Richardson Co. of Hollywood.

The most powerful single arc ever used was a giant 13 940 amp, 325 million candlepower lamp used by Colonel Tim McCoy on the western *California* (US 27). The lamp was 40 times the strength of the most powerful arc available today (see above), 54 times as powerful as the most brilliant lighthouse beam, and said to have a beam that would radiate for 90 miles (145 km).

LOCATION

The largest number of different locations used on a motion picture was 168 in the case of Sergei Bondarchuk's four-part *War and Peace* (USSR 1963–67), of which the most prominent were the Battle of Borodino sequence, filmed at Borodino; the 'Moscow on Fire' sequence, filmed at Volokolamsk; and the 'Hunting in Otradnoye' sequence, filmed in the village of Boguslavskiy, near Kashira.

The largest number of films set in an English provincial city is 19, in Liverpool: *Her Benny* (GB 20); *Grass Widowers* (GB 21); *Old English* (US 30); *The House of the Spaniard* (GB 36); *Souls at Sea* (US 37); *Penny Paradise* (GB 38); *Spare a Copper* (GB 40); *Atlantic Ferry* (GB 41); *It Happened One Sunday* (GB 44); *Waterfront*

Stanley Baker in *Violent Playground* (GB 58)

(GB 50); *The Magnet* (GB 50); *These Dangerous Years* (GB 57); *Violent Playground* (GB 58); *Sapphire* (GB 59); *In the Wake of a Stranger* (GB 59); *Ferry Across the Mersey* (GB 64); *The Little Ones* (GB 64); *Charlie Bubbles* (GB 67); *The Birth of the Beatles* (GB 80). Ten films have been set in Brighton and Blackpool, nine in Glasgow, eight in Manchester and Edinburgh and seven in Oxford.

TAKES AND RETAKES

The longest take in a movie comprises the whole of the second reel of Andy Warhol's *Blue Movie* (US 68) and consists of a 35-minute uninterrupted scene of Viva and Louis Waldon making love.

The longest take in a commercially-made feature movie is a 14-minute uninterrupted monologue by Lionel Barrymore in *A Free Soul* (US 31). Since a reel of camera film only lasts ten minutes, the take was achieved by using more than one camera. Alfred Hitchcock's *Rope* (US 48), the story of two homosexual college men who kill a third for the intellectual thrill of it, was shot in eight ten-minute takes. The effect was of one continuous shot, since the action of the story occupied the same period of time – 80 minutes – as the length of the film.

Retakes: most. The record for the most retakes of a scene has never clearly been established, but there are three known occasions on which over 100 takes were required before the director was satisfied:

The scene in *A Woman of Paris* (US 23) in which the French Sureté question Lydia Knott about the death of her child had to be shot over a hundred times because director Charles Chaplin wanted a reaction drained of all emotion and Miss Knott, the only performer ever to argue with the Master (according to Chaplin's assistant Eddie Sutherland), insisted on playing the scene with resolute fortitude. After retakes occupying a whole week's shooting Miss Knott lost her temper and became sullen, with the result that Chaplin obtained exactly the kind of deadpan response he was demanding.

Animal scenes often involve protracted shooting. More than 100 retakes were needed for a sequence in the Douglas Fairbanks' *Robin Hood* (US 24) in which a falcon pursues and brings to earth a pigeon carrying a vital message.

Howard Hughes demanded over a hundred takes of a scene in *Hell's Angels* (US 30) in which a Zeppelin crew were abandoning their cabin. He then ordered the first take to be printed. Prodigious extravagance in reshooting scenes tended to diminish with talkies, but dialogue presented its own problems. One scene in *Dr Strangelove* (GB 63) was shot 48 times because Sterling Hayden, playing the mad base commander, fluffed his lines 47 times. Marilyn Monroe did 59 takes of a scene in *Some Like It Hot* (US 59) in which her only line of dialogue was 'Where's the Bourbon?' Even less demanding scenes can occupy a whole day's shooting. On *Journey into Fear* (US 42), Orson Welles insisted on 49 takes of himself simply climbing a gangplank. He never explained what had so dissatisfied him about the first 48. John M. Stahl tried Margaret Sullavan's patience with 67 attempts to get her to smile naturally in *Only Yesterday* (US 33). On the first 66 occasions the smile lapsed into a squint.

At the other end of the scale, there have been those who earned themselves reputations as **'one-shot' directors**, notably G.W. Pabst, Cecil B. DeMille and D.W. Griffith. According to Lillian Gish, Griffith's masterwork *The Birth of a Nation* (US 15) was made with only one retake of one scene. The single repeat shot was necessitated, much to Mr Griffith's displeasure, by the fact that Mae Marsh forgot to drape herself in the Confederate flag for her suicide scene.

MAKE-UP

Make-up: Little attention was paid to make-up in films before the advent of the close-up (q.v.). **The earliest motion picture in which it is apparent that the actors are wearing make-up** (other than

---

Above left: Boris Karloff's make-up for *Frankenstein* (US 31) was a four-hour job

Above right: Fredric March's transformation from Jekyll to Hyde took four hours

Below left: It took 4½ hours daily to transform Bull Montana into an apeman for *The Lost World* (US 25)

Below right: Four hours were required for applying Jean Marais' whiskers in *La Belle et la Bête* (Fr 45)

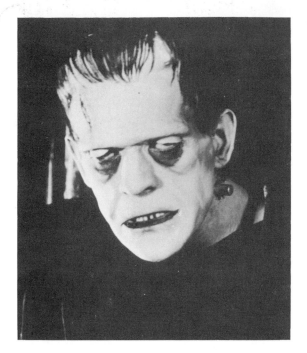

black-face or whiskers) is Edwin S. Porter's *The Whole Dam Family and the Dam Dog* (US 05), in which the cast are made-up to create the illusion of a family resemblance. The pioneer of special make-up techniques for film as opposed to stage performances was D.W. Griffith, who began experiments to achieve a more naturalistic appearance for his performers at Biograph in about 1910. Stage actress Olga Petrova recalled of her film debut in *The Tiger* (US 14): 'I noticed immediately that my co-workers wore a make-up much darker, almost a beige, whereas I wore the usual light Leichner's 1'. There was a good reason for her co-workers' departure from stage practice. The orthochromatic film stock used at this date was insensitive to the red end of the spectrum (scarlet registered as black) and consequently a heavy application of yellow make-up was necessary to create an impression of natural skin tone on screen. In British studios *c.* World War I Leichner No. 5 was most in favour.

The first studio make-up department was established at First National in 1924 under British-born Perc Westmore (1904–70). Perc later became head of make-up at Warner's, his brother Bud became head of make-up at Universal, and his other brother Wally spent 38 years in make-up at Paramount.

The largest make-up budget was $1 million for *Planet of the Apes* (US 68), which represented nearly 17 per cent of the total production cost. A team of 78 make-up artists worked under the direction of Fox's make-up specialist John Chambers, who won a special Oscar for his remarkable achievement of creating wholly credible ape faces sufficiently mobile to register the full range of human emotions.

The longest make-up job ever performed on a single artiste was the tattooing applied to Rod Steiger in Warner Bros' *The Illustrated Man* (US 69). It took make-up artist Gordon Bau and his team of eight assistants ten hours to complete the torso and another full day was spent on the lower body, hands and legs. Bau's longest job previously had been Charles Laughton's make-up for the title role of *The Hunchback of Notre Dame* (US 39), which he finished in a mere $5\frac{1}{2}$ hours.

Other marathon make-up jobs have included the 4 hours daily spent by Wally Westmore on

Klaus Kinski in *Nosferatu* (W.Ger 79)

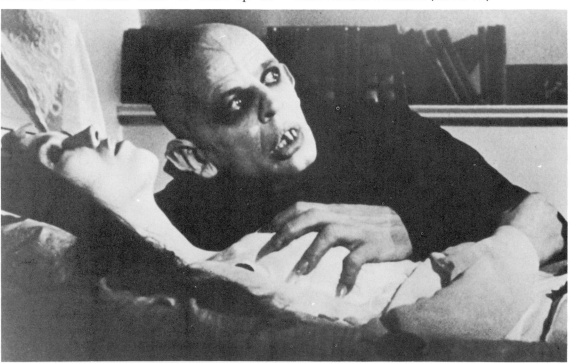

Dustin Hoffman after a five-hour make-up job for *Little Big Man* (US 70)

Fredric March's Hyde in *Dr Jekyll and Mr Hyde* (US 32); 4 hours for Boris Karloff's monster in *Frankenstein* (US 31), and a similar time for Jean Marais' make-up in *La Belle et la Bête* (Fr 45); 4½ hours on Bull Montana's ape-man in *The Lost World* (US 25) and the same for Lon Chaney in *The Hunchback of Notre Dame* (US 23); 5 hours for the principal apes in *Planet of the Apes* (US 68) and also for the 121-year-old character played by Dustin Hoffman in *Little Big Man* (US 70); Klaus Kinski's Dracula make-up for *Nosferatu* (Ger 79) also took 5 hours daily to apply as did John Hurt's deformed features in *The Elephant Man* (GB 80). Boris Karloff's make-up for *The Bride of Frankenstein* (US 35), an elaboration of Jack Pierce's original monster make-up for the 1931 *Frankenstein*, took 7 hours to complete each day. Shooting of scenes involving Karloff – he was in most – had to be delayed until 1 p.m. In the same film Elsa Lanchester's make-up as the female monster was so rigid she had to be fed lunch through a tube.

NIGHT SHOOTING

The first film shot at night out-of-doors was Edwin S. Porter's *Panorama of the Esplanade at Night* (US 01), taken at the Pan-American Exposition at Buffalo, NY, on 5 September 1901. Each frame required a ten-second exposure and it took Porter several hours to expose 27 ft of film.

The first night shooting in Britain was for *The Exhibition of Fireworks on the Occasion of the Visit of the Channel Fleet to Liverpool* (GB 07), taken by Films Ltd for the Australian Bioscope Co. and premièred at the Picton Lecture Hall in August 1907.

Feature films which played entirely at night include *Crossfire* (US 47), *The City that Never Sleeps* (US 50), and *La Notte* (It 61). Most Philippine silent movies of the 20s were made entirely at night, as the ill-paid part-time actors had to take day jobs to support themselves.

PRODUCER

The youngest producer to produce a feature-length film for commercial exhibition was 16-year-old George Palmer of Melbourne, Vic., whose thriller *The Mail Robbery* (Aus 25) was released in Victoria and New South Wales. The following year he produced, directed and starred in *Northbound Ltd* (Aus 26), a railroad drama he had written himself. On reaching man's estate Palmer retired from the film business to establish a successful travel agency, but retained an interest in experimental film-making.

Britain's youngest producer was 22-year-old Norman Hope-Bell, who made his professional debut at Cricklewood Studios with an Ernie Lotinga comedy called *Love Up the Pole* (GB 36).

The first woman producer was Alice Guy (see p. 133), who founded the Solax Co. at Flushing, New York, on 7 September 1910. The first of nearly 300 short films produced by her in the next three years was *A Child's Sacrifice* (US 10), starring 'The Solax Kid' (Magda Foy), which was released on 21 October 1910.

The first feature film produced by a woman was Eros Films' *The Definite Object* (GB 20), a gangster movie set in New York produced by Countess Bubna.

The first talkie produced by a woman was Elinor Glyn's Talkicolor production *Knowing Men* (GB 30), with Carl Brisson and Elissa Landi. She also directed. **The first Hollywood talkie by a woman** was Elsie Janis's *Paramount on Parade* (US 30), which was released in April 1930, two months after Miss Glyn's picture.

SCHEDULES

The longest production schedule for a feature movie was the 18 years it took to complete Alvaro Henriques Goncalves' *Presente de Natal* (Br 71). Goncalves, a lawyer by profession, worked on his full-length animated feature single-handed.

The longest production schedule for a dramatic film in terms of start date and completion date was 13 years for Leni Riefenstahl's *Tiefland* (W.Ger 53). Production of what promised to be the most expensive talkie then made was suspended in 1942 after expenditure of 5 million RMs and the complete breakdown of the director's health. At the end of the war Frl. Riefenstahl was banned from working in the film industry, but following her de-Nazification in 1952 she succeeded in reassembling the original cast and completed the film. It recouped its cost but Frl. Riefenstahl, dissatisfied with her work, then withdrew the picture from distribution and it has not been shown since.

The longest continuous production schedule for a dramatic film was the 8 years 20 days (6 May 1956–26 May 1964) it took Kevin Brownlow and Andrew Mollo to complete their fantasy of a Nazi-occupied Britain, *It Happened Here* (GB 66).

Other protracted production schedules have included 11 years (1925–36) for Ladislas Starewitch's animated puppet film *Le Roman de Rénard* (Fr 40), 9 years for Léon Delbrove's documentary *Un Jour, Le Genie des Hommes* (Belg 47), 7 years for Michael Kohler's *The Experiencer* (GB 77) and Harry Hoyt's *The Lost World* (US 25), 5 years for George Stevens' *The Greatest Story Ever Told* (US 65) and *Eraserhead* (US 77), 4 years for Mel Ferrer's *Vendetta* (US 50), Rudall Hayward's *On the Friendly Road* (NZ 36), Francis Ford Coppola's *Apocalypse Now* (US 79) and Joseph L. Mankiewicz's *Cleopatra* (US 63), and over 3 years for Howard Hughes' *Hell's Angels* (US 30), John Carpenter's *Dark Star* (US 74), Jack Hazan's *A Bigger Splash* (GB 74) and *The Fate of Lee Khan* (HK 73).

Potentially the longest production schedule for a dramatic film is the 15 years that David Carradine anticipates his *Mata Hari* (US) will be in production. Begun in 1978, the film stars Carradine's daughter Calista, who is playing the title role from her own and Mata Hari's age of 16 through to 31, the age at which the Dutch-born spy was executed – a unique instance of natural ageing over the time-span of a single film.

The shortest shooting schedule for a full-length, commercial feature film made without the use of stock footage was two days in the case of Roger Corman's *The Little Shop of Horrors* (US 60). The story is about a Jewish florist (Jonathan Haze) on New York's Lower East Side who accidentally revives a withering plant of indeterminate species when he waters it with blood from a cut finger. The plant's insatiable and ever-growing appetite for human blood can only be satisfied by feeding it corpses and the florist proceeds to exterminate his neighbours in order to accommodate it. Retribution comes in a not unexpected dénouement when the predator falls victim and is consumed by the object of his adoration.

The shortest production schedule for a full-length feature film was for *Twist Around the Clock* (US 61), released 28 days after Chubby Checker reached No. 1 in the charts and gave Sam Katzman the idea of making a movie to cash in on the new dance craze. Chubby Checker starred.

SET

The largest film set ever built was the 1312 by 754 ft (400 × 230 m) Roman Forum designed by Veniero Colosanti and John Moore and built on a 55-acre site at Las Matas, outside Madrid, for the last great Hollywood epic of the ancient world, Samuel Bronston's production of *The Fall of the Roman Empire* (US 64). Commencing 10 October 1962, 1100 workmen spent seven months laying the surface of the Forum with

170000 cement blocks, erecting 22000ft (6705m) of concrete stairways, 601 columns and 350 statues, and constructing 27 full size buildings. The highest point on the set was the Temple of Jupiter, whose bronze equestrian statues surmounting the roof soared 260ft (79m) above the paving of the Forum.

The largest indoor set was the UFO landing site built for the climax of Stephen Spielberg's *Close Encounters of the Third Kind* (US 77). With a height of 90ft (27m), length of 450ft (137m) and 250ft (76m) breadth, the set was constructed inside a 10 million cubic ft dirigible hangar at Mobile, Alabama, which had six times the capacity of the largest sound stage in Hollywood. The structure included four miles (6·4km) of scaffolding, 16900 sq ft of fibreglass, 29500 sq ft of nylon canopy and 'enough concrete to make a full-scale replica of the Washington monument'.

Samuel Bronston's massive set for *The Fall of the Roman Empire* (US 64). It was the largest ever built

The largest single structure ever built as a movie set was the vast 450ft (137m) long, 90ft (27m) high medieval castle designed by Wilfred Buckland and erected at Pasadena, California, for Douglas Fairbanks' version of *Robin Hood* (US 22). No record survives of its other dimensions, but to be in proportion it must have been at least as big as the *Close Encounters* set (see above), which was exactly the same height and length.

The smallest set used for the entire action of a movie – in terms of confined acting space – was the lifeboat containing the nine protagonists of Alfred Hitchcock's *Lifeboat* (US 44).

Films which have been made on a single set include the submarine drama *Umini sul fondo* (It 41), the underground railway dramas *Subway Express* (US 31) and *Dutchman* (GB 66) and the Spanish pictures *Historia de una escalera* (Sp 50), set on a staircase, and *Noventa minutos* (Sp 50), which took place in a cellar. Alfred Hitchcock's *Rope* (US 48), the story of an unmotivated murder by two homosexual college men, takes place entirely in the room of the

apartment in which the crime was perpetrated and his *Lifeboat* (US 44) was confined to the craft of the title. Another Hitchcock movie, *Rear Window* (US 54), has been described as a single set movie, but there is a brief scene in the murderer's apartment. Roman Polanski's *Repulsion* (GB 65) was set in the London flat in which Catherine Deneuve nurses her psychosis and murders sundry visitors, and Fassbinder's *The Bitter Tears of Petra von Kant* (W.Ger 72) was another study of flat-bound neurosis. *La Morte al lavoro* (It 78), *Inserts* (GB 75), *La Droleuse* (Fr 78) and *Yaadein* (India 64) were one-room dramas, while Kostas Sfikas' *Model* (Greece 74) took place entirely in a factory yard unpeopled by human beings (there were some robots). *The Office Party* (GB 76) is set, as the title

suggests, in an office: an economy further enhanced by the fact that Oppidan Films used the freshly-painted production office of Oppidan Films as their single location.

STUDIOS

The first film studio in the world was Thomas Edison's *Black Maria*, a frame building covered in black roofing-paper, built at the Edison Laboratories in West Orange, NJ, and completed at a cost of $637·67 on 1 February 1893. Here Edison made short vaudeville-act films for use in his Kinetoscope, a peep-show machine designed for amusement arcades. The building was so constructed that it could be revolved to face the direction of the sun.

The first studio in Europe and **the first in the world in which films were made by artificial light** was opened by Oskar Messter at 94a Friedrich Strasse, Berlin in November 1896. For illumination Messter used four Körting & Matthiessen 50-amp arc-lamps on portable stands. His earliest productions by artificial light included *From Tears to Laughter* (Ger 96) and *Lightning Artist Zigg* (Ger 96). The first artificially lit studio in the USA, the Biograph Studio at 11

Above left: The largest structure ever built for a movie – the medieval castle erected at Pasadena, California, for Douglas Fairbanks' *Robin Hood* (US 22)

Below left: The single set of Hitchcock's *Rope* (US 48)

Above: Universal Studios – the world's largest

East 14th Street, New York, was not opened until 1903.

The first film studio in Britain was built at the back of the Tivoli Theatre in the Strand in 1897 by the Mutoscope & Biograph Co. Like Edison's *Black Maria*, the studio was mounted on a cup-and-ball fixture that enabled it to be turned in the direction of the sun. It could also be rocked to and fro for 'storm at sea' sequences and similar effects. The glass panels that made up the sides of the studio could be dismantled for 'outdoor' scenes.

The first purpose-built sound stage was Stage Three at Warner Bros Studios, Sunset Boulevard, Hollywood, erected in April 1927. Shooting of *The Jazz Singer* (US 27) commenced on Stage Three the following month.

The largest film studio in the world is Universal City, California, whose 34 sound stages and other buildings cover an area of 420 acres. As many as 6000 staff are employed at times of peak production. Built by Carl Laemmle, the studio was originally opened on a 230-acre lot on 15 March 1915 and had the unique distinction of being a municipality in its own right. Besides the outdoor stages, indoor studio, prop stores, processing labs, zoo and stables, Universal City had its own Town Hall, fire station and police department.

The largest studio stage in the world is the 007 Stage at Pinewood Studios, Buckinghamshire, England, which was built in 1976 at a cost of £350 000. It is 374 ft (114 m) long by 160 ft (49 m) wide and 53 ft (16 m) high. Designed by Ken Adam and Michael Brown, the stage was originally built for the James Bond film *The Spy Who Loved Me* (GB 77) and accommodated 1·2 million gallons of water, a full-scale 600 000-ton oil-tanker and three nuclear submarines. The 007 Stage is owned by United Artists and Eon Productions and is rented out to other film production companies.

SWORDFIGHTS

The longest swordfight sequence was the 22-minute climax to *Beach of the War Gods* (HK 73), in which Wang Yu as the Chinese super-patriot and swordsman Hsiao Feng destroys large numbers of hated Japanese before dropping dead himself.

The longest swordfight in a Hollywood picture – *Scaramouche* (US 53)

Surprisingly **the longest clash-of-steel sequence in a Hollywood movie** does not exceed 6½ minutes. Stewart Granger was crossing swords with an ignoble marquis (Mel Ferrer) in *Scaramouche* (US 53).

SUBLIMINAL IMAGES

Subliminal images, carried on a single frame of film remaining on the screen for 1/24th of a second, have been used in three feature films – *My World Dies Screaming*/GB: *Terror in the Haunted House* (US 58), *A Date with Death* (US 59) and *The Exorcist* (US 73). In the first named, an image of a skull was flashed on screen to invoke the concept of death, two beating hearts to represent love, and a snake to conjure up hatred. The passage of the image is too rapid for the audience to be consciously aware of what they have seen, but they are supposed to register the idea subliminally. The original system was called the Precon Process, or 'Psychorama' for commercial purposes. The subliminal shots in *The Exorcist* included images of Fr Karras's face distorted to look like a death mask and others of the word 'PIG' emblazoned on a set, but cut in and out so quickly that the audience only perceived it subconsciously.

TANK

The largest tank ever built for movie making was erected in a disused Zeppelin hangar at Berlin under the direction of art director Max Heilbronner for UFA's *Volga, Volga* (Ger 29), an historical epic about Cossack pirate Stenka Rasin. The tank, which was constructed to represent the Volga river, was 2000 ft (600 m) long.

TECHNIQUES

Unusual techniques and ideas that have been used only once:

Two versions of *The Impossible Convicts* (US 05) were made, both with the same cast and story-line, but one was shot by the curious technique of having all the actors walk and perform backwards while the camera was run in reverse, giving much the same effect as if they had performed normally. No logical explanation of this strange experiment has ever been offered.

Hollywood's only original screenplay in blank verse was by Ira Wolfert for *Force of Evil* (US 48), an MGM 'B' thriller directed by Abraham Polonsky. S.N. Behrman and Ben Hecht's script for *Hallelujah, I'm a Bum* (US 33) was in rhymed dialogue.

In *Sign of the Rose* (US 22), the hero of the film, played by George Beban, appeared live on stage for sequences in which he conducted a dialogue with himself on screen.

Broadwest's *The Merchant of Venice* (GB 16) opened with a scene of the star, Matheson Lang, negotiating his contract with the producers at his private house. *I am Curious Yellow* (Sw 67) opens beyond the contract signing stage, but the initial scene shows director Vilgot Sjöman leaving the offices of Sandrews, the production company, together with Lena Nyman, the star of the film.

A number of stage plays have been filmed without adaptation, but the only feature picture to include curtain breaks throughout was *Top Banana* (US 54).

Werner Herzog is alleged to have used the unusual technique of placing his actors under hypnosis to obtain the detached performances he required for *Heart of Glass* (W. Ger 78).

An unnamed Plasticon short premièred at the Rivoli Theater, New York in December 1922 allowed audiences a choice of story line, including a happy and an unhappy ending. Dual images were incorporated in a single print and the audience wore red and green anaglyph (3-D type) spectacles. When the patron looked through the red glass he saw one image on the screen; or a different image when he looked through the green glass.

André Cayatte's *Anatomy of a Marriage* (Fr 64) consisted of two full-length features about the marriage of a young French couple (Jacques Charrier and Marie-Jose Nat), one related from the point of view of the husband (subtitled *My Nights with Françoise*), the other related the same incidents from the wife's vantage point *(My Nights with Jean-Marc)*. When the film opened in New York, the two parts were shown in two cinemas half a block apart and the $3 admission was good for both.

Tom Tom the Piper's Son (US 69) was akin to a filmic version of 'ready-made art'. Director Ken Jacobs took a nine-minute film of that title dating from 1905 and stretched it into a feature-length film by showing parts of it in slow motion, freezing the action, repeating the action, dwelling on particular figures and other techniques designed to heighten the sense of anarchy he had identified in the original film.

Peter Wechsburg's *Deafula* (US 75) was a horror movie about Dracula's illegitimate son made in sign language for the deaf.

A number of one-off experiments have been made in the use of colour, some of them effective, like William Wellman's attempt to heighten the effect by using largely colourless background in *Track of the Cat* (US 54), such as snow-clad landscapes and forests, so that the occasional flash of bright colour would register more strongly. Less successful was John Huston's 'desaturated colour' in *Reflections of a Golden Eye* (US 67), which he considered to be in keeping with its story of neurosis in a claustrophobic military camp in the deep south. Objections were so loud and clear it was restored to full and glorious Technicolor. In *Il Deserto Rosso* (It 64), Antonioni painted natural objects in unnatural colours to 'alter their emotional connotations'. At the other end of the artistic as well as the colour spectrum, *Teenage Millionaire* (US 61) was made in 11 different colours by the Multicolor process, but each colour was presented separately for each of its eleven musical numbers.

The hero of *The Lady in the Lake* (US 46), played by Robert Montgomery, was never seen except in mirrors, the whole action of the film being seen through his eyes.

Cameraman David Watkin collected some mid-19th century camera lenses for use on Tony Richardson's Crimean War epic *The Charge of the Light Brigade* (GB 68). Placed behind the Panavision anamorphoser or 'squeeze lens', they helped to convey the period ambience of early photography. René Clement achieved a similar effect of an old daguerreotype by different means in *Gervaise* (Fr 55), printing his black-and-white negative on Eastman colour stock.

Split screen technique is commonly used to show simultaneous action in two places at once, but it has only once been used for the full length of a movie – in Richard L. Bare's horror film *Wicked, Wicked* (US 73). It was billed as being in 'Duo-Vision'.

John Chamberlain's feature-length *Wide Point* (US 69), starring Taylor Mead, ran on seven screens simultaneously with three different soundtracks.

Underground films have naturally spawned the most 'one-offs' – indeed almost every underground movie aims to achieve an effect that has not been presented on screen before. Thus Robert Breer's *Images by Images I* (US 54) contains a different image on each frame of the film, while Tony Conrad's *The Flicker* (US 66) consists of black-and-white frames alternated. It is claimed that the film will cause one in every 15000 people seeing it to have an epileptic seizure, though it is doubtful whether that number of people have actually seen it. No such fear should arise from viewing Nam June Paik's *Zen for Film* (Jap 6?), which contains no images at all – the film itself is perfectly clear.

Another film made without a camera was Stan Brakhage's *Mothlight* (US 63), which was 'shot' by pasting a line of moth wings and fragments of plant life onto a transparent tape and running it through an optical printer. The subject matter of George Landow's *Film in which There Appear Sprocket Holes, Edge Lettering, Dirt Particles Etc.* (US 66) is encompassed by the title.

The underground has perhaps attained its ultimate exponent with Takehisa Kosugi, whose

Film and Film #4 (Jap ??) is not a film at all – Kosugi simply runs the projector with no film in it, throwing a rectangle of light on to a paper screen.

TIME SPAN

Films with an uninterrupted narrative are few, the most celebrated example being Fred Zinnemann's classic western *High Noon* (US 52), about a marshal (Gary Cooper) preparing during the course of 90 minutes to defend the town unaided against the baddies who are due to arrive on the noon train (though actually the movie runs for 85 minutes). Others have been: Alfred Hitchcock's *Rope* (US 48), which takes place in one room during the 80 minutes running time of the film – the story is of a university professor (James Stewart) who deduces during the course of a cocktail party that two of the other guests, homosexual former students of his, have murdered their absent host; Antonio de Amo's *Noventa Minutos* (Sp 50), about people trapped in a cellar for *noventa minutos* during the Spanish Civil War; Alessandro Blasetti's *First Communion* (It 50), which takes place during the hour and a half preceding a young girl's first communion on Easter morning and is mainly concerned with the non-delivery of her white communion dress; Agnès Varda's *Cléo de Cinq à Sept* (Fr/It 62) was a 90-minute film which recorded 90 minutes (despite the title) in the life of a nightclub singer (Corinne Marchand) as she wanders through Paris awaiting the result of a cancer test; *Tant Qu'il y aura un Espoir/While Hope is Alive* (Br 71) relates the story of two poor children in the remote town of Pariquera-acu who are bitten by a venomous snake and the desperate attempts of the authorities to locate and airlift an antidote to the local hospital within the 90 minutes before the children will die.

Carsten Brandt's *92 minutter af i gaar/92 Minutes of Yesterday* (Den 78) is unique in occupying more screen time than the action of the story. The 117-minute movie tells of the encounters of a French businessman during a 92-minute stop-over in Copenhagen.

UNDERWATER FILM

The first underwater film was *The Underwater Expedition of the Brothers Williamson* (US 14), made by American cinematographer J.E. Williamson off Watling Island (the site of Columbus's first landfall in the New World) in the Bahamas in March 1914. The filming was done from a four-ton 'photosphere', a spherical chamber designed by Williamson himself which was suspended by a flexible tube from the base vessel lying on the surface. The six-reel documentary feature, which included a scene of a fight between a man and a killer shark (Williamson himself volunteered to fight the shark after the native swimmers hired for the job had deserted), was premièred at the Smithsonian Institution prior to a successful commercial release, running for seven months in Chicago and attracting capacity audiences in London and New York.

The first undersea footage shot for a fiction film was by J.E. Williamson for Universal's *Twenty Thousand Leagues Under the Sea* (US 16).

The first underwater feature in colour was MGM's *The Mysterious Island* (US 29), a Technicolor version of Jules Verne's story of a pioneer submarine journey.

WOMEN

The first film made with an all-female crew was a comedy titled *Sally Sallies Forth* (GB 28), produced with a women-only cast by the lady members of the Amateur Cinema Association. The 'directress' (as she was called) was Frances Lascott, the camerawoman Mrs A.E. Low and the title role – an inexperienced maidservant who disrupts a pompous tea party – played by Sadie Andrews. It was premièred at the Camera Club on 12 December 1928 and *Film Weekly's* male critic declared it 'a rattling good effort'.

The first professionally-made feature by women was Savithri Ganesh's *Chinnari Pappalu* (India 67), produced and scripted in Telegu by Mrs Sarojini Madhusudana Rao, with music by Mrs P. Leela and art direction by Mrs Mohana. **America's first femme production** was *The Waiting Room* (US 73), a psychological drama produced and directed by Karen Sperling (grand-daughter of Harry Warner) and Doro Bachrach. The 32-woman crew was selected from 300 applicants attracted from California, Canada, Europe and New York (where the film was made). **Other all-women features include**

Ta det Som en Mand, Frue!/Take It Like a Man, Ma'am! (Den 75), *Io sono mia/I Belong to Me* (It 78), directed by Sofia Scandurra and starring Maria Schneider, and *Rapunzel Let Down Your Hair* (GB 78).

BLUNDERS

The most frequent mistakes made in movies are microphone booms visible within the frame, and camera crews reflected in plate-glass windows. Other blunders are legion. Some of the choicest include:

● In *Jaws* (US 75), when the citizens of Amity celebrate 4 July, there are no leaves on the trees. (The scene was shot in May.)

● The dramatic scene at the Mount Rushmore cafeteria in Hitchcock's *North by Northwest* (US 59), where Eve Marie Saint fires a gun loaded with blanks at Cary Grant in order to simulate murder, is marred by the fact that an onlooker, a small boy, is sitting with his fingers in his ears *before* Miss Saint aims and fires.

● In another Hitchcock movie, *Psycho* (US 60), a bad blunder was happily spotted by the director's wife Alma at the final print stage. She noticed that Janet Leigh swallowed *after* being murdered in the shower. The scene was doctored and the film released without flaw.

● In *Where Love Has Gone* (US 64) Michael Connors upsets a cup of coffee at breakfast; the stain has mysteriously disappeared by the next scene.

● A possibly unique example of an incorrectly spelt main title is Francois Truffaut's *La Sirène du Mississipi* (Fr 69). The American state has two p's.

● In *Fury* (It/GB 73) a Russian female serf is flogged supposedly to the point of death, but when her naked back is exposed it bears but a single welt.

● Mikhail Romm's *The Thirteen* (Rus 36) was so titled because it was supposed to be about a desert patrol of 13 soldiers. In fact anyone in the audience who bothered to count would have noticed that there were only twelve soldiers.

● In *Ohm Krüger* (Ger 41), a nurse is seen reading the news to the exiled Kruger from the *front* page of *The Times*, London.

● The action of *The Sound of Music* (US 65) is set in the 1930s, yet in one scene an orange box can be discerned stamped 'Produce of Israel'.

● In *War Hawks* (GB 27), an RFC plane rams another in mid-air and then lands undamaged. In another flying picture of the same year, *The Flight Commander* (GB 27), the hero takes off in a Moth and lands in a DH50.

● The Good King in *Saint Wenceslas* (Cz 29) wore a wristwatch.

● In *Eye of the Cat* (US 69), Gayle Hunnicutt is barefoot one moment and wearing tights the next.

● Director Stephen Spielberg is visible standing at the side of a shot during the final car chase sequence of *Duel* (US 71). The reason for the error getting through was because the film was shot in widescreen, but the rushes were viewed in 'academy frame' format – hence the sides of the picture did not show.

● A tablecloth on which Jeanne Moreau is attempting to play cards keeps disappearing and reappearing again in *The Immortal Story* (Fr 68); in *Seconds* (US 66) Rock Hudson's headrest on his aeroplane seat does a similarly recurring vanishing trick.

● Wendy Barrie pays for a 75c jar of preserves with a single coin in *Love on a Bet* (US 36).

● One character in *Cruisin' '57* (US 75), set in 1957, is seen wearing an Evel Knievel T-shirt.

● In *Cry Terror* (US 58) the car driven by Rod Steiger and the car carrying the FBI both have the same licence plate number. *Come to the Stable* (US 49) is set in Bethlehem, NH; the jeep driven by the local nuns had a licence plate with the registration Bethlehem, Pa.

● The prehistoric man thawed back to life in *Return of the Ape Man* (US 44) is wearing cotton underwear beneath his animal skins.

● At the end of *Viva Villa* (US 34), Wallace Beery is ceremoniously invested with a medal he has been seen wearing earlier in the film.

● Maid Marian wears a dress with a zip fastener in *The Story of Robin Hood and His Merrie Men* (GB 52).

● In *Written on the Wind* (US 56), Dorothy Malone's apartment starts as a basement and later elevates itself to the second floor.

● Hugh Griffith utters the words 'By the Beard of the Prophet' in *Ben-Hur* (US 59). The Prophet, Mohammed, was born 600 years after the period of the film.

● In *Shop Worn Angel* (US 30), set in 1917, a maid tells her mistress she can only have one lump of sugar in her tea because 'President Hoover says we must economise'. Woodrow Wilson was President in 1917, Hoover at the time the film was made.

● As Lee Remick and George Segal travel down the Hudson River in a police launch in *No Way to Treat a Lady* (US 68), they pass the stationary Queen Mary twice – without turning round.

● Tyre tracks are clearly visible on the stagecoach route in *Stagecoach* (US 66).

● In a scene set in 1945 in *The Godfather* (US 72) there is an American flag with 50 stars.

● The number of the address on a telegram received by Rose in *Gypsy* (US 62) does not correspond with the number on the front door.

● In a scene in *Butterfield 8* (US 60) Elizabeth Taylor stands alone in front of a mirror – alone except for the crew member whose hairy arm is also reflected in the mirror.

● Jackie Cooper tore open a sealed envelope in *Buttons* (US 28), read the letter, then put it back in the envelope and *stuck the flap down*.

● In *A Girl in Every Port* (US 28), Victor McLaglen fell into the water, climbed out, reached for cigarettes and matches from his pocket and lit up.

● The main titles of Paramount's *Badge 373* (US 73) stated that the film was 'inspired by the exploits of Eddie Egan' (the real life NY cop also depicted in *The French Connection* (US 71)); the end titles warn that 'any similarity to actual persons or events is unintentional'. A similar disclaimer at the end of *Marie Antoinette* (US 38) was spotted by an historically minded MGM executive and removed in time.

● A calendar in *This Property is Condemned* (US 66) identifies the period as August 1931. When Natalie Wood and Robert Redford go to the cinema it is to see *One Way Passage* (US 32), released 14 months later. In *Bridge of the Sun* (US 61), set in 1935, Carroll Baker and James Shigeta see Garbo's *Camille* (US 36). Tom Drake, playing Richard Rodgers in *Words and Music* (US 48), also went to see *Camille*. He was able to take in the movie at Radio City Music Hall, even though it was playing the Capitol.

● In *The Barbarian and the Geisha* (US 58) John Wayne absentmindedly addressed Sam Jaffe, playing a character called Henry Heuken, as Sam instead of Henry.

● In *The White Heather* (US 19) a *fox-hound* retrieves grouse.

CHAPTER 8

COLOUR, SOUND AND SCOPE

COLOUR

The first commercially successful natural colour process was two-colour Kinemacolor, developed by George Albert Smith of Brighton for the Urban Trading Co., London. Smith made his first colour film by this process outside his house at Southwick, Brighton, in July 1906. It showed his two children playing on the lawn, the boy dressed in blue and waving a Union Jack, the girl in white with a pink sash.

The first commercially produced film in natural colour was G.A. Smith's *A Visit to the Seaside* (GB 08), an eight-minute short featuring the White Coons pierrot troupe and the Band of the Cameron Highlanders which was trade shown in September 1908. Taken at Brighton, it showed children paddling and eating ice cream, a pretty girl falling out of a boat, and men peeping at the Bathing Belles changing in their bathing machines. The first public presentation of Kinemacolor before a paying audience took place at the Palace Theatre, Shaftesbury Avenue, on 26 February 1909 and consisted of 21 short films, including scenes taken at Aldershot, sailing at Southwick, the Water Carnival at Villefranche and the Children's Battle of Flowers at Nice.

The first dramatic film in natural colour was the Kinemacolor production *Checkmated* (GB 10), directed by Theo Bouwmeester, who also played the lead role of Napoleon. **The first American dramatic film in natural colour** was Eclair's Kinemacolor production *La Tosca* (US 12), with Lillian Russell. A total of 54 dramatic films were produced in Kinemacolor in Britain from 1910–12. In the USA there were only three dramatic productions in Kinemacolor besides *La Tosca*. These were *Mission Bells* (US 13), *The Rivals* (US 13) and *The Scarlet Letter* (US 13), the latter starring D.W. Griffith's wife Linda Arvidson.

The first full-length feature film in colour was a five-reel melodrama, *The World, the Flesh and the Devil* (GB 14), produced by the Union Jack Co. in Kinemacolor from the play by Laurence Cowen. Starring Frank Esmond and Stella St Audrie, it opened at the Holborn Empire on 9 April 1914 billed as 'A £10 000 Picture Play in Actual Colours' in 'four parts and 120 scenes'. Like most of the Kinemacolor dramas, the acting and direction (F. Martin Thornton) were execrable, the colour impressive.

Kinemacolor was an additive process in which both filming and projection were done through red and green filters. The drawbacks were the cost of the special projector used and the wear on the film, which passed through the projector at twice normal speed. Nevertheless, it was installed at some 300 cinemas in Britain and achieved success overseas as well, notably in the United States and Japan. On the production side Kinemacolor was limited in its application because it could not be used for indoor work. There was also a virtue to this, since it encouraged location shooting at a time when black-and-white productions were becoming progressively more studio-bound. One enterprising Kinemacolor venture was **the first colour western**, Theo Bouwmeester's *Fate* (GB 11), set in Texas but filmed in Sussex! Kinemacolor

The first all-colour talkie – Warner's *On With the Show* (US 29)

was particularly well suited for films of pageantry, two of the most successful releases being a newsreel of King Edward VII's funeral in May 1910 – at which no less than nine kings were present – and a spectacular two-hour presentation of the 1912 Delhi Durbar. Others included the Coronation of King George V, the Naval Review of June 1911 and the Investiture of the Prince of Wales at Caernarvon. Production came to a halt when Charles Urban, the guiding spirit behind Kinemacolor, left for the US in 1914 to propagate the British war effort through films.

The first colour talkie was Frans Lundberg Films' *Vals ur Solstrålen* (Sw 11), directed by Ernst Dittmer and starring Rosa Grünberg, which was premièred at the Stora Biografteatern in Malmö, Sweden, on 1 May 1911. The 215 ft short was made by the Biophon synchronised-disc sound process. The colour process is not recorded, but it was probably stencilled.

The first feature-length sound film in colour was MGM's two-colour Technicolor production *The Viking* (US 28), directed by R. William Neill with Donald Crisp as Leif Ericsson, the

legendary discoverer of America, and Pauline Starke as the lovely Helga. It was premièred on 2 November 1928 with synchronised score and sound effects.

The first all-colour talkie feature was Warner Bros' two-colour Technicolor musical *On With the Show* (US 29), directed by Alan Crosland with Betty Compson and Joe E. Brown, which was premièred at the Winter Garden, New York, on 28 May 1929.

The first British talking feature in colour was Talkicolor's *Knowing Men* (GB 30), produced, directed and scripted by Elinor Glyn from her own novel in French and English versions with Danish star Carl Brisson playing opposite Austrian actress Elissa Landi. Although made in colour, the film was released in black-and-white. The first to be released in colour was BIP's *A Romance of Seville* (GB 29), which was originally shown as a silent in 1929 but had sound added in July 1930. Colour process unknown. **The first film made as a talkie to be**

released in colour was BIP's *Harmony Heaven* (GB 30), a musical about a composer (Stuart Hall) who wins fame and the hand of his girl (Polly Ward) despite the attentions of a flirtatious socialite (Trilby Clark).

The first Technicolor film was *The Gulf Between* (US 17), a five-reeler starring Grace Darmond and Niles Welch, produced by the Technicolor Motion Picture Corporation in a two-colour additive process and premièred at the Aeolian Hall, New York, on 21 September 1917. It was **the first full-length colour feature produced in the USA** and the third in the world.

The first feature in subtractive Technicolor was Chester Franklin's *The Toll of the Sea* (US 22),

---

Britain's first colour talkie – *Harmony Heaven* (GB 30). Director Thomas Bentley had directed the first British feature film 18 years earlier *(Backnumbers)*

Two-colour Technicolor achieved success with the development of the subtractive process – now the print itself was coloured, whereas before the colour had to be added with filters. First Technicolor picture in the subtractive process was Chester Franklin's *The Toll of the Sea* (US 22)

---

starring Anna May Wong, which was premièred at the Rialto Theatre, New York, on 26 November 1922. **The first Technicolor interior shots** were taken for a colour sequence in *Cytherea* (US 24).

The Technicolor Motion Picture Corporation had been founded by Dr Herbert Kalmus of the Massachusetts Institute of Technology in 1915. The earliest Technicolor process was not unlike Kinemacolor and depended on the use of filters on both camera and projector. Following his development of a reasonably successful two-colour subtractive process, Dr Kalmus took Technicolor to Hollywood in 1923. The main problem was that the double-coated film was given to cupping and scratched more easily than monochrome. To most producers the cost at 27¢ a foot was prohibitive, compared with 8¢ a foot for monochrome stock, but with the coming of talkies the feverish search for novelty by the major studios encouraged its use and 33 all-colour Technicolor features were made in the three years 1929–31.

The first film in three-colour Technicolor was Walt Disney's Silly Symphony cartoon *Flowers and Trees* (US 32), premièred 17 July 1932 at Grauman's Chinese Theatre, Hollywood. The first dramatic subject was *La Cucaracha* (US 34), released at the RKO-Hill Street Theater, Los Angeles, on 15 November 1934 and the first three-colour Technicolor sequence in a feature was in MGM's *The Cat and the Fiddle* (US 34).

The first feature made entirely in three-colour Technicolor was Rouben Mamoulian's *Becky Sharp* (US 35) with Cedric Hardwicke and Miriam Hopkins. **The first in Britain** was *Wings of the Morning* (GB 37), a race-track drama starring Henry Fonda and French actress Annabella, which opened at the Gaumont, Haymarket, in May 1937.

The first three-colour film stock which could be used in any standard 35mm camera was Technicolor Monopack, which was used for the first time on the exterior shots of *Lassie Come Home* (US 42). Formerly special cameras had to be rented for colour work.

Best Technicolor film: Natalie Kalmus, head of the Technicolor colour consultants seconded to all productions in Technicolor, nominated as the best Technicolor film of all time *The Red Shoes* (GB 48).

The last two-colour films were the Republic B movies *Daniel Boone* (US 57), *Trailblazer* (US 57), *Spoilers of the Forest* (US 57), and *Accused of Murder* (US 57), released in Cinecolor.

Cinecolor and similar two-colour processes were able to reproduce hues of orange, pink, green, blue-green, brown and muted red. Three-colour processes like Technicolor added pure red, pure blue, pure yellow, violet, purple and grey to the range attainable.

Most widely used colour process: Technicolor held almost a monopoly of the three-colour field from 1932 until 1952, when *Royal Journey* (Can 52) was released in Kodak's new Eastman Color process. Within three years Technicolor had fallen into second place, with 112 films being produced in Eastman Color in 1955 against 90 in Technicolor. Eastman Color is now used for virtually all colour films produced in the West. Metrocolor, Warnercolor and De Luxe are all processes using Eastman Color stock and films credited 'Color by Technicolor' are generally made with Eastman Color negative but printed by Technicolor laboratories.

Shooting *Becky Sharp* (US 35) with the giant three-colour Technicolor camera

The shortest colour sequence consisted of two frames of Alfred Hitchcock's *Spellbound* (US 45). Towards the end of the film, a split-second scene of a gun blast was presented in vivid red Technicolor.

Decline of black and white films: Not surprisingly the USA was the first country to produce more films in colour than black and white, the 50–50 stage being reached *c.* 1955. Elsewhere colour was not considered appropriate to naturalistic, 'social realism' films or to subjects of serious concern. It was only in the 1960s, when colour television and the increasing use of colour in magazines made anything in monochrome unacceptable, that colour movies became omnipresent. In Britain colour became predominant in 1965, when 46 colour films were produced against only 34 monochrome. Only three years later monochrome production was down to a single picture, with 72 colour releases. 1969 was the first year in which British production was 100 per cent colour. France, long the bastion of grainy monochrome effects, had succumbed by 1967, when only four out of 120 films were shot in black and white. Japan had reached a 50–50 stage by 1965, but within three years the proportion of monochrome features had dropped to 25 per cent. Italy maintained some black-and-white feature production up to 1968, when seven out of 153 films were shot in monochrome, but very few after that. In 1978 *Variety*, which reviews virtually all films either made in or imported to the USA, covered only five 35 mm pictures shot in monochrome. Two of these were from Germany, one from Italy, one from Vietnam, and one a domestic product – *Hot Tomorrows* (US 78).

COLOUR FILM PRODUCTION: GREAT BRITAIN 1937–69		
	Colour	*B & W*
1937	2	174
1938	3	131
1939	3	81
1940	1	49
1941	0	46
1942	1	38
1943	1	46
1944	1	34
1945	2	37
1946	6	35
1947	3	55
1948	7	67
1949	6	95
1950	5	76
1951	7	68
1952	14	87
1953	14	88
1954	32	78
1955	33	62
1956	35	56
1957	31	84
1958	23	88
1959	24	75
1960	20	90
1961	32	77
1962	25	101
1963	31	76
1964	34	41
1965	46	34
1966	58	11
*1967	84	6
1968	72	1
1969	86	0

Since 1970 nearly all production has been in colour.

* Colour television introduced in Britain

SOUND

The first presentation of sound films before a paying audience was made by Oskar Messter at 21 Unter den Linden, Berlin, in September 1896. The sound system employed synchronised Berliner discs, but there is no record of the titles of the films or the performers in them. **The first artistes known to have performed in a**

Oskar Messter making an early sound film at his Berlin studios in 1906. This was probably a synchronised song picture

sound film were Giampetro and Fritzi Massary, who appeared in a scene from an operetta filmed by Max Skladanowski, probably before the end of 1896.

The earliest known talking films were presented by Clément Maurice of the Gaumont Co. at the Phono-Cinéma-Théâtre of the Paris Exposition on 8 June 1900. They included: Sarah Bernhardt and Pierre Magnier in the duel scene from *Hamlet*, playing Hamlet and Laertes respectively; Coquelin in Rostrand's *Cyrano de Bergerac*; Coquelin and Mesdames Esquilar and Kervich in Molière's *Les Précieuses Ridicules*; Felicia Mallet, Mme Reichenberg and Gabrielle Réjane of the Comédie Française in scenes from *Madame Sans-Gêne* and *Ma Cousine*. In addition there were synchronised opera films (q.v.) and ballet films (q.v.).

The earliest known talking film with original dialogue was *Lolotte* (Fr 00), a comedy written and directed by Henri Joly and premièred at the Théâtre de la Grande Roue at the Paris Exposition. The scene takes place in a hotel bedroom and is played by three characters, a newly-married couple and the patron of the hotel, the latter performed by Joly himself. The dialogue script survives.

The first sound films produced in Britain were a series of song subjects made by Walter Gibbons in the autumn of 1900 under the name of Phono-Bio-Tableaux Films. They included Vesta Tilley singing *The Midnight Son, Algy the Piccadilly Johnny* and *Louisiana Lou* and G.H. Chirgwin giving a soulful rendering of *The Blind Boy*. There was also an actuality with sound effects titled *Turn Out the Fire Brigade*. **The earliest British talking film** was Hepworth's Vivaphone version of *Cinderella* (GB 13) with Gertie Potter.

The first sound-on-film process was patented by French-born Eugene Lauste of Stockwell, London, on 11 August 1906. It was not until 1910, however, that Lauste succeeded in recording and reproducing speech on film, employing an electromagnetic recorder and string galvanometer. He used a French gramophone record, selected at random, for the initial trial, and by coincidence the first words to be heard in the playback were 'J'entends très bien maintenant' ('I hear very well now'). A colleague in the film business, L.G. Egrot, recalled visiting Lauste at his home in Benedict Road about this time: 'He had already started building his camera to take pictures and sound together, the front part of the camera allowing to test the different systems he was experimenting with for sound recording . . . Very often on a Sunday, a bandmaster friend of his, Mr Norris, would come along with his band and play in the garden of the house where, in 1911, Mr Lauste had had a wooden building erected as an experimenting studio. The machine was taken out, with all leads, some pictures would be made and some sound recorded.'

Lauste completed his sound-on-film projector and reproducing apparatus in 1913, and was about to embark on the commercial exploitation of the process when war broke out. In 1916 he went to the USA with the idea of obtaining

Eugene Lauste with his sound camera *c.* 1911

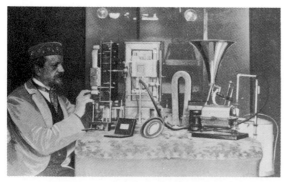

financial backing, but the entry of America into the war the following year put an end to his hopes.

The first sound-on-film productions to be presented in public were shown at the Alhambra Kino in Berlin on 17 September 1922 before an invited audience of 1000 people. The films were made by the Tri-Ergon process developed by Joseph Engl, Joseph Massolle and Hans Vogt and included **the first sound-on-film dramatic talkie.** Titled *Der Brandstifter/The Arsonist* (Ger 22), and adapted from Von Heyermann's play of the same name, it had a cast of three with Erwin Baron playing seven of the nine parts. The other films were mainly orchestral with vocal accompaniment. Press reaction was mixed, criticism being levelled not so much against the level of technical achievement, but at the notion of talking films, which it was said would destroy the essential art of the motion picture – mime – and detract from the cinema's international appeal.

The first American sound-on-film motion picture was *Lincoln's Gettysburg Address* (US 22), a monologue delivered by Ellery Paine, made by Polish-born Prof. Joseph Tykocinski-Tykociner, research professor of electrical engineering at the University of Illinois, and presented in the Physics Building on 9 June 1922. The film was not released commercially.

The first presentation of sound-on-film productions before a paying audience took place at the Rialto Theater, New York, on 15 April 1923, when Lee De Forest showed a number of singing and musical shorts made by the Phonofilm process. The sound films formed a supporting programme to the main (silent) feature, *Bella Donna* (US 23) with Pola Negri. During the following 12 months, 34 cinemas in the eastern United States were wired for Phonofilm sound. The films made at the De Forest Studios between 1923 and 1927 included monologue numbers by Eddie Cantor, George Jessel and Chic Sale; dialogues between Gloria Swanson and Thomas Meighan and between Weber and Fields; Folkina's *Swan Dance*; playlets with Raymond Hitchcock; and orchestral subjects featuring Ben Bernie, Paul Sprecht and Otto Wolf Kahn.

The year 1924 saw three notable sound-on-film 'firsts' from Phonofilm. President Coolidge was

Making a Tri-Ergon sound-on-film talkie in Berlin in 1923 *(Backnumbers)*

filmed delivering a campaign speech on the White House lawn, **the first time that a President of the USA had spoken from the screen; the first Technicolor film with a sound-track was made**, the subject being Balieff's *Chauve Souris* danced in the open air; and **the first dramatic talkie film to be released commercially**, *Love's Old Sweet Song*, a two-reeler directed by J. Searle Dawley with Mary Mayo and Una Merkel in the leading roles. Although the first to exploit sound-on-film commercially, De Forest failed to establish talking pictures as a major entertainment medium and the Phonofilm patents were eventually taken over by William Fox together with those of the Tri-Ergon system.

The first public demonstration of sound-on-film in Britain took place at the Finsbury Park Cinema on 14 June 1923, when a programme of Phonofilm shorts was trade shown. The *Bioscope*

reported: 'Several pictures were projected, including a vocalist rendering a song from *Carmen*, a dancer imitative of Pavlova with dying swan musical effects, and others. The synchronisation was as near perfect as possible, but the articulation sounded to me somewhat throaty.'

The first sound-on-film production shown before a paying audience in Britain was the Technicolor dance subject *Chauve Souris* (US 24), which was shown with musical sound-track at the Tivoli in London in the summer of 1925. **The first talking film seen by a paying audience** introduced a programme of Phonofilm singing and orchestral shorts prèmiered at the Empire, Plumstead on 4 October 1926 and consisted of Sidney L. (now Lord) Bernstein explaining how Phonofilm worked.

The first sound-on-film talkie produced in Britain was De Forest Phonofilms' *The Gentleman* (GB 25), a comedy short directed and scripted by William J. Elliott. The following year four short dramas were produced at the Clapham Studios by the De Forest Phonofilm Co. of Great Britain and in 1927 there were films of Edith Sitwell reading her own poems and Sybil Thorndike in a scene from Shaw's *Saint Joan*

The first full-length feature film with sound (in part) was D.W. Griffith's *Dream Street* (US 21), a United Artists release. Described by one cinema historian as 'a dreadful hodgepodge of allegory and symbolism', it was a total failure when originally presented as an all-silent picture at the Central Theater, New York, in April 1921. After it had closed, Griffith was persuaded by Wendell McMahill of Kellum Talking Pictures to add a sound sequence. On 27 April the star, Ralph Graves, was brought to the Kellum Studios on West 40th Street to record a love song on synchronised disc, and this was included when the film reopened at the Town Hall Civic Centre on 1 May. A fortnight later a second sound sequence was added, consisting

Not an early monster movie — simple the 'horse-blankets' used at Fox Studios to sound-proof the cameras for *Song o' My Heart* (US 29)

Enterprising cinema managers with an Allefex machine could achieve almost any sound effect back in 1912 from rattling chains to a Force 9 gale

of the shouts and whoops of Porter Strong shooting craps together with other background noises, and this version opened in Brooklyn on 29 May 1921.

The only other feature movie with vocal sound prior to *The Jazz Singer* (see below) was José A. Ferreya's *La Muchacha del Arrabal* (Arg 22), starring Lidia Lis.

The first talking feature film (in part) was Warner Bros' Vitaphone (sound-on-disc) production *The Jazz Singer* (US 27), directed by Alan Crosland and starring Al Jolson, which opened at the Warner Theatre on Broadway on 6 October 1927. The initial, historic talking sequence takes place in Coffee Dan's, where Jack Robin (Al Jolson) has been singing *Dirty Hands, Dirty Face*. Amidst the applause, Jolson holds up his hands and urges: 'Wait a minute. Wait a minute. You ain't heard nothin' yet! Wait a minute, I tell you. You ain't heard nothin'. You wanna hear *Toot-toot-tootsie*? All right. Hold on.' Turning to the band, Jolson says: 'Now listen: you play *Toot-toot-tootsie*. Three choruses, you understand, and in the third chorus I whistle. Now give it to 'em hard and heavy. Go right ahead...'

The second and only other talking sequence was longer and involved a conversation between Jack Robin and his mother (Eugenie Besserer). In view of the many conflicting claims concerning the amount of dialogue in *The Jazz Singer,* it is worth recording that exactly 354 words are spoken in the two talking sequences, 60 in the first and 294 in the second. Jolson speaks 340, Eugenie Besserer 13 and Warner Oland (as the father) one – 'Stop!' The dialogue sequences were unscripted, because Warner Bros had only intended to make a film with synchronised music and singing, not a talkie. Jolson, however, ad libbed – the famous line 'You ain't heard nothin' yet' was in fact a catch-phrase he used in his stage performances – and studio head Sam Warner liked the snatches of talk enough to keep them in.

Warner Bros overcame the problem of how to take the camera booth on location with these cumbersome vehicles (*c.* 1929)

The first all-talking feature was Warner Bros' *Lights of New York* (US 28), which was premièred at the Strand Theater, New York, on 6 July 1928. Starring Helene Costello, the picture was so determinedly all-talking that the dialogue continued non-stop from opening credits to end title. Warner's billed it as '100% Talking!'; *Variety* commented '100% Crude'.

The first sound-on-film feature was Fox's *The Air Circus* (US 28), with Louise Dresser and David Rollins, which opened at New York's Gaiety on 1 September 1928. The dialogue sequence lasted 15 minutes. **The first all-talking sound-on-film feature** was Raoul Walsh and Irving Cummins' Fox western *In Old Arizona* (US 28), with Edmund Lowe and Warner Baxter, which was also **the first talkie shot outdoors**. It opened 26 December 1928 at the Criterion, Los Angeles.

The first British talking feature was Marshall Neilan's *Black Waters* (GB 29), a melodrama about a mad captain posing as a clergyman to murder people aboard a fog-bound ship. Starring John Loder and Mary Brian, the

A sound-proof camera booth at Warner's in the early Vitaphone days

picture was produced in the USA by Herbert Wilcox for British & Dominions Sono Art World Wide.

The first talkie made in Britain was Alfred Hitchcock's *Blackmail* (GB 29), produced by British International Pictures at Elstree with Anny Ondra and John Longden and premièred at the Regal, Marble Arch, on 21 June 1929. The first reel had incidental sound and music only, but the characters began to speak in the second as the plot unfolded. It was billed as '99 per cent talking', a pardonable exaggeration. The posters also carried the slogan 'See and Hear It – Our Mother Tongue As It Should Be Spoken' – a sideswipe at the American-English that had dominated the screen hitherto.

Britain's first all-talking feature was *The Clue of the New Pin* (GB 29), adapted from the Edgar Wallace novel of the same name and produced by British Lion in association with British Photophone. The film was directed by Arthur Maude, starred Donald Calthrop and Benita Hume, and was released on 16 December 1929. An undistinguished production, the film is chiefly memorable for the fact that a rising young stage performer called John Gielgud played a bit part in it.

The first dubbed film was Lee De Forest's Phonofilm production *Love's Old Sweet Song* (US 24). The film contains one exterior scene, in which Una Merkel is strolling down a street when she hears the title song being sung by Mary Mayo from indoors. Since the exterior

footage had to be shot silent, the song was dubbed in afterwards.

The first occasion on which another actor's voice was substituted for that of a member of the cast was in *The Patriot* (US 28). The performer concerned, Emil Jannings, threatened legal proceedings if the new sound-track was not erased, and the dubbed voice was removed. The first film released with a substitute voice was *The Wolf of Wall Street* (US 29), in which the heavily accented Hungarian actor Paul Lukas played a partner in a firm of stockbrokers. His dialogue was dubbed by Lawford Davidson. Happily Lukas's accent did not hinder the development of his career – he continued to play major roles in Hollywood pictures for another 40 years.

The first British film to be dubbed was Alfred Hitchcock's *Blackmail* (GB 29). The female lead, Czech actress Anny Ondra, spoke almost no English and her voice was dubbed by Joan Barry (later the mother of heiress Henrietta Tiarks). This was done by the novel method of having Miss Barry read Miss Ondra's lines into a microphone while the latter was performing.

Post-synchronisation with the same actors was first used in a feature film by Ernst Lubitsch for *The Love Parade* (US 29), as a means of freeing the camera from the constraints of the immobile sound-proof booth used in early talkies. By using a silent camera, he was able to counter the static camera positions that marred most of the pioneer sound productions and dub in the dialogue afterwards.

A new motion picture technique, borrowed from television, is **para-dubbing**. It was used for Richard Attenborough's and other English roles in Satyajit Ray's *Shatranj ke Khilari/The Chess Players* (India 78). Since Attenborough dubbed in Hindi by the normal dubbing system would have sounded absurd, a voice speaking Hindi was dubbed *over* the English voice, which was specially moderated. The effect was the same as in TV interviews where an interpreter does a voice-over translation.

The first film with stereophonic sound was the re-edited version of Abel Gance's *Napoleon Bonaparte* (Fr 27), which was presented with added dialogue and sound effects at the Paramount Cinema, Paris, in 1935. The stereophonic process used had been patented by Gance and André Debrie three years earlier.

The first American productions with stereophonic sound were the Warner Bros' productions *Santa Fe Trail* (US 40) and *Four Wives* (US 40), presented in Vitasound. The first successful system of stereophonic musical accompaniment was Fantasound, developed by Walt Disney Studios in association with RCA and first employed for the sound-track of Disney's feature-length cartoon *Fantasia* (US 41), with music by the Philadelphia Orchestra under the direction of Leopold Stokowski.

Sensurround was first used for the 'quake effects in Universal's *Earthquake* (US 74). A more sophisticated version with Sensurround music was used for *Rollercoaster* (US 77) and this was also the first time that sound effects had been recorded in the process live. Previously, both in *Earthquake* and in *Midway* (US 76), the Sensurround effects were dubbed in at the post-production stage.

Overlapping dialogue: The talking picture borrowed the stage convention, far removed

A very young John Gielgud in Britain's first all-talkie, *The Clue of the New Pin* (GB 29)

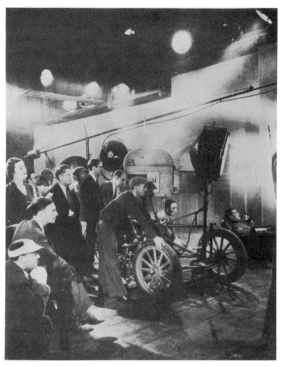

By 1931 the 'blimp' (sound-proof camera casing) had freed the camera from its confining booth and the camera dolly came into its own again. The actor in the armchair is Ramon Novarro – the picture *Daybreak* (US 31)

from reality, whereby no more than one character speaks at once. Credit for introducing overlapping dialogue in the interests of naturalism is usually given to Orson Welles for *Citizen Kane* (US 41), but in fact the technique had been used a year earlier in Howard Hawks' wild and witty *His Girl Friday* (US 40), with Cary Grant and Rosalind Russell.

Film stock with magnetic sound track was first produced experimentally by Du Pont for RCA in 1947. It was adopted by Warner Bros in 1949 and Paramount in 1950, but at this stage was used for recording only, the sound being transferred to optical tracks for projection. **The first commercially released film with magnetic track** was *This is Cinerama* (US 52).

The first use of radio microphones – 'neck mikes' – by performers on set was in *My Fair Lady* (US 64). The use of concealed microphones worn on the person enables a vocalist who is

Hollywood's last silent picture – Richard Talmadge in *The Poor Millionaire* (US 30)

moving about the set to perform a whole number in one take.

The last wholly silent film (ie without a soundtrack) **produced in America** for general distribution was George Melford's *The Poor Millionaire* (US 30), with Richard Talmadge (who played both the hero and the villain) and Constance Howard. It was released by Biltmore Pictures on 7 April 1930, just thirty months and a day after the presentation of the first talkie feature. Only four other silents had been issued in 1930, all of them low budget westerns. The following year there were no silents but four films with synchronised music and sound effects only, including Chaplin's *City Lights* and F.W. Murnau's *Tabu*. Silent production in America, however, was not finished for good. In 1950 Georges Sadoul reported that silent features in colour were being produced in San Francisco for the Chinese population of the United States.

The last British silent feature was Argyle Art Pictures' *Paradise Alley* (GB 31), starring John Argyle and Margaret Delone, the story of a miner who takes the blame when his brother shoots a man during a robbery. It was released in March 1931.

European production had made virtually a complete change-over to sound by the end of 1931. Elsewhere, the last silent feature from Soviet Russia – Alexander Medvekin's *Schastye/*

Happiness – was released in 1935 and the last seven Indian silents were issued the same year. Japan took longer to make the change. In 1937, 209 out of 524 movies were without dialogue – 50 with sound effects and music, 159 silent. The following year saw the virtual demise of the silent, with 16 'sound effects only' films and 15 wholly silent. As late as 1952 in Burma, where only two of the 22 production companies were equipped to make sound films, production totalled 40 silents and 6 talkies.

The last silent feature films for commercial distribution were produced in Thailand at the end of the 1960s. Although talkies had been produced in the 1930s, World War II totally disrupted both the Thai economy and its film industry and subsequently all films were shot silent on 16mm stock until 1965. Dialogue was supplied by actors and actresses 'live dubbing' in cinemas from a cubicle next to the projection booth. After 1965 the popularity of Indian-style musicals stimulated producers to shoot sound song-and-dance sequences on 35mm stock for interpolation with otherwise silent 16mm footage. According to the Thai Motion Picture Producers' Association 'by 1970 all Thai films were shot on 35mm with sound'.

Post-sound silents: A small number of non-dialogue dramatic films (usually with synchronised music and sound effects) have been produced since the last war. The following list excludes ballet films and similar mime productions and also the Burmese, Thai and Chinese-American silents referred to above: Russel Rouse's atomic spy thriller *The Thief* (US 52) with Ray Milland; the Bengali production *Ingeet* (India 61); the slapstick comedies *A Home of Your Own* (GB 64) and *San Ferry Ann* (GB 65); Luiz Rosemberg Filho's $2\frac{1}{4}$ hour *Imagens* (Br 72), which had no music nor sound effects; Yoichi Takabayashi's *Gaki Zoshi* (Jap 72); Andrej Brzozowski's *Obszar Zamkniety/The Closed Area* (Pol 72); the cast-of-one *Vase de noces* (Belg 73); the cast-of-none *Model* (Greece 74), directed by Kostas Sfikas; Morton Hellig's *Once* (US 74) with Christopher Mitchum; Milos Radivojević's *Testament* (Yug 75); *Robinson Columbus* (Den 75); Jérôme Savetry's *La Fille du garde barrière/The Gatekeeper's Daughter* (Fr 75); James Scott's *Coilin and Platonida* (GB 76); V. Miroshnichenko's *Lone*

Wolf (USSR 77), from the Turgenev story about a giant woodsman endeavouring to bring up his two motherless children as well as care for the estate; Gérard Myriam Benhamou's *Adom ou le sang d'Abel* (Fr 77), about Cain and Abel; and *Pentimento* (Neths 78). Mel Brooks' *Silent Movie* (US 76) nearly qualifies, but there was one word of dialogue.

LANGUAGES

Hollywood's foreign language output was confined principally to the early talkie period, the largest proportion being in Spanish for the Latin American market. Beginning with a dubbed version of RKO's *Rio Rita* (US 29), a total of 96 Spanish language movies were produced in the USA during the ensuing six years, the majority by Fox, and another 17 were made by Paramount at their Joinville studios in France 1930–33. **The first foreign language feature made in America with live dialogue** was *Sombras de Gloria/Blaze of Glory* (US 30), a Sono Art-World production.

During the period 1930–35 a total of 63 French language pictures were produced by MGM, First National, Paramount, Warner Bros, RKO, Universal, Fox, Columbia and Twentieth Century. The Paramount productions were made at Joinville, outside Paris, where they also produced in Spanish, German, Italian, Swedish, Portuguese, Romanian, Polish, Czech and Dutch.

The first foreign language talkie to be subtitled in English was *Two Hearts in Waltz Time* (Ger 29). The titles were written by Herman Weinberg (an American), who sub-titled a record number of over 400 films during the ensuing 40 years.

The first talkie produced in different language versions was British International Pictures' trilingual *Atlantic* (GB 29), which was released with separate English, French and German sound-tracks. Besides its overseas release, the German version was shown at the Alhambra, Leicester Square, to cater for the large German population living in London prior to World War II.

Multilingual films, in which foreign characters speak in their own language, were comparatively rare before *The Longest Day* (US 72) broke with former Hollywood practice by having the Germans speaking German and the French speaking French. There had been occasional examples, however, from the earliest days of sound, starting with G.W. Pabst's *Westfront 1918* (Ger 30), with dialogue in French and German. Others included Pabst's *Kameradschaft* (Ger 31), about a mining disaster involving French and German miners; Luis Trenker's *Der verlorene Sohn/The Prodigal Son* (Ger 34), in German and English; Jean Renoir's *La Grande Illusion* (Fr 37), in French, English and German; Nyrki Tapiovaara's *Stolen Death* (Fin 38), a thriller in Finnish, Swedish and Russian; *Carl Peters* (Ger 41), in German and English; *Die Letze Chance* (Swz 45), in German and French; Guy Hamilton's *The Colditz Story* (GB 54), in English and German; *La Chatte* (Fr 58), in French and German; and Jean-Luc Godard's quadrilingual *Le Mépris/Contempt* (Fr/It 63), in which Michel Piccoli spoke Italian, Brigitte Bardot spoke French, Jack Palance spoke American and Fritz Lang spoke German, the need for sub-titles being effectively reduced by Giogia Moll's role as the interpreter.

Even silent films could be multilingual. Rex Ingram stated in *Motion Picture Directing* (New York 1922) that when making films with foreign settings, he made his principals speak the language of the country. Explaining that 'it helps them materially in keeping to the required atmosphere', he admitted ruefully 'few of them like to go to this trouble . . .'

The most multilingual film producing country is India, which has produced films in the following 40 languages since 1931: Angami Naga, Arabic, Assamese, Avadhi, Bengali, Bhojpuri, Burmese, Chhattisgadhi, Coorgi, Dogri, English, German, Gorkhali, Gujarati, Haryanavi, Hindi, Kannada, Kashmiri, Konkani, Magadhi, Maithili, Malay, Malayalam, Manipuri, Marathi, Marwari, Nepalese, Oriya, Persian, Punjabi, Pushtu, Rajasthani, Sindi, Sinhalese, Swahili, Tamil, Telegu, Thai, Tulu, Urdu. Currently, the highest proportion of films are made in Tamil (1979: 140 or 19·6 per cent) and Telegu (1979: 133 or 18·6 per cent).

The only film made in a classical or 'dead' language was Derek Jarman's *Sebastiane* (GB 76), a homophile interpretation of the legend of St Sebastian, which was entirely in Latin. The translator, Jack Welch, used ingenious shifts to put Roman barrack-room language of the third century AD into comprehensible Latin, but in one instance had to resort to a Greek word, rendering the epithet *Motherfucker* as *Oedipus*. *Sebastiane* enjoys the unique distinction of being the only English film ever to have been released in Britain with English sub-titles.

The first talking film made in dialect was *Mieke* (Belg 30), a comedy made in Antwerp by Felix Bell (Gaston Schoukens) in the Anversois patois.

The only feature film made in Esperanto was *Incubus* (US 65), whose star William Shatner is familiar to TV viewers as Capt Kirk of *Star Trek*. The avowed purpose of using Esperanto dialogue was to give the movie an air of the supernatural. It is one of the few American films to have been released with English sub-titles.

Sagir Rahi starred in Britain's first Hindi movie – *Bhaag Re Bhaag* (GB 78)

The first Hindi film produced in Britain was the Cabana Film Co.'s comedy-thriller *Bhaag Re Bhaag* (GB 78), which had its world première at Leytonstone State Cinema on 4 February 1978. Produced and directed by M.A. Qayyum, it was a cops and robbers caper set in London and Epping Forest, starring Saghir Rahi and an overweight young English lady credited only as Patsy.

The first feature film in Irish was Bob Quinn's *Poitin/Poteen* (Eire 78), with Cyril Cusack as a poteen maker attempting to evade the attentions of the Garda in Connemara.

The only full-length feature film made in pidgin English was *Wokabout Bilong Tonten* (Aus 73), filmed in New Guinea with Anton Sil and Taruk Wabei in the lead roles.

The first feature film in Welsh was Tom Haydon's documentary reconstruction *The Last Tasmanian* (Aus/GB/Fr 79). The curious circumstance of a film set in Tasmania being filmed in Welsh (there were also English and French language versions) is explained by the fact that Haydon's partner in the enterprise was the Welsh anthropologist Rhys Jones.

The first feature film in Yiddish: *see* Jewish Films, p. 73.

The first Zulu language feature film was *U'Deliwe* (SA 75).

WIDE SCREEN

The first wide screen process used for a feature film was Panoramico Alberini, devised by Filoteo Alberini in 1914, which was employed by Enrico Guazzoni for a sequence of *Il Sacco di Roma* (It 23).

The first wide screen system to employ the use of an anamorphic lens – a lens that squeezes a wide image onto standard gauge film as in Cinemascope (see below) – was Henri Chretien's Hypergonar, used by Claude Autant-Lara in making *Construire un feu* (Fr 27).

The first wide screen system to use wide gauge film for feature productions was 70mm Fox Grandeur, used for *Happy Days* (US 29) and *Fox Movietone Follies of 1929* (US 29).

The first wide screen system to incorporate both wide gauge film and the anamorphic lens was

Wide screen is almost as old as the movies. This wrestling match was filmed by the Lamda Co. in 1895 for showing on the Eidoloscope projector

of almost 3 : 1. The first production in the perfected process was *This is Cinerama* (US 52), which opened in New York on 30 September 1952 and ran for 122 weeks. **The first full-length Cinerama feature** was MGM's *The Wonderful World of the Brothers Grimm* (US 62).

The widest wide screen system ever was Raoul Grimoin-Sanson's Cineorama, presented at the Paris Exposition of 1900. Ten synchronised projectors threw a 360° image onto a screen 330 ft (100 metres) in circumference. The audience sat on the roof of the projection booth, which was designed to simulate the basket of a giant balloon. The hand-coloured film took the audience on an aerial voyage of discovery, looking down on the great capitals of Europe. Unfortunately, the show had to be terminated after three performances, since the heat of the ten projectors constituted a fire risk. The concept of 'cinema-in-the-round' was not revived until Walt Disney introduced Circarama at the Brussels World Fair in 1958, though on a screen of more modest circumference.

Camera 65, later renamed Ultra-Panavision, which was originally employed on *Raintree County* (US 57).

Cinemascope was developed by the French inventor Henri Chretien from his original anamorphic Hypergonar system of 1927. Fox bought the patent rights in 1952 and the first Cinemascope feature film, *The Robe* (US 53), was premièred at Grauman's Chinese Theater in Hollywood on 24 September 1953. **Britain's first Cinemascope production** was also her first wide screen feature: MGM's *Knights of the Round Table* (GB 54), with Robert Taylor and Ava Gardner.

Cinerama was developed by self-taught inventor Frederick Waller of Huntington, New York, who had originated the idea as early as 1939 for an oil exhibit at the New York World's Fair. His intention had been to project moving pictures all over the interior surface of the oil exhibit building, but technical difficulties persuaded him to compromise with a half-dome, using eleven 16mm projectors to cover the vast area of screen. After the war he resumed work on the process, reducing the number of projectors to three and adopting a wide screen ratio

SMELLIES

The first attempt at combining an appropriate odour with a film was made by S. L. Rothapfel – the celebrated showman 'Roxy' – at the Family Theater, Forest City, Pa., in 1906. Roxy dipped cotton wool in a rose essence and strung it in front of a powerful electric fan during the showing of a news film of the Pasadena Rose Bowl Game. Similar experiments were made in 1929, when Albert E. Fowler, manager of the Fenway Theater, Boston, used a pint of lilac scent tipped into the ventilating system to accompany the credits of *Lilac Time* (US 29). Synthetic orange blossom perfume was sprayed from the ceiling when *Broadway Melody* (US 29) opened on Broadway.

The first film made as a 'smellie' was a wide-screen travelogue about China, *Behind the Great Wall* (US 59), filmed in Totalscope, DeLuxe Color, stereophonic sound and the new wonder of Aromarama. Premièred at the DeMille Theatre, New York, on 2 December 1959, the film was accompanied by a range of 72 smells that included incense, smoke, burning pitch, oranges, spices and a barnyard of geese. The process, devised by Charles Weiss, involved circulating the scents through the ventilating system. Unlike most novelty films, *Behind the Great Wall* had the smell of success even without the gimmicks. It won two awards when it was shown at the Brussels Film Exposition unaccompanied by Aromorama.

The first feature 'smellie' was Michael Todd Jnr's *Scent of Mystery* (US 60), a 70mm Technicolor thriller made in Smell-O-Vision and premièred at the Cinestage, Chicago, on 12 January 1960. The scents used – ocean ozone, pipe tobacco, garlic, oil paint, wine, wood shavings, boot polish, etc – were piped to each individual cinema seat on cue from the 'smell-track' of the film.

THREE-DIMENSIONAL FILMS

The first presentation of three-dimensional films before a paying audience took place at the Astor Theater, New York, on 10 June 1915. The programme consisted of three one-reelers, the first of rural scenes in the USA, the second a selection of scenes from Famous Players' *Jim, the Penman* (US 15), with John Mason and Maria Doro, and the third a travelogue of Niagara Falls. The anaglyphic process used, developed by Edwin S. Porter and W. E. Waddell, involved the use of red and green spectacles to create a single image from twin motion picture images photographed $2\frac{1}{2}$ in apart. The experiment was not a success, for much the same reason that 3-D failed 40 years later. Lynde Denig wrote in *Moving Picture World*: 'Images shimmered like reflections on a lake and in its present form the method couldn't be commercial because it detracts from the plot'.

The first 3-D film in colour was *Rêve d'Opium* (Fr 21), produced by the Société Azur in the System César Parolini.

The first 3-D feature film was Nat Deverich's 5-reel melodrama *Power of Love* (US 22), starring Terry O'Neil and Barbara Bedford, premièred at the Ambassador Hotel Theater, Los Angeles, on 27 September 1922. Produced by Perfect Pictures in an anaglyphic process developed by Harry K. Fairall, it related the adventures of a young sea captain in California in the 1840s. The only other American feature in 3-D prior to *Bwana Devil* (US 52) was R. William

Neill's *Mars* aka *Radio Mania* (US 22), with Grant Mitchell as an inventor who succeeds in making contact with Mars via television. It was produced in Laurens Hammond's Teleview process.

The first 3-D talkie was a De Forest Phonofilm comedy short titled *Lunacy* (US 24), which opened at the Rivoli and Rialto theaters in New York as part of the supporting programme on 22 September 1924. The 3-D process was called Plastigram.

The first feature-length talkie in 3-D was Sante Bonaldo's *Nozze vagabonde* (It 36), starring Leda Gloria and Ermes Zacconi, which was produced by the Società Italiana Stéréocinématografica at the Cines-Caesar studios. The 3-D cameraman was Anchise Brizzi.

The first 3-D talkie in colour was an UFA short titled *Zum Greifen Nah/You Can Nearly Touch It* (Ger 37), premièred at the UFA Palast in Berlin on 27 May 1937.

The first feature-length talkie in colour and 3-D was Alexander Andreyevsky's Soyuzdetfilm production *Robinson Crusoe* (USSR 47), starring Pavel Kadochnikov as Crusoe and Y. Lyubimov as Friday. The process used, Stereokino, was the first to successfully dispense with anaglyphic spectacles. Developed by S.P. Ivanov, it employed what were known as 'radial raster stereoscreens' – a corrugated metal screen with 'raster' grooves designed to reflect the twin images separately to the left and right eye. The most difficult technical problem encountered during the production of *Robinson Crusoe* was persuading a wild cat to walk along a thin branch towards the camera. After five nights occupied with this one scene, the cameraman succeeded in getting a satisfactory shot. The effect, according to accounts, was riveting, the animal seeming to walk over the heads of the audience and disappear at the far end of the cinema.

Right: The Russian process used for *Robinson Crusoe* (USSR 47), the first feature-length colour talkie in 3-D, gave stereoscopic relief without the audience having to wear special glasses

OUR VILLAGE CINEMA.

Showman. "'ERE, I SAY, IT BE 'ORSES' 'OOVES, NOT 'ORNS OR 'AIL-STORMS."

Silent movies were never wholly silent. Even the most primitive halls could usually manage something in the way of sound effects, as *Punch* portrayed in 1913

The first British 3-D films were five Stereo-Techniques shorts directed by Raymond Spottiswoode and presented in the Tele-Cinema (now the National Film Theatre) at the Festival of Britain in 1951: *A Solid Explanation*; *Royal River*; *The Black Swan* (ballet with Alicia Markova); *Now is the Time*; and *Round is Around* (animated). **The first British feature in 3-D** was Montgomery Tully's *The Diamond*/US: *The Diamond Wizard* (GB 54), a thriller with Dennis O'Keefe and Margaret Sheridan. It was released 'flat'.

The first 3-D feature with stereophonic sound was Warner Bros' *The Mystery of the Wax Museum* aka *House of Wax* (US 53). When it was premièred at the Paramount Theater, New York, with 25 speakers, the *Christian Science Monitor* was moved to deplore the 'cacophony of sound hurtling relentlessly at one from all directions'. André de Toth, director of the movie, may have been able to hear the cacophony, but was unable to see the 3-D effect, as he only had one eye.

3-D Output: During the 3-D boom that began with the low budget *Bwana Devil* (US 52), over 5000 cinemas in the USA were equipped to show 3-D movies, but the fad was short-lived. 3-D production figures were: 1952 – 1; 1953 – 27; 1954 – 16; 1955 – 1. In addition there were 3-D movies produced in Japan, Britain, Mexico, Germany and Hong Kong, but many of these (as well as some of the US productions) were released flat. Since then there have been occasional revivals, including: *September Storm* (US 60) – the first Cinemascope movie in 3-D; *The Mask* (US 61); *Wondrous Encounters of a Magician* (China 62); *La Marca del Hombre Lobo* (Sp 69); *The Stewardesses* (US 70); *Flesh for Frankenstein* (It/Fr 73); *Prison Girls* (US 73); *SoS over the Tayga* (USSR 75); *The Lollipop Girls in Hard Candy* (US 76); *Ape* (S. Korea 76); *Dynasty* (Taiwan 77); *Thirteen Nuns* (Taiwan 77); *The Porno Hostess in Three D* (It 79); *Remi* (Jap 79).

HOLOGRAPHY

The first successful demonstration of holographic film was given before the Twelfth Congress of the International Union of Technical Association Cinematographers in Moscow in 1977. The system was developed by Prof. Victor Komar of the Cinema and Photo Research Institute and gives an illusion of three-dimensional substance without the use of anaglyphic spectacles. Komar's method involved the deployment of laser beams to create a representation of objects in depth based on wave interference. If a spectator moved from one vantage position to another, he would see the object represented from a different angle, as in natural vision. **The first film made in holography** was a 30-second experimental subject showing a beautiful girl putting jewellery into a glass case. It could be viewed by a maximum of four spectators at a time.

CHAPTER 9

MUSIC

Cinema music is almost as old as cinema. Felicien Trewey's presentation of films at the Regent Street Polytechnic in February 1896, the first before a paying audience in Britain, had a piano accompaniment described in a contemporary newspaper report as 'a trifle meagre'. It was not long before presenters began to recognise the virtue of appropriate music, though whether the quartet of saxophones engaged by the Cinématographe Lumière when it opened in the Boulevard Saint-Denis, Paris, in March 1897 was able to produce something apposite for every item on the programme is not recorded. In America, Albert E. Smith of Vitagraph recalled that the first of their productions to be shown with musical accompaniment was a news film of the burial of the victims of the sinking of the *USN Maine*, premièred at a disused opera house on Lexington Avenue, New York, in March 1898 with an orchestra playing a funeral dirge. Similarly, Henry Hopwood recorded in his book *Living Pictures* (London 1899) that a news film of the Albion launch disaster, screened only 30 hours after the event, was accompanied by an orchestra playing *Rocked in the Cradle of the Deep*.

The resident cinema orchestra is recorded as early as 1901, when Britain's first picture house, Mohawk's Hall, in Islington, appointed the 16-piece Fonobian Orchestra under the direction of Mr W. Neale. This remained rare, though, until the advent of the super-cinemas after 1914, which generally employed large orchestras under competent if not distinguished conductors. At the smaller houses, a single

pianist would do the job, sometimes far from competent, but occasionally brilliant – Shostakovich supported himself while writing his first symphony in 1924 by playing the piano in an 'old, draughty and smelly' back-street cinema in Leningrad. (He lost the job a year later because he stopped playing during an American comedy to roar with laughter.) Less brilliant at the keyboard, but later to achieve celebrity in another walk of life, was the pianist at the Market Street Cinema in Manchester, about the same time. She was Violet Carson, the hair-netted Ena Sharples of television's *Coronation Street*.

Picture houses that could not afford even the meagre wages of a pianist might fall back on the humble phonograph, which was adequate only if there was no intention that the music should relate to the mood of the film being shown. The manager of the first cinema in Leicester, opened in 1906, recalled that he installed a gramophone (later replaced by a mechanical organ) operated by the girl in the pay-box, but that the choice of records bore no relation to the action on the screen, their only purpose being to drown the noise of the projector.

Inappropriate music could easily destroy the enjoyment of an otherwise meritorious picture, and in the USA the usual practice was for production companies to issue 'cue sheets' of suitable mood music with screen cues, an idea inaugurated by the Edison Co. in 1910 and copied by Vitagraph the following year. The consequence of leaving the choice of music to individual accompanists could be disastrous.

Paul McCartney's father Jim McCartney recalls leading a small orchestra providing the music for *The Queen of Sheba* (US 21) when it was presented in Liverpool. For the chariot race sequence they played *Thanks for the Buggy Ride* and for the tragic culmination of the picture, the death of the Queen, they chose *Horsey Keep Your Tail Up*.

The cinema organ had its origins in the mechanical organs acquired by the French travelling showmen of the 1890s. The earliest recorded was a Gavioli organ purchased by Jérôme Dulaar of Lyon at a price of 15000 francs (about £750) for his Théâtre Mondain in 1898.

The first cinema in Britain with an organ was the Palace, Tamworth, Staffs, where a Harper electric piano was installed *c*. 1909 with six ranks of pipes and drums believed to have been added by the John Compton Organ Co.

The first purpose-built cinema organ (ie a unit organ) was designed by Robert Hope-Jones, a Liverpudlian who joined the Wurlitzer Co. of North Tonawanda, New York, in 1910 and killed himself four years later after his employers, exasperated at the expense incurred by his constant improvements in design, had locked him out of the factory on full salary. The first Wurlitzer cinema organs were installed in theatres in 1911.

The first unit organ in Britain was a Compton 3/14 (14 units available on three manuals) installed at the Surrey County Cinema, Sutton in 1921.

Britain's first Mighty Wurlitzer was a Model D Unit Orchestra Organ, with six units on two manuals, installed at the Picture House, Walsall, Staffs, in January 1925. Although removed in 1955, the organ is still in use at the Congregational Church at Beer, South Devon.

The largest cinema organ in the world was the Wurlitzer installed at Radio City Music Hall, New York, in 1932. Still in use, it has 58 ranks of pipes controlled from either or both of the twin four-manual consoles.

Left: The Mighty Wurlitzer – a 1933 advertisement from *The Cinema Organ Herald (Backnumbers)*

The largest organ ever installed in a cinema in Britain was a Christie 4/30 (30 units on four manuals), installed at the Regal (now Odeon), Marble Arch and first played by Quentin Maclean in 1928. It incorporated a piano and a carillon, the latter feature being unique.

Mr Maclean also inaugurated **the largest British Wurlitzer**, a £15000, 15-ton, 4/21 Wizard at the Trocadero, Elephant and Castle, in 1930. Removed from the cinema when it closed in 1961, it now belongs to the Cinema Organ Society and is sited at the South Bank Polytechnic, SE1.

The only cinemas still equipped with cinema organs in Britain are the Dome, Brighton; Majestic, Cradley Heath; Regal, Eastleigh; Palace, Gorleston; State, Grays; Odeon, Hammersmith; Regal, Henley-on-Thames; Forum, Jersey; Gaumont State, Kilburn; Odeon, Leicester Square; Odeon, Southport; Granada, Sutton; Odeon, Weston-super-Mare. **The only Mighty Wurlitzer still operational in a cinema** is the 4/15 at the Gaumont State, Kilburn.

The first film music to be specially composed **for the screen** was by Romolo Bacchini for the Cines productions *Malia dell 'Oro* (It 06) and *Pierrot Innamorato* (It 06). Italy was the first country whose major films were regularly supplied with an original score, a practice that did not become widespread elsewhere until the 1920s. Notable early examples were *Lo Schiavo di Cartagine* (It 10), with music by Osvaldo Brunetti, *La Legenda della Passiflora* (It 11), for which Mazzuchi composed the music, and rival scores by Walter Graziani and Colombio Aron for the two simultaneous productions of *The Last Days of Pompeii* (It 13). Ildebrando Pizetti composed the *Sinfonia de Fuoco* to accompany the epic sequences in *Cabiria* (It 14) in which Carthage and the Roman Fleet are seen in flames, Mario Costa wrote a distinctive score for *Storia del Pierrot* (It 13) and Tosti lent prestige to *A marechiare ce sta 'na fenesta* (It 15).

The first composition for a French film was Wormser's score for Michel Carré's six-reel production of *L'Enfant prodigue* (Fr 07), the longest film made anywhere in the world at that date. It preceded by a year the score which is usually said to have been the world's first specially composed film music, written by Camille Saint-Saëns for Film d'Art's inaugural production *L'Assassinat du Duc de Guise* (Fr 08). This was an arrangement for piano, two violins, viola, cello, bass violin and harmonium. Other pioneer film composers were: Mikhail Ippolitov-Ivanov, who composed scores for *Stenka Razin* (Rus 08), Russia's first dramatic film, and for Vasili Goncharov's *Song About the Merchant Kalashnikov* (Rus 08); R.N. McAnally, whose composition, originally thought to be for the Salvation Army's *Soldiers of the Cross* (Aus 00), is now believed to have been for their similarly titled religious feature *Heroes of the Cross* (Aus 09); the Brazilian Costa Junior, composer of a score for *Paz e Amor* (Br 10), a two-reel 'talkie' with dialogue spoken by actors behind the screen; and another Russian, V. Strizhevsky, who wrote the music for *Zaporozhskaya Syetch* (Rus 11).

America and Britain trailed behind the countries mentioned above. **The first original score to accompany an American production** was composed by Walter Cleveland Simon for Sidney Olcott's *Arrah-Na-Pough* (US 11), while **the first for a full-length American feature production** was by Victor Schertzinger for *Civilization* (US 15). The same year Joseph Carl Breil became **the first American composer to receive screen credit**, for his score to accompany D.W. Griffith's *The Birth of a Nation* (US 15), but this was not a wholly original work. The 151-page score comprised excerpts from the works of a dozen famous composers, including Beethoven, Schubert, Schumann, Weber and Wagner, together with some original themes by Breil himself, notably the *Love Strain* reflecting the final love scene of the Little Colonel (Henry B. Walthall) and Elsie Stoneman (Lillian Gish).

The first composer to write music for a British film was Sir Edward German, who was paid 50 gns by W.G. Barker for 16 bars of music to accompany the Coronation scene in *Henry VIII* (GB 11). It was reported at the time that Barker 'personally supervised rehearsals of special music which he thinks important in adding to the effectiveness of the subject', which suggests that there may have been a rather more complete score than the single theme by German.

The first film music composed for a sound film was commissioned by Erich Pommer, Gaumont manager for Central and Eastern Europe, for *Les Heures* (Fr 13) aka *Die Stunden*, a 55 minute non-acted 'visual impression' of a day – morning, noon and night. The score was recorded on disc and synchronised with the film. The name of the composer is not known.

The first sound-on-film score was Hugo Riesenfeld's music for Fritz Lang's *Siegfried* (Ger 22), recorded on Phonofilm for its presentation at the Century Theater, New York, in 1925. This was a year earlier than the sound-on-disc Vitaphone accompaniment to Warner Bros' *Don Juan* (US 26), usually claimed as the first synchronised sound feature film.

The first British feature film with synchronised music was Lupu Pick's *A Knight in London* (GB 29), a Blattner Pictures production starring Lilian Harvey.

The first film in which the music was dubbed (ie post-recorded) was *Innocents of Paris* (US 29), a Maurice Chevalier confection whose success was mainly attributable to the theme song *Louise*.

The Philharmonia Orchestra recording Sir William Walton's score for *Hamlet* (GB 48) at Denham

Garbo liked to be serenaded on set. In this 1927 photograph, the girl with the megaphone is singing to her to create 'mood'

The first song specially composed for a motion picture was *Mother I Still Have You*, written by Louis Silvers and sung by Al Jolson in *The Jazz Singer* (US 27).

The first hit-song from a movie was *Sonny Boy*, also an Al Jolson number, from *The Singing Fool* (US 28), composed by Buddy De Sylva, Lew Brown and Ray Henderson. The film was released on 28 September 1928 and within nine months the sales of *Sonny Boy* records had reached 2 million, and sheet music sales $1\frac{1}{4}$ million.

The first record of a song from a movie was *Mother o' Mine* from *The Jazz Singer* (US 27), sung by Al Jolson and released on the Brunswick label on 6 October 1927 concurrently with the film's première.

The first complete score to be issued on records was Sir Arthur Bliss's music for *Things to Come* (GB 36).

The first complete score from an American film to be issued on records was Victor Young's music for *For Whom the Bell Tolls* (US 43).

The first woman film composer was Jadan Bai, founder of the Sangeet Film Co. and mother of India's superstar Nargis, who made her musical debut with the score of *Talash-e-Huq* (India 35).

The first woman composer to write a complete score for a Hollywood feature was Elizabeth Firestone, daughter of tyre magnate Harvey S. F. Firestone, who did the music for the Robert Montgomery comedy *Once More, My Darling* (US 47).

The first woman to compose for a British feature was Angela Morley, whose score accompanied *Watership Down* (GB 78).

Music on set to provide 'mood' for the performers, a common practice during the production of silent dramas, is usually said to have originated with D.W. Griffith's *Judith of Bethulia* (US 14), though the star of the film, Blanche Sweet, says she has no recollection of it. In fact the idea had originated in Europe at an earlier date, pioneer woman director Alice Guy playing a gramophone on set to assist the actors in emoting during the production of *La Vie du Christ* (Fr 06). In Britain George Pearson was the first to try it, employing a three-piece orchestra – piano, violin and viola – on set in 1916.

On occasions the practice got out of hand. Garbo was not satisfied with unadorned orchestral music and insisted on being sung to on set, it was reported in 1927. A soloist would join the studio orchestra and serenade her through a megaphone. Another demanding star caused an even greater onslaught of melody, though not entirely of her own volition. During an epic feud between Pola Negri and Gloria Swanson, whose respective egos were too great to be accommodated together in one studio, Swanson's director Allan Dwan hired a 70-strong brass band to drown the noise being made on Negri's adjacent set and persuade his opposite number to control the temperamental Polish star. In another instance the practice was itself instrumental in inflating a performer's ego to the point of affecting his career. Erich von Stroheim had commanded that whenever Anton Wawerka, who played the Emperor Franz Josef in *The Merry-Go-Round* (US 22) and in *The Wedding March* (US 28), appeared on set, the orchestra should strike up the Austrian national anthem. The custom even prevailed off set, all the Hollywood restaurants honouring Wawerka with the anthem whenever he entered their doors. The actor became so accustomed to this regal treatment that he suffered a breakdown when *The Wedding March* was completed and his imperial privileges withdrawn.

CHAPTER 10

TITLES AND CREDITS

TITLES

The Fifteen Longest Film Titles

●Lina Wertmüller's *Un Fatto di sangue nel commune di Siciliana fra due uomini per causa di una vedova si sospettano moventi politici. Amore·Morte·Shimmy. Lugano belle. Tarantelle. Tarallucci é vino.* (It 79). The English language title was *Revenge*.

●*The Persecution and Assassination of Jean-Paul Marat as Performed by the Inmates of the Asylum of Charenton under the Direction of the Marquis de Sade* (GB 66).

●*Les yeux ne veulent pas en tout temps se fermer ou peut-être qu'un jour Rome se permettre de choisir à son tour* (Fr/W.Ger 70).

●*La' il cielo é la terra si univano, la' le quattro stagioni si ricongiungevano, la' il vento é la pioggia si incontravano* (It 72).

●*Those Magnificent Men in their Flying Machines; or, How I Flew from London to Paris in 25 Hours and 11 Minutes* (GB 65).

●*Film d'amore é d'anarchia, ovvero stamattina alle 10, in via dei Fiori, nella nota casa di tolleranza* (It 72).

●*Cafeteria or How Are You Going to Keep Her Down on the Farm after She's Seen Paris Twice* (US 73). Described as 'the short and sweet story of a girl and her 26 cows', this, the longest titled American fiction film, runs precisely one minute.

●*You've Got to Walk It if You Like to Talk It or You'll Lose That Bear* (US 71).

●*Break into the Formidable Realm of Deaf Mutes under the Guidance of Mao Tse Tung Thought* (China 71).

●*I Could Never Have Sex with any Man who Has so Little Regard for my Husband* (US 73).

●*Lina Braake – Die Interessen der Bank koennen nicht die Interessen sein, die Lina Braake hat* (W.Ger 75).

●*Die Unterdrueckung der Frau ist vor allem an dem Verhalten der Frauen selber zu erkennen* (W.Ger 69).

●*The End of the World is our Usual Bed in a Night Full of Rain* (W.Ger 78). NB: English language movie.

●*Riuscia l' Avv. Benenato a sconfiggere il suo acerrimo nemico, il Pretore Ciccio de Ingras* (It 72).

●*Oh Dad, Poor Dad, Mama's Hung You in the Closet and I'm Feeling so Sad* (US 67).

The Shortest Titles have all had one letter or digit:

A (Fr 64); *A* (It 69); *B* (It 69); *C* (It 70); *D* (It 70); *G* (US 72); *G* (GB/W.Ger 74)*; *H* (US 60); *I* (Rom 66); *I* (Sw 66)*; *M* (Ger 31)*; *M* (US 51)*; *M* (Cz 64); *O* (GB 32); *O* (Jap 75); *P* (Neths 64); *Q* (Fr/It/Belg 74)*; *W* (US 73)*; *X* (US 62); *Z* (Fr/It 68)*; *$* (US 72)*; *3* (US 56).
*Features

Numbers as Titles: *1,2,3* (Hung 62); *2½* (Can 75); *3* (US 56); *3,2,1,0* (Belg 6?); *5:5* (Israel 80); *007* (India 75); *7–9–13* (Den 34); *8½* (It 63); *08/15* (W.Ger 54); *9.25* (Pol 29); *10* (US 79); *10.32* (Neths 65); *11:1* (DDR 55); *12–10* (GB 19); *13–13* (Sp 43); *14–18* (Fr 63); *21–87* (Can 63); *25* (Mozambique 76); *27A* (Aus 73); *30* (US 59); *33* (USSR 67); *33* (GB 7?); *36–26–36* (US 67); *42* (India 48); *42:6* (Swz 69); *'49–'17* (US 17); *50–50* (US 23); *58/2b* (Fr 57); *66* (US 66); *66* (US 68); *69* (US 68); *69* (US 69); *69* (Fin 69); *'70* (US 70); *96* (USSR 19); *97·217* (GB 75); *99* (Hung 18); *111* (Hung 19); *113* (Sp 35); *298* (Swz 65); *322* (Cz 69); *329* (US 15); *413* (US 14); *491*

(Swz 64); *625* (W.Ger 67); *666* (US i.p.); *813* (Jap 23); *911* (US 70); *5000* (US 70); *7254* (US 71); *7362* (US 67); *13,000* (Sp 41); *33,333* (Sw 24); *33,333* (Sw 33); *77,297* (Cz 63); *750,000* (Greece *c.* 68).

Arithmetical Titles: *1+1* aka *Sympathy for the Devil* (GB 69); *1+1* (Can 61); *1+1 = 1* (Yug 64); *1+1 = 2* (Neths 72); *1+1 = 3* (Ger 29); *1+1 = 3* (W.Ger 79); *1 = 2?* (Fr 75); *2+1* (US 68); *2+2 = 5* (Tunisia 70); *2+2 = 69* (US 68); *2×2* (Hung 44); *2×2×2 (= 2)* (It 68); *3×1 = 1* (Ger 13); *5+5* (Israel 80); *6×6* (Jap 62); *8×8* (US 57); *8½×11* (US 74); *11×14* (US 77); *12+1* (Fr/It 70); *16+1* (Jap 74).

Word Number Titles: *Two* (India 65); *Three* (GB 69); *Five* (US 51); *Seven* (US 79); *Ten* (Jap 71); *Fifteen* (Swz 68); *Sixteen* (It 73); *Seventeen* (US 16); *Twenty One* (GB? 15).

Date Titles: *1740* (Can 77); *1776* (US 06); *1776* (US 72); *1778* (Fr 78); *1789* (Fr 73); *1810* (Arg 60); *1812* (Rus 12); *1812* (Ger 23); *1812* (GB 65); *1812* (Hung 73); *1814* (Fr 11); *1860* (It 32); *1866* (It 33) – English language title; *1861* (US 11); *1880* (Fr 63); *1900* (US 72); *1900* (It/Fr/W.Ger 77); *1905* (USSR 52); *1907* (Rom 76); *1914* (GB 15); *1914* (Ger 31); *1917* (GB 70); *1918* (Fin 55); *1918* (USSR 58) – English language title; *1922* (Greece 79); *1925* (Bulg 76); *1929* (Cz 74) – English language title; *1931* (GB 32); *1933* (Can/US 67); *1941* (US 41); *1941* (US 79); *1945* (Ger 45); *1948* (Fr 48); *1958* (Nor 80); *1967* (US 67); *1968* (US 68); *1970* (US 70); *1971* (Ven 71); *1972* (W.Ger 73); *1984* (GB 56); *1985* (US *c.* 70).

The only full date title, *9/30/55* (US 77), refers to the date that James Dean was killed.

Odd titles: Writing in *Films and Filming*, David McGillivray nominated *Betta, Betta in the Wall, Who's the Fattest Fish of All* (US 69) and *She Ee Clit Soak* (US 71) as 'the most preposterous movie titles ever conceived'. Other unusual titles include *Ojojoj* (Sw 66); *RoGoPaG* (It 63); *I-Ro-Ha-Ni-Ho-He-Yo* (Jap 60); *Ha Ha, Hee Hee, Hoo Hoo* (India 55); *Sssssssss* (US 73); *Phffft* (US 54). Rather more comprehensible curiosities are *Telephone Girl, Typist Girl or Why I Became a Christian* (India 25); *After the Balled-Up Ball* (US 17); *In My Time Boys Didn't Use Hair Cream* (Arg 37); *The Film that Rises to the Surface of Clarified Butter* (US 68), but some explanation might be needed for *Egg! Egg?* (Sw 75) and *Cash? Cash!* (Belg 69). *Yes* (Hung 64) was followed by *No* (Hung 65) and the situation remained equally unclear with *Yes No Maybe Maybenot* (GB 75). Among the more disagreeable titles was the one adopted by Yoshitaro Nomura for a gangster movie he made in which the hero was a night soil collector, *A Tale of Dung and Urine* (Jap 57). Wordless titles include Warhol's well-known **** (US 67); ... (Arg 71) – the English language title was *Dot Dot Dot*; and Michael

Snow's ⟷ (Can 69). *Film without Title* (W.Ger 47) was the title of a Rudolph Jugert movie, but it was not apparent whether Vincenzo Ferrari's *Untitled* (It 73) had one or not. The makers of *Don't Worry, We'll Think of a Title* (US 65) evidently had trouble in doing so.

Title Changes

● *Livingstone* (GB 25), was reissued in America in 1933 as *Stanley*. (Livingstone was British; Stanley an American.) Numerous British films have needed title changes for the USA – *Carleton Browne of the F.O./*US: *Man in a Cocked Hat* (GB 59) and *Never Take Sweets from a Stranger/*US: *Never Take Candy from a Stranger* (GB 60) are two obvious examples, but there is only one recorded instance of a title change *within* Britain. *This England* (GB 41), a wartime flagwaver with Emlyn Williams and Constance Cummings, was retitled *Our Heritage* for release in Scotland.

● In China *Great Expectations* (GB 46) was released as *Bleeding Tears of Lonely Star*, *Nicholas Nickleby* (GB 46) as *Hell on Earth*, and *Oliver Twist* (GB 48) as *Lost Child in Foggy City*. Olivier's *Hamlet* (GB 48) became *The Prince's Revenge*.

● *Peyton Place* (US 57) played in Paris as *The Pleasures of Hell*, in Munich as *Glowing Fire Under the Ashes* and in Hong Kong as *The Cold and Warmth in the Human World*. *Guys and Dolls* (US 55) was *Heavy Youths and Light Girls* in Germany, Indonesia changed *I'll Cry Tomorrow* (US 55) to *To Relieve Yourself From the Grief of Your Passions*, while Hong Kong looked for something catchier than *Not as a Stranger* (US 55) and came up with *The Heart of a Lady as Pure as a Full Moon Over the Place of Medical Salvation*.

● *Chicago, Chicago* was not the mid-west release title of *New York, New York*, but the Spanish title of Norman Jewison's *Gaily, Gaily* (US 69).

● *Dracula 72* (GB 72) did not reach France until a year after its release in Britain. When it did, the title had become *Dracula 73*. Similarly *Airport '79* (US 78) became *Airport '80* on its belated arrival in the UK.

● The working title of *Foxes* (US 80) was *Twentieth Century Foxes* until another film company intervened.

● The Spanish word for *Grease* (US 78) is *grasa*, but this translates literally as 'fat'. In Spain the movie was released as *Brillantina/Brilliantine* and in Venezuela as *Vaselina/Vaseline*.

The only film with the main title at the end instead of the beginning was Henry King's *Who Pays?* (US 16). The picture, King's first, was about a girl who has an illegitimate baby and marries another man after the father has been erroneously reported killed. The father eventually reappears. King decided it would be more appropriate to pose the question when the audience knew why it was being asked.

Meaningless or Misleading Titles

● *The Bible* (It 13) was not a biblical epic as its title suggested, but a 6-reel melodrama which included a riot in a theatre, a revolver fight on stage, a car chase, a motorcycle blowing up, and people falling out of trains, fighting to the death in rivers, and kidnapping children. Somewhere amongst all this activity a bible was worked into the plot. Warner's *Tracked by the Police* (US 27) was a Rin Tin Tin vehicle whose title was decided before the script was written. The completed film was certainly about tracking, but the tracker was Rin Tin Tin with never a policeman in sight from first reel to last. Edgar Ulmer's *The Black Cat* (US 34) had nothing to do with the Poe story of the same name (despite a credit to Poe) and nothing to do with a black cat other than the fact that a cat crept in and out of a few scenes, irrelevantly, to justify the title.

● In the early 1930s, piracy of ideas was rife in the Indian film industry and director Dhiren Ganguly was wont to evade questions about the title of his next film with a courteous 'Excuse me, Sir' before hastily switching to another topic. After a while people began asking him when *Excuse Me, Sir* was due to be released, so he decided to call his current project by that title. *Excuse Me, Sir* (India 31), released in Hindi and Bengali versions, was one of the most successful pre-war Indian comedies.

● Equally meaningless, and for not dissimilar reasons, was the title of a Warner movie starring Errol Flynn. During the 30s there was a Hollywood convention of using the wholly fictitious title of *Another Dawn* for films purportedly showing at any cinema in a film story. When Warner's ran out of ideas for something catchy to title the somewhat slender story scheduled for Flynn's next exhibition of sexual bravado, they tagged it *Another Dawn* (US 38).

● Universal executives admitted that they had no idea what relevance *You Can't Cheat an Honest Man* (US 39) had on the subject matter, nor what writer-star W.C. Fields meant by this scarcely tenable aphorism.

● Boris Karloff barely appeared in *Abbott and Costello Meet the Killer, Boris Karloff* (US 48) and somebody else turned out to be the killer.

● Warner's *The Return of Dr X* (US 39), in which Bogart played a vampire, was not, as the title suggested, a sequel to their earlier horror pic *Dr X* (US 32), which was about a quite different kind of monster, a murderer with no arms. *Beyond the Valley of the Dolls* (US 70) was equally deceptive; it had no connection with Jacqueline Susann's *Valley of the Dolls* (US 67).

● *The Amorous Prawn* (GB 62) was about a general's wife who opens their official home in the Highlands to American paying guests. In America the title was changed to *The Playgirl and the War Minister*, despite the fact that there was no playgirl and no War Minister in the film – the date explains the choice, since 1962 was the height of the Profumo affair. Similarly *Marilyn and the Senator* (US 75) had nothing to do with Marilyn Monroe and Senator Kennedy, despite its promotors' obvious intention to mislead, and the girl entangled with a senator is not even called Marilyn.

● *The Trygon Factor* (GB 66) was about bogus nuns pulling a million pound bank raid. The words of the title were never mentioned nor explained. The title of *I'll Never Forget Whatshisname* (GB 67) had no discernable bearing on the story, nor did *Olly, Olly Oxen Free* (US 78) or *A Clockwork Orange* (GB 71). Woody Allen gave a succinct explanation of the title of *Bananas* (US 71): 'Because there are no bananas in it'.

The least compelling title: The editor would like to nominate *Chairman Mao Reviews the Mighty Contingent of the Cultural Revolution for the Fifth and Sixth Times* (China 67).

INTER-TITLES AND SUBTITLES

The earliest known use of inter-titles was by R.W. Paul in *Our General Servant* (GB 98), at 320ft the longest story film then produced in Britain. Presented in four scenes, with linking inter-titles, it related how a new maid was compromised by the master of the house. **The earliest known European example** is Georges

Méliès' *L'Affaire Dreyfus* (Fr 99) and **the earliest American example**, Edwin S. Porter's *Uncle Tom's Cabin* (US 03). **The earliest known use of dialogue in inter-titles** occurs in Edwin S. Porter's *The Ex-Convict* (US 04).

Subtitles superimposed over action – as in foreign language films today – were first used in a Lubin serial *Road o' Strife* (US 15) in order to avoid interrupting the fast-paced narrative. The only other silent picture examples known are another serial, *Judex* (Fr 17), the monumental *Ben Hur* (US 25) and *Walking Back* (US 28). The reason it was not done more often appears to be the problem presented with foreign language versions.

The silent film with the most inter-titles in relation to its length was *Every Woman's Problem* (US 25), starring Dorothy Davenport. Nat Levine, then sales manager with a Kansas City film exchange, bought the 2300 ft negative, with no titles, for a bargain basement $10000. By adding 2600 ft of inter-titles he increased it to acceptable feature length and, by choosing an enticing main title, did well enough at the box office to gross four times his investment. Levine used his profit to go into production on his own account, founding the famous Poverty Row studio of Mascot Pictures. *Every Woman's Problem* was probably the only film in which the titles occupied more time than the action.

Silent films with no inter-titles: Murnau's *The Last Laugh* (Ger 25) has often been described as the first feature-length silent movie to rely solely on the action for the development of the narrative, to the exclusion of explanatory titles. Those that preceded it were Max Reinhardt's *Eine Venzianische Nacht* (Ger 14); Alexander Tairov's *Le Mort* (Rus 15); *A Page from Life* (It 16); *Remorse* (Den 20); *The Rail* (Ger 21); *The Old Swimming Hole* (US 21); *Warning Shadows* (Ger 22); Karl Grune's *The Street* (Ger 23); Lupu Pick's *Sylvester* (Ger 23); *Lily of the Alley* (GB 23); *The Audacious Mr Squire* (GB 23).

CREDITS

The first screen credits went to André Heuzé for the films he wrote for the French production company Pathé Frères from 1906.

In the USA **the first person to receive screen

No titles were needed to convey Charles Ray's intentions in *The Old Swimming Hole* (US 21)

credits** was G.M. Anderson, as the leading man of the Broncho Billy westerns in 1908. As producer and author of the films, and part-owner of the Essany studio, Anderson was in a strong position to promote his own name. Generally performers in American films did not receive screen credit until 1911, when the Edison Co. and Vitagraph Co. led the way.

The first British film known to have included screen credits was the Gaumont Co.'s *Lady Letmere's Jewellery* (GB 08), with Maisie Ellis in the title role. The credits were pictorial, each leading character being portrayed next to a card bearing his or her name and role. It is possible that Gaumont had adopted the practice of screen credits earlier the same year when they released a film version of the Lyceum Theatre production of *Romeo and Juliet* (US 08), with Godfrey Tearle and Mary Malone. In this case the cast had been billed in the advertising for the film.

The film-maker with most screen credits was Cedric Gibbons (1893–1960), whose name appeared as art director on over 1500 films between 1917 and 1955. The feat was achieved by Gibbons' insistence on a clause in his 1924 contract with MGM to the effect that every film produced by the studio in the USA would credit him as art director. In practice the art direction for the majority of these films was in the hands of his subordinates.

The first pre-credit sequence belongs to *Destry Rides Again* (US 39). Nearly a minute of action precedes the title and credits.

The longest pre-credit sequence lasted for 17 minutes, preceding the titles of Irvin Kershner's *The Return of a Man Called Horse* (US 76), in which Richard Harris played a 19th-century English nobleman saving an Indian tribe from extinction.

The longest credit sequence lasted for 12 minutes in Sergio Leone's *Once Upon a Time in the West* (Italy/US 68).

The largest number of names credited was 457 for *Superman the Movie* (GB 78).

Unusual credits

In *The Terror* (US 28), the novelty of sound inspired Warner's to have the credits spoken by a caped and masked Conrad Nagel. Other films in which the credits have been spoken rather than written include Orson Welles' *The Magnificent Ambersons* (US 42), Truffaut's *Fahrenheit 451* (GB 66), Tony Richardson's *Hamlet* (GB 69) and Robert Altman's *M*A*S*H* (US 70). The last named had a recurring theme of the front line field hospital's nightly film show being announced over the Tannoy. The last film to be so announced is *M*A*S*H* itself, with full credits. A film called *Episode* (Austria 35) was released with conventional credits at home, but with spoken credits in Nazi Germany. In this case the reason was more sinister than a mere desire for novelty. The director of the picture, Walter Reisch, was Jewish. The credits were spoken against a musical background and when Reisch's name was reached, the music swelled to make it inaudible.

The only recorded example of *sung* credits features in *Por que te engana tu marido/Why Does Your Husband Deceive You* (Sp 69). The vocalists are a priest and his choir-boys.

Slim Carter (US 57) had novelty credits whereby the cast signed their own names on the screen.

Although performer credits have often been superimposed over the image of each performer named, only once have production credits been treated in this way. In the Douglas Fairbanks movie *When the Clouds Roll By* (US 20), the director's credit pictures him wielding his microphone, the cameraman's credit shows him grinding the camera, the scriptwriter's credit has him hunched over the typewriter and so on.

In Mike Snow's curiously titled ←——————→ (Can 69), the credits appear in the middle of the film.

Notorious credits include two for authors. *The Taming of the Shrew* (US 28) bore the attribution 'by William Shakespeare, with additional dialogue by Sam Taylor'; while *The Black Cat* (US 34) was credited to Edgar *Allen* Poe, a misspelling of his middle name. (The fact that the film had absolutely nothing to do with Poe's story did not seem to trouble anyone.)

Fritz Lang's *Hangmen Also Die* (US 43) is probably the only film with credits distinguishing the scriptwriter who wrote the script that was used (Fritz Lang) from the scriptwriter who wrote the script that was not (Bertold Brecht). Incensed that Lang had departed so far from his intended ideas, Brecht won a court decision that allowed him a credit disassociating his script from the shooting script.

Some of the odder individual credits are for 'First Aid' in Clint Eastwood's mayhem chase film *Gauntlet* (US 77); 'Technical Consultant on Vampire Bats' in *Chosen Survivors* (US 74); 'Ant Consultant' in *Empire of the Ants* (US 77); for the perfume worn by the leading players in *Marjorie Morningstar* (US 58); for the shoe polish brightening the cast's shoes in *Scent of Mystery* (US 60); for 'Spiritual Counsel' in *Hallelujah the Hills* (US 63); for 'The Assistant to the Assistant to the Unit Publicist' in *The Greek Tycoon* (US 78); and to Federico Fellini, who was not on the picture, 'for encouragement at the right time' in *The World's Greatest Lover* (US 77). 'Fangs by Dr Ludwig von Krankheit' in Polanski's *Dance of the Vampires* (GB 67)

Above: Birth of the star system. Asta Nielsen, who made a sensation with her screen debut in *Afgrunden*/*The Abyss* (Den 10), was one of the first performers to be credited by name. (See p. 86). *Below:* With *Traffic in Souls* (US 13) American movies discovered a new theme – sex! *(Backnumbers)*

Above: The Blue Lamp (GB 49) started the trend in television spin-offs. *Below: Illustrated* paid Victor Fleming's *Joan of Arc* (US 50), with Ingrid Bergman, the tribute of a cover story. *Harvard Lampoon* gave the picture a special award as 'The Worst Picture of the Century'. (See p. 240) *(Backnumbers)*

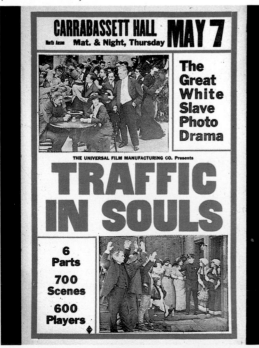

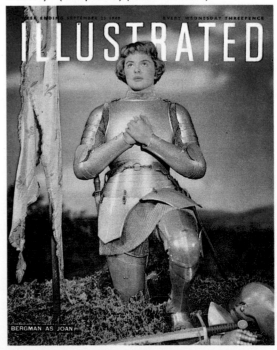

FAN MAGAZINES·
In both Britain and America the fan magazine
emerged with the beginnings of the star system.
The examples shown here are among the popular
titles which flourished in the days when the cinema
meant escape from the workday world for millions
of fans *(Backnumbers)*

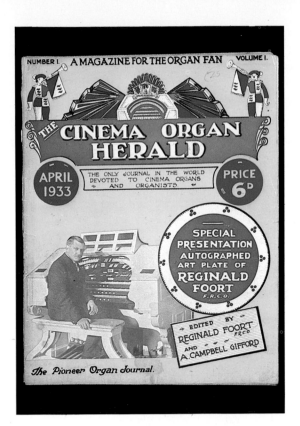

Stars of the Thirties

should probably be taken with a pinch of garlic salt.

DEDICATIONS

Dedications are still comparatively rare in movies. Among the earliest was in Dorothy Davenport's anti-narcotics film *Human Wreckage* (US 23), which was dedicated 'to the memory of A MAN who fought the leering curse of powdered death and, dying, was victorious'. The MAN was the director's late husband, Hollywood romantic lead Wallace Reid, who had died of morphine addiction at the age of 31. Other actors who have had films dedicated to them posthumously include Harry Carey (1880–1947), who played 'Cheyenne Harry' in many early John Ford westerns; Ford's *Three Godfathers* (US 49) bore a screen credit to his memory as a 'Bright Star of the early Western sky'. *The Silent Flute* (US 78) was dedicated to Bruce Lee (1940–73). Perhaps the most discreet dedication was the end credit to Robert Altman's *California Split* (US 74), which read simply 'For Barbara'. It commemorated Barbara Ruick (1933–73), wife of *Star Wars* composer John Williams, who played the character role of the casino barmaid and died suddenly on location in Las Vegas before the film was completed.

Two of Truffaut's movies have been dedicated to living performers. *L'Enfant Sauvage* (Fr 70) was dedicated to his protégée and star of the Antoine Doinel series, Jean-Pierre Léaud (1944–), while *La Nuit Américaine/Day for Night* (Fr 73) was a tribute to Lillian Gish (1896–) and her sister Dorothy (1898–1968).

The film in which Léaud had made his debut, Truffaut's *Les Quatre cents coups* (Fr 59), was dedicated to the distinguished critic and founder of *Cahiers du Cinéma*, André Bazin (1918–58). Raj Kapoor's *Satyam Shivam Sundaram* (India 77) was 'Dedicated to my beloved friend Mukeshchand'. Blake Edwards' *10* (US 79) was in memory of stunt co-ordinator Dick Crockett, who died during production. *The Flight of the Phoenix* (US 65) was dedicated to stunt aviator Paul Mantz, who was killed in one of the flying sequences, while *Superman* (GB 78) also commemorated stuntmen killed during the film, Terry Hill and John Bodimeade. *Superman* was unique in having two separate dedications, another one at the beginning being to the

memory of Geoffrey Unsworth, the film's cinematographer who had died before it was released. Unsworth had filmed the train sequence in *The First Great Train Robbery* (GB 79) and this picture was also dedicated to him, with the epitaph 'His Friends Miss Him'.

The Good Earth (US 36) carried the credit 'To the Memory of Irving Grant Thalberg, we dedicate this picture – his last great achievement'. Thalberg, production supervisor at MGM, had died of pneumonia that year at the age of 37.

A number of directors, both alive and dead, have been honoured with dedications. Mel Brooks' *High Anxiety* (US 77) honours 'the master of suspense, Alfred Hitchcock', while Chabrol's *Alice ou la dernière fugue* (Fr 76) is a tribute to Fritz Lang (1890–). Jacques Demy's *Lola* (Fr 60) was dedicated to the German director Max Ophüls (1902–57), whose last film had been *Lola Montès* (Fr/W. Ger 55). Federico Fellini (1920–) was the dedicatee of *The World's Greatest Lover* (US 77) and Tomas Gutieirrez Alca's *Los Sobreviventes/Survivors* (Cuba 79) was dedicated to Luis Buñuel (1900–).

Martin Scorsese's *Taxi Driver* (US 76) was in memory of composer Bernard Herrman (1911–75), who died a day after completing the

California Split (US 74) was dedicated to Barbara Ruick, seen here tending bar. She died on location

recording of the score. Jean Cocteau dedicated *Orphée* (Fr 50) to the designer of some of his most distinguished films, Christian Bèrard (1902–49).

Probably the only film dedicated to stage performers was *Dark Manhattan* (US 37), the first black production made in Hollywood. Besides a tribute to Bert Williams (1867–1922), pioneer black screen performer, it commemorated Richard B. Harrison, the black actor who had played 'De Lawd' in the stage version of *Green Pastures*, and *Blackbirds* star Florence Mills (1895–1927).

At least two films have been made in honour of production companies, though in neither case the company producing the film. Jean-Luc Godard, whose undying devotion to Hollywood 'B' movies created a trend among cinema buffs, dedicated his first feature *A Bout de souffle* (Fr 60) to Monogram Pictures. Dutch director Pim de la Parra followed suit when he dedicated his *Obsessions* (Neths/W.Ger 69) to Republic Pictures.

The only film dedicated to another film was *Robin Hood Jr* (US 23), which paid respectful tribute to the picture it parodied, the epic *Robin Hood* (US 22) with Douglas Fairbanks.

Not all dedications are concerned with film-making. War films in particular tend to be dedicated to their subjects, such as *Kozara* (Yug 60), which commemorated the partisan heroes whose story the movie presented. *Henry V* (GB 44) was dedicated to all those serving in World War II, and *The Sands of Iwo Jima* (US 49) to the US Marines. Sometimes such a dedication was seen to be contrived, *Box Office* magazine remarking of *South of Panama* (US 41): 'There is questionable taste in dedicating this film to the RAF just because the plot tumbles over a secret paint formula for planes and some misplaced aerial manouevre stock footage'. *Horizons sans fin* (Fr 52), Jean Dreville's story of pioneer aviatrix Helène Boucher, was dedicated to test pilots. The dedication of *The Vanishing Frontier* (US 54)

was 'To Men like Wyatt Earp'.

La Bandera (Fr 35), a Spanish Foreign Legion picture starring Jean Gabin, was dedicated to General Franco (1892–1975).

Communist director Pier Paolo Pasolini dedicated his *Gospel According to St Matthew* (It 64) to Pope John XXIII (1881–1963). Pasolini was inspired to make the film after reading the Gospel in a hotel Bible when he was held up in Florence due to traffic jams caused by the visit of the Pope.

The Sea Wolves (GB/US/Swz 80), about the last action of the Calcutta Light Horse, was dedicated to Earl Mountbatten of Burma (1900–79) in appreciation of his help in pre-production, shortly before his assassination by the IRA.

The Discovery of America (US 70) sounds as if it should have been dedicated to Christopher Columbus, but was in fact dedicated to Andy Warhol (1926–). Jose Maria Garci's *Asignatura pendiente* (Sp 76) was to the memory of Spanish poet Miguel Hernández (1910–42), 'who died without us ever knowing of his existence'. A posthumous tribute in more lighthearted vein was made by the Beatles in *Help!* (GB 65), which was 'respectfully dedicated to Elias Howe who, in 1846, invented the sewing machine'. The English writer and opponent of Marxist totalitarianism George Orwell (1903–50) received a posthumous dedication from Vera Belmont, whose *Prisonniers de Mao* (Fr 79) was based on the true experiences of a Frenchman imprisoned in Red China.

Greed (US 23) was dedicated by Erich von Stroheim to his mother and *Umberto D* (It 51) by Vittorio De Sica to his father. *Daaera* (India 53) was 'To Mothers and Daughters'.

Preston Sturges ranged wide when he dedicated *Sullivan's Travels* (US 42) to 'all the funny men and clowns who have made people laugh', but the most all-embracing dedication of all must be Val Lewton's for *I Walked with a Zombie* (US 43), with the sepulchral words 'To all those alive or dead...'

CHAPTER 11

CENSORSHIP

The first film known to have been suppressed was taken by Lumière cameraman Francis Doublier in Moscow in the summer of 1896 and showed Prince Napoléon dancing with the 'lady of his affections', a professional dancer. The film was seized by the Russian police and destroyed.

Later the same year *Delorita's Passion Dance* (US 96) became **the first film to be banned in the USA** when it was prohibited from exhibition in Atlantic City, NJ, by order of the Mayor.

The world's first regulated film censorship was introduced under a Chicago City Council Ordinance of 4 November 1907 'prohibiting the exhibition of obscene and immoral pictures'. Effective 19 November 1907, the Ordinance required that every film be shown to the Chief of Police before it was exhibited publicly and an exhibition permit obtained. Penalty for violation was a fine of $50–100 (£10–20), each day of exhibition without a permit to be regarded as a separate offence. One of the first films to fall foul of the censorship in Chicago was a Vitagraph production of Shakespeare's *Macbeth* (US 08), banned by a zealous police lieutenant on the grounds that 'Shakespeare is art, but it's not adapted altogether for the five cent style of art'. He explained: 'The stabbing scene in the play is not predominant. But in the picture show it is the feature.'

The first country to establish a State Censorship Board was Sweden. The Statens Biografbyrå was founded on 4 September 1911 and all films released in Sweden after 1 December 1911 were required to be certified by the Board.

Censorship USA: The USA is one of four countries where the film industry has a self-regulatory censorship independent of government (the others are Britain, Germany and Japan). The following is a brief chronology of American censorship as regulated by the Motion Picture Producers of America (MPPA).

1922: The Motion Picture Producers and Distributors of America founded March under the presidency of former Postmaster General Will H. Hays in an attempt to regulate the industry from within and combat growing demands for government intervention. At this date there were already eight State Censorship Boards (Maryland, New York, Florida, Ohio, Pennsylvania, Virginia, Kansas, Massachusetts) plus 90 municipal boards of varying degrees of severity.

Roscoe 'Fatty' Arbuckle, the world's highest paid entertainer, became **the first screen star to be banned**. The announcement was made by Will H. Hays of the MPPDA on 18 April, six days after Arbuckle had been acquitted of the manslaughter of 'good time girl' Virginia Rappe. Shortly afterwards Hays drew up a list of 200 people considered morally dangerous whom it was intended to bar from the industry. Heading the list was Wallace Reid, probably the most popular male star in America prior to Fairbanks' ascendancy, whose drug habit was to finish his career before the MPPDA was able to finish it for him.

1924: The 'Hays Formula' introduced – members agreed to submit scripts in advance for comment and guidance. Few did so unless the script was known to be innocuous.

The 'Index' of forbidden books and plays was introduced.

1927: Hays' list of 'Don'ts and Be Carefuls' adopted 8 June. Eleven 'Don'ts' included 'any licentious or suggestive nudity', 'miscegenation', 'ridicule of the clergy', 'any inference of sex perversion' and 'the illegal traffic of drugs'. 'Be Carefuls' included 'brutality and possible gruesomeness' and 'the sale of women, or of a woman selling her virtue'. Largely ineffective.

1930: First Production Code – known as 'The Hays Code' – drawn up by Martin Quigley, publisher of *Motion Picture Herald*, and Fr Daniel A. Lord of St Louis University. Introduced 31 March. No penalties for evasion.

1931: Prior submission of scripts made binding on members.

1934: Production Code Administration Office established in June. 'Resolution for Uniform Interpretation' required producers to abide by Code. Penalties for evasion introduced.

First Seal of Approval granted by Hays Office to Fox's *The World Moves On* 11 July.

1943: Howard Hughes caused the first serious breach of the Code when he exhibited *The Outlaw* (US 43) without a Seal of Approval. Billy the Kid, a criminal and moral transgressor, and his girl Rio, a moral transgressor only, were able to ride off into the sunset without reaping any of the just deserts demanded by the Code. (Or by history – in reality Billy the Kid was shot.)

1954: Code seriously breached again when Preminger distributed *The Moon is Blue*, a comedy about virginity, without a Seal of Approval.

1955: *The Man with the Golden Arm* awarded Seal despite explicit treatment of drug addiction.

1956: Revised Code introduced. The only two subjects now positively prohibited were venereal disease and sexual perversion, though restrictions retained on language.

1961: *The Children's Hour* granted Seal despite theme of sexual deviation – in this case lesbianism.

1966: The 'blue language' barrier finally crashed by *Who's Afraid of Virginia Woolf,* the Produc-

Margaret Lockwood had British audiences sitting on the edge of their seats in *The Wicked Lady* (GB 45), but for US distribution her *décolletage* had to be lifted to a more circumspect elevation

tion Code Administration agreeing to give it a Seal (with audiences restricted to over 18's) because it reflected 'the tragic realism of life'.

Code revised again, with no positive prohibitions remaining. Approved films were now divided into 'general audience' and 'mature audience'.

1968: Production Code Administration defied when they refused to approve two British films which contained scenes of oral sex: Michael Winner's *I'll Never Forget Whatshisname* (GB 67) and Albert Finney's *Charlie Bubbles* (GB 68). They were released through subsidiary companies of the intending distributors which were not members of the Association. This device enabled any major distributor to circumvent the Administration and hastened its end.

Code replaced by ratings system under the Motion Picture Association of America Ratings Board, effective 1 November. Four classifications: G = General Audience; M = Mature Audience; R = Restricted (over 18); X = Over 21 only. M was replaced by GP (General Patronage) in 1970, as 'mature' was being misinterpreted as meaning 'X+'. By 1975 R had changed to allow accompanied children under 17, the X restriction had been lowered to over 17, and GP had become PG (Parental Guidance). The X rating can be self applied to obviate any request for cuts. An XX rating has been devised to designate sexploitation movies.

Censorship GB: The British Board of Film Censors (BBFC) was inaugurated by the Kinematograph Manufacturers' Association in October 1912 with powers effective from 1 January 1913. The moving spirit behind the venture was the film producer Will Barker, who was concerned at the increase in the number of films being produced 'for the smoking room', which he considered would bring the whole industry into disrepute. Together with Col A.C. Bromhead and Cecil Hepworth, two leading pioneer film-makers, he persuaded the Kinematograph Manufacturers' Association that it was up to the trade to put its own house in order, and with the approval of the Home Secretary the Board was established under the Presidency of G.A. Redford, formerly a playreader for the Lord Chamberlain.

The original classification was into 'U' (Universal) and 'A' (Adult). **The first U Certificate** was granted to the Barker production *Mary of Briarwood Dell* (GB 13) and **the first A Certificate** to the Clarendon picture *A Strong Man's Love* (GB 13), both on 1 January 1913. The A Certificate was originally advisory only (as it is today). It was not until 1923 that the London County Council prohibited children under 16 from attending A films. Most other local authorities in England and Wales followed suit by the end of the decade, though in Scotland the A Certificate always remained advisory only.

The BBFC began life with only two firm prohibitive rules: no film depicting the living figure of Jesus Christ and no film which contained scenes of nudity would be granted a Certificate. During the first year of operation, the Board examined 7510 films (6861 'U'; 627 'A'), of which only 22 were rejected outright. Reasons included 'indelicate or suggestive sexual situations', 'holding up a Minister of Religion to ridicule', 'excessive drunkenness' and the portrayal of 'native customs in British lands abhorrent to British ideas'. In 1917 the new Chairman, T.P. O'Connor, declared that he would not grant a Certificate to any film in which crime was the dominant feature and warned producers that no criminal was to be portrayed as a victim of social deprivation. By 1925 the following were also among the 'Don'ts': 'Women fighting with knives'; 'Animals gnawing men, women and children'; 'Insistence upon the inferiority of coloured races'; and 'Salacious wit'.

An 'H' Certificate (advisory only) was introduced in 1930 to designate horror films, and 'X' for 'Adult Only' in 1951 (*see* First 'X' Film, below). A revised rating system took effect in July 1970 as follows:

U: Passed for general exhibition (no change).

A: Reverted to advisory status. Passed for general exhibition, but parents/guardians are advised that the film contains material they might prefer children under 14 years not to see.

AA: New classification. No children under 14 admitted.

X: Admission age raised from 16 to 18.

A recent *aide-mémoire* indicates that the Board's function and powers have remained fundamentally unchanged since its inception, despite modification of its criteria for certification in line with changing social and moral standards: 'The power of censorship is in the hands of Local Authorities. The BBFC exists to act as an intermediary between Local Authorities and the film industry. Its success or failure can be measured simply in terms of the acceptability of its judgements to the majority of Local Authorities in Britain.'

Local Authorities have the power to alter the Certificate issued by the BBFC or to permit the showing of an uncertified film. They also remain the only agency with the power to refuse the right of exhibition.

The first film to receive an X-rating (adults only) under the British Board of Film Censors system of classification was *La Vie commence demain/Life Begins Tomorrow* (Fr 50), which opened in London on 9 January 1951. The reason for the X Certificate was a sequence dealing with artificial insemination. Previously the film would have had to have been either banned or cut.

The first British film to receive an X Certificate was a 20-minute short of the Edgar Allan Poe story *The Tell-Tale Heart* (GB 53). **The first British feature film to be X-rated** was Rene Clement's *Knave of Hearts* (GB 54), about a Frenchman (Gerard Philipe) who tries to seduce his wife's friend by recounting his affairs with various English girls.

The first film to receive an X-rating under the Motion Picture Association of America system of classification was Brian de Palma's anti-establishment *Greetings* (US 68) with Robert de Niro, which opened in New York on 15 December 1968.

The largest number of cuts known to have been ordered by a censor to one film is 103 in respect of Faria de Almeida's *Catembe* (Port 64), a critical film by a Mozambique director about the then Portuguese Colony. The most cuts to a Hollywood film was 60 in the case of D.W. Griffith's *Way Down East* (US 20), a heart-rending Victorian melodrama which had been reducing stage audiences to tears for the previous thirty years without apparently undermining their morals. The pivot of the story concerns the waiflike heroine's (Lillian Gish) illegitimate baby and it was this to which the Pennsylvania State Censorship Board took grave exception. Scenes ordered to be cut in their entirety included the mock marriage (the heroine having been deceived), the mock honeymoon, the heroine announcing that she was with child, and all sequences relating to its birth. Indeed the baby made its first, unheralded appearance in the cut version only shortly before it expired, much to the bewilderment of Pennsylvania audiences. (The Board also insisted, for reasons undisclosed, that the title 'I can never be any man's wife' be changed to 'I can never marry any man'.)

The British Board of Film Censors is unable to confirm a British record, but acknowledges that the 31 cuts, totalling 30 minutes running time, made in the exploitation shocker *Uncle Tom* (It 72) was exceptional.

The first country to abolish censorship of films was Russia under the Kerensky government in March 1917. It was formally reimposed in 1922, though in practice there had been a strong measure of control since the accession of the Bolsheviks to power. In the Stalinist era the Soviet censorship became the most rigorous in the world, to the point of nearly extinguishing the film industry in the 1950s. It probably remains so.

The brief flowering of liberty in the revolutionary Russia of 1917 had resulted in nothing more stimulating than a spate of anti-Tsarist films, most of them centering on the depraved monk Rasputin as the architect of decay. When Germany abolished censorship in December 1918, the worst fears of its upholders were confirmed by the rash of sex films that followed. Their titles in no way belied their content: *Frauen, die der Abgrund verschlingt/Women Engulfed by the Abyss* (Ger 18), *Verlorene Töchter/Lost Daughters* (Ger 19), *Die Prostitution* (Ger 19), *Hyänen der Lust/Hyenas of Lust* (Ger 19), etc. Homosexuality (q.v.) was also treated on the screen for the first time. It is doubtful whether anything so explicitly sexual was encountered again in films until the 1960s. Censorship was restored by the National Assembly in May 1920.

No other country abolished censorship for adult audiences until 1969, when Denmark took a lead which was to be followed in the 1970s by Austria, Uruguay, Portugal and Upper Volta. Belgium is unique in never having exercised any censorship of films for adults.

The Unkindest Cuts

The vagaries of censorship have taken many forms. Here are some of them.
● The State of Illinois demanded excision of the scene in *The Kid* (US 20) in which Jackie Coogan smashes windows. For similar reasons the censorship board of Ohio tried to ban *Treasure Island* (US 20) altogether lest it should encourage children to piracy.
● A song sequence by Myrna Loy in *Love Me Tonight* (US 32) was cut because her navel was visible through her negligee. Navels were by no means the only part of the body subject to the censor's scissors. Paul Poiret, the Paris fashion designer, made a fashion film in 1913 which was seized by US Customs as obscene when he tried to bring it into America. Poiret's models in the film were wearing dresses which revealed the ankle. Over exposed legs were taboo in most American states in the 20s, but Ohio went so far as to have a newsreel censored – it presented a fleeting glimpse of Mistinguet's celebrated 'million dollar legs'.
● 20th Century Fox was obliged to cut a shot of a Botticelli nude from its art documentary *Birth of Venus* (US 52) at the insistence of the Hays Office.
● The films of Libertad Lamarque, one of Argentina's major stars of the 30s, were banned in Argentina when Perón came to power in

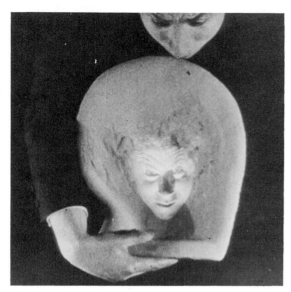

La Coquille et la Clergyman (Fr 28) was banned in Britain on the grounds that if there was any meaning to the film, 'it is doubtless objectionable'

1945. The reason was that Senorita Lamarque had slapped the face of Perón's mistress Eva Duarte – Evita – on the set of *Circus Cavalcade* (Arg 43) because the aspiring actress had sat in the star's personal chair. When Eva Duarte became the nation's First Lady as Eva Perón, Libertad Lamarque had to flee into exile.

● *Bloody Cry* (China 34) was banned by the Kuomintang censors because the villain bore a certain physical resemblance to Chiang Kaishek.

● Chicago was particularly sensitive to sexual inferences, real or imagined. The local censorship board cut a scene in *The Devil Within* (US 21) in which a father-to-be is seen pacing up and down outside a bedroom, pulling petals from a flower and murmuring 'boy-girl-boy-girl'. A scene in *Bobbed Hair* (US 22) of a family man drawing the curtains of his own house was cut lest the idea might be conveyed to the impressionable that he was going to kiss his wife – or worse.

● When the script of *Zaza* (US 39) was returned from the Hays Office, a line in which the heroine screams at the villain 'Pig! Pig! Pig! Pig! Pig!' had noted in the margin against it: 'Delete two pigs'. The Hays Office permitted the saloon queen Frenchie (Marlene Dietrich) to push money down her cleavage in *Destry Rides Again* (US 39), but insisted on the deletion of the accompanying line 'There's gold in them thar hills!'

● The Egyptian censor declared that *Cleopatra* (US 63) would be banned unless all scenes with Elizabeth Taylor were cut. Miss Taylor was a convert to the Jewish religion. Egypt banned 352 foreign films between 1955 and 1967, 120 of them because they featured Jewish stars.

● *La Coquille et la Clergyman* (Fr 28), the surrealist fantasy directed by Germaine Dulac, was banned by the British Board of Film Censors with the comment: 'This film is so cryptic as to be almost meaningless. If there is a meaning, it is doubtless objectionable.'

● The British Board of Film Censors banned only one British film outright between the two World Wars. *Blow Bugles Blow* (GB 36), produced by the Progressive Film Institute, was about a right-wing Prime Minister who aims to declare war on France, but war is averted when a General Strike is called by militant unionists. The action of the Board in this case reflected its upholding of the establishment credo during the thirties.

● Even the most vigilant censorship could be circumvented. When a whole scene of crucial importance to the story was cut from *The Battle Cry of Peace* (US 15), the New York cinema at which it opened had the screen raised and the episode mimed by actors on the stage.

● Censors might even, on rare occasions, be persuaded to change their mind. Clark Gable's farewell line of dialogue to Scarlett in *Gone with the Wind* (US 39) – 'Frankly, my dear, I don't give a damn' – aroused the ire of the Hays Office, who wanted it altered to 'I don't give a darn'. Producer David O Selznick flew to New York to see Will Hays personally and spent four hours persuading him that the concluding word was essential to convey Rhett Butler's feelings. Hays capitulated and the offending word remained in what has become one of the most memorable lines ever spoken from the screen.

● All scenes of people smoking were banned in Kansas in the 20s, as well as views of girls in bathing costumes or 'fancy stockings'. Male attire could also arouse the censor's displeasure in the USA. Respecting D.W. Griffith's *Drums of Love* (US 28), one censorship board ordered: 'Cut scenes showing hero in tight trousers bowing and standing at top of stairway. Cut view of him walking (still in tight trousers).'

● Spitting was taboo in Australia in the 1940s.

● In 1964 the Peking Cinema Institute banned, along with *Hamlet* (GB 48), *Othello* (US/Fr 51) and *The Three Musketeers* (US 48), an educational film titled *Elementary Safety in Swimming in Rivers, Lakes and Seas*. The safety element was considered a bourgeois tendency likely to undermine revolutionary daring.

● The Pennsylvania censorship board refused to pass *The Branding Iron* (US 20) until an intertitle reading 'A Hidden House built for Love' was changed to 'A Hidden House built for Inspiration'.

● *The Wicked Lady* (GB 45), in which Margaret Lockwood played a high-born lady highwayman, had to be almost entirely reshot for the USA due to the depth of Miss Lockwood's *décolletage*.

● Cartoons are by no means exempt from censorship. In *Fantasia* (US 40), the barebreasted girl centaurs in the Pastoral Symphony sequence had to be redrawn with flower leis draping the offending parts. Early Clarabelle Cow cartoons had the cow's udder discreetly draped with an apron, while another cow, appearing opposite Donald Duck, had to have the pink tips of her teats recoloured a more neutral hue as the original was held to be indelicate for child audiences. However, in the 1950s Bugs Bunny was allowed to be married off to his traditional enemy Elmo, and the two were seen slipping off to a honeymoon cottage for what can only have been a night of homophile passion.

● A scene of a wife being kissed on the shoulder by her husband in *The Last Payment* (US 21) was ordered to be cut in Maryland. Shoulders had exercised the censor's attention before. An over-exposed pair in *The Man who had Everything* (US 20) fell foul of the Pennsylvania board's scissors.

● *The Grapes of Wrath* (US 40) was allowed to be shown in the USSR, because the authorities considered it painted a sufficiently unattractive picture of the life of the American proletariat during the depression. It was later banned when they found that audiences were immensely impressed by the fact that the itinerant family of the story, intended to represent America's dispossessed, owned an automobile.

● After 1942 no photos of Gandhi were allowed on the screen in Indian films, even as incidental props. Prior to World War II many Indian producers and directors had demonstrated their support of the outlawed Indian National Congress by using the Gandhian symbol – the spinning wheel – as decoration, or by having pictures of Gandhi and Nehru on the walls, or by introducing a few bars of a Congress anthem into the soundtrack.

● In Russia in 1915 all scenes with Jews were cut and Biblical films were banned altogether on the grounds that it would be 'very dangerous to see so many Jews on the screen'. In contrast, David Lean's much acclaimed *Oliver Twist* (GB 48) was banned in Quebec because Alec Guinness's portrayal of Fagin was thought to be antisemitic.

● *Ben-Hur* (US 25) was banned in China in 1930 on the grounds that it was 'propaganda of superstitious beliefs, namely Christianity'. In Italy the film was also banned when Mussolini found to his dismay that the Roman, played by Francis X. Bushman, was not the hero and that he is eventually defeated in the chariot race. Other countries could be equally sensitive on matters of national pride. *The Millionairess* (GB 60), in which Peter Sellers played an unworldly but benign Indian doctor, was banned in Egypt because the character's nationality had been switched – in Shaw's play he was an Egyptian doctor.

● Hatred has been a regrettably potent factor in censorship. All German films were banned in Britain after World War I (a ban imposed by the exhibitors themselves) and until recent years no German film was admitted into Israel. *All Quiet on the Western Front* (US 30), generally acknowledged as one of the greatest pacifist films, was banned in France until 1962 because of its moderate stance towards the Germans. When it was finally released it was booed by Paris audiences. Local censorship boards in the southern states of America between the wars customarily demanded cuts in films that depicted blacks in any role other than a menial one. Even after World War II the Memphis censor cut Lena Horne sequences from MGM musicals and a scene from *The Sailor Takes a Wife* (US 46) in which a white character tips his hat to a black.

● It is salutary that censorship can also be

Die Reiter von Deutsche Ost-Afrika (Ger 34) – banned first as pacificist, then banned again as militarist

employed to counter hatred. A boycott of all films in which Ben Hecht was involved was organised by British exhibitors in the UK in 1946 after the Hollywood scenarist had publicly rejoiced at the killing of British peace-keeping troops in Palestine by Zionist terror squads.

● Films have sometimes been banned by different censors for diametrically opposite reasons. *Die Reiter von Deutsche Ost-Afrika/The Riders of German East Africa* (Ger 34) was banned by the Nazi government in 1939 as pacifist and by the Allied authorities in Germany in 1945 as militarist.

● Political censorship has taken some strange turns. Scenes in which the American flag appeared were ordered to be cut in Canada at the time of a boundary dispute in 1919. The British Board of Film Censors refused to certify *The Battleship Potemkin* (USSR 25) on the grounds that it dealt with 'recent' controversial events. ('Recent' being 20 years earlier.) The DDR banned *Thunderball* (GB 65) because James Bond 'personifies the ideals of Fascism and is the incarnation of all the wrong and dangerous ideals provided to the youth of the western world'. Agent 007 is also *persona non grata* in the Arab States, where all United Artists releases are banned (on account of the fact that they maintain an office in Israel). The March of Time newsreel titled *Inside Nazi Germany* (US 38) and Chaplin's *The Great Dictator* (US 40), both strongly anti-Nazi, were banned in Chicago for 'political bias'. All Chaplin's films were banned in Tennessee in the early 50s, because the State Censor objected to his morals and his politics.

● *The Cow* (Iran 69) was produced under the auspices of the Iranian Ministry of Culture and Arts. On completion it was promptly banned – by the same Ministry of Culture and Arts.

● In 1918 the burghers of Villefranche-sur-Rhône banned *Othello* (It 14) from local exhibition because they objected to Desdemona being killed in it.

● Titles are not immune from censorship. In 1928 the Hays Office mysteriously insisted that the title of Somerset Maugham's *Rain* should be changed to *Sadie Thompson* (the prostitute heroine), justifying the demand on unspecified moral grounds. The British Board of Film Censors would not certify *Underworld* (US 28) unless the title was changed (it was released in Britain as *Paying the Penalty*). The same week it cheerfully passed *Undressed* (US 28). *The Greeks had a Word for Them* (US 32) was originally called *The Greeks had a Word for It*, but the Hays Office objected that the word 'it' was suggestive.

● There was a unique instance in American censorship of a ban on a particular individual being portrayed on the screen. It applied to gangster John Dillinger, whose heroic stature in the mass consciousness had considerably unnerved the American authorities by the time he was gunned down in 1934. For ten years the Hays Office would consider no scripts featuring the gangster, though seven Dillinger movies have been made since 1945.

● The British Board of Film Censors refused to pass a scene in *The Little Shepherd of Kingdom Come* (US 28) because it showed an elderly gentleman clambering out of a double bed (to investigate a night noise) which also contained his equally elderly wife. Representations from the Hays Office being of no avail, its director, who happened to be in London at the time, personally took the print to a laboratory and asked them to reprint the offending scene so dark that it was impossible to distinguish a bed. After that date twin beds were used in nearly all Hollywood productions with bedroom scenes, to avoid problems in penetrating the lucrative British market.

●Britain's sensitivity about double beds was matched by America's sensitivity about, among other things, raindrops. The scene in *The Stars Look Down* (GB 39) in which extra-marital relations between the hero and heroine (Michael Redgrave and Margaret Lockwood) are decorously suggested by two raindrops coursing down a windowpane and merging into one, fell victim to the Hays Office.

●Probably the most liberal censorship on sexual content during the thirties was that of Nazi Germany. It is doubtful whether such erotic comedies as *Der Ammenkönig* (Ger 35) or Carl Froelich's *Wenn wir alle Engel wären/If We were All Angels* (Ger 36) would have passed any foreign censor. This may well have been because of Josef Goebbels' own sexual predelictions and he was the Chief Censor not only in name but in practice. During the twelve years of the Third Reich he personally viewed every one of the 1363 feature films produced, as well as all newsreels, cartoons, documentaries and other shorts, before they were passed for public showing. There was one exception to the generally permissive tone. Hitler himself had personally ordered that any woman character in a film who broke up a marriage must die before the end, a retribution that exceeded even the just desserts demanded by the Hays Office for moral transgressors.

●A rare example of sound effects being cut by the censor occurred in Spain in 1975, when the farts were excised from Mel Brooks' *Blazing Saddles* (US 74).

●*The Great Missouri Raid* (US 50) originally began with a narrator saying: 'This is the story of Frank and Jesse James, who were not born bad...' On release, the preface began: 'This is the story of Frank and Jesse James, who were born bad...'

●One local police chief in Sweden about the time of World War I censored all films in which china was smashed – presumably to prevent housemaids from getting the idea that the practice had the endorsement of moviemakers.

●In August 1913 Russia banned films showing strikes, 'the life of indentured peasants' and 'difficult forms of labour'. Mexico banned imported films that depicted Mexicans as villains in 1926. The ban was ignored by Holly-wood, but the effect on exports south of the border was sufficiently serious for the Hays Office to order no more Mexican heavies in 1930. As a quid pro quo, the censors let it be tacitly understood that it would be quite acceptable for the stock foreign undesirable to be portrayed as Russian, in retaliation for Soviet restrictions on Hollywood imports. France in the 20s had an instruction written into its code 'No displeasing Mexicans, Chinese or Niggers', while Poland at this time banned 'films tending to provoke emigration agitation'. India, meanwhile, had accumulated a list of 50 prohibited subjects, including 'representation of nude statues', 'references to race suicide', 'unnecessary exhibition of female underclothing', 'bathing scenes passing the limits of propriety', 'indecorous dancing', 'vulgar accessories', 'references to controversial politics', 'unpleasant details of medical operations', and 'scenes . . . bringing into disrepute British prestige in the Empire'. The latter piece of chauvinism was matched by Mussolini in 1928. He banned all foreign war films from Italian screens because they gave insufficient credit to Italy's contribution in World War I.

●Unusual prohibitions still exist in censorship today. South Korea will not permit teachers to be ridiculed on screen and revenge must not be justified in any film unless it is a western. The latter requirement effectively restricts the showing of Kung-fu movies; in Iraq and Iran they are banned outright. Among the subjects which 'may be objectionable' to the Indian censors are 'accentuation of class distinctions' and 'depoverty'. The meaning of the latter is unclear; Pakistan straight-forwardly forbids the depiction of poverty in films. The Indian censor has an unusual power of being able to decertify a film after it has been released. This happened in the case of *The African Queen* (GB 51), *The Snows of Kilimanjaro* (US 52) and *The King and I* (US 56), possibly for diplomatic reasons. The Turks have a prohibition against 'hurting the pride of the armed forces or security police'. Both the Guatemalan and the Egyptian censors may ban films of low creative standards. *Anguish* (Egypt 62) and *Youth* (Egypt 62) were each refused certificates because of poor scripts and inept direction.

CHAPTER 12

AUDIENCES AND EXHIBITORS

CINEMAS

The first cinema was the Cinématographe Lumière at the Salon Indien, a former billiard hall in the Grand Café, 14 Boulevard des Capucines, Paris, opened under the management of Clément Maurice on 28 December 1895. The proprietors of the show were Auguste and Louis Lumière, the pioneer cinematographers whose films made up the programme. The opening performance included *Le Mur, L'Arrivée d'un train en gare, La sortie des Usines Lumière, Le goûter de Bébé, La pêche des poissons rouges, Soldats au manège, M. Lumière et le jongleur Trewey jouant aux cartes, La rue de la République à Lyon, En mer par gros temps, L'arroseur arrosé* and *La destruction des mauvaises herbes*. Returns from the box office on the day of opening were disappointingly low, as only 35 people had ventured a franc to see the new form of entertainment. This barely covered the rent of 30 francs a day, and the owner of the Grand Café, M. Borgo, doubtless congratulated himself that he had refused Maurice's offer of 20 per cent of the receipts in lieu of rent. Later he was to come to regret his decision, when the Cinématographe Lumière became the sensation of Paris and box office receipts rose to 2500 francs a day. Most historians have assumed that the Cinématographe Lumière at the Grand Café was simply a temporary show and consequently it has usually been claimed as the first presentation of films before a paying audience (which it was not) instead of the first cinema. Although the exact date of its closure is not known, there is contemporary evidence that it was still functioning as late as 1901. The fact that it operated continuously for at least five years should be sufficient to justify any claim based on permanence.

The first cinema in the United States was Vitascope Hall, opened at the corner of Canal Street and Exchange Place, New Orleans on 26 June 1896. The proprietor of the 400-seat theatre was William T. Rock and his projectionist was William Reed. Most of the programme was made up of short scenic items, including the first British film to be released in America, Robert Paul's *Waves off Dover* (GB 95), but there was sometimes more compelling fare, such as *The Irish Way of Discussing Politics* (US 96) or *The Lynching Scene* (US 96). A major attraction was the movie *May Irwin Kiss* (US 96), which may be said to have introduced sex to the American screen. Admission to Vitascope Hall was 10¢ and for another 10¢ patrons were allowed to peep through the door of the projection room and see the Edison Vitascope projector. Those possessed of a liberal supply of dimes could also purchase a single frame of discarded film for the same price.

The first cinema in Britain: The earliest attempt at establishing a cinema in Britain was made by Birt Acres, whose Kineopticon opened at 2 Piccadilly Mansions at the junction of Piccadilly Circus and Shaftesbury Avenue on 21 March 1896. The manager was Mr T.C. Hayward. The opening programme (admission 6d) consisted of *Arrest of a Pickpocket, A Carpenter's*

The earliest known photograph of the interior of a cinema with audience – the Maailman Ympäri Kino, Helsinki, Finland 1906

Shop, *A Visit to the Zoo*, *The Derby*, *Rough Seas at Dover* (original title of *Waves off Dover* mentioned above), *The Boxing Kangaroo* and *The German Emperor Reviewing his Troops*. After only a few weeks operation, Acres' cinema was gutted by fire.

The first cinema in Britain of any permanence was Mohawks' Hall, Upper Street, Islington, opened by the Royal Animated & Singing Picture Co. on 5 August 1901. The manager was Henry N. Phillips. Principal attractions of the inaugural programme were *The Rajah's Dream or The Enchanted Forest* (Fr 00), billed as 'the

The only known photograph of the Volta Picture Theatre in Dublin, the cinema managed by James Joyce. It was Ireland's first permanent cinema *(Liam O'Leary Film Archives)*

finest mysterious picture ever placed before the public', and a number of primitive 'talkies' featuring vocalists Lil Hawthorne, Vesta Tilley and Alec Hurley. There were also war films from South Africa and China, scenes of rush hour at the Angel, a 'graphic representation of the sensational sporting spectacle *Tally Ho* taken at the London Hippodrome', a newsreel of King Edward VII presenting medals to the South African war heroes, and scenes of a motor car explosion, Count Zeppelin's airship and 'a visit to a spiritualist'. The show was nightly at 8 p.m., with matinees on Thursdays and Saturdays, and prices of admission were 6d, 1s, 2s and 3s – considerably more than the average of 3d or 6d that most cinemas charged at the time of World War I. The Mohawk, though, was an ambitious enterprise, for while later cinemas were content to offer a piano accompaniment to the films, the Royal Animated & Singing Picture Co. engaged the 16-piece Fonobian Orchestra under the direction of Mr W. Neale. Within a few days of opening, the Mohawk advertised that it was 'besieged at every performance'. Evidently the cinema-going public was fickle, for within a few months the Mohawk had been forced to close its doors. After a period as a music hall, it was reopened as a cinema in 1908 as the Palace, changed hands ten years later to become the Blue Hall Cinema, and finally became a Gaumont before closing in 1962. The building still stands, an empty and derelict shell.

FIRST CINEMAS WORLDWIDE

The cinemas listed below were the first to be established permanently (or intended to be permanent) in their respective countries.

Country	Date	Cinema	Locale
Argentina	1901	–	467 Calle Maipu, Buenos Aires
Australia	Dec 1896	Salon Cinématographe	237 Pitt St, Sydney
Austria	1903	Münstedt-Kino	the Prater, Vienna
Belgium	1897	Théâtre de Cinématographie	Boulevard du Nord, Brussels
Brazil	31 Jul 1897	Salão de Novidades	141 Rua do Ouvidor, Rio de Janiero
Bulgaria	1908	The Modern Theatre	Sofia
Canada	1 Jan 1906	The Ouimetoscope	Montreal
China	1903	–	estab. Shanghai by Antonio Ramos
Cuba	c. 1904	Florodora	Palationo, Havana
Denmark	1903	–	27 Frederiksberggade, Copenhagen
Egypt	1904	Pathé Cinema	Cairo
Finland	1901	Kinematograph International	Helsinki
France	28 Dec 1895	Cinématographe Lumière	14 Boulevard des Capucines, Paris
Germany	Jul 1896	–	21 Unter den Linden
Greece	1907	–	Constitution Square, Athens
India	1907	Elphinstone Cinema	Calcutta
Iran	1905	–	Avenue Cherâq Gaz, Teheran
Ireland (Eire)	1909	Volta Cinema	Dublin (manager: James Joyce)
Italy	c. 1898	Cinema Silenzioso	21 Corso Vittorio Emanuele, Milan
Japan	Oct 1903	Denkikan	Asakusa
Lebanon	1909	Zahret Sourya	Beirut
Mauritius	1912	Luna Park	Port Louis
Mexico	1901	Salon Pathé	5 Calle de la Profesa, Mexico City
New Zealand	1910	King's Theatre	Auckland
Norway	1 Nov 1904	Kinematograf-Teatret	12 Storthingsgd, Oslo
Portugal	1904	Salão Ideal	Lisbon
Romania	May 1909	Volta	Bucharest
South Africa	19 Dec 1908	New Apollo Theatre	39 Pritchard Street, Johannesburg
Spain	c. 1897	Salón Maravillas	Glorieta de Bibaô, Madrid
Sweden	27 Jul 1902	Arkaden Kino	Gothenburg
Switzerland	11 May 1906	Grand Cinématographe Suisse	17 Croix d'Or, Geneva
Syria	1916	Janak Kala'a	Damascus
Thailand	1907	The Bioscope	Bangkok
Tunisia	16 Oct 1908	Omnia Pathé	Tunis
Turkey	1908	Pathé	Istanbul
United Kingdom	5 Aug 1901	Mohawk's Hall	Upper Street, Islington
United States	26 Jun 1896	Vitascope Hall	Canal Street, New Orleans
USSR (Russia)	1903	The Electric Theatre	Moscow
Yugoslavia (Croatia)	1900	Znasstveno Umjetničko Kajilšte	Zagreb

It is apparent from this list that the oft repeated claim that the first cinema in the world was the Nickelodeon opened by Harry Davis in Pittsburgh, Pa. in June 1905 is wholly without foundation.

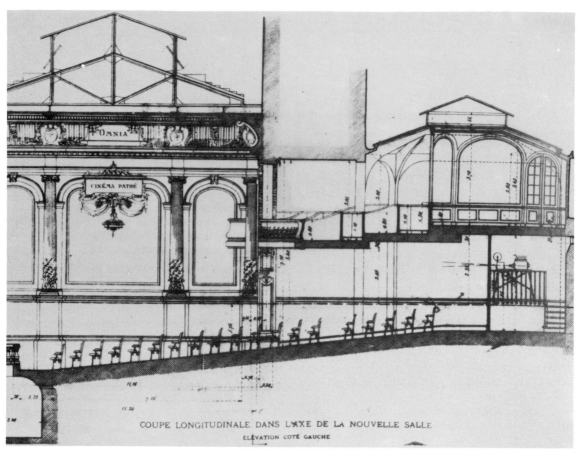

COUPE LONGITUDINALE DANS L'AXE DE LA NOUVELLE SALLE

ELÉVATION COTÉ GAUCHE

An artist's impression of Britain's first purpose-built cinema as it looked when it first opened in 1907

The first purpose-built cinema was the Cinéma Omnia Pathé, on the Boulevard Montmartre, Paris, which opened with *Le Pendu* (Fr 06) and supporting programme on 1 December 1906. The world's first luxury cinema, and the first with a raked floor so that everyone could see above the heads in front, it was decorated in classical style with columns and Grecian friezes. The screen, measuring 20ft (6m) by 13ft (4m), was one of the largest ever installed in a cinema at that time. Admission for the two-hour show ranged from 50c–3fr – prices at other cinemas were generally in the range of 25c–2fr.

The first purpose-built cinema in Britain was established by Joshua Duckworth of the Premier Picture Co., a former magic lantern showman and kinetoscope proprietor, whose Central Hall, Colne, Lancs, was erected at a cost of £2000 and opened on 22 February 1907. At first Duckworth presented both films and variety, but abandoned the latter when he found that pictures alone were a sufficient attraction. In his two-hour programme, he always liked to 'include an

Top left: Architect's drawing of the first purpose-built cinema – the Omnia-Pathé, Paris, 1906

Bottom left: The luxury cinema was beginning to emerge by 1912. This tapestried interior graced the Picture House in Leeds

educational or travel subject; this I find gives dignity to the show. Good drama and pathetic subjects are always appreciated. The greatest difficulty is experienced in satisfying an audience to which you are playing week after week, with humorous and comic subjects – breaking crockery, tumbling over furniture, or running against the banana cart fails to draw a smile if not positive disapproval.' (*Kinematograph Weekly* 2.7.08). The building continued in operation as a cinema until 1924, then became a Spiritualist chapel; in recent years its only use has been as an engineering training workshop.

The first British cinema with a sloping floor was the Picture Palace at St Albans, Hertfordshire, opened by Arthur Melbourne-Cooper of the Alpha Trading Co. in 1908. It was also the first to depart from standard theatre practice by charging more to sit at the back of the stalls than the front. The *Bioscope* reported: 'This arrangement was somewhat resented at first by patrons of the higher-priced seats, but when they found the specially raised floor gave them a better view than could be got from the front, they appreciated the innovation'. The idea was suggested to Melbourne-Cooper by his usherette, whom he later had the good sense to marry.

Social Acceptance of The Cinema

Although the cinema was primarily a proletarian form of entertainment in the USA and UK prior to World War I, elsewhere it achieved social acceptance at an earlier date. The first countries in which this was manifest were Russia and Japan, a phenomenon partly accounted for by high admission charges. In Japan seat prices of the earliest cinemas (*c.* 1903) were generally in a range equivalent to 6d (12c)–3s 9d (90c), well out of the reach of peasants or artisans. The respectability of the cinema in Russia was attested by the fact that the exclusive Hotel Metropole in Moscow saw fit to open its own cinema in 1906. The interest of the Tsar and Tsarina in films – the court photographer was kept constantly employed filming the Royal Family at leisure – did much to make movies fashionable. An American wrote to a US trade publication in 1913 that the audiences he saw in Russia were of a far better class – and the seats more expensive – than elsewhere in Europe. Cinemas were attended, he said, even by 'very high officials in uniform'.

THE CINEMA AS AN EDUCATIVE FORCE.

Tommy (a regular attender at cinematograph shows, during the performance of a society drama). "Is that the trusting husband or the amorous lover?"

In France the stage-bound but much admired productions of Film d'Art, with casts drawn from the illustrious Comédie Française, catered from 1908 for the kind of audiences who looked to film as a silent record of great theatre drama. Around 1910, at a time when even minor American players would only deign to appear in films under the strictest cloak of anonymity, the fact that the leading stars of the Budapest National Theatre were prepared to be seen on screen gave the Hungarian cinema its artistic imprimatur. In Germany *Der Andere* (Ger 12), directed by Max Mack with the distinguished stage actor Albert Basserman in the lead, was the first film to receive serious critical attention in the press and consequent patronage from a new type of cinema audience. The emergence of Denmark's Asta Nielsen as the first star specialising in tragic roles had a profound influence on the cinema in Scandinavia and Central Europe from 1910 onwards, demonstrating the drawing power of original screen drama and 'name' stars to middle-class audiences. As the artistic quality of motion pictures

The cartoon weekly *Punch* has always been something of a social barometer. When *Punch* publishes a cartoon about a new trend, it is probably here to stay. Note the middle class audience in this 1912 drawing

improved, new luxury cinemas opened designed to accommodate the kind of audiences at which these films were aimed. Foremost was the giant Gaumont-Palace in Paris (1911), with a seating capacity of 5000; others included Berlin's 2000-seat Alhambra Platz (1911), the Panellinion in Athens (1911), also with 2000 seats, and Copenhagen's majestic 3000-seat Palads-Teatret (1912).

In America the era of the 'super cinema' began a little later, dating from the opening of the Regent on 116th Street and 7th Avenue in February 1913 and the Vitagraph Theater and the Strand on Broadway in 1914. There has been a tendency to oversimplify American film history by suggesting that the cinema remained a primitive entertainment controlled by unlettered immigrants and largely aimed at immigrant

US and UK CINEMAS from 1945					
	USA	UK		USA	UK
1945	20457	4723	1963	12800	2181
1946	19019	–	1964	13750	2057
1947	18607	–	1965	14000	1971
1948	18395	4706	1966	14350	1847
1949	18570	4800	1967	13000	1736
1950	19016	4584	1968	13190	1631
1951	18980	4581	1969	13480	1581
1952	18623	4568	1970	13750	1529
1953	17965	4542	1971	14070	1482
1954	19101	4509	1972	14370	1450
1955	19200	4483	1973	14650	1530
1956	19003	4391	1974	15384	1535
1957	19003	4194	1975	15969	1530
1958	16000	3996	1976	15976	1525
1959	16103	3414	1977	16554	1547
1960	16999	3034	1978	16755	1563
1961	–	2711	1979	16965	1604
1962	–	2421			

audiences until the advent of D.W. Griffith, whereupon, it is said, the movies became an art form. In fact the influence of Griffith in making the cinema socially acceptable is probably less significant than the emergence of the feature-length film in the United States in 1912–13, a development that took place later than it did in Europe. While the simple one-reeler remained standard, the primitive nickelodeon was an appropriate showplace. The rise of the full-length drama, which was contemporary with the creation of the 'star system', broadened the appeal of the movies and stimulated the erection of theatres adequate to their presentation in an atmosphere of 'comfort and refinement'.

In Britain the feature film was also late in supplanting the modest one-reel melodramas and comedies of predominantly back-street picture houses. Significantly the humour weekly *Punch*, generally alert to social trends, did not publish its first cartoon about cinema-going until 1912. By that date artist Charles Pears was able to show what was clearly intended to represent a sophisticated, middle-class audience. Few of the 4000 cinemas estimated to be operating in Britain by 1912, however, would have

aspired to such a level of patronage unless they were of the standard of London's first luxury cinema, Cinema House in Oxford Street (1910), with its oak-panelled auditorium, adjoining restaurant, and seats upholstered in a 'delicate shade of Rose du Barri velvet'. Generally speaking middle-class cinema going in Britain came in with World War I and was due to a combination of circumstances: the relaxation of chaperonage, the provision of better appointed and more luxurious cinemas, the feverish desire for entertainment by officers home on leave, and not least, the vastly improved standard of film-making after 1914.

CINEMAS WORLDWIDE

The countries listed below are those for which statistics are available. Few countries issue figures regularly; the last date given in each case is the latest for which figures are obtainable.

Albania 1935–10; 1939–18; 1950–14; 1960–176; 1970–189; 1979–450 (includes mobile).

Algeria 1935–130; 1939–165; 1950–200; 1972–550; 1979–304.

Afghanistan 1939–1; 1952–9; 1972–20; 1977–45.

Argentina 1923–800; 1930–1608; 1939–1021; 1950–1855; 1960–1739; 1970–1767; 1979–1794.

Australia 1919–760; 1925–1216; 1930–1250; 1935–1090; 1939–1371; 1945–1600; 1950–1674; 1960–1800; 1970–1349; 1978–900.

Austria 1921–516; 1925–580; 1930–736; 1935–850; 1949–957; 1956–1210; 1964–1248; 1970–820; 1977–533.

Bangladesh 1976–230.

Belgium 1920–811; 1930–700; 1939–1100; 1950–1550; 1960–1550; 1972–1081; 1979–545.

Bolivia 1925–16; 1935–23; 1947–60; 1954–60; 1976–41.

Brazil 1930–1431; 1939–1450; 1947–1514; 1958–3113; 1968–3234; 1978–3200.

Bulgaria 1920–93; 1925–48; 1935–128; 1939–111; 1947–240; 1957–1400; 1967–2957; 1979–3529.

Burma 1939–131; 1950–150; 1960–380; 1979–400.

Cambodia	1933–4; 1951–15; 1975–50; 1979–0.
Canada	1922–1078; 1937–1121; 1947–1493; 1955–2085; 1960–1756; 1968–1142; 1977–1392.
Chile	1930–215; 1939–243; 1947–268; 1960–450; 1972–336; 1979–160.
China	1925–120; 1930–185; 1935–276; 1939–275; 1949–596; 1953–770; 1958–1386; 1965–2000; 1979–4000.
Colombia	1930–207; 1939–276; 1947–435; 1972–819; 1980–1000.
Costa Rica	1930–21; 1939–40; 1947–52; 1950–77; 1972–136.
Cuba	1939–375; 1947–450; 1950–515; 1972–444.
Czechoslovakia	1919–490; 1925–680; 1930–1200; 1939–1254; 1945–1656; 1951–1928; 1955–2268; 1966–3584; 1972–3469; 1978–3248.
Denmark	1930–270; 1935–340; 1939–370; 1947–430; 1955–458; 1960–500; 1970–382; 1978–442.
Dominican Rep.	1980–150.
Ecuador	1930–25; 1935–29; 1939–37; 1950–75; 1960–260; 1977–330.
Egypt	1925–40; 1930–60; 1935–89; 1939–118; 1946–285; 1950–226; 1960–389; 1972–384; 1979–215.
Eire	1945–212; 1950–345; 1955–327; 1960–290; 1970–300; 1975–230; 1980–131.
Ethiopia	1939–33; 1950–11; 1972–35.
Finland	1911–80; 1922–120; 1927–245; 1932–195; 1937–274; 1942–421; 1947–460; 1952–523; 1957–613; 1962–581; 1970–330; 1979–314.
France	1920–1525; 1925–2947; 1930–3113; 1935–4000; 1939–4600; 1950–5300; 1955–5732; 1960–5821; 1965–5454; 1970–4381; 1975–4328.
Germany	1912–1500; 1918–2299; 1920–3731; 1925–3878; 1930–5266; 1935–5100; 1940–6900; 1945–11 150. W.Ger: 1950–5930; 1955–5100; 1960–6950; 1965–5209; 1970–3634; 1975–3094; 1979–3110. DDR: 1960–1550; 1968–1300; 1975–880; 1980–839.
Greece	1915–147; 1925–138; 1930–224; 1935–122; 1939–170; 1947–300; 1955–450; 1960–1000; 1970–1034; 1979–1504.
Guatemala	1930–25; 1939–34; 1950–42; 1972–195.
Honduras	1925–6; 1930–27; 1950–28; 1972–60; 1979–c. 100.
Hong Kong	1920–6; 1950–27; 1954–62; 1972–99; 1978–73.
Hungary	1907–127; 1912–270; 1921–362; 1930–495; 1939–524; 1945–972; 1951–586; 1960–1200; 1972–981; 1979–1045. (NB: Figs refer to 35mm cinemas only.)
Iceland	1979–25.
India	1910–5; 1920–148; 1924–171; 1930–309; 1936–910; 1941–1136; 1946–1700; 1950–1950; 1960–3200; 1970–4500; 1975–5363; 1979–6232. (NB: Excluding mobile cinemas.)
Indonesia	1930–196; 1939–170; 1950–260; 1960–750; 1972–675; 1977–406.
Iran	1925–4; 1930–10; 1939–35; 1945–78; 1950–80; 1972–520; 1976–438.
Iraq	1935–7; 1939–20; 1950–71; 1972–137; 1979–87.
Israel	1947–216; 1960–226; 1970–257; 1975–227; 1980–230.
Italy	1907–500; 1922–2019; 1930–2405; 1935–3794; 1939–4049; 1955–9543; 1960–10 500; 1970–9680; 1979–7495.
Jamaica	1930–19; 1939–17; 1950–28; 1972–54.
Japan	1920–600; 1925–1050; 1930–1120; 1935–1600; 1930–1749; 1947–1477; 1950–2157; 1955–7400; 1960–8477; 1963–6164; 1966–4119; 1970–3246; 1973–2974; 1975–2443; 1977–2453; 1979–2392.
Jordan	1950–17; 1972–34.
Kenya	1935–8; 1950–44; 1972–28; 1979–35.
Korea	1935–45; 1939–60; 1950–116; South Korea: 1960–273; 1970–658; 1977–752.
Kuwait	1979–10.
Lebanon	1949–48; 1960–82; 1972–170.
Libya	1951–12; 1972–60.
Luxembourg	1933–26; 1939–30; 1950–39; 1955–41; 1972–52; 1975–36; 1979–17.

Madagascar	1925–5; 1933–14; 1950–24; 1972–21.
Malaysia	1925–10; 1935–58; 1939–97; 1950–100; 1960–220; 1972–430; 1975–522.
Malta	1915–30; 1950–26; 1960–49; 1972–39; 1979–35.
Mexico	1930–615; 1935–701; 1939–823; 1946–1369; 1950–1726; 1960–2232; 1972–1850; 1979–2567.
Morocco	1933–51; 1939–62; 1950–90; 1972–155; 1977–276.
Netherlands	1925–264; 1930–236; 1935–308; 1939–333; 1950–461; 1955–573; 1960–565; 1966–490; 1970–435; 1975–387; 1980–507.
New Zealand	1925–350; 1930–443; 1935–366; 1939–576; 1945–568; 1950–570; 1960–581; 1970–260; 1975–228; 1979–200.
Nicaragua	1925–11; 1939–24; 1950–47; 1972–85.
Nigeria	1939–11; 1950–25; 1973–112; 1979–131.
Norway	1925–252; 1930–212; 1935–241; 1939–247; 1947–291; 1951–452; 1955–508; 1960–668; 1971–442; 1975–464; 1979–455.
Outer Mongolia	1952–50; 1977–60.
Pakistan	1947–250; 1957–360; 1960–419; 1970–527; 1975–623; 1979–725.
Paraguay	1930–9; 1939–15; 1950–40; 1972–30.
Peru	1925–60; 1930–70; 1935–110; 1939–205; 1950–235; 1960–400; 1972–363; 1977–400.
Philippines	1935–273; 1950–450; 1960–634; 1972–704; 1977–900; 1980–1200.
Poland	1925–383; 1935–728; 1939–769; 1950–574; 1967–3694; 1977–3232. (NB: 1967 and 1977 figs inc. 16mm cinemas.)
Portugal	1925–127; 1939–215; 1950–301; 1967–336; 1975–410.
Puerto Rico	1980–98.
Romania	1925–304; 1930–357; 1935–380; 1939–372; 1948–383; 1955–350; 1968–573; 1972–462; 1977–578.
Senegal	1975–87; 1979–75.
Singapore	1979–73.
South Africa	1925–380; 1935–350; 1945–465; 1950–470; 1970–521; 1979–700.

Spain	1914–900; 1921–570; 1925–1500; 1930–2074; 1935–3252; 1939–3500; 1948–3251; 1955–7325; 1960–6459; 1970–6627; 1974–5178; 1978–4430.
Sri Lanka	1930–24; 1939–19; 1950–82; 1960–206; 1970–315; 1975–365.
Sweden	1920–600; 1930–1182; 1935–843; 1939–1907; 1947–2493; 1955–2494; 1966–1733; 1975–1192; 1979–1210.
Switzerland	1920–178; 1930–302; 1941–351; 1950–410; 1960–615; 1972–539; 1977–494.
Syria	1925–14; 1935–26; 1950–50; 1960–70; 1972–90; 1977–70.
Taiwan	1960–542; 1972–668.
Tanzania	1972–65.
Thailand	1915–3; 1925–42; 1935–68; 1939–80; 1950–118; 1960–238; 1970–340; 1977–415.
Trinidad	1978–68.
Tunisia	1933–61; 1950–50; 1972–65; 1979–76.
Turkey	1925–40; 1930–104; 1939–120; 1950–275; 1960–700; 1970–790; 1979–3000 (claimed).
Uruguay	1925–101; 1930–122; 1935–137; 1945–175; 1950–177; 1972–223; 1979–94.
United Kingdom	1914–3170; 1928–3760; 1934–4305; 1939–4901. For 1945–1979 see p. 205.
United States	1910–9480; 1913–15700; 1923–15000; 1929–23344; 1935–15273; 1940–19042. For 1945–1979 see p. 205.
USSR	1977–14700. (NB: At the time of the revolution in 1917 the number of Russian cinemas was 1045. No reliable figures are available for the interim years because the USSR counts projection points, not cinemas proper.)
Yugoslavia	1921–231; 1930–397; 1939–383; 1950–736; 1960–1585; 1967–1172; 1977–1385.
Venezuela	1930–121; 1939–147; 1950–350; 1954–575; 1964–741; 1975–650.
Vietnam	1912–10; 1925–29; 1930–34; 1939–110; 1950–80; 1960 (S. Vietnam only)–189; 1970 (S. Vietnam only)–102.

The largest cinema in the world is the Radio City Music Hall, opened in New York on 27 December 1932 with an original seating capacity of 5945. A number of seats were removed during renovations in the spring of 1979, leaving the present seating capacity of the Music Hall at 5882.

The largest cinema ever built was the Roxy, built in New York at a cost of $12 million and opened under the management of Samuel Rothapfel (after whom it was named) on 11 March 1927. With an original seating capacity of 6214, the Roxy employed a total of 300 staff, including 16 projectionists and 110 musicians. By 1957, however, the number of seats had been reduced to 5869, leaving Radio City Music Hall as the world's largest cinema. The Roxy closed on 29 March 1960.

Europe's largest-ever cinema was the Gaumont Palace, opened in Paris with a 6000 seat auditorium in 1931.

The largest cinema in Britain is the Odeon Theatre, Hammersmith, with 3485 seats.

The smallest cinema in the world to operate as a

Radio City Music Hall – currently the world's largest cinema

regular commercial venture was the Miramar at Colon, Cuba, which was reported in 1926 to have 25 seats.

The smallest cinema in the USA was the Silver Star Theater in Silver Star, Montana, which had a seating capacity of 26 in 1925. Silver Star, population 75, boasted two cinemas, with a total seating capacity (126) exceeding the number of citizens. Only eleven of the 15000 cinemas operating in the US at that date had under 100 seats, of which five were in the State of Montana.

The highest cinema attendance in the world is in India, with 3285 million seats sold in 1978 (about 9 million daily). This compares with 1130 million in the USA, 317 million in Italy, 177 million in France, 166 million in Japan, 130 million in West Germany and 127 million in Britain (1978 figures).

The largest cinema ever built – New York's 6214 seat Roxy (plan starts at top and continues on bottom)

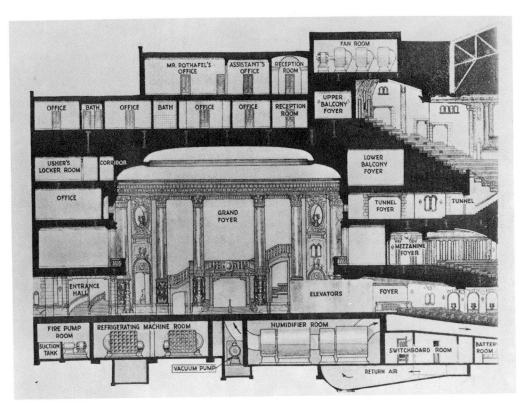

FAN ROOM

MR. ROTHAFEL'S OFFICE ASSISTANT'S OFFICE RECEPTION ROOM

UPPER BALCONY FOYER

OFFICE BATH. OFFICE BATH OFFICE OFFICE RECEPTION ROOM

USHER'S LOCKER ROOM CORRIDOR

LOWER BALCONY FOYER

OFFICE

GRAND FOYER

TUNNEL FOYER TUNNEL

MEZZANINE FOYER

ENTRANCE HALL

ELEVATORS FOYER

FIRE PUMP ROOM REFRIGERATING MACHINE ROOM HUMIDIFIER ROOM

SUCTION TANK

SWITCHBOARD ROOM BATTERY ROOM

VACUUM PUMP

RETURN AIR

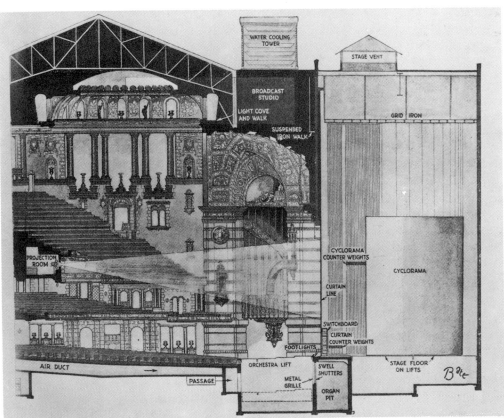

WATER COOLING TOWER

STAGE VENT

BROADCAST STUDIO

LIGHT COVE AND WALK

GRID IRON

SUSPENDED IRON WALK

PROJECTION ROOM

CYCLORAMA COUNTER WEIGHTS

CURTAIN LINE

CYCLORAMA

SWITCHBOARD

CURTAIN COUNTER WEIGHTS

FOOTLIGHTS

AIR DUCT

ORCHESTRA LIFT

SWELL SHUTTERS

STAGE FLOOR ON LIFTS

PASSAGE

METAL GRILLE

ORGAN PIT

WEEKLY CINEMA ATTENDANCE: USA AND UK

	USA (m)	UK (m)		USA (m)	UK (m)
1922	40	–	1951	54	26·2
1923	43	–	1952	51	25·2
1924	46	–	1953	46	24·7
1925	46	–	1954	49	24·5
1926	50	–	1955	46	22·7
1927	57	–	1956	47	21·2
1928	65	25·2	1957	45	17·6
1929	95	–	1958	40	14·5
1930	90	–	1959	42	11·2
1931	75	–	1960	40	9·6
1932	60	–	1961	42	8·6
1933	60	–	1962	43	7·6
1934	70	18·3	1963	44	6·9
1935	75	–	1964	–	6·6
1936	88	–	1965	44	6·3
1937	85	–	1966	38	5·6
1938	85	–	1967	17·8	5·1
1939	85	–	1968	18·8	4·6
1940	80	–	1969	17·5	4·1
1941	85	25·2	1970	17·7	3·7
1942	85	28·7	1971	15·8	3·9
1943	85	29·6	1972	18	3·0
1944	85	30·3	1973	16·6	2·6
1945	90	30·5	1974	19·4	2·7
1946	90	31·4	1975	19·9	2·2
1947	90	28·1	1976	18·4	2·0
1948	90	29·1	1977	20·2	2·1
1949	87·5	27·5	1978	21·7	2·4
1950	60	26·8	1979	22·1	2·5*

*Estimated

The all-time record figure for any country was 4940 million seats sold in the USA in 1929. The European record is 819 million in Italy in 1955.

The country with the highest per capita cinema attendance in the world is the Philippines (pop. 44 million), with an average of 19·06 visits annually per head of population (1979–80 figures).

The country with the largest number of cinemas in relation to population is San Marino, with one cinema for every 1512 inhabitants (a total of 8). In comparison the USA has one cinema for every 13750 inhabitants, the USSR has one cinema for every 14250 inhabitants and the UK, television dominated, is content with one cinema for every 36000 inhabitants.

At the other end of the scale comes Saudi Arabia (pop. 8 million) with no cinemas, the public presentation of films being illegal as contrary to strict Islamic belief.

Incentives to encourage cinema-going were part of the huckstering tradition of enterprising showmanship. Among the earliest such schemes was free transport. W. Hilton Perkin of the South African Biograph & Mutoscope Co. made an arrangement with the Cape Government Railway Department in 1899 by which anybody residing between Wynberg and Cape Town would receive a free first-class return ticket to attend 'Biograph Night' at Good Hope Hall. Walter Jeffs, a pioneer British showman who presented the first all-film programmes to be seen outside London, drew patrons to his 'New Century Pictures' at the Curzon Hall in Birmingham c. 1905 by arranging with Birmingham Tramways to issue special combined tram-fare and cinema-admission tickets. The concessionary 1s ticket, purchased from the tram conductor, admitted a patron to the 1s seats at Curzon Hall. In 1925 the Aurora, Calcutta, offered 'a free motor bus service up to Sham Bazaar, after the night shows, for those buying tickets above four annas'.

The earliest cinema audiences in Hong Kong had to be paid to attend. An Englishman had opened the first cinema for Chinese inhabitants, but they were so superstitious of the possible evil power of the 'moving spirits' on the screen that they would not come. For three weeks the proprietor hired audiences by the day, paying each person a stipulated sum for attendance, until the superstitious fears were shown to be groundless. By 1913 the enterprising proprietor was running a chain of ten cinemas.

Competitions were popular with many exhibitors. The proprietor of the Stuart Hall, a cinema in Wood Green, London, inaugurated a weekly competition in 1908 with a prize of half a guinea for the patron who came nearest to guessing the *number of frames* in the main picture. *Curly's Holiday* (GB 17) was presented in Blackpool (where the film was set) with the actor who played Curly, J.F. Carr, always somewhere in the audience. The first person to recognise him won £5. At Rawtenstall in industrial Lancashire, the unemployed were induced into the local cinema during the depression of the early 30s by prizes of tea, sugar, packets of bacon and other groceries for the holders of 'lucky tickets'. A showman at Dubbo, NSW, was prosecuted under the Lotteries Act in 1910 when he offered a cake to whoever correctly guessed what time the show was over. He was able to convince the magistrate that 'the exercise of forethought was demanded' and that therefore his competition was not a lottery.

In 1904 H. Howard, an itinerant Bioscope showman, announced that he would give three consecutive performances at Durban Town Hall and the person who succeeded in guessing the total of the combined audiences would be given the projector and accessories, value £400. If the winner was a clergyman, he would receive a copy of the 2400 ft *Horitz Passion Play* film as a bonus. Two men correctly guessed the meagre total of 572 and were awarded the whole cinema enterprise, to split between them as they saw fit.

During the 1918 'flu epidemic the Royal Opera House, Calcutta, which had been converted into a cinema, gave away a bottle of medicine with the ticket to anyone brave enough to attend.

In 1912 the American Tobacco Co. began offering these coupons towards the price of a cinema seat (*Backnumbers*)

Alexander Khanzhonkov, collecting for Russian war charities in 1915, put a motion picture camera in front of the collecting box in the foyer of his Moscow cinema and filmed everyone who contributed. The film was shown the following week and encouraged not only generosity but also renewed attendance. The New Zealand showman T.J. West had done something similar when he presented a show in Sydney on 21 April 1906 consisting of scenes of the city. Press advertisements contained a special message to the employees of Anthony Hordern's, one of Sydney's largest department stores: 'You left business at 1 p.m. today. Come and see yourself doing it again tonight.'

Cinemas run by China Theatres Ltd in the twenties resorted to the habit of letting the audience in without payment – Chinese would not pay for something they had not seen – and then running the film for half a reel or so before stopping and collecting the admissions in a basket. In 1921, during a temporary recession in the cinema industry, a theatre in Portland, Oregon, allowed patrons to pay on the way out.

At the Batley Co-operative Hall (Yorks) *c.* World War I, patrons of the Saturday children's matinee received a stick of rock or a bar of Mazawattee chocolate on the way in and an orange on the way out. All this plus the show

for a penny. Since the cinema could only be reached by climbing 250 stone steps, some added inducement may have been necessary.

In 1912 the American Tobacco Co. began offering movie coupons with Tokio cigarettes. Worth ½¢ each towards the cost of admission, they were accepted (it was claimed) at all cinemas in the USA. Many smaller cinemas only charged a nickel in 1912, so ten coupons would secure free admission. The scheme was operated in reverse when the Brazilian film industry inaugurated a system in 1968 by which all ticket stubs counted towards free gifts on the trading stamp principle.

Free gifts will always draw an audience. There are many Americans still eating off the free dishes which were given to audiences during the depression. On occasion the film itself has been the medium of the gift. When a topical called *Moving Melbourne* (Aus 06) came to the end of its run at Melbourne Town Hall, the film was cut up into short lengths which were then presented to the members of the audience. The promoters of *Blitzkrieg Operation Number Eleven* (Jap 57), a war-newsreel compilation feature, offered Japanese audiences 'free stills of any scene in which your relatives or friends appear'.

The first cinema to present a double bill was the Glacarium in Melbourne, Australia, on 15 May 1911. The programme for the week was *The Lost Chord* (Aus 11) and *The Fall of Troy* (It 10).

The first cinema in the USA to offer two features in the same bill was the Knickerbocker Theater, New York, on 23 September 1915, when Thomas Ince's *The Iron Strain* (US 15), with Dustin Farnum, was the supporting picture to D. W. Griffith's *The Lamb* (US 15), with Douglas Fairbanks. Generally the double feature remained rare in the United States until 1931, when the practice began to spread beyond the New England states where it had begun to take root in the late twenties. Previously, exhibitors had generally shown a supporting programme consisting of a two-reel comedy, a travelogue or other 'general interest' subject, a cartoon and a newsreel. In 1931 some 1800 cinemas in the US, or about 12½ per cent, were showing double features; by 1947 the proportion had risen to about 67 per cent.

The triple feature was introduced by the Nikkatsu Co. of Japan about 1920 in its chain of cinemas. The programme was generally made up of a period movie, followed by a film of contemporary life, followed by a foreign feature.

The quadruple feature appeared a few years later, when the financially pressed Taikatsu Co. found production had outstripped the capacity of its outlets.

During the 1950s small cinemas in Japanese villages would show up to six features on a single programme. This invariably rose from competition between two rival cinemas, one advertising a triple feature, the other outbidding it with a quadruple, and so on.

The oldest cinema in Britain is the Alexandra Cinema, Blackburn, which opened on Easter Tuesday 1909. It now shows Asian films only.

The oldest building ever converted to use as a cinema was the Music Hall Cinema, Chester, England, which was in service as a 'common hall' as early as 1280 and as a place of entertainment by 1616. The building was converted into a legitimate theatre in 1773 and a music hall in 1855. Films were first exhibited there in 1910, but only in 1921 was it reconstructed as a permanent cinema. It closed in 1962 to undergo yet another conversion, this time an ignominious transformation into a supermarket.

The largest cinema chain in the world is GCC Theatres Inc. of Chestnut Hill, Mass., a subsidiary of General Cinema Corporation, which controls 892 screens throughout the USA. This represents approximately 5 per cent of the total number of American cinemas. The USA has 312 cinema chains each controlling three or more cinemas.

The largest cinema chain in Britain is controlled by EMI/ABC with 320 screens, 18 per cent of the total in the country. Odeon/Rank follows with 273 screens (17 per cent), while the Star chain numbers 140 screens, and Classic Cinemas 126.

The highest box office gross for a cinema in any one week was the $468 173 receipts for *Crossed Swords*/UK: *The Prince and the Pauper* (US 78) at New York's Radio City Music Hall during the week commencing 2 April 1978.

The last silent cinema in Britain was the Electra at Royton, Lancs, run by the Progress Film Co. In contrast to their name the proprietors refused to countenance anything so new-fangled as talkies and only closed down in 1935 when the renters were unable to maintain a supply of silent films.

Elsewhere the silent cinema survived longer. According to US statistics, there were 36 silent picture houses remaining in 1937, though it is possible that some of these were buildings still licensed to show films, but which had ceased to operate. Finland is said to have had some silent houses running during World War II and as late as 1952 only 50 out of the 150 cinemas in Burma were wired for sound. Thailand continued to produce silent films until the mid-1960s (*see* Silent Film, p. 168).

The longest continuous run of any film at a single cinema was achieved by *The Cabinet of Dr Caligari* (Ger 19), which ran in Paris for seven years from 1920.

It is claimed that *The Birth of a Nation* (US 15) was on continuous release in the southern states of the US (though at different cinemas) between 1915 and 1927.

The longest run in Britain was that of *Gone with the Wind* (US 39), which ran for four years and 29 weeks at the 450-seat Ritz Cinema, London, from 18 April 1940. *South Pacific* (US 58) ran for four years 22 weeks, 21 April 1958–30 Sept 1962, at the much larger Dominion, Tottenham Court Road, and was the first film in Britain to gross over £1 million at one cinema.

The longest running film currently on exhibition is *Emmanuelle* (Fr 74), which is still showing (1980) at the Champs Elysées cinema where it opened on 26 June 1974.

The longest name ever given to a cinema was conferred on a mobile picture show operated by Spanish showman José Fessi Fernandez in the Bordeaux region of France in 1902. It was called the Lentielectroplasticromomimocoliserpentographe. **The longest name of a cinema currently in operation** is the comparatively terse Cinema-I-Anjuman-I-Khairiya-I-Niswan, a 200-seat picture house in Kabul, Afghanistan. **The longest single word name** is borne by the Kannikaparameswari in Turyvegere, India.

The shortest name ever given to a cinema was borne by the K in Mattoon, Ill. in 1925.

Unusual cinema names have abounded since the Cabbage opened in Liverpool in 1914 and the Decadence in Harbin, China, the same year. A Bradford clergyman, the Rev S. Thomas, opened The World's Window about this date and while Brussels offered High Life, Moscow promised Magic Dreams. Brno, Czechoslovakia made an honest declaration with The Illusion, while Estonia's Bi-Ba-Bo may have meant anything at all, even in Estonian. A name which definitely cloaked a secret was the 555 at Brown's Bay, New Zealand, owned by Mrs Olga Brown – it was 'a private family joke, believed to concern cards'. The first cinema in Peking to show talkies was inappropriately called the Peace and Quiet. The Yank Theatre was located far from any indigenous Yanks, in the Grand Duchy of Luxembourg, and it was unnecessary to travel to Milan to attend La Scala when there was one in the Irish village of Letterkenny, Co. Donegal. Greenland Theatre was nowhere near Greenland, but in Palacode, India. The image of suburban gentility conjured up by Bristol's Kosy Korner Kinema was matched by Mon Repos, only the latter was located in the untamed frontier atmosphere of Russia's Baku oilfield in 1916. In India many cinemas are still called 'Talkies', such as Swastika Talkies in Bihar, Tip Top Talkies at Gopichettipalayam, Jolly Talkies in Muttom and Molly Talkies in Nedunganpara, or Baby Talkies, Thiruvarar. English Talkies in Ahmedabad shows movies in Gujarati, not English. The Roxy, now no more than a fading memory to New Yorkers, lives on in Motihari, Champaran, Bohar, and Bombay. The White Elephant and the Black Cat both belonged to World War I Glasgow, as did a Cinerama long before today's wide-screen spectacle was ever thought of. The Buffalo in Ashington, Northumberland, opened about 1912, was so named because it specialised in westerns.

The oddest names are undoubtedly those found in the United States: Amusu (Lincolntown, Ga.); Hobo (Shawneetown, Ill.); The No Name (Moreauville, La.); Tootles (St Joseph, Mo.); U-No-Us (Rensselaer Falls, NY); Muse-Us (Dayton, Ohio); Tar Heel (Plumtree, NC); Dazzleland (Philadelphia); Glory B (Miami, Okla.); C-It (Ashtabula Harbor, Ohio); The Vamp (Barnwell, SC); Fo To Sho (Ballinger, Texas); Ha Ha (Minneapolis);

Hoo Hoo (Doucette, Texas); The Herring (Winton, NC); Cinderella (Detroit); OK (Simpson, Ill.); My (Indianapolis); Your (Detroit); Our (Sparta, Mich.); Why Not (Greenfield, Ind.); It (Huntingdon, W. Va.); Try-It (Buffalo, NY); Hi-Art (Lockport, NY); Good Luck (Seattle, Wash.); Sour Wine (Brazil, Ind.); Oh Gee (Edwardsville, Ill.); Happy Jack (Abilene, Texas); Uses Pictures (Butlerville, Ind.); No Home (Dalton City, Ill.); Pa and Ma's (Cobsden, Ill.); Red Apple (Omak, Wash.); Fattie's (Winchester, Texas); Silent Prayers (Sprigg, W. Va.); Za Za (Plainfield, Ind.); Zim Zim (Cumberland, W. Va.). The Norka in Akron and the Idol in Lodi were simply the town name spelt backwards. In Thibodaux, La., there were two cinemas before the war. The larger was the Grand. Its smaller rival was the Baby Grand.

The Americans have also had a penchant for giving cinemas girls' names: Adele (Eatonton, Ga.); Alice (Vincennes, Ind.); Annette (Cicero, Ill.); Besse (Red Cloud, Neb.); Bertha (Chicago); Cecile (Cokato, Minn.); Daisy (Memphis, Te.); Dawn (Detroit; Dorothy (Hotcoal, W. Va.); Edith (Port Allen, La.); Elizabeth (Falmouth, Mass.); Eloise (Ashley, Ill.); Emma (Payette, Idaho); Enid (Donnybrook, NC); Ethel (Ethel, Mo.); Evelyn (Social Circle, Ga.); Fay (Olympia, Wash.); Flora (Elizabeth, NJ); Florence (Bedford, Ky.); Gayle (Angelton, Texas); Gloria (New York); Grace (Martinsville, Ind.); Hortense (Indianapolis); Iris (Chicago); Imogene (Milton, Fla.); Ivy (Cleves, Ohio); Janet (Chicago); Katherine (Monticello, Fla.); Lillian (Greenville, Ky.); Lily (Long Is. City); Lois (Toppenish, Wash.); Louisa (Louisa, Va.); Lucille (Chicago); Mabel (Chicago); Marion (Clarksdale, Miss.); Margaret (Huntingdon, W. Va.); Martha Jane (Malakoff, Tex.); Maxine (Croswell, Mich.); May (Mayville, Wisc.); Mildred (Barnesville, Ga.); Myrtle (New York); Paulina (Chicago); Polly Anna (Maryland, Okla.); Priscilla (Toledo, Ohio.); Rose (Chelan, Wash.); Shirley (Richmond, Va.); Sylvia (Sylvester, Ga.); Thelma (Kenbridge, Ga.); Violet (Brookston, Ind.); Zelda (Duluth, Minn.).

The largest number of cinemas in one city was 986 in New York in 1913.

The post-war record was held by Tokyo, which had over 600 cinemas in 1958, two and a half times as many as New York.

The largest number of cinemas showing the same film in the same city at the same time was 246 in New York when the sensational sex film *Traffic in Souls* (US 13) was first released.

The largest multiple cinema in the world is Cineplex, a complex of 18 auditoria under one roof, which opened at Eaton Centre, Toronto, Canada, on 19 April 1979. The individual cinemas have a seating capacity of 60–130, with an aggregate of 1600. Cineplex specialises in foreign and minority interest pictures, including undubbed Italian films aimed at Toronto's 400 000 strong Italian community.

Europe's largest multiple cinema is the Palads in Copenhagen, Denmark, with 15 cinemas under one roof. One of Europe's oldest picture houses, it was converted into a multiple by A/S Nordisk Film on 1 September 1978.

The northernmost cinema in the world is the 329-seat North Cape Municipal Kino at Honningsvåg (pop. 5000), Norway, which lies on latitude 71° 1′, 300 miles north of the Arctic Circle.

The southernmost cinema in the world is the Cine San Martín in Ushuaia (pop. 2200), Tierra del Fuego, Argentina, which lies just north of latitude 55°.

Unusual Cinemas: Cinemas have been located in odd places ever since someone thought of putting one on top of Mt Portofino, Genoa, in 1907. Motion pictures entered the Arabian harem the same year when one Mehdi Russi Khan persuaded Shah Mohammed Ali to allow him to relieve the boredom of the many royal wives with a 'ladies only' cinema showing Pathé films imported from France. Meanwhile in the less exotic atmosphere of one of London's ancient churches, St Mary Axe, the Rev Wilson Carlisle was relieving the ennui of his parishioners by introducing elevating and instructive movies into his Sunday services. Some years later, in the early 1920s, the Crawford Memorial Methodist Church at 218th Street, New York, began doubling as a cinema. The Rev Lincoln Caswell was worried about dwindling congre-

Right: The LNER introduced talkies on trains in 1935

The Commercial Film

UNDER
THE DIRECTION OF
SYDNEY W. CARROLL

JUNE 1935
VOL. I. No. 5.

6D MONTHLY

PROPAGANDA · PUBLICITY · INSTRUCTION

gations and started up Saturday night cinema performances with full-length features plus a supporting programme of comedies and a newsreel, borrowing the films for nothing from an obliging neighbourhood theatre. The following night he would preach on the moral pointed by the 'big picture'. As a further inducement the stars themselves were invited along, one notable patron being Lillian Gish. The first feature films to be shown in a cathedral were *The Sower* (GB 37), starring Eliot Makeham, and *Where Love Is, God Is* (GB 37), which formed part of a special service held at Chichester Cathedral, England, on 9 December 1937.

There have been occasional misguided attempts to establish open-air cinemas in Britain, among them the Garden Cinema at Hull, which opened for business on a balmy summer's night in July 1912. Patrons sat on deck chairs in an open-sided marquee. Not surprisingly the cinema was forced to close with the onset of winter and never reopened again. Another attempt was made in 1915, when a roof-top cinema seating 150 was established by Pathé Frères on a building in Wardour Street, London. Two years later an open-air cinema was inaugurated in the middle of Trafalgar Square for the benefit of soldiers and sailors on leave.

In 1913 Secretary of State William Jennings Bryan established a cinema inside the State Department, Washington, for the leisure-time entertainment of the staff.

There is no record of cinemas in prisoner of war camps, but Allied civilians interned at Ruhleben Internment Camp during World War I enjoyed the benefit of a well-appointed picture house.

One Nazi concentration camp is known to have had a cinema. In November 1944 a barracks at Dora, a concentration camp adjacent to Buchenwald, was converted into a cinema as a special privilege for the slave labourers engaged on the assembly of Hitler's V1 and V2 rockets.

Various attempts have been made to establish specialist cinemas. One that thoroughly deserved to fail was the Patriotic Cinema Theatre, founded in Moscow in 1908 by a proto-Fascist group called the 'Union of Russian People' with the object of showing anti-semitic films. The cinema enjoyed special police protection, but closed for lack of suitable material after the

Union had been unable to find a producer willing to make films justifying the pogroms. The Crystal Hall on 14th Street, New York, showed only Chaplin movies for nine years 1914–23, with the exception of one week when they decided to vary the programme. Business was so bad they reverted to Chaplin. In Moscow in 1925 there was a cinema devoted entirely to old Clara Kimball Young movies, despite the fact that Miss Young's career was already over by this date. (She had refused to diet when the fashion for slim figures overtook America. In Russia the rotund look never went out.) In May 1931 the Grand Cinema in Auckland, New Zealand, changed its name to the London and initiated a policy of showing only British films 'for the first time in the whole Empire'. It was also the last time.

One man who succeeded in defying contemporary taste was John Hampton, who opened Hampton's Silent Movies on Fairfax Avenue, Los Angeles, in 1942 – long before the silents were treated with the reverence they are today. Hampton claimed that the difference between what he was offering and what film archives and societies offered was that he tried to present programmes of *typical* silent films, not just the great classics. Having survived the lean years, Hampton's now thrives on the nostalgia cult.

The first cinema in a train was established on the Trans-Siberian Railway by a French company in 1913. Admission was 50 kopeks (12½c or 1s). In Britain cinema coaches on trains were introduced by the LNER on the *Flying Scotsman* between Kings Cross and York in March 1924. The premier presentation was *Ashes of Vengeance* (US 23) with Norma Talmadge. 'Talkie Trains' were inaugurated by the LNER in May 1935 and continued in service till outbreak of war.

A floating cinema was instituted in the USA on the Erie Canal between Troy and Newark, NY in 1907. Called the *Star Floating Palace*, it was a converted canal boat with a 'wainscoted inside' which plied the canal towns giving shows at each. In later years the idea was borrowed by Soviet Russia. When the 'agit-steamboat' *Red Star* was despatched on a propaganda tour down the Kama and Volga Rivers in 1919, Molotov and Lenin's wife Krupskya, who were in charge, arranged for the construction of a 800-seat cinema on a barge, which was towed behind the *Red Star*.

A conventional cinema run in an unconventional way was the Picture House in the little Yorkshire village of Denholme, established as a co-operative venture in 1935 and operated entirely by voluntary labour. A hundred villagers contributed the £200 capital needed and the management of the cinema was in the hands of a committee elected annually. Old Age Pensioners were admitted free, others paid 3d–9d.

A cinema called the Fly-In was opened at Asbury Park, NJ, in 1948 with space for 500 cars and 50 aeroplanes.

There is nothing unusual about watching movies in the air, but cinemas are curiously rare at airports. The only one in Europe is at Prague, where it is greatly appreciated by those subjected to the haphazard scheduling of East European airlines. It shows full-length features, mainly Italian westerns with Czech sub-titles, and admission is free to bona fide passengers.

The first children's Saturday matinees were inaugurated by Sidney Bernstein (now Lord Bernstein) of the Bernstein Group of Theatres (later Granada Theatres) with a performance at the Empire, Willesden, on 23 March 1928. Two thousand children paid 3d each to attend a programme which included *Robinson Crusoe* (GB 27), a *Topical Budget* and two short films on items of general interest.

The first cinema club for children in Britain was the Mickey Mouse Club, the earliest recorded branch being established at the Arcade Cinema, Darlington, in 1933. There were 200 Mickey Mouse Clubs by May 1937. Gaumont-British cinema clubs were in being by 1936 and the Granadiers, organised by the Granada circuit, were founded in 1937.

The first gaol to institute film shows for prisoners was Goulburn Gaol, Sydney, New South Wales, commencing on 3 January 1911 with a programme presented by the Methodist chaplain, the Rev. J.H. Lewin. The *Melbourne Argus* reported: 'Some of the long-sentence prisoners had never previously seen moving pictures and they more especially enjoyed the entertainment. The pictures were of course of an elevating character, including *Waterways of Holland, Dogs of Various Countries,* and *The Visit of the American Fleet*'.

In Britain the first regular film shows for gaol inmates were instituted on a weekly basis at Maidstone Prison in November 1937. The inaugural programme was rather dauntingly described as 'three hours of educational and cultural films, specially selected for reformative treatment of prisoners'. The shows were held in the 100-seat prison chapel, admission accord-

A children's Saturday matinée somewhere in the North of England. The year is 1936

ing to a three-weekly rota (Maidstone held 350 prisoners) being permitted to inmates who had earned a certain number of good conduct marks. The projector was operated by 'lifers'.

The first drive-in cinema was the Camden Drive-In, opened by Richard Hollingshead on a 10-acre site off Wilson Boulevard, Camden, NJ, on 6 June 1933. The screen measured 40ft (12m) by 30ft (9m) and there was accommodation for 400 cars. The sound came from high-volume screen speakers provided by RCA-Victor.

The 'In-Car' speaker was introduced by RCA-Victor in 1941. The screen speakers of the pioneer drive-ins had been replaced in the meantime by multiple-site speakers providing sound for two cars side by side.

The expansion of drive-ins began very slowly; twelve years after the opening of the Camden there were still only 60 in the whole of the United States. The growth years were conterminous with that of television, for no clear reason. In 1949 there were 1000 drive-ins; by 1953 the figure had quadrupled. Ten years later there were 6000, accounting for 20–25 per cent of US box office receipts.

The largest drive-in cinema in the world is Loew's Open Air at Lynn, Mass., which has accommodation for 5000 cars. Assuming at least two occupants per car, a capacity audience would exceed that of any conventional cinema. The average size of drive-ins in the USA is 550 car places.

The smallest drive-in cinema is the Starnite at New Rockford, North Dakota, with accommodation for 75 cars.

Birth of the in-flight movie – Imperial Airways, April 1925

The first in-flight movie was First National's production of Conan Doyle's *The Lost World* (US 25), shown during a scheduled Imperial Airways flight from London to the Continent in April 1925.

America's first in-flight presentation was a more modest affair consisting of a *Universal Newsreel* and a couple of cartoon shorts shown aboard a transcontinental Air Transport Inc. Ford transport aircraft on 8 October 1929.

The first airline to introduce regular in-flight movies was TWA, commencing with the presentation of *By Love Possessed* (US 61), with Lana Turner and Efrem Zimbalist Jnr.), in the first-class section during a scheduled New York–Los Angeles flight on 19 July 1961.

The averages given above have been rounded to the nearest cent or penny. A clearer idea of *typical* seat prices in Britain may be obtained from the changes made at the Electric Cinema, Portobello Road, between its opening in 1910 and initial closure in the 1960s. The 1962 figure is untypically low and most cinemas would have had price increases in the 1950s. Otherwise, the prices probably accord with those charged by the majority of older, small picture houses in London's suburbs and the provinces.

1910 3d, 6d, 1s (reserved)	1942	8d–1s 2d
1921 5d–1s 3d	1943	10d–1s 6d
1927 3d–1s 2d	1945	10d–1s 9d
1933 5d–1s 0d	1962	1s 6d–2s 0d

The $2 seat: Contrary to orthodox wisdom, *The Birth of a Nation* (US 15) was not the first motion picture presentation to carry a $2 price tag. Admission to the Miles Bros' *Great American Biograph* touring show in the mining camps of Alaska had been $2 as early as 1901.

The lowest seat price recorded was a farthing by a cinema in London's Whitechapel Road in 1909, though the concessionary admission applied only to four children purchasing tickets together. The regular price for children at the Star Kinema in Newcastle upon Tyne about the time of World War I was $\frac{1}{2}$d, but admission could be obtained by presenting a clean glass jam jar instead. In 1925, during a temporary slump in movie-going, a desperate cinema manager in Covington, La., admitted patrons in exchange for empty beer bottles. He took $23 and 1812 empties. The cheapest seats noted in the Report of the Indian Cinematograph Committee (1928) were priced at one anna – slightly over one penny. These were 'seats' in a figurative sense, since the lowly price meant only a lowly place on the ground. In the late 1930s some cinemas in Karachi were wont to give free shows, consisting of shorts and long trailers, when their rivals were showing a blockbuster. A cinema opened in Cardiff in 1935 for 'coloured people' only charged a flat rate admission of 1d. Even cheaper was a picture house on Sixth Avenue, New York, which advertised *c.* 1912 a movie of a negro lynching for 1c. On at least one occasion any price for a seat has been accepted. In Victoria, BC, a patriotic cinema

---

AVERAGE CINEMA SEAT PRICES

	USA	UK		USA	UK
1933	23c	10d	1957	50c	2s 4d
1934	23c	10d	1958	65c	2s 4d
1935	24c	10d	1959	66c	2s 4d
1936	25c	10d	1960	69c	2s 6d
1937	23c	10d	1961	69c	2s 8d
1938	23c	10d	1962	70c	2s 10d
1939	23c	10d	1963	74c	3s 1d
1940	24c	11d	1964	76c	3s 4d
1941	25c	1s 0d	1965	85c	3s 8d
1942	27c	1s 2d	1966	87c	4s 1d
1943	29c	1s 4d	1967	$1·19c	4s 5d
1944	27c	1s 5d	1968	$1·31c	4s 10d
1945	29c	1s 5d	1969	$1·42c	5s 5d
1946	33c	1s 5d	1970	$1·55c	6s 1d
1947	33c	1s 5d	1971	$1·65c	34p
1948	34c	1s 5d	1972	$1·70c	38p
1949	38c	1s 5d	1973	$1·76c	43p
1950	44c	1s 6d	1974	$1·88c	50p
1951	44c	1s 7d	1975	$2·05c	61p
1952	50c	1s 8d	1976	$2·12c	73p
1953	50c	1s 8d	1977	$2·23c	83p
1954	45c	1s 9d	1978	$2·34c	94p
1955	50c	1s 10d	1979	$2·46c	£1·14p
1956	50c	1s 11d		(June)	

The largest per cent American increase was 36·8 per cent from 1966 to 1967; the largest British was 22 per cent from 1974 to 1975.

manager running *The Luck of Ginger Coffey* (Can 64) allowed patrons to pay whatever they thought the film was worth on their way out.

Currently the lowest admission charges are in China, where seat prices for first run pictures in Peking and Shanghai are equivalent to 18c (US) or 8p and slightly less for older films. In the country areas admission is often free.

The highest tax on cinema admission prices is levied by the state government of the Punjab in Pakistan, where it was raised to 150 per cent on 1 July 1978.

AUDIENCES

The largest audience ever to view a film simultaneously in the same locale was 110000 on the occasion of the screening of D.W. Griffith's *Boots* (US 19) at the Methodist Centenary celebration held at the Oval Amphitheater, Columbus, Ohio, on 4 July 1919. Fifty thousand of the audience were accommodated in the stands, the remainder in the arena. The film was projected on a giant screen, with a picture size of 100×75 ft ($30 \cdot 5 \times 22 \cdot 9$ m).

The highest number of times a patron has seen the same film is 940 by Mrs Myra Franklin of Cardiff, Wales, whose favourite picture can only be *The Sound of Music* (US 65).

Fan mail began to be sent to the uncredited performers of the early silents even before the advent of named stars. Mary Pickford recalled an occasion at the Biograph Studios in about 1912 when she enquired about a letter she was expecting, and was told that it had probably been thrown away together with the hundreds of other letters addressed simply to 'the Girl with the Curls' or 'the Biograph Girl'. She was amazed to learn that people she had never met should feel impelled to write to someone who had no more substance for them than a mute shadow on a silver screen. Biograph's high-handed method of disposing of unsolicited correspondence did not long survive the onslaught of the fan magazines, which soon took to publishing the stars' studio addresses in response to eager enquiries from the fans. Producers came to realise that a mail count was

one method of assessing a rising star's popularity and consequently his or her box office potential, while the stars themselves knew that it was in their own interest to maintain a devoted fan following, even at the cost of the $250 a week it was estimated in the 20s that a major star would need to spend on photographs and postage.

The largest fan mail of the immediate post-World War I period was received by 'America's Sweetheart' Mary Pickford, with an average of 18000 letters a month. It was maintained that Miss Pickford employed a fleet of 18 secretaries to answer them.

Mary Pickford's popularity began to decline in the 'flapper era' and in 1927 it was reported that Colleen Moore was leading the fan mail league table with 15000 letters a month. Miss Moore was obliged to despatch an average of 12000 photographs of herself monthly at a cost of 12c each, including postage. A year later she had been overtaken by Clara Bow, whose count for the month of April 1928 was no less than 33727 items of mail. The cost of replying was $2550 including $450 for three full-time secretaries. The most popular male star at that time was, somewhat surprisingly, Charles 'Buddy' Rogers, with 19618 letters. Douglas Fairbanks, generally thought of as the most consistently popular male star of the 20s, rated only 8000 letters, which gave him equal place in the league table with a dog, Rin Tin Tin. Chaplin, who had once created a fan mail record with 73000 letters in the first three days of his return home to London in 1921, could muster no more than 5000.

The coming of sound virtually ended the screen careers of Colleen Moore and Clara Bow, but ushered in a host of new stars, one of whom was to create a fan mail record which has never been broken. Mickey Mouse, reported Walt Disney at the end of 1933, had received 800000 letters that year, an average of 66000 a month. He stressed that all these communications had been addressed to Mickey personally, and not to his creator.

In that heady period of Hollywood history known as 'the era of the Great Stars', neither Gable nor Garbo could compete with a mouse, a child and a singing cowboy. By 1936 seven-year-old Shirley Temple was receiving just over 60000 letters a month, an all-time record for a mere human being. As age crept up on the

Left: It is a well known fact that *Gone with the Wind* (US 39) held the box office record for over 25 years, but which film held the record before the advent of Rhett Butler and Scarlett O'Hara? The most successful talkie in the 1930s was Walt Disney's *Snow White and the Seven Dwarfs* (US 37), which displaced silent blockbuster *The Big Parade* (US 25) as the film with the highest worldwide rentals. (See p. 243) (© Walt Disney Productions)

Below: In spite of the fact that he has already been off screen longer than he was ever on it – the 118 MM cartoons were made between 1928 and 1953 – Mickey Mouse probably remains the world's best loved cartoon character. By 1934 he was receiving more personal fan mail than any live Hollywood star. (See p. 220) (© Walt Disney Productions)

Above: For children of the 1940s, the Saturday matinée was often the highpoint of the week. The idea had been introduced by the present Lord Bernstein in 1928. (See p. 218) *(Backnumbers)*

The longest make-up job in the history of movies — it took nine men some 20 hours to apply the tattooing to Rod Steiger's body. (See p. 146)

golden-curled moppet, the fickleness of film fans once again asserted itself. By the time she had reached the mature age of ten, Miss Temple was no longer at the top. Her place had been taken by the guitar-strumming cowboy Gene Autry, though it may have been some consolation that his peak of 40 000 letters a month came nowhere near her best.

World War II brought a new element into star appeal with the advent of the pin-up picture, and it is probable that a high proportion of the dog-faces who wrote from far-away places to the new record holder, the fighting forces' own Betty Grable, had never seen any of her films. The attraction of her million dollar legs, however, was attested by the average of 30 000 letters a month they inspired.

A number of factors contributed to the decline of fan mail after World War II, chief amongst them the parallel decline in the star system, the rise of other cult heroes such as pop singers and sportsmen, and dwindling audiences in the wake of television. Even in recent years, however, it has been possible for stars held high in public esteem to inspire prodigious quantities of mail at times when they are the focus of news attention, as evidenced by the 150 000 letters received by John Wayne from loyal fans during the two months following his heart operation in June 1978.

The nature of the fan letter writer has seldom been examined, but in April 1927 *Variety* published the results of a survey in which they reported that 10 per cent of all fan mail sent from within the USA came from Poles (or people with Polish names), while up to 8 per cent of the 32 250 000 letters received annually from fans worldwide by Hollywood studios originated from South American countries. The greater proportion of requests for photographs, said *Variety*, came from people who never went to the movies – 'they are of the poor kind who cannot afford it and simply pick up coupons or read names on billboards of the various stars . . .'. An analysis made the following year at Paramount, the studio which received the most fan mail, revealed that 75 per cent of the correspondents were women, despite the fact that female stars received more letters than men.

Fan mail being traditionally associated with film stars, it is worthy of note that no actor or actress has received in the course of a career the number of letters delivered to Charles Lindbergh following his transatlantic flight – a total of 3 500 000.

Space precludes more than the briefest selection of the last 60 years of fan mail:

- To Kathlyn Williams 1916: 'Dear Miss Williams, You are my favourite moving picture actress. I would appreciate it so much if you would give me one of your old automobiles, any one, I wouldn't care how small.'
- To Enid Bennett 1920: 'I am making a collection of pictures of the most notorious actresses. Please send me yours.'
- To Emil Jannings (whose looks were certainly subordinate to his artistry) 1928: 'Dear Miss Jannings, You are my favourite actress. I go to see all your pictures because I like the way you wear your clothes. To me you are the best-dressed actress on the screen, as well as the most beautiful. I try to imitate your clothes and your stylish way of wearing your hair.'
- To Una Merkel (following a request for a signed photo) 1933: 'Do not send picture. Am moving and decided I don't want it.' Miss Merkel to fan: 'Picture is sent. You'll take it and like it.'
- To Glenn Ford 1946: 'I am 22, pretty, but I never saved my money. You did. That is the real reason I would like to marry you. Please let me know soon, as I have also written to Dick Powell and Larry Parks.'
- To Virginia Mayo from Arab Sheik 1948: 'You are the surest proof to me of the existence of God.'

Film Fans, Famous and Infamous

Royalty have been among the most fervent supporters of the cinema since its earliest days. At a time when 'animated pictures' had scarcely moved out of the fairground, Queen Victoria was enjoying frequent film shows at Windsor Castle. An ardent film fan, the Queen had a special predilection for movies about children and her favourite was said to be a Riley Bros production called *The Pillow Fight* (GB 98), in which four mischievous schoolgirls bombarded each other with pillows in their bedroom.

The first royalty with private cinema theatres in their palaces were the Crown Prince of Siam and Tsar Nicolas II, both in about 1913. When war broke out and the Tsar took command of his forces in the field, he missed his cinema at the Tsarkoye Selo palace so much that he had another one installed at the Stavka, headquarters of the Russian Army. The Tsar's favourite film was *The Exploits of Elaine* (US 14), a cliff-hanger type serial which he watched weekly at Stavka throughout the second half of 1916. The deposed Emperor of China, Henry P'u Yi, had a cinema built at the Palace of Established Happiness about 1920, where a steady flow of Charlie Chaplin and Fatty Arbuckle films was maintained, until the emergence of Harold Lloyd, who displaced them as Imperial Favourite. The Emperor's owlish horn-rimmed glasses were said to have been acquired in tribute to the American comedian.

Queen Alexandra's favourite film was *True Heart Susie* (US 19), in which Lillian Gish played the kind of simple, joyful country girl the Queen sometimes wished she could have been. A private print of the film was kept at Buckingham Palace. Queen Mary's taste, on the other hand, ran to rather more robust fare, her favourite star being the romantic and extremely athletic hero of Hollywood adventure movies Eddie Polo. (Reputedly Queen Mary was the only member of the Royal Family who was not a Charlie Chaplin fan – the reason, according to one fan magazine writer, being the fact that she was not endowed with a very developed sense of humour.) The Queen was said to be the Royal Family's most enthusiastic filmgoer and during World War II, when living at Badminton, she gave a weekly film show for servicemen. However, her youngest son, the Duke of Kent, seems to have rivalled her in his passion for the pictures. When he married Princess Marina in 1934, the Earl of Dudley had a squash court converted into a cinema at his seat, Himley Hall, where the Royal Couple were to spend their honeymoon. During the twelve days of their stay, the Duke and Duchess watched 18 feature films, nine comedies, an unspecified number of documentaries, five news-reels and a specially made life-story of His Royal Highness. Every night of the honeymoon was spent at the movies reported an ecstatic Gaumont-British, who had supplied the 202 reels of film shown.

Both the Duke's brothers shared his delight in the cinema. The Duke of York, later King George VI, was reported in America to have a particular weakness for the films of Nancy Carroll. A greater sensation, though, was the revelation in *Photoplay* in 1931 that the Prince of Wales (later Edward VIII) was in the habit of making incognito visits to one of London's less exclusive suburban cinemas, the Grand in Edgware Road, at least once or twice a week. The Prince always attended with the same girl, it was alleged, she taking her seat at 8.45 p.m. and he slipping into his at precisely 9 p.m., after the house lights had gone down.

No recent information is available about H.M. The Queen's taste in films, the Palace being prepared to say only that 'she most often asks to see those of which she has read favourable reviews'. According to a newspaper report of the late 1950s, however, her favourite stars were then Gary Cooper, Laurence Olivier and Dirk Bogarde. Curiously Her Majesty does not have a private cinema. At Sandringham the shows are held in the Ballroom, at Balmoral in the Large Drawing Room and at Windsor Castle in the Waterloo Room. Films are not shown at Buckingham Palace. Royal film shows are the responsibility of the Equerry in Waiting, who selects the films unless the Queen has made a particular request.

World leaders have also been in the forefront of the world's film fans. Both Stalin and Churchill named *Lady Hamilton* (GB 41) as their favourite film, the British Prime Minister seeing it four times. Churchill's passion for films was not shared by all his wartime colleagues, a number of whom have testified to their displeasure at the PM's habit of breaking off the evening's work to watch the ritual movie and then expecting them to match his alertness and vigour as top-level discussions continued until three in the morning. At Kremlin film shows, according to Khruschev, Stalin 'used to select the movies himself. The films were usually what you might call captured trophies: we got them from the West. Many of them were American pictures. He liked cowboy movies especially. He used to curse them and give them their proper ideological evaluation but then immediately order new ones.'

Hitler's favourite movie at the time he became Chancellor of Germany was *The Blue Angel* (Ger 30), of which he had a private print. Trenker's *The Rebel* (US 33), was said to be his favourite American film. *The Blue Angel* was later displaced in his affections by Willi Forst's *Mazurka* (Ger 35), which he watched as often as two or three times a week in the small hours of the morning when he was suffering from insomnia. Such was the Führer's devotion to the film, a rumour spread that its star, the bewitching Pola Negri, was under his special protection. In fact Miss Negri had never met Hitler, but found that whenever she went to Nazi Germany she was treated with the kind of privileged deference accorded only to intimates of the Reich's Chancellor. (She later won a libel action against the French cinema magazine *Pour Vous*, which alleged she was Hitler's mistress.)

The Führer is said to have indulged in film shows of a less conventional kind. Pauline Kohler, who served on the staff at Berchtesgaden, claimed that Hitler had a special film made of a prominent German star (whom she named, but is still alive) stripping and exhibiting 'various exercises' which 'threw a terrible light on the perversity of Hitler's sexual desires'. This was shown in the Führer's private cinema at Berchtesgaden, where a selected group of staff were invited to view it on Christmas Day 1937.

Probably the most devoted film fan of world leaders was President Tito, who watched an average of 200 films a year – one virtually every night he was in Belgrade. His favourite was the Humphrey Bogart-Bette Davis movie *The Petrified Forest* (US 36), a melodrama about a group of travellers at a way-station in Arizona who are held up by gangsters.

American Presidents have been enjoying films at the White House since June 1914, when Giovanni Pastrone's epic *Cabiria* (It 14) was screened before President Wilson and his Cabinet. The President's favourite star was the statuesque Katharine MacDonald, known as 'The American Beauty'. It is not recorded whether President Truman was obliged to sit through *The Scarlet Pimpernel* (GB 34) the 16 times his daughter Margaret – a devotee of Leslie Howard – had it screened at the White House. Eisenhower's favourite films while President were *Angels in the Outfield* (US 52) – described by Leslie Halliwell as 'unamusing, saccharine whimsy' – *Springfield Rifle* (US 52), *To Catch a Thief* (US 55), and *Rear Window* (US 54). The latter two starred his favourite actress, Grace Kelly. President Kennedy left the selection of films to aide Arthur Schlesinger, who arranged a show every Sunday evening at the White House. *Patton* (US 69) was President Nixon's favourite, while President Carter seems unwilling to declare himself. According to the White House Media Liaison Section, the President 'enjoys a wide range of movies, and does not have one preference over others'. Films selected for showing at the Family Theatre in the White House and at Camp David appear to be exclusively American and generally major box-office successes. Neither has Mr Carter revealed a favourite star, though it has not escaped notice on the other side of the Atlantic that he is enrolled as an honorary member of Britain's Errol Flynn Fan Club.

The first British Prime Minister to attend a cinema was Mr Herbert Asquith (father of the noted director Anthony Asquith) during a visit to Cannes in 1914. It would seem from the *Bioscope's* report (23.7.14) that the PM was the kind of patron one prefers not to have sitting nearby: 'Mr Asquith was delighted with his first version of a cinematograph production . . . From time to time he laughed heartily and continually made witty comments.'

PREMIÈRES

The largest audience to attend a world première were the 23930 persons who paid $2·50–$50 each to see Robert Altman's *Brewster McCloud* (US 70), starring Bud Cort and Sally Kellerman, at the Houston Astradome on 5 December 1970. A special 70 mm print was made exclusively for the première at a cost of $12000, since a standard gauge film would have given insufficient definition on the 156 × 60 ft (47·5 × 18·3 m) 'astroscreen'. The *Houston Chronicle* reported in inimitable Texan style: 'The reaction was what you might call mixed. The audience was mostly your younger hip crowd, but the low intelligibility and the film's weirdness in general caused things to be a bit subdued. Miss Kellerman runs around nekkid a lot and there are what you might call bad words . . . .'

The largest number of simultaneous openings was by the Clint Eastwood movie *Bronco Billy* (US 80), which premièred at 1316 US sites on 11 June 1980.

The most belated world première took place at Bristol Arts Centre in February 1979, when the completed version of a one-reel comedy by the Yorkshire firm of Bamforth called *Finding His Counterpart* (GB 14) was presented for the first time. The unedited rushes of the film had been discovered in the National Film Archive by Allan T. Sutherland and edited as he perceived the producer had intended.

ROYALTY

The first occasion on which a ruling monarch attended a public film performance was on 11 June 1896, when King Christian IX of Denmark (reigned 1863–1906) visited Vilhelm Pacht's exhibition of Lumière films at his Kinoptikon in Copenhagen's Raadhuspladsen.

The first member of the British Royal Family to visit a public cinema was Queen Alexandra (1844–1925), daughter of King Christian IX of Denmark (see above), who attended a performance at the Kinomatograph Theatre, Christiania (Oslo), in September 1907 accompanied by the Dowager Empress of Russia.

The first British monarch to attend a public cinema performance was King George V (reigned 1910–36) who, accompanied by Queen Mary, saw a matinee showing of *Quo Vadis?* (It 13) at the Albert Hall on 5 May 1913. The visit was described as 'strictly private', meaning it was not a Command Performance.

The first Royal Command Film Performance was held at Marlborough House on 21 July 1896 before 40 royal guests who had assembled for the marriage of Princess Maud the following day. The show was occasioned by a request from pioneer cinematographer Birt Acres of New Barnet, Herts, to be allowed to exhibit publicly a film he had taken the previous month of the Prince and Princess of Wales attending the Cardiff Exhibition (*see* News Film, p. 250). Before giving his permission, the Prince of Wales commanded Acres to bring the film to Marlborough House for inspection. It was screened in a specially erected marquee together with 20 other short films, including Tom Merry the Lightning Artist drawing Mr Gladstone and Lord Salisbury, the Derby races of 1895 and 1896, Henley Regatta, and scenes showing a boxing kangaroo, a Great Northern Railway express train, and the pursuit of a pickpocket. The royal film was shown twice by popular demand.

The first Royal Command Performance before the Sovereign was held in the Red Drawing Room at Windsor Castle on 23 November 1896, when HM Queen Victoria (reigned 1837–1901) saw a film of the Royal Family taken by W. Downey at Balmoral the previous month (*see* News Film: Monarch to be Filmed, p. 250). The Queen brought her opera glasses with her to ensure that she missed none of the action. This was the first of many such performances before the aged Queen, who became something of a cinema addict in the closing years of her long life.

The first feature film presented by Royal Command was Cecil Hepworth's production of *Comin' Through the Rye* (GB 16), starring Alma Taylor, which was shown before Queen Alexandra (1844–1925) in the State Dining Room of Marlborough House on 4 August 1916. Hep-

Vivien Leigh being presented to Queen Elizabeth at the first annual Royal Command Film Performance in 1946 *(Illustrated London News)*

worth was no stranger to Command Performances, having been present at the very first one when he had acted as assistant to Birt Acres.

The first feature film to be presented by Command of the Sovereign was *Tom Brown's Schooldays* (GB 17), which Lew Warren exhibited before King George V (reigned 1910–35) and Queen Mary at Buckingham Palace on 25 February 1917.

The first Royal Command Performance at a public cinema and the first of the present series of annual Command Performances took place at the Empire, Leicester Square, on 1 November 1946, when King George VI (reigned 1936–52) and Queen Elizabeth, accompanied by Princess Elizabeth and Princess Margaret, saw David Niven and Marius Goring in *A Matter of Life and Death* (GB 46). The novelty of seeing the King 'going to the pictures' caused crowds to gather ten hours before his arrival. Since then the following films have been chosen for the Royal Command Performance:

1947 *The Bishop's Wife* (US)
1948 *Scott of the Antarctic* (GB)
1949 *The Forsyte Saga* (US)
1950 *The Mudlark* (GB)
1951 *Where No Vultures Fly* (GB)
1952 *Because You're Mine* (US)
1953 *Rob Roy the Highland Rogue* (GB)
1954 *Beau Brummel* (GB)
1955 *To Catch a Thief* (US)
1956 *The Battle of the River Plate* (GB)
1957 *Les Girls* (US)
1958 No Performance
1959 *The Horse's Mouth* (GB)
1960 *The Last Angry Man* (US)
1961 *The Facts of Life* (US)
1962 *West Side Story* (US)
1963 *Sammy Going South* (GB)
1964 *Move Over Darling* (US)
1965 *Lord Jim* (GB)
1966 *Born Free* (GB)
1967 *The Taming of the Shrew* (It/US)
1968 *Romeo and Juliet* (GB)
1969 *The Prime of Miss Jean Brodie* (GB) – first X film
1970 *Anne of the Thousand Days* (GB)
1971 *Love Story* (US)
1972 *Mary Queen of Scots* (GB)
1973 *Lost Horizon* (US)

Rigg's motorised Kinematograph of 1896
(Barnes Museum of Photography)

1974 *The Three Musketeers* (Panama)
1975 *Funny Lady* (US)
1976 *The Slipper and the Rose* (GB)
1977 *Silver Streak* (US)
1978 *Close Encounters of the Third Kind* (US)
1979 *California Suite* (US)
1980 *Kramer vs Kramer* (US)

PROJECTORS

The first projector manufactured for sale was the Lumière Cinématographe, produced under licence by Jules Carpentier of Paris, early in 1896.

The first British machine manufactured for sale was the Theatrograph, produced by R.W. Paul at his Saffron Hill factory, of which the first model to be sold was purchased by conjurer David Devant for £100 and installed at the Egyptian Hall, Piccadilly, on 19 March 1896. It was at just about this time that Paul Cingqueralli arrived in London to offer the Edison Vitascope, which had yet to make its American debut, to prospective purchasers at $25000 each. Not surprisingly the margin between £100 ($500) and $25000 effectively dissuaded anyone from purchasing what was later reported to be an inferior projector.

The first motorised projector was the Kinematograph designed and manufactured by J.H. Rigg of Skinner Lane, Leeds, and demonstrated publicly at the Royal Aquarium, London, on 6 April 1896. Powered by a four-volt electric motor, it was available for sale by the end of the year through the Anglo-Continental Phonograph Co. of London and Rigg's American agent in Philadelphia.

The most powerful projector ever built was the Canadian developed IMAX, made by the Multi-screen Corporation for use at Japan's *Expo '70*, where the Fuji Group used it to show the specially produced multi-image film *Tiger Child* (Can/Jap 70). The projector's ten-element Canon 150mm F/20 high-precision lens and 25000 watt Xenon short arc lamp were capable of reproducing a high fidelity image nine storeys tall. The illumination was four times as great as the most powerful lamp hitherto available. Although the size of the Fuji Co.'s pavilion at *Expo '70* limited the screen size to 60×40 ft ($18 \cdot 3 \times 12 \cdot 2$ m), the projector was theoretically capable of rendering a sharp image on a screen measuring 126×88 ft ($38 \cdot 4 \times 26 \cdot 8$ m).

FILM REEL

The largest film reel holds 20 200 ft (6157 m) of film, against the 1000 ft (305 m) capacity of a standard 35mm reel. Produced by the IMAX Systems Corporation of Cambridge, Ontario, for use with IMAX projectors, the reel is 4 ft (1·2 m) in diameter. IMAX is proposing to introduce a $6\frac{1}{2}$ ft (2 m) diameter reel with a capacity of 50 500 ft (15 322·5 m).

SCREEN

The largest screen image ever achieved with a single projector under demonstration conditions was 79 ft 2 in $\times$ 99 ft ($24 \cdot 1 \times 30$ m) – the height of a six-storey building – at the Galérie des Machines on the Paris Exposition site in 1898. The picture throw was 650 ft (198 m) and the screen was kept wet to increase its reflection of light, a task undertaken by the Paris Fire Brigade, who trained their hoses on the mammoth sheet before the show began. The purpose of the demonstration, which was given by Louis Lumière, was

The giant screen used by the Lumière brothers at the Paris Exposition of 1900. Note the two figures in the foreground

to prove to the General Secretary of the Paris Exposition that large screen movies were feasible. Having proved that they were, Lumière was invited to exhibit such films at the Exposition in 1900. Unfortunately, a decision was taken to partition the Galérie des Machines, reducing the seating capacity to 25000 and halving the picture throw, with the result that the Lumière films had to be presented on a smaller screen allowing only an image of 52 ft 8 in $\times$ 69 ft 3 in ($16 \times 21 \cdot 1$ m).

The largest screen in the world today belongs to the Parques Interama cinema in Buenos Aires, Argentina, and measures 74 ft 9 in $\times$ 100 ft 6 in ($22 \cdot 8 \times 30 \cdot 6$ m).

The largest screens in the USA are two identical 70 ft 6 in $\times$ 96 ft ($21 \cdot 5 \times 29 \cdot 3$ m) screens at Marriott's Great America Parks at Santa Clara, California and Gurnee, Illinois. They were manufactured by Harkness Screens of Boreham Wood, Herts, England, and are used in conjunction with Canadian IMAX projection systems. By comparison the original Cinerama screen size was 26×90 ft ($7 \cdot 9 \times 27 \cdot 4$ m).

The widest screen ever used for projecting motion pictures was erected at the Palais d'Electricité et de la Lumière at the Paris Exposition of 1937 for showing Henri Chretien's *hypergonar* films, the precursor of Cinerama. The concave screen had a breadth of 195 ft (59·5 m) and was 32 ft 6 in (9·9 m) high.

CHAPTER 13

PRESS AND PRINT

The first book on cinematography was *The History of the Kinetograph, Kinetoscope and Kineto-Phonograph,* by W.K.L. and Antonia Dickson, New York, 1895. Dickson was Thomas Edison's assistant and the inventor of the Kinetoscope 'peep show' motion picture apparatus and Kinetograph camera patented in his employer's name. The book was published in Britain in October of the same year by the Continental Commerce Co. of New York as a give-away to publicise their Oxford Street Kinetoscope parlour.

The first British work on the subject of cinematography was *Animated Photography, or the ABC of the Cinematograph* by Cecil Hepworth, published by Hazell, Watson & Viney Ltd of London in 1897.

The first work on the aesthetics of cinema was Vachel Lindsay's *The Art of the Moving Picture,* published in the USA in 1915.

The first work of fiction about motion pictures was Mrs Henry Mansergh's short story *An Idyll of the Cinematograph,* which was published in the *Windsor Magazine* for February 1898. It concerned an unsuccessful private detective, Ronson, who decides to bolster his failing business by offering to take films of 'subjects' clandestinely on behalf of his clients. His first commission is from Mr John Webb, who has been separated from his fiancée, Daisy Ray, for 15 years since he left for India. He is about to invite Miss Ray to India for the nuptials, but is full of anxiety that his affianced might have lost the sweet bloom of youth. Accordingly, he engages Ronson, the detective, to make a film

of her. When the film arrives in India, he arranges with a photographer to show it to him on a 'magic lantern'. Evidently Mrs Mansergh had only the sketchiest knowledge of cinematography, as she referred to film as 'cinematographic slides'. However, there was in reality a photographer's studio in Bombay in 1898 which had a projector for hire, though it is unlikely the authoress knew this. Webb's worst fears are confirmed: Miss Ray at forty has become fat and fussy. Meanwhile, in England, Daisy Ray has commissioned Ronson to make a film of John Webb. This is achieved by bribing one of Webb's Indian servants to take the film. (He does this at night and Mrs Mansergh assumes the ability of the servant not only to operate the camera, but also to light the scene without arousing his master's suspicions.) The film arrives in England and Daisy is horrified when reality is beamed onto the screen: her fiancée is bald, liverish and slovenly; he throws things at his servants; and worst, he *drinks*. The protracted engagement is terminated to the satisfaction of both parties, but the only one to truly benefit, writes Mrs Mansergh, is the private detective, who waxes prosperous on the proceeds of his cunning and dexterity as a keyhole cameraman.

Mrs Mansergh's short story is herein identified as the earliest work of cinematographic fiction for the first time. Hitherto, Rudyard Kipling's *Mrs Bathurst*, a short story about a bioscope show in South Africa which was published in his *Traffics and Discoveries* in 1904, has generally been regarded as the pioneer work of fiction about the cinema.

The earliest allusion to the cinema in a novel appears in E.F. Benson's *Mammon and Co* (London 1899), in which Mrs Murchison, an elderly lady given to malapropisms, visits the Palace Theatre to 'see the Biography'. She reports that 'Most interesting it was, and the one from the front of the train made me feel quite sick and giddy – most pleasant'.

The first book-of-the-film was a special illustrated 'photoplay edition' of Ralph Ince's Vitagraph three-reeler *The Mills of the Gods* (US 12), published by Grosset and Dunlap of New York at 50c in 1912.

The first original work of literature based on a film was Stuart Edward White's *Oil on Troubled Waters*, published in the *Saturday Evening Post* in 1913. Director Alan Dwan had written the film scenario and approached White, a distinguished novelist, with the idea of paying him simply for the use of his name as the supposed author. White was so impressed with the plot, however, that he decided to turn it into a genuine short story for publication. One of the most notable examples of literature derived from a motion picture is Budd Schulberg's novel *On the Waterfront*, adapted from the screenplay of his 1954 film. Novels had been written from screenplays before, but as with cheap paperback adaptations today this was simply a means of publicising a film at the same time as producing a book with high readership potential. Schulberg's 'book-of-the-film' was probably the first to be conceived as a serious work of literature exploring themes beyond the capacity of the movie camera.

Economically, the book-of-the-film is seldom more than a subsidiary merchandising operation. In what is believed to be a unique case, however, respecting the Faye Dunaway starrer *The Eyes of Laura Mars* (US 78), the highly-successful paperback is reputed to have made a larger profit than the lacklustre movie.

Perhaps the most bizarre 'book-of-the-film-of-the-book' episode centred round the non-existent novel on which a film titled *Zane Grey's Western Union* (US 41) was based. Zane Grey's estate authorised the deception, though the western writer had never written a novel with this title. The film was, in fact, based on a scenario by a member of the Fox script department. It proved sufficiently successful to create a

The first novelisation of a movie. Harold MacGrath had written the scenario of the successful 1913 Selig serial on which the novel was based.
Published in 1914, it was illustrated with stills from the film

demand for the book, so a novel based on the film was hastily concocted by a hack and published under the name of Zane Grey, who had died two years earlier.

Another book born of a film was *The Jazz Singer*. In this case a newspaper serial was adapted from the novel (by Arline De Haas), which was based on the film script (by Alfred A. Cohn) of the 1927 talkie, which in turn was a rendering of the Broadway show (by Samson Raphaelson), which had been dramatised from a short story called *The Day of Atonement* (also by Samson Raphaelson).

Similarly, the 1972 TV series *Anna and the King* was a spin-off of the film musical *The King and I* (US 56), an adaptation of the stage musical of the same name, derived from the straight movie version of the story, *Anna and the King of Siam* (US 46), taken from Margaret Landon's fictionalised biography which was based on the autobiography of Anna Leonowens.

Not even Shakespeare is immune. Huddersfield Theatre Royal advertised *Hamlet* in April 1952 as 'The Play of the Famous Film'.

The first university thesis written on the subject of the cinema was sociology major Ray LeRoy Short's *A Social Study of the Motion Picture*, which earned its author an MA degree from the University of Iowa in 1916.

The first autobiography of a star was Pearl White's *Just Me*, published by Doran of New York in 1916. It is a lively and wholly unreliable account of her rise as the Queen of the Silent Serials.

The star with the largest number of biographies is Charles Spencer Chaplin (1889–1977), whose life and art have been expounded in 58 book-length works published as far afield as London, Barcelona, Leipzig, Paris, Buenos Aires, Moscow, Boston, New York, Lisbon, Padua, Munich, Charlottesville, Brescia, Stockholm, Berlin, Prague, Rio de Janiero, Gaud, Mexico City, Chicago, Vienna, Amsterdam, Copenhagen, Hamburg, Oslo and Algiers. **The most biographied female star** is Marilyn Monroe (1926–62), with 29 life stories, followed by Greta Garbo (1905–) with 23.

The first film journal was *Le Bulletin Phonographique et Cinématographique*, established in Paris as a fortnightly during the summer of 1899. **The first in Britain** was *The Optical Lantern and Cinematograph Journal*, monthly, price 3d, which commenced publication in November 1904. The opening number included an interview with pioneer producer Charles Urban, in which he deplored films 'depicting crime, immorality, foolhardiness, drunkenness and other vices'; reviews of *Lady Plumpton's Motor* (GB 04), *The Jonah Man* (GB 04) and a rather daring Gaumont offering (of which Mr Urban was doubtless disapproving) called *Mixed Bathing* (GB 04); and such items of trade intelligence as 'The National Sunday League have introduced animated pictures into their Sunday programmes' and 'Look out for a new style of home cinematograph projector, at two guineas'. **The**

first **American publication** was *Views and Film Index* in 1906.

The first fan magazines were Italy's *Il Cinematagrafo* and Spain's *El Cinematagrafo*, both established in 1907. **The first in Britain** was *Pictures*, weekly 1d, founded on 21 October 1911. It consisted mainly of fiction based on film scenarios, illustrated with stills from the films summarised, but a regular feature called 'Picture Notes from All Parts' retailed such interesting snippets of information as the fact that four million people went to the pictures daily (1911), that Florence Lawrence was making 300 films a year and was America's highest paid star at £50 a week, that newsreel producers had paid £200 for special positions on the Coronation route, and that Leyton Public Library was blaming local cinemas for a decline in the number of books issued. **America's first fan magazine** was *Motion Picture Story Magazine*, founded by J. Stuart Blackton of Vitagraph as a monthly in February 1911.

Shopgirl's choice 1931

The most extensive cinema press in the world belongs to India, which had 315 film magazines of all kinds at the latest count. During the silent period, Japan had the most prolific film press, with 104 fan magazines existing in 1926, including one of the only journals ever devoted solely to a single star – *Kurishima Notebook*, for fans of the Japanese 'Queen of the Silents' Sumiko Kurishima.

The first newspaper cartoon about the cinema was a political lampoon in the *Cape Register* (Cape Town, South Africa) for 19 September 1896 which used the Edison Vitascope as the 'vehicle' to make its point.

Britain's earliest cinema cartoon in a non-trade paper was a 'Wiles of Wily Willy' subject in *The Sketch* for 15 February 1908. Willy is seen filming the new comet.

The first regular film column in a newspaper began appearing in the *New York Morning Journal* in 1909. **The first in Britain** was a weekly feature titled 'Around the Cinema Palaces' written by W.G. Faulkner for the *Evening News*, commencing 17 January 1912. It was to be many years, though, before editors were to regard screen journalism as having any connection with the arts. In 1921 the editor of a leading London newspaper remarked that their film page was intended solely for East End readers, the only film news worthy of attention outside slumdom being the activities of Mary Pickford or Charlie Chaplin.

Film criticism was born with a brief review of *May Irwin Kiss* (US 96) in the *Chap Book* for 15 June 1896: '. . . absolutely disgusting'.

In the early days of screen journalism the trade journals used to carry plot outlines, but there was little attempt to assess the merits of the new films. **The first regular film critic** was Frank Woods, who began reviewing for the *New York Dramatic Mirror* with the issue of 1 May 1909. Woods used the pen-name 'Spectator'. His salary was $20 a week.

The first newspaper to carry film reviews was *Vilag* (*World*), a Budapest daily, which engaged Sándor Kellner as its critic in August 1912. Kellner's sojourn with the paper was brief, since he was determined to get into the production side of the movie business, which he did with spectacular success as (Sir) Alexander Korda.

The first American newspaper to employ a regular film critic was the *Chicago Tribune* with the appointment of John Lawson in 1914. Lawson was killed in an accident soon after and his place was taken by Miss Audrie Alspaugh, who wrote under the by-line 'Kitty Kelly'. Movie historian Terry Ramsaye recalled: 'Kitty Kelly could make or break a picture in the Middle West . . . Her column was a large success, and she became the best disliked name in the world of the film studios'.

CHAPTER 14

AWARDS AND FESTIVALS

AWARDS

The first film awards were made in respect of a competition held in Monaco in February 1900. According to a report in *The Optical Magic Lantern Journal* (March 1900), eleven prizes had been 'awarded during the last few days by the Prince to the successful competitors'. No other information about the contest is obtainable. The first award winning film known by name was Giovanni Vitrotti's *Il Cane riconescente* (It 07), an Ambrosio production which won a gold plaque awarded by the Lumière brothers at an international contest held in Italy in 1907. Ambrosio was also successful in winning **the first award made to a feature film**, the Grand Prix of 25000 francs at the International Exhibition at Turin in 1912, which went to *After Fifty Years* (It 12), an historical drama set in the Austro-Italian War of 1859.

The first film festival was held as part of the Venice Biennale and took place at the Hotel Excelsior from 6 to 21 August 1932, the purpose behind it being an attempt to revive the depression-hit tourist trade. A total of 18 pictures were entered by Germany, the USA, France, Italy and the UK, three of them directed by women. No awards were made, but judging was by popular vote, with the following results:

● *Which actress did you like best?* – Helen Hayes in *The Sin of Madelon Claudet* (US 31).
● *Which actor did you like best?* – Fredric March in *Dr Jekyll and Mr Hyde* (US 32).
● *Which director seemed the most convincing?* – Nicolai Ekk, *The Road to Life* (USSR 31).

● *Which film was the most entertaining?* – *A nous la liberté* (Fr 31).
● *Which film moved you most?* – *The Sin of Madelon Claudet* (US 31).
● *Which film had the most original sense of fantasy?* – *Dr Jekyll and Mr Hyde* (US 32).

Official awards were instituted for the second festival, held in 1934, when the main prize for Best Foreign Film went to *Man of Aran* (GB 34). For table of results, *see* under Awards, p. 238.

The first award-winning film by a woman was Dorothy Arzner's *Fashion For Women* (US 27), which won first prize at the International Festival of Women's Films held in London in 1928.

Ambrosio's feature-length *After Fifty Years* (It 12) was the first major award winner

No woman director has succeeded in winning an Academy Award, but the Oscar for Best Picture won for *The Sting* (US 73) was shared by Julia Phillips with her co-producers Tony Bill and Michael Phillips.

ACADEMY AWARDS

These were instituted by the Academy of Motion Picture Arts and Sciences and first presented on 16 May 1929. The awards that year were to dignify the efforts of film-makers during the twelve months August 1927–July 1928 – and at the same time to dignify, so the Academy hoped, the somewhat tarnished reputation the film industry had earned itself in the 'roaring twenties'.

Oscar, the Academy Award trophy, is the figure of a man with a crusader's sword standing on a reel of film. Until 1931 it was known simply as 'The Statuette', but in that year Academy librarian, Margaret Herrick, chanced to remark 'He looks like my Uncle Oscar' and the name stuck. Plated in 10 carat gold, Oscar has always stood $13\frac{1}{2}$ inches tall, except in war time when the trophy consisted of a gold-plated plaster plaque with the Oscar figure in relief. The value of an Oscar is about $150. Recipients pledge never to sell their statuette except back to the Academy, who will pay $10 for it. Between 1936 and 1939 the members of the Board of the Academy had to pay for the Oscar statuettes out of their own pockets as the Academy was so short of funds. Double Oscar winning scriptwriter Frances Marion says that she sees the statuette as 'a perfect symbol of the picture business: a powerful athletic body clutching a gleaming sword, with half of his head, that part which held his brains, completely sliced off'.

The most awards in any category have been won by Walt Disney (1901–66), who was honoured with 24 regular and 6 special trophies.

The most awards won by any one film went to *Ben Hur* (US 59) and numbered 11. These were: Best Picture; Best Director: William Wyler; Best Actor: Charlton Heston; Best Supporting Actor: Hugh Griffith; Cinematography: Robert L. Surtees; Art Direction: William A. Horning, Edward Carfango, Hugh Hunt; Sound: MGM Sound Department; Music Score: Miklos Rozsa; Film Editing: Ralph D. Winters, John D.

Dunning; Special Effects: Arnold A. Gillespie, Robert MacDonald, Milo Lory; Costume: Elizabeth Haffenden.

The most awards won by a British film went to *Lawrence of Arabia* (GB 62) and numbered 7: Best Picture; Best Director (David Lean); Cinematography – Color; Music Score – Substantially Original; Art Direction; Sound; and Film Editing.

The most nominations for awards were made in respect of *All About Eve* (US 50) with 14. It won six (1950).

The most Best Director Awards have been made to John Ford, who won four times: *The Informer* (US 35); *The Grapes of Wrath* (US 40); *How Green was my Valley* (US 41); *The Quiet Man* (US 52).

The most Best Actor Awards have been won by four actors, each with two Oscars: Spencer Tracy for *Captains Courageous* (US 37) and *Boys Town* (US 38); Fredric March for *Dr*

The most Academy Awards for individual creative achievement are the eight won by costume designer Edith Head

Jekyll and Mr Hyde (US 32) and *The Best Years of our Lives* (US 46); Gary Cooper for *Sergeant York* (US 41) and *High Noon* (US 52); and Marlon Brando for *On the Waterfront* (US 54) and *The Godfather* (US 72). Tracy, though, received nine nominations during his career, against seven for Brando and five each for March and Cooper. Sir Laurence Olivier has equalled Tracy's nominations, but won only a single Best Actor Award for *Hamlet* (GB 48). Perhaps Tracy should also take first place by virtue of the fact that Katharine Hepburn is on record as saying that one of her Academy Awards was doubtless intended for both of them.

The most Best Actress Awards have been won by Katharine Hepburn, whose three Oscars were awarded for *Morning Glory* (US 33), *Guess Who's Coming to Dinner* (US 67) and *The Lion in Winter* (GB 68). Miss Hepburn also enjoys the distinction of having received the most nominations of any performer (12), and of having the longest award-winning career, spanning 35 years.

The only co-stars to win Best Actor and Best Actress Award in the same year were Clark Gable and Claudette Colbert, for *It Happened One Night* (US 34). Miss Colbert was so sceptical of her chances of winning the Oscar that she decided not to postpone a trip to New York on a train scheduled to leave on the evening of the ceremony. She was just stepping into the carriage when officials of the Academy arrived to tell her she had won. A motorcycle escort rushed her to the Biltmore Bowl to receive the Award, still dressed in her travelling clothes.

The shortest performance to win an Oscar was Anthony Quinn's eight-minute *tour de force* as Gauguin in *Lust for Life* (US 56), which won him the 1956 Best Supporting Actor Award.

The first Oscar winning debut performance was by Mercedes McCambridge in *All the King's Men* (US 49), for which she won the Best Supporting Actress Award.

The youngest Oscar winner was Shirley Temple, who won a Special Award at the age of 6 'in grateful recognition of her outstanding contribution to screen entertainment during the year 1934'.

The youngest person to receive a regular Academy Award was 9-year-old Tatum O'Neal, who won the Oscar for Best Supporting Actress for her role in *Paper Moon* (US 73).

The first black Oscar winner was Hattie McDaniel, who was awarded Best Supporting Actress for her role as Mammy in *Gone with the Wind* (US 39). Twenty-four years elapsed before another black performer won a regular Oscar: Sidney Poitier was awarded Best Actor for *Lilies of the Field* (US 63).

The first posthumous Award was a Special Award to James Baskette for his characterisation of Uncle Remus in *Song of the South* (US 47). The first regular Award to be won posthumously was Best Actor by Peter Finch for his role in *Network* (US 76).

The first Award winner to refuse an Oscar was Dudley Nichols, voted Best Writer (Screenplay) for *The Informer* (US 35). Nichols gave as his reason loyalty to the Writers Guild, which together with other unions was trying to force a boycott of the Academy Awards in their fight for recognition by the studios.

The first performer to refuse an Oscar was George C. Scott, winner of Best Actor for *Patton* (US 70). His example was followed by Marlon Brando, who refused his Best Actor Award for *The Godfather* (US 72).

The only unclaimed Oscar remained so for 19 years. In 1957 one 'Robert Rich' won an Academy Award for Best Writer (Motion Picture Story) for the screenplay of *The Brave One* (US 56). No one came forward to claim the statuette at the Awards Ceremony and nobody knew a screenwriter called 'Rich' (or were not prepared to say so if they did). It was only in 1975 that the producers of the film, the King Brothers, sent the Academy an affidavit that 'Rich' was in fact Dalton Trumbo, one of the 'Hollywood Ten' (q.v.) who had been black-listed by the studios for alleged communist sympathies. Trumbo was presented with his belated Oscar by Academy President Walter Mirisch.

The longest acceptance speech was made by Greer Garson on receiving the Best Actress Award for *Mrs Miniver* (US 42) – it lasted over an hour.

The Academy Award for the Best Film
(Dates given are year award was made)

1929	*Wings* (US)
1930	*Broadway Melody* (US)
1931	*All Quiet on the Western Front* (US)
1932	*Cimarron* (US)
1933	*Grand Hotel* (US)
1934	*Cavalcade* (US)
1935	*It Happened One Night* (US)
1936	*Mutiny on the Bounty* (US)
1937	*The Great Ziegfeld* (US)
1938	*The Life of Emile Zola* (US)
1939	*You Can't Take It With You* (US)
1940	*Gone with the Wind* (US)
1941	*Rebecca* (US)
1942	*How Green was my Valley* (US)
1943	*Mrs Miniver* (US)
1944	*Casablanca* (US)
1945	*Going my Way* (US)
1946	*The Lost Weekend* (US)
1947	*The Best Years of Our Lives* (US)
1948	*Gentlemen's Agreement* (US)
1949	*Hamlet* (GB)
1950	*All the King's Men* (US)
1951	*All About Eve* (US)
1952	*An American in Paris* (US)
1953	*The Greatest Show on Earth* (US)
1954	*From Here to Eternity* (US)
1955	*On the Waterfront* (US)
1956	*Marty* (US)
1957	*Around the World in 80 Days* (US)
1958	*The Bridge on the River Kwai* (GB)
1959	*Gigi* (US)
1960	*Ben-Hur* (US)
1961	*The Apartment* (US)
1962	*West Side Story* (US)

The only co-stars to win Oscars for Best Actor and Best Actress were Clark Gable and Claudette Colbert in *It Happened One Night* (US 34)

1963	*Lawrence of Arabia* (GB)
1964	*Tom Jones* (GB)
1965	*My Fair Lady* (US)
1966	*The Sound of Music* (US)
1967	*A Man for All Seasons* (GB)
1968	*In the Heat of the Night* (US)
1969	*Oliver!* (GB)
1970	*Midnight Cowboy* (US)
1971	*Patton* (US)
1972	*The French Connection* (US)
1973	*The Godfather* (US)
1974	*The Sting* (US)
1975	*The Godfather, Part Two* (US)
1976	*One Flew Over the Cuckoo's Nest* (US)
1977	*Rocky* (US)
1978	*Annie Hall* (US)
1979	*The Deer Hunter* (US)
1980	*Kramer vs Kramer* (US)

The Academy Award for Best Foreign-Language Film
(Dates given are year award was made)

1957	*La Strada* (It)
1958	*The Nights of Cabiria* (It)
1959	*Mon Oncle* (Fr)
1960	*Black Orpheus* (Fr)
1961	*The Virgin Spring* (Sw)
1962	*Through a Glass Darkly* (Sw)
1963	*Sundays and Cybele* (Fr)
1964	*8½* (It)
1965	*Yesterday, Today, and Tomorrow* (It)

1966   *The Shop on Main Street* (Cz)
1967   *A Man and a Woman* (Fr)
1968   *Closely Observed Trains* (Cz)
1969   *War and Peace* (USSR)
1970   *Z* (Algeria)
1971   *Investigation of a Citizen above Suspicion* (It)
1972   *The Garden of the Finzi-Contini's* (It)
1973   *The Discreet Charm of the Bourgeoisie* (Fr)
1974   *Day for Night* (Fr)
1975   *Amarcord* (It)
1976   *Dersu Uzala* (USSR)
1977   *Black and White in Colour* (Ivory Coast)
1978   *Madame Rosa* (Fr)
1979   *Get Out Your Handkerchiefs* (Fr)
1980   *The Tin Drum* (W.Ger)

The American Film Institute's 'Life Achievement in Motion Pictures' Award has been won by the following:

1973   John Ford
1974   James Cagney
1975   Orson Welles
1976   William Wyler
1977   Bette Davis
1978   Henry Fonda
1979   Alfred Hitchcock
1980   James Stewart

The Berlin Film Festival Award for Best Film

The Berlin Film Festival was established in 1951. There was no overall Best Film award in the first year and from 1952–55 the films were voted for by the audience. The Golden Bear award for Best Picture was inaugurated in 1956.

1952   *She Danced for the Summer* (Sw)
1953   *The Wages of Fear* (Fr)
1954   *Hobson's Choice* (GB)
1955   *The Rats* (W.Ger)
1956   *Invitation to the Dance* (GB)
1957   *Twelve Angry Men* (US)
1958   *The End of the Day* (Sw)
1959   *The Cousins* (Fr)
1960   *Lazarillo de Tormes* (Sp)
1961   *La Notte* (It)
1962   *A Kind of Loving* (GB)
1963   *Oath of Obedience* (W.Ger); *The Devil* (It)
1964   *Dry Summer* (Turkey)
1965   *Alphaville* (Fr)
1966   *Cul de Sac* (GB)
1967   *Le Depart* (Belg)
1968   *Ole Dole Doff* (Sw)
1969   *Early Years* (Yug)
1970   No award
1971   *The Garden of the Finzi-Continis* (It)
1972   *The Canterbury Tales* (It)

1973   *Distant Thunder* (India)
1974   *The Apprenticeship of Duddy Kravitz* (Can)
1975   *Orkobefogadas* (Hung)
1976   *Buffalo Bill and the Indians* (US) – award declined
1977   *The Ascent* (USSR)
1978   *The Trouts* (Sp); *The Words of Max* (Sp)
1979   *David* (W.Ger)
1980   *Heartland* (US);
       Palermo Oder Wolfsburg (W.Ger)

British Film Academy 'Best British Film' Award/ Best Film Award *(The award is for the best film of the previous year)*

1948   *Odd Man Out*
1949   *The Fallen Idol*
1950   *The Third Man*
1951   *The Blue Lamp*
1952   *The Lavender Hill Mob*
1953   *The Sound Barrier*
1954   *Genevieve*
1955   *Hobson's Choice*
1956   *Richard III*
1957   *Reach for the Sky*
1958   *The Bridge on the River Kwai*
1959   *Room at the Top*
1960   *Sapphire*
1961   *Saturday Night and Sunday Morning*
1962   *A Taste of Honey*
1963   *Lawrence of Arabia*
1964   *Tom Jones*
1965   *Dr Strangelove*
1966   *The Ipcress File*
1967   *The Spy who Came in from the Cold*
1968   *A Man for All Seasons*
(In 1969 the 'best British Film Award' was discontinued and replaced by a 'Best Film Award')
1969   *The Graduate* (US)
1970   *Midnight Cowboy* (US)
1971   *Butch Cassidy and the Sundance Kid* (US)
1972   *Sunday Bloody Sunday* (GB)
1973   *Cabaret* (US)
1974   *La Nuite Americaine/Day for Night* (Fr)
1975   *Lacombe, Lucien* (Fr)
1976   *Alice Doesn't Live Here Anymore* (US)
1977   *One Flew Over the Cuckoo's Nest* (US)
1978   *Annie Hall* (US)
1979   *Julia* (US)
1980   *Manhattan* (US)

Cannes Film Festival: Palme d'Or for Best Film

1946   *La Bataille du Rail* (Fr)
1947   *Antoine et Antoinette* (Fr)
1948   No festival
1949   *The Third Man* (GB)
1950   No festival

1951 *Miracle in Milan* (It); *Miss Julie* (Sw)
1952 *Othello* (Morocco); *Two Cents Worth of Hope* (It)
1953 *Wages of Fear* (Fr)
1954 *Gate of Hell* (Jap)
1955 *Marty* (US)
1956 *World of Silence* (Fr)
1957 *Friendly Persuasion* (US)
1958 *The Cranes are Flying* (USSR)
1959 *Black Orpheus* (Fr)
1960 *La Dolce Vita* (It)
1961 *Viridiana* (Sp); *Une aussi longue absence* (Fr)
1962 *The Given Word* (Brazil)
1963 *The Leopard* (It)
1964 *The Umbrellas of Cherbourg* (Fr)
1965 *The Knack* (GB)
1966 *A Man and a Woman* (Fr); *Signore e Signori* (It)
1967 *Blow-Up* (GB)
1968 Festival disrupted; no awards
1969 *If* (GB)
1970 *M*A*S*H* (US)
1971 *The Go-Between* (GB)
1972 *The Working Class Goes to Paradise* (It); *The Mattei Affair* (It)
1973 *Scarecrow* (US); *The Hireling* (GB)
1974 *The Conversation* (US)
1975 *Chronicle of the Burning Years* (Algeria)
1976 *Taxi Driver* (US)
1977 *Padre Padrone* (It)
1978 *L'Albero Degli Zoccoli* (It)
1979 *The Tin Drum* (W.Ger); *Apocalypse Now* (US)
1980 *All That Jazz* (US); *Kagemusha* (Jap)

Venice Film Festival: Best Foreign Film Award (1934–42) Best Film Award (1946–68)

1932 No official award
1933 No festival
1934 *Man of Aran* (GB)
1935 *Anna Karenina* (US)
1936 *Der Kaiser von Kalifornien* (Ger)
1937 *Un Carnet de Bal* (Fr)
1938 *Olympia* (Ger)
1939 No award
1940 *Der Postmeister* (Ger)
1941 *Ohm Kruger* (Ger)
1942 *Der grosse König* (Ger)
1943 No festival
1944 No festival
1945 No festival
1946 *The Southerner* (US)
1947 *Sirena* (Cz)
1948 *Hamlet* (GB)
1949 *Manon* (Fr)
1950 *Justice is Done* (Fr)
1951 *Rashomon* (Jap)
1952 *Forbidden Games* (Fr)

1953 No award
1954 *Romeo and Juliet* (It/GB)
1955 *Ordet* (Den)
1956 No award
1957 *Aparajito* (India)
1958 *Muhomatsu no Issho* (Jap)
1959 *Il Generale della Rovere* (It)
1960 *Le Passage du Rhine* (Fr)
1961 *Last Year at Marienbad* (Fr)
1962 *Childhood of Ivan* (USSR)
1963 *Le Mani sulla citta* (It)
1964 *Red Desert* (It)
1965 *Of a Thousand Delights* (It)
1966 *Battle of Algiers* (It)
1967 *Belle de Jour* (Fr)
1968 *Die Aristen in der Zirkuskuppel* (Ger)
Jury and award system discontinued 1969

New York Times Film of the Year

From 1924 the *New York Times* has made an annual selection of the Ten Best Films reviewed during the year. Until 1968 they were listed in order of preference; since 1969 alphabetically. The list below, of the *New York Times'* choices of 'Best Film of the Year', is therefore confined to the former years. (Foreign-language films were excluded 1956–61.)

1924 *The Dramatic Life of Abraham Lincoln* (US)
1925 *The Big Parade* (US)
1926 *Variety* (Ger)
1927 *The King of Kings* (US)
1928 *The Circus* (US)
1929 *The Love Parade* (US)
1930 *With Byrd at the South Pole* (US)
1931 *The Guardsman* (US)
1932 *Mädchen in Uniform* (Ger)
1933 *Cavalcade* (US)
1934 *It Happened One Night* (US)
1935 *The Informer* (US)
1936 *La Kermesse Heroique/Carnival in Flanders* (Fr)
1937 *The Life of Emile Zola* (US)
1938 *Snow White and the Seven Dwarfs* (US)
1939 *Made for Each Other* (US)
1940 *The Grapes of Wrath* (US)
1941 *The Lady Eve* (US)
1942 *In Which We Serve* (GB)
1943 *Air Force* (US)
1944 *Destination Tokyo* (US)
1945 *A Tree Grows in Brooklyn* (US)
1946 *Open City* (It)
1947 *The Yearling* (US)
1948 *The Treasure of the Sierra Madre* (US)
1949 *Command Decision* (US)
1950 *The Titan – Story of Michelangelo* (US)
1951 *Fourteen Hours* (US)

1952   *The Greatest Show on Earth* (US)
1953   *Moulin Rouge* (GB)
1954   *The Glenn Miller Story* (US)
1955   *The Bridges of Toko-Ri* (US)
1956   *Richard III* (GB)
1957   *The Great Man* (US)
1958   *Teachers' Pet* (US)
1959   *The Diary of Anne Frank* (US)
1960   *I'm All Right, Jack* (GB)
1961   *The Facts of Life* (US)
1962   *Lover Come Back* (US)
1963   *Heavens Above* (GB)
1964   *Dr Strangelove* (GB)
1965   *The Pawnbroker* (US)
1966   *The Shop on Main Street* (Cz)
1967   *La Guerre est finie* (Fr)
1968   *Charlie Bubbles* (GB)

The Best American Films of All Time (1962)

A poll of 292 film critics resulted in the selection of the following 14 'Best American Films of All Time' (in chronological order) for showing at the 1962 Seattle World's Fair:

The Birth of a Nation (1915)
The Gold Rush (1925)
All Quiet on the Western Front (1930)
Anna Christie (1930)
I Am a Fugitive from a Chain Gang (1932)
It Happened One Night (1934)
David Harum (1934)
Gone with the Wind (1939)
The Wizard of Oz (1939)
Wuthering Heights (1939)
Citizen Kane (1941)
Sunset Boulevard (1950)
Shane (1953)
Seven Brides for Seven Brothers (1954)

The Greatest American Films of All Time (1977)

These were selected in 1977 by means of a ballot of the 35000 members of the American Film Institute, each of whom was asked to name his or her Top Five. A total of 1100 films were nominated, from which the AFI compiled a list of 50 which had received the most 'votes'. A second ballot was then held, the members being asked to select their Top Five from the list of 50. Considering the effort put into this survey, it is less than reassuring to find that four British productions were included amongst the 50 'Greatest American Films' and that two of these *(2001: A Space Odyssey* and *The African Queen)* emerged in the final Top Ten listing, a permutation based on the results of the second ballot. The titles of the AFI's Top Ten Greatest American Films of All Time are, in order of greatness:

1   *Gone with the Wind* (1939)
2   *Citizen Kane* (1941)
3   *Casablanca* (1942)
4   *The African Queen* (1952)
5   *The Grapes of Wrath* (1940)
6   *One Flew Over the Cuckoo's Nest* (1975)
7   *Singin' in the Rain* (1952)
8   *Star Wars* (1977)
9   *2001: A Space Odyssey* (1968)
10   *The Wizard of Oz* (1939)

National Board of Review Best Films of all Time

In 1929 the National Board of Review, a voluntary censorship board active in the USA since 1909, named its four 'Greatest Films of All Time': *The Birth of a Nation* (US 15); *The Cabinet of Dr Caligari* (Ger 19); *The Battleship Potemkin* (USSR 25); *The Passion of Joan of Arc* (Fr 28).

It is worthy of note that Sergei Eisenstein's *The Battleship Potemkin*, which features in all three Sight and Sound 'Ten Best' polls (1952, 1962 and 1972) as well as in the above list, and was voted 'Best Film of All Time' in the Cinématheque Belgique directors' poll of 1952 and the Brussels World's Fair film historians' poll of 1958, was dismissed in the report written after its first screening to Sovkino, the Soviet state film organisation, as only 'suitable for workers' clubs'.

Cinématheque Belgique Best Films of All Time

In 1952 the committee of the Festival Mondial du Film et des Beaux Arts Belgique asked 100 film directors to select their individual 'Ten Best Films of All Time'. Permutation of the directors' choices gave the following overall result:

1   *The Battleship Potemkin* (USSR 25)
2   *The Gold Rush* (US 25)
3   *Bicycle Thieves* (It 49)
4   *City Lights* (US 31)
     La Grande Illusion (Fr 37)
     Le Million (Fr 31)
7   *Greed* (US 24)
8   *Hallelujah!* (US 29)
9   *Die Dreigroschenoper/The Threepenny Opera* (Ger 31)
     Brief Encounter (GB 45)
     Intolerance (US 16)
     Man of Aran (GB 34)

Sight and Sound Ten Best Polls

In 1952, 1962 and 1972 the British film quarterly *Sight and Sound* conducted international polls of critics in which they were invited to select 'The Ten Best Films of All Time':

1952	**1962**	**1972**
1 *Bicycle Thieves* (It 49)	1 *Citizen Kane* (US 41)	1 *Citizen Kane* (US 41)
2 *City Lights* (US 31)	2 *L'Avventura* (It 59)	2 *La Règle du Jeu* (Fr 39)
The Gold Rush (US 25)	3 *La Règle du Jeu* (Fr 39)	3 *Battleship Potemkin* (USSR 25)
4 *Battleship Potemkin* (USSR 25)	4 *Greed* (US 24)	4 *8½* (It 63)
5 *Louisiana Story* (US 47)	*Ugetsu Monogatari* (Jap 53)	5 *L'Avventura* (It 59)
Intolerance (US 16)	6 *Battleship Potemkin* (USSR 25)	*Persona* (Sw 66)
7 *Greed* (US 24)	*Bicycle Thieves* (It 49)	7 *The Passion of Joan of Arc* (Fr 28)
Le Jour se lève (Fr 39)	*Ivan the Terrible* (USSR 46)	8 *The General* (US 26)
The Passion of Joan of Arc (Fr 28)	9 *La Terra Trema* (It 48)	*The Magnificent Ambersons* (US 42)
10 *Brief Encounter* (GB 45)	10 *L'Atalante* (Fr 33)	10 *Ugetsu Monogatari* (Jap 53)
Le Million (Fr 30)		*Wild Strawberries* (Sw 57)
La Règle du Jeu (Fr 39)		

Brussels World's Fair Best Films of All Time

On the occasion of the Brussels World's Fair of 1958, the 'Twelve Best Films of All Time' were selected by 117 film historians from 26 countries under the auspices of the Bureau International de la Recherche Historique Cinématographiques. The results, with the number of votes cast for each film, were as follows:

		Votes
1	*The Battleship Potemkin* (USSR 25)	100
2	*The Gold Rush* (US 25)	85
	Bicycle Thieves (It 49)	85
4	*The Passion of Joan of Arc* (Fr 28)	78
5	*La Grande Illusion* (Fr 37)	72
6	*Greed* (US 24)	71
7	*Intolerance* (US 16)	61
8	*Mother* (USSR 26)	54
9	*Citizen Kane* (US 41)	50
10	*Earth* (USSR 30)	47
11	*The Last Laugh* (Ger 25)	45
12	*The Cabinet of Dr Caligari* (Ger 19)	43

Worst Film Awards

Since 1940 the *Harvard Lampoon* has made annual 'Movie Worsts' awards in a range of categories designed to undermine the pretentiousness and sentimentality that mars much of Hollywood's output. An award for 'The Worst Picture of the Century' was made in 1950 to Victor Fleming's *Joan of Arc* (US 48), with Ingrid Bergman as an Americanised and worldly Joan. The award was repeated in 1958, going to Otto Preminger's *Saint Joan* (US 57), in which Jean Seberg had failed to illuminate the mysticism of the Maid. In 1964 it was won by *Cleopatra* (US 63). The *Harvard Lampoon* has presented its award for 'The Worst Film of the Year' to the following:

1940   *The Rains Came* (US)
1941   *The Howards of Virginia* (US)
1942   *Hudson's Bay* (US)
1943   No award
1944   No award
1945   *Kismet* (US)
1946   *Weekend at the Waldorf* (US)
1947   *Night and Day* (US)
1948   No award
1949   *Winter Meeting* (US)
1950   *Joan of Arc* (US)
1951   *Our Very Own* (US)
1952   *Tales of Hoffman* (US)
1953   *Jumping Jacks* (US)
1954   *The Robe* (US)
1955   *Haaji Baba* (US)
1956   *Not as a Stranger* (US)
1957   *The Ten Commandments* (US)
1958   *Raintree County* (US)
1959   *South Pacific* (US)
1960   *The Best of Everything* (US)
1961   *Butterfield 8* (US)
1962   *King of Kings* (US); *Parrish* (US)
1963   *The Chapman Report* (US)
1964   *Cleopatra* (US)
1965   *The Greatest Story Ever Told* (US); *The Carpetbaggers* (US); *Sylvia* (US); *Cheyenne Autumn* (US); *Station Six Sahara* (US); *Kiss Me Stupid* (US)
1966   *The Sandpiper* (US)
1967   *Is Paris Burning?* (Fr/US)
1968   *Guess Who's Coming to Dinner* (US)
1969   *The Lion in Winter* (GB)
1970   *Easy Rider* (US)
1971   *Love Story* (US)
1972   *A Clockwork Orange* (GB)
1973   *Last Tango in Paris* (Fr/It/US)
1974   *The Great Gatsby* (US)
1975   *Lenny* (US)
1976   *Barry Lyndon* (GB)
1977   *A Star is Born* (US)
1978   *Looking for Mr Goodbar* (US)
1979   *Sgt. Pepper's Lonely Hearts Club Band* (US)

CHAPTER 15

ANIMATION

The first animated film using the stop-motion technique to give the illusion of movement to inanimate objects was Vitagraph's *The Humpty Dumpty Circus* (US 98?). Albert E. Smith, who conceived the idea, borrowed his small daughter's toy circus and succeeded in animating the acrobats and animals by shooting them in barely changed positions one frame at a time – the same principle as that used for animated cartoons.

The earliest known British example of animation is an untitled advertising film made by Arthur Melbourne Cooper of St Albans, Herts, for Messrs Bryant & May. Dating from 1899, it consists of an appeal for funds to supply the troops in South Africa with matches, as it seems this was something the Army authorities had overlooked. The animated 'performers' are match-stick men who climb up a wall and form themselves into the legend: 'Send £1 and enough matches will be sent to supply a regiment of our fighting soldiers'. Some years later, Melbourne Cooper made two charming films featuring animated toys, *Noah's Ark* (GB 08) and *Dreams of Toyland* (GB 08). Strutting teddy bears were featured in the latter with particularly engaging effect. Meanwhile, in the United States J. Stuart Blackton, Albert E. Smith's co-partner at Vitagraph, had produced an unusual novelty with *The Haunted Hotel* (US 07), in which furniture moved about seemingly by its own agency. The following year Pathé pioneered the animation of paper cut-outs in *Paper Cock-a-Doodle* (Fr 08) – the cut-outs being in the shape of exquisitely wrought birds. The pioneer of animation in Russia was Ladislas Starevitch, who applied the stop-motion technique to bring dead insects 'alive' in *The Grasshopper and the Ant* (Rus 11) and *The Stag-Beetles* (Rus 11).

The first silhouette film was Bray Picture Corporation's *Inbad the Tailor* (US 16), drawn by C. Allan Gilbert. The most celebrated exponent of the silhouette film is undoubtedly Lotte Reiniger, whose *Die Abenteuer des Prinzen Achmed/The Adventures of Prince Ahmed* (Ger 26) was the first feature-length animated film produced in Europe.

Pin screen technique: An unusual technique for animation was used for the first time by Alexandre Alexcieff in *Une Nuit sur le Mont Chauve* (Fr 34). Together with Clair Parker he devised a 'pin screen' consisting of 500000 pins which could be raised or lowered by hand to create an image of varying density. The pins were changed in height from frame to frame to create an illusion of movement. The technique was later used by Alexcieff for advertising films, and the prologue to Orson Welles' *The Trial* (US 62) was also made with the pin screen.

The first cartoon film was J. Stuart Blackton's *The Enchanted Drawing* (US 00), copyrighted by the Edison Co. on 16 November 1900. The film shows artist Blackton at his easel drawing an outline face. The artist then pours himself a drink and the face registers a glum expression, changing to happiness when Blackton pours another drink for the drawing. The film continues in this vein, the artist causing the expression on the drawn face to change according to the various gifts he draws on the paper – a top hat, cigars,

Lotte Reiniger's *The Adventures of Prince Ahmed* (Ger 26) is the only feature-length silhouette film ever made

etc. It culminates in the face contentedly puffing away on a cigar. This film is nearly six years older than the hitherto earliest recorded cartoon, Vitagraph's *Humorous Phases of Funny Faces* (US 06), also by Blackton. It was discovered by Kemp R. Niver when he undertook the restoration of the Library of Congress Paper Print Collection.

The first British cartoon film was the Urban Trading Co.'s *The Hand of the Artist* (GB 06). Made by ex-conjurer Walter Booth, it showed an artist (Booth) drawing a coster and his donna who come to life and dance the cake-walk.

The first cartoon film to tell a story was Emile Cohl's *Fantasmagorie* (Fr 08), which was premièred at the Théâtre du Gymnase in Paris on 17 August 1908. Cohl made the film for Léon Gaumont, by whom he was employed as a scenarist. Prior to this, nearly all cartoon films were of the artist-drawing-a-living-picture genre. Robert Desnos has described Cohl as the first to 'cut the umbilical cord which still linked the life of the characters on the screen with the secretions of the fountain pen'. He made about 100 cartoons between 1908 and 1918 and can thus be regarded as **the first professional screen animator.**

The first cartoon series was inaugurated by Emile Cohl with the debut of his character Fantôche, a kind of match-stick man combatting the cruel world, in *Le Cauchemar du Fantôche* (Fr 09). **America's first regular cartoon character** was Colonel Heeza Liar, whose initial appearance was in Bray Studios' *Colonel Heeza Liar in Africa* (US 13). The series ran till 1917, then resumed in 1922.

The first animation studio was the Bray-Hurd Studio, established on 42nd Street, New York, by John R. Bray and Earl Hurd in 1911. Bray and Hurd devised the 'cel' process of animation, by which the moving elements of a scene were drawn onto a celluloid sheet, which was then superimposed on a static background. The introduction of this technique, first used for Pathé's *The Artist's Dream* (US 13), enabled the production of longer cartoon films at lower cost and considerably less labour.

The first cartoon talkie was *The Audion* (US 22), an animated physics film on the working of the three-element vacuum tube. Made by E.B. Craft of Western Electric, it was premièred at Woolsey Hall, Yale University, on 27 October 1922. The synchronised disc sound system used later developed into Vitaphone.

The first cartoon talkie for theatrical release was Max Fleischer's Koko Song Kar-Tune *My Old Kentucky Home* (US 25?), in which Bimbo the dog plays a trombone and speaks the words: 'Now let's all follow the bouncing ball and sing along'. It was produced by Inkwell Studio Productions with sound-on-film accompaniment by DeForest Phonofilm.

The first all-talking cartoon was Walt Disney's *Steamboat Willie* (US 28), which marked the debut of Mickey Mouse. It was premièred at the *Colony Theater*, New York, on 18 November 1928. Another Mickey Mouse talkie, *Plane Crazy* (US 28), had in fact been completed before *Steamboat Willie,* but was released later.

The first colour cartoon was *The Debut of Thomas Kat* (US 16), a Paramount release produced by the Bray Pictures Corporation of New York in the Brewster natural-colour process. The drawings were made on transparent celluloid and painted on the reverse, then filmed with a two-colour camera. An unfortunate kitten, Thomas Kat, had been taught by his mother to catch mice, but inadvertently mistook a rat for the smaller breed of rodent. There was no follow-up to this remarkable pioneering endeavour until 1930, when the otherwise live-action Universal feature *King of Jazz* (US 30) contained an opening cartoon sequence by Walter Lanz filmed in two-colour Technicolor.

The first colour cartoon talkie was Ted Esbaugh's *Goofy Goat* (US 31), made in two-colour Multi-color and previewed at Warner's Alhambra Theater, Los Angeles, on 6 July 1931. **The first Disney colour cartoon** (often erroneously claimed as 'the world's first colour cartoon'), and the first cartoon made in a three-colour process, was the Silly Symphony *Flowers and Trees* (US 32), made in Technicolor and premièred at Grauman's Chinese Theater on 15 July 1932.

Britain's first cartoon talkie in colour was Reunion Films' *Sam and His Musket* (GB 35), made by Anson Dyer in the Dunning two-colour process with voice-over by Stanley Holloway.

The first feature-length cartoon film was Don Frederico Valle's 60-min *El Apostol* (Arg 17). Based on the book by Alfredo de Lafarrere, the film was a political satire on Argentina's President Irigoyen. The team of five animators was headed by Diogones Tabora, a well known caricaturist, and between them they produced 50000 drawings for the completed film. Surprisingly **the first full-length cartoon talkie** was also produced in Argentina. Made by Quirino Cristiani in 1931, *Peludopolis* was another satire on President Irogoyen and used the Vitaphone sound-on-disc system of synchronised sound. Running time was one hour. These two Argentinian cartoon features, and an Italian production *The Adventures of Pinocchio* (It 36), preceded the film which has generally been hailed as the world's first full-length cartoon feature. In fact Walt Disney's *Snow White and the Seven Dwarfs* (US 37) was only the first American cartoon feature, though the world's first to be made in both sound and colour. (A curiosity with the uninviting title of *Einstein's Theory of Relativity* (US 23), produced by Premier Productions in 7 reels, has sometimes been claimed as America's first cartoon feature. According to recent research by Denis Gifford, it would appear that this lost film was mainly live action, with some animated sequences by Max Fleischer.)

Britain's first feature-length cartoon was *Handling Ships* (GB 46), an instructional film made for the Admiralty by Halas and Batchelor. The first made for commercial release was Halas and Batchelor's *Animal Farm* (GB 54), from George Orwell's savage satire on Soviet repression. It was also **the first cartoon to be X-rated.**

Halas and Batchelor's *Animal Farm* (GB 54) was the first cartoon to be X-rated

The first 3-D cartoon was Norman McLaren's abstract subject *Around is Around* (GB 51).

The first cinemascope cartoon was Walt Disney's *Lady and the Tramp* (US 56).

The most expensive cartoon ever made is Walt Disney's *The Fox and the Hound* (US i.p.) at $10 million.

The longest cartoon ever made was Osamu Tezuka's erotic feature *A Thousand and One Nights* (Jap 69), which had a running time of 2 hr 30 min in the original Japanese version.

  The longest American cartoon, and the only one to date to exceed 2 hr, was the 2 hr 5 min John Wilson production *Shinbone Alley* (US 70), which told of the love of a cockroach for a sex-pot alley cat.

The multiplane camera, which registers degrees of depth in animation, **was used for the first time** on Walt Disney's *Fantasia* (US 40).

Feature Cartoon Output: Up to the end of 1979, a total of 204 all-cartoon feature films had been made worldwide. The most prolific country was the USA with 49 full-length cartoon features, followed by Japan (47), Italy (12), USSR (12), France (10), GB (9), Spain (9), Germany (9), Belgium (7), South Korea (6), China (5), Argentina (4), Australia (4), Hungary (4), Denmark (3), Canada (2), Sweden (2). Poland, Czechoslovakia, Israel, Thailand, Colombia, Cuba, Finland, Hong Kong, Mexico and the United Nations each produced one.

The highest grossing cartoon film of all time is Walt Disney's *The Jungle Book* (US 67), with worldwide rentals of $69·7 million to the end of 1979.

CARTOON DEBUTS

Betty Boop
Max Fleischer's boop-boop-a-doop flapper of the 30s debuted in *Dizzy Dishes* (US 30). Betty started life as a small dog with long ears and only became a human girl in 1932. Her baby-talk voice was done by five different actresses, of whom Little Ann Little (who spoke in boop-boop-a-doop language in real life) and Mae Questel were the best known.

Bugs Bunny
Started as a hare rather than a 'wabbit' in Ben Hardway and Cal Dalton's Looney Tune *Porky's Hare Hunt* (US 38). The character only began to assume his real Brooklyn bunny persona in Tex Avery's *Wild Hare* (US 40).

Daffy Duck
Tex Avery's Looney Tune *Porky's Duck Hunt* (US 37).

Donald Duck
Walt Disney's *The Wise Little Hen* (US 34). His opening (and only) words were: 'Who – me? Oh no! I got a bellyache!' Clarence Nash, always Donald's voice, recalled: 'I had an ambition to be a doctor and somehow or other I became the biggest quack in the country'.

Droopy Dog
Created by Tex Avery in MGM's *Dumb-Hounded* (US 43).

Felix the Cat
Created *c.* 1917 by Australian cartoonist Pat Sullivan in *The Adventures of Felix the Cat*, but film not released until 1922, when it was tagged onto the end of a *Pathe Screen Magazine*. First of the anthropomorphic animal characters to attain the kind of celebrity accorded to human stars. Television debut WXB2S New York 1930.

Goofy
Walt Disney's *Mickey's Revue* (US 32).

Mickey Mouse
Born 18 November 1928 with première of *Steamboat Willie* (*see* also Cartoon Talkie). The artist for the MM cartoons was not Disney

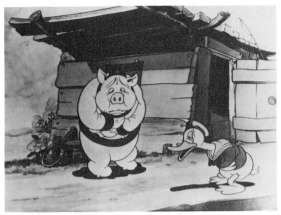

Donald Duck suffered a bellyache when he made his screen debut in *The Wise Little Hen* (US 34) (© *Walt Disney Productions*)

but Ub Iwerks, though Walt himself did Mickey's voice. By 1934 the Mouse was receiving more fan mail than any other Hollywood star. There were a total of 118 MM cartoons, of which the majority – 87 – were made in the 30s. The last was *The Simple Things* (US 53).

Mr Magoo
United Productions of America's *Ragtime Bear* (US 49).

Pluto
Walt Disney's *The Chain Gang* (US 30).

Popeye
Debuted in Max Fleischer's *Popeye the Sailor* (US 33); head animator Seymour Kneitel. The voice was that of William Costello, better known as Red Pepper Sam, whose experience as a talking gorilla on a radio show was thought to qualify him for the role. Success went to his head and he was fired as too temperamental, so Jack Mercer, an artist at the Fleischer Studio with a bent for imitations, took over. Popeye's friend Wimpy gave his name to a disagreeable type of British hamburger.

Porky Pig
Warner Bros Looney Tune *Haven't Got a Hat* (US 35).

Road Runner
Together with the Coyote, created by Chuck Jones and Michael Maltese in *Fast and Furry-ous* (US 48).

Speedy Gonzales
The Fastest Mouse in all Mexico debuted in Warner Bros' *Speedy Gonzales* (US 55).

Sylvester
Kitty Kornered (US 45). His constant prey Tweety Pie had preceded him on screen (see below).

Tom and Jerry
Hanna-Barbera's *Puss Gets the Boot* (US 39). The love-hate relationship of the amiable adversaries was condemned in the 70s for its 'mindless violence'.

Tweety Pie
Birdie and the Beast (US 44). American essayist S.J. Perelman held Tweety Pie personally responsible for what he regarded as a reprehensible British habit of referring to all felines as 'puddy tats'.

Woody Woodpecker
Knock Knock (US 40). The distinctive woodpecker voice was that of Grace Stafford, wife of Woody's creator Walter Lanz.

The earliest use of puppets and live action together in a full-length feature film was by Segundo de Chomon in *La Guerra e il sogno di Momi* (It 16).

The first all-puppet feature film was Frederico Valle's political satire *A Full-Dress Night at the Colon Theatre* (Arg 19). The first in Europe was Ladislas Starewitch's *Le Roman de Renard* (Fr 40). Electronically-controlled puppets were first used in Lou Bunin's *Alice in Wonderland* (GB/Fr 50).

CHAPTER 16

SHORTS AND DOCUMENTARIES

ADVERTISING FILMS

The first advertising films were made in France, Britain, and the USA, in 1897. The single surviving American example of that year was copyrighted by the Edison Co. of West Orange, NJ, on 5 August 1897. The Library of Congress Catalogue records: 'The film shows a large, poster-type backdrop with the words "Admiral Cigarettes". Sitting in front of the backdrop are four people in costume: Uncle Sam, a clergyman, an Indian, and a businessman. To the left of the screen is an ash-can size box that breaks apart and a girl, attired in a striking costume, goes across the stage towards the seated men and hands them cigarettes. Then she unfolds a banner that reads, "We all Smoke".'

Advertising films were also made that year by the International Film Co. of New York, who were the first company to specialise in such productions. Their clients included Haig Whisky, Maillard's Chocolate and Pabst's Milwaukee Beer, and the films advertising these products were interspersed with entertainment films, in the manner of modern TV commercials, in a grand open-air free movie show in the centre of New York. The giant screen was set on top of the Pepper Building at 34th Street and Broadway and the films rear projected with a powerful Kuhn & Webster 'Projectorscope'. The projectionist was Edwin S. Porter, later to achieve fame as director of *The Great Train Robbery* (US 03). On this occasion, however, the only celebrity he achieved was in the police court, where he was charged with being a public nuisance and causing an obstruction by encouraging people to block the sidewalk.

Three different advertising films are known to date from 1897 in Britain. Walter D. Welford made a film called *The Writing on the Wall* for John Samuel Smith and Co. of Borough High Street, Southwark, manufacturers of bicycle tyres. This was shot in Tottenham and showed a man painting the words 'Ride Smith Tyres' on a brick wall. Rather more ambitious was a production by Arthur Melbourne Cooper of St Albans, which brought to light a contemporary poster for Bird's Custard. An old man is seen walking down stairs bearing a large tray of eggs. He misses his footing, trips, and the eggs cascade onto the floor. Cook has no need to worry, though, because she has a liberal supply of Bird's Custard Powder. The company made an agreement with Melbourne Cooper that he should be paid £1 for every copy of the film distributed. The third example comes from Nestlé and Lever Bros, who joined forces in 1897 to purchase 12 Lumière Cinématographes for a combined promotional exercise. Their initial effort was called *The Sunlight Soap Washing Competition* and was available free to showmen. Besides producing their own advertising films, Lever Bros and Nestlé's also sponsored films with no advertising content. On 7 February 1898 they premièred a film of the recent Test Match in Australia at the Alhambra, Leicester Square. This was so successful that it was followed in March by films of the Cambridge crew in training for the Boat Race and later by the Boat Race itself. Mellin's Baby Food also

A Victorian 'commercial' – one of the earliest
advertising films made by Edwin S. Porter in 1897

Above: The world's most beautiful woman? Nobody would have said so when this 16-year-old appeared in an advertising short called *How Not to Wear Clothes* (Sw 21), but they did when she conquered Hollywood as Greta Garbo

Right: Britain's first advertising film in full colour

Here's a Film You *must* see

Look out for this beautiful
all-colour Film at your Cinema

"It's an ill wind."

Enter the office boy with INK

He slips and her Jumper is ruined

I'll show you how to put it right

So simple— Tintex Colour Remover takes the colour and stain out

Dip into Tintex Dye and . . .

Voila! . . . a new Jumper in the latest shade

THANKS TO:

Tintex

The Astonishing New Dye

"Tints as you rinse"

30 GLORIOUS LASTING TINTEX COLOURS!
GREY BOX.—For tinting and dyeing silk, cotton, wool and linen.
BLUE BOX.—For lace-trimmed real silks (tints the silk—cotton lace remains white or original colour).
COLOUR REMOVER.—For taking out dark colour when you want to dye things lighter.

Send for Free Home Testing Outfit and see for yourself how easy it is to use Tintex. Sold at Chemists, Grocers, Drapers and all Stores. In case of difficulty in obtaining, send remittance with name of your dealer to BRITISH TINTEX & DYE PRODUCTS, LTD., Suite 33x, 252-260 Regent Street, London, W.1.

began giving 'advertising entertainments' with the cinematograph the same year.

The most sophisticated of the pioneer advertising films were made by the great French innovator Georges Méliès, who also made the earliest trick films and the earliest 'blue movies'. Méliès' first advertising film, made at his studio at Montreuil-sous-Bois, was for Bornibus mustard. The scene was a restaurant. Two diners get into an argument which grows so heated that they begin to pelt each other with mustard. The camera then cuts to a black table top on which a jumble of white letters are scattered at random. The letters are seen to form themselves into the slogan *Bornibus, sa moutarde et ses cornichons à la façon de la mère Marianne* – all except the 's' of 'Bornibus', which is unable to find its correct place and keeps bumping into the other letters. Méliès recalled that the erratic 's' was always greeted with gales of laughter.

Subsequent Méliès productions advertised shoe polish, flour, Chocolat Ménier, tortoiseshell combs, Moritz Beer, Mystère corsets, Xour Lotion (hair restorer), Delion hats and Dewar's Whisky. In the last named, ancestors step down from family portraits to sample the product. The Delion commercial showed live rabbits being pushed into one end of a Heath Robinson-type machine and emerging as fur hats at the other. An attempt was made to placate the animal lovers in the audience by then reversing the film to show the hats entering the machine and becoming live rabbits again. These films were projected on an open-air screen in the Boulevard des Italiens in Paris by Méliès' young daughter Georgette.

The earliest known advertising film in colour was *Das Wunder/The Wonder* (Ger 25), an animated cartoon coloured directly onto the prints by means of a stencilling process. Directed by Julius Pinschewer, the two-minute film advertised 'World-renowned Kantorwicz Liqueur' and was notable not only for its colour but also its use of expressionism in the animated designs, some of them wholly abstract, of animator Walter Ruttmann.

The first British all-colour advertising film was *It's An Ill Wind* (GB 29), made for Tintex Dyes of London. The film related the drama of an office boy emptying a bottle of ink over the typist heroine's jumper. However, with the aid of Tintex Colour Remover and Tintex Dye, the jumper is made like new in the latest fashionable colour.

The first talkie advertising film was *Die Chinesische Nachtigall/The Chinese Nightingale* (Ger 28), an animated silhouette version of the Hans Andersen fairy tale made by the Tri-Ergon Co. of Berlin to advertise a new process they had developed for disc recording. Although the use of synchronised discs was common to many early sound film systems, the process Tri-Ergon were promoting had no apparent connection with film-making, their advertising talkie being made by the sound-on-film process they had pioneered six years earlier.

Britain's first advertising talkie was *Meet Mr York* (GB 29), a cartoon with animation by John Noble which was directed by Bertram Phillips of British Publicity Talking Pictures for Rowntree & Co. of York.

Between 1914 and 1942 the standard length for advertising films in Britain was five minutes. Generally they contained some element of narrative and often featured famous stars, such as Jack Hulbert and Cicely Courtneidge in a 1926 comedy made for Rufflette Curtain Tape. Shortage of film stock brought the 'story' advertising film to an end in World War Two. In the USA, the use of major stars was rarer, partly due to the contract system but also because most advertising films were made in New York. One notable example, however, was a General Electric advertising film of 1933 which had Dick Powell and Bette Davis cast as a suburban couple extolling the virtues of dishwashers and garden floodlighting. Advertising films could also be an entrée for those who had yet to receive the summons to Hollywood. When the Bergström Department Store of Stockholm allowed a 16-year-old salesgirl to play a small role in *How Not to Wear Clothes* (Sweden 21) they were unwittingly launching the screen career of Greta Garbo.

AERIAL FILM

The first film shot from an aeroplane was taken by L.P. Bonvillain, a Pathé cinematographer, piloted by Wilbur Wright at Camp s'Auvours, France, in September 1908. This was over a year before the first still photograph from an aeroplane was taken at Rheims.

The first aerial film of a topical event (non-aeronautic) was made by the Warwick Trading Co. for its *Bioscope Chronicle* newsreel on 21 April 1913. The film showed the Royal Yacht *Victoria and Albert* bearing King George V across the Channel on a visit to Paris, and the arrival at Calais. The pilot, B.C. Hucks, flew the cameraman straight back to Hendon, where a representative of the film company was waiting to rush the canister back to the laboratories. The complete film of the King's journey from London to Paris, including the aerial sequences, was shown during the matinée performance at the Coliseum at 5.20 p.m. the same day.

DOCUMENTARY

The term 'documentary' was first used by L. d'Herbeumont in the January 1924 issue of *Cinéopse* (Paris), referring to sponsored and industrial films. Its earliest use in English was by John Grierson in February 1926 in his review of Robert Flaherty's *Moana* (US 26) for the *New York Sun*. Flaherty is generally acknowledged as the first to have brought form and structure to documentary films, commencing with his study of Eskimo life, *Nanook of the North* (US 22); while Grierson himself is regarded as the father of Britain's between the wars 'documentary movement'.

The first documentary film: The majority of pre-1900 films were actualities, but the first of sufficient length to be considered a legitimate documentary record of its subject was *The Cavalry School at Saumur* (Fr 97), which ran for 1330 ft (405·4 m) or about 20 min. At around the same time Joseph Perry of the Salvation Army's Limelight Division at Melbourne, Vic., Australia, began shooting some 2000 ft (609 m) of film illustrating the social work of the Salvation Army. Melbourne had been the first place in the world where the Salvation Army embarked on an organised programme of social work in addition to its traditional evangelism.

The first British documentary was Robert Paul's one-reel production *Army Life, or How Soldiers are Made* (GB 00), premiered at the Alhambra in London on 18 September 1900.

The earliest known American documentary of comparable length was American Mutoscope & Biograph's *Baby's Day* (US 05). The Library of Congress Catalogue notes: 'The subject is a day in the life of an infant supervised by a nurse. The film illustrates the various tasks necessary to properly enhance the growth and security of a small child, such as awakening, supervised play, companionship with other children, exposure to sights and scenes other than those of a nursery, bathing, and sleeping.'

The first feature-length documentaries were Paul Rainey's eight-reel *African Hunt* (US 12) and a dramatised production in five reels called *One Hundred Years of Mormonism* (US 12).

The first government grant in support of film-making was a sum of 300 crowns awarded by the Austrian Minister of Culture and Education in 1907 to Prof. Alto Arche, professor of chemistry and natural history at Staadsrealschule Wien XX, to produce educational films for distribution to schools. Arche's documentaries on manufacturing and crafts were so well made that they are still being used in Austrian schools today.

INDUSTRIAL FILMS

The first industrial film was taken by the American Mutoscope & Biograph Co. for the American Ball Nozzle Co. of Atlantic City on 18 July 1896. The production was supervised by 'agent Stewart' of the American Ball Nozzle Co. and showed the company's product in use in a States fire-engine discharging its jet at maximum pressure. The demonstration took place on North Carolina Avenue before Chief Whippey, ex-Chief Lackey and other prominent members of the Atlantic City Fire Department. The cameraman was W.K.L. Dickson, inventor of the Edison Co.'s Kinetoscope, and the film was used by agents of the American Ball Nozzle Co. as a sales aid which could be shown in a portable Mutoscope. According to D.W. Griffith's cameraman, Billy Bitzer, who joined the American Mutoscope & Biograph Co. in 1896, the firm made other industrial films of 'loom-weaving materials which the travelling salesmen could use to show merchants what they were buying' and 'very large machines, whose working parts could be demonstrated by this method better than they could by chart'.

The first British industrial film was made by Messrs Lever Bros in 1898 and showed the work carried out in the various departments of their Port Sunlight soap factory. Admission to the showing of this film, which was accompanied by variety acts, was open to those producing a coupon enclosed with packets of Sunlight Soap. Mellin's Food gave similar exhibitions the same year, with free samples for every member of the audience.

Other early sponsored films included an 1898 production by the Canadian Pacific Railroad designed to encourage emigration to Manitoba, a sales film of agricultural horse-rakes and self-binders in action made by a firm of Toronto agricultural engineers in 1899, and a documentary about the Alaskan Gold Rush of 1898–99 commissioned by the North West Transportation Co. The latter cost $40 000 to shoot, making it **the most expensive motion picture production on record at that date.** In 1904 the North Borneo Co. commissioned the Urban Trading Co. of London to make a film in Borneo as 'a way of bringing the shareholders into a direct knowledge of the country and usages where their money was invested'. Shareholders of America's Diamond Match Co. also had cause to be grateful for industrial films. In 1903 the Japanese government was negotiating with the company for the purchase of match-making machinery, but the board of the Diamond Match Co. suspected that the Japanese only wanted to see the machines in operation in order to copy them and so were unwilling to show them working. The Japanese insisted on a demonstration before purchase. Having reached stalemate, the Diamond Co. called in the Vitagraph Co. of New York to make a demonstration film showing the process without revealing details of the mechanism. The motives of the Japanese proved honourable; after seeing the film they signed a contract worth a million dollars.

NEWS FILMS

The first news film (other than sporting events, q.v.) was made by photographer Birt Acres of High Barnet, Herts, on the occasion of the opening of the Kiel Canal by Kaiser Wilhelm II (1859–1941) on 20 June 1895. Besides the arrival of the Kaiser at Holtenau aboard his yacht *Hohenzollern*, Acres took films of the

laying of a memorial stone, and of a number of other events held as part of the celebrations, including scenes of the Kaiser reviewing his troops at Hamburg and leading a procession through the streets of Berlin. He also filmed a charge of Uhlan Lancers at the Tempelhof Feld in Berlin, starting a news cameraman's tradition of taking risks in the cause of film reportage by arranging with their commander that the horsemen should charge direct at the camera. Seized with the desire to run for his life as the troop thundered towards him with drawn lances, he nevertheless continued to grind the handle of his camera and was afterwards congratulated by the CO as 'the pluckiest fellow he had ever met'. The first public screening of the films took place before the Royal Photographic Society on 14 January 1896.

The first news film shot in Britain was taken by Birt Acres on 27 June 1896 and showed the arrival of the Prince and Princess of Wales at the Cardiff Exhibition. Acres secured special permission to film the Royal party, on the proviso that he himself was not seen. Accordingly, a small aperture was cut in a canvas screen forming one side of a private walkway along which the Prince and Princess would approach the exhibition entrance. Since there was no corresponding hole for the viewfinder, Acres had to begin shooting on receipt of a signal from an official. He filmed the whole scene without being able to see anything of his subject. The film was premièred at a special Command Performance at Marlborough House on 21 July 1896.

The first British monarch to be filmed was Queen Victoria (1819–1901) during her autumn holiday at Balmoral in 1896. She recorded the event in her diary for 3 October: 'At twelve went down to below the terrace, near the ballroom, and we were all photographed by Downey by the new cinematograph process – which makes moving pictures by winding off a reel of film. We were walking up and down, and the children jumping about. Then took a turn in the pony chair, and not far from the garden cottage Nicky and Alicky planted a tree.'

Downey was the Royal Photographer. The children who jumped about included the late Duke of Windsor, who must consequently have had one of the longest records of film appearances (including three acting roles) when he died in 1972. 'Nicky and Alicky' were the Emperor Nicholas II (1868–1918) and the Empress Alexandra Feodorovna (1872–1918) of Russia, who had arrived at Balmoral for an informal visit ten days earlier. The film was 'premièred' in the Red Drawing Room at Windsor Castle on 23 November 1896.

The first American President to be filmed was Grover Cleveland (1837–1908), outgoing President on the occasion of President-designate William McKinley's inauguration at Washington DC on 4 March 1897. The inaugural parade, covered by Edison, Biograph and Lumière cameramen, and by one E.H. Amet, included shots of Cleveland, then in the last hour of his Presidency. McKinley had been filmed by

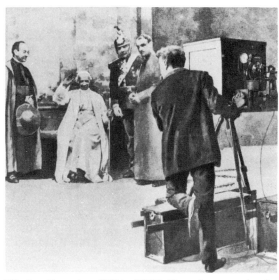

The title frame of *The Gaumont Graphic* (GB 11), one of Britain's earliest newsreels

Filming Pope Leo XIII in 1898. Note the motorised camera, powered by electricity

Biograph cameraman Billy Bitzer on 18 September 1896, shortly before the Presidential election.

The first President to speak from the screen was Calvin Coolidge (1872–1933) in an experimental newsreel made by Theodore Case on 25 July 1924 using the then embryonic Fox-Case sound-on-film system.

The first Pope to be filmed was Pope Leo XIII (reigned 1878–1903) by Biograph cameraman W.K.L. Dickson in 1898. The film, which showed the Pope in his carriage, riding in his sedan chair, walking, seated on his favourite bench in the Vatican gardens, and bestowing the Papal blessing on an audience, was premièred at Carnegie Hall in New York on 14 December 1898 in the presence of Archbishop Corrigan. Price of the best seats was $1·50 for this gala occasion.

NEWSREELS

The first newsreel was *Day by Day*, produced by Will G. Barker and presented at the Empire Theatre, Leicester Square, in 1906. It was issued daily except when fog prevented filming.

The first newsreel produced for general distribution was *Pathé-Faits Divers*, founded in Paris early in 1908 under the direction of Albert Gaveau. There were originally five cameramen, Messieurs Rischmann, Maes, Stuckbert, Keyler and Fouquet. The name was soon changed to *Pathé-Journal*. Japan's *Daimai News* is variously claimed to have been founded in 1908 and 1909. This was literally intended as a moving-picture newspaper, having been established by the influential daily *Osaka Mainichi*. *Pathé-Journal* did a reverse operation, founding a weekly illustrated newspaper of the same name in November 1912. The photographic news reportage consisted of stills from the newsreel.

The first general newsreel in Britain was *Pathé's Animated Gazette,* founded in 1910, which survived, as *Pathé News*, until February 1969.

The first newsreel in the United States was *Pathé's Weekly*, of which the first issue came out on 8 August 1911, just ten days before its rival *The Vitagraph Monthly of Current Events*. In 1914 it was replaced by *Pathé Daily News*, but in 1917 it was no longer possible to obtain the safety film stock from France which gave

It was not often that the newsreel was billed above the feature. In this case though the slaying of Bonnie and Clyde took precedence over any horse opera

Pathé the advantage over its rivals of being able to distribute daily by mail, and the newsreel reverted to weekly issue as *Pathé News* until its closure in 1956.

The first regular sound newsreel was *Movietone News*, presented at the Roxy Theater, New York, on 28 October 1928. The subjects covered included Niagara Falls, the Army-Yale football game, 'Romance of the Iron Horse', and Rodeo in New York. Regular weekly issue of *Movietone*

News to cinemas throughout the USA commenced 3 December 1928. The previous year Fox-Movietone had produced a number of 'specials', the most significant being a sound news report of Charles Lindbergh's take-off from Roosevelt Field, Long Island, for his solo transatlantic flight, shown at the Sam H. Harris Theater on 25 May 1927.

The first British sound newsreel was *British Movietone,* commencing with an issue showing the Derby and the Trooping of the Colour which was released on 9 June 1929. It survived as the last remaining newsreel produced in Britain (see below).

The first unscheduled event to be captured by the sound newsreel camera was the assassination attempt on Prince Humbert of Italy on 24 October 1929. Cameraman Jack Connolly of *Movietone* had hidden himself behind the Tomb of the Unknown Warrior in Rome in order to secure forbidden pictures of the Prince and Princess paying tribute to the Italian war dead. He had just been discovered by the police when a shot was fired at the Prince, but fortunately the camera was still running and the sound equipment operating.

The last newsreel in the United States was *Universal Newsreel*, founded as *Universal Animated Weekly* in 1913, of which the final issue was released on 22 December 1967. At its peak it was showing in 3300 cinema theatres, but with the competition of television declined to a circulation of 1100.

The last newsreel in Britain was *Movietone News*, founded as *British Movietone* in 1929 (see above), which suffered a decline from its circulation of over 2000 a week at the peak in World War II to only 200 a week when the final issue was released on 27 May 1979. The sign-off items were the Chelsea Flower Show, 'Our Capital City' (London from the air) and 'Highlights of 50 Years'.

The most costly newsreel ever made was the *Gaumont British* edition of 24 October 1934, which included scenes of the Centenary Air Race shot at Melbourne, Victoria. The Australian footage was transmitted to Britain frame by frame by beam wireless for 68 hours at a cost of some $4000 a foot or $30 264 for the brief sequence of 160 frames. The newsreel was on show in 1500 cinemas within 48 hours of transmission.

The only woman news cameraman was Dorothy Dunn, who was a member of the crew of *Universal Animated Weekly* in America during World War I.

The specialised newsreel has catered to various minorities and sectional interests since the early 20s. The first all-black newsreel was produced by the Renaissance Co. of New York in 1922 and a sound newsreel for blacks called *All-American News* was established in 1942. The last newsreel to be established anywhere in the western world, Heyns Films' *Topical News*, was founded as recently as 1975 to cater to the black population of South Africa. A number of newsreels for women were produced in America, including *Eve's Film Pictorial* in the early 1920s, the world's first colour newsreel, *McCall Fashion News* (1925), and Fox's *Fashion Forecast*, which ran from 1938–40.

Children were catered to in America by *The Junior Newsreel* (1934). Other newsreels were made by young people themselves. In England the boys of Mill Hill public school started the *Mill Hill School Animated News* in 1920. On the other side of the Atlantic *Dartmouth College News* (1928) was a regular 16 mm newsreel made by the college film club for circulation to alumni, and Culver Military Academy was producing a weekly newsreel in 1929.

A sponsored newsreel, the *Ford Animated Weekly*, was produced by the Ford Motor Co. between 1914–21, succeeded by the *Ford News*, which was for circulation to Detroit theaters only, in 1934. A different type of sponsored newsreel, *Kinograms*, which had commercials interspersing the news items, was introduced on 28 August 1931. The sound was recorded on disc – the only sound newsreel ever to use the synchronised disc system.

Naked capitalism was matched by a socialist newsreel called *The Workers' Newsreel*, of which 16 issues were produced in the USA (1931–32) by the Film & Photo League, an offshoot of the militant Workers' International Relief.

The William J. Ganz Co. of New York began issuing a monthly *Highlights of the News* for home movie buffs in 1927. A similar enterprise in Britain was Fox Photos' *Film-at-Home News*,

Hazards of the newsreel cameraman. This intrepid newsman of the thirties missed death by nine inches as the 'plane roared past

inaugurated in September 1933 at an annual subscription of £25 for a 200 ft reel monthly.

Israel produced a *Monthly Newsreel for Immigrants* between 1966–68.

The only all-cartoon newsreel was *Topical Sketch*, founded in Britain in July 1915. A regular comedy newsreel, titled *Crazy Newsreel*, was issued by 'Gaumont-Skittish News' – otherwise Gaumont-British – from 1937–39.

Soviet Russia has a satirical newsreel called *Fitil/The Fuse*, which deals chiefly with the shortcomings of the bureaucracy. Established in the days of Khruschev's 'thaw', and allowed to survive as a safety valve against discontent, each ten-minute monthly issue comprises a playlet, a documentary report and a cartoon. The documentary sequence of a recent *Fitil* showed children walking to school in the rain, despite regulations enjoining local authorities to supply transport. When the bureaucracy replied that the situation had now been rectified, another issue of *Fitil* showed the same schoolchildren still walking to school, this time in a snowstorm.

SCIENTIFIC FILMS

The first anthropological film was made by F. Reynault in 1895 of an African negress making pottery at the Colonial Exhibition in Paris. An analysis of the technique revealed by the film was published under the title 'Poterie crue et origine du tour' in the *Bulletin Société Anthropologique Paris*. The following year Reynault made film studies of the attitudes adopted by recumbent and sleeping negroes and

in 1897 he followed this with a film demonstrating tree climbing methods. In 1900 he secured the adoption of this resolution at the International Ethnographic Congress in Paris: 'All anthropological museums should add suitable film archives to their collections. The mere possession of a potters' wheel, a number of weapons or a primitive loom is not sufficient for a full understanding of their functional use; this can only be handed down to posterity by means of precise cinematographic records.'

The first anthropological film shot on location was a 3000 ft study of the tribal rites of Australian aborigines, taken by Univ. of Melbourne biologist Baldwin Spencer in 1901 with a Warwick Biograph camera at Charlotte Waters, Northern Territory. The film was accompanied by a 'sound-track' of didgeridoo music, recorded on an Edison wax cylinder as the film was being shot.

The first medical films were made by pioneer Polish cinematographer Boleslaw Matuszewski at hospitals in St Petersburg and Warsaw, beginning in May 1897. The subject matter of his earliest attempts included surgical operations – one of them a leg amputation – difficult births and the behaviour of mental patients. Matuszewski was dissatisfied with the results because his camera was defective, but the following year he purchased one of French make and in April–May 1898 he filmed at the Saint-Antoine and de la Pitié hospitals in Paris under the direction of Drs Ballet, Brissaud and Balinski. The results were shown before an invited audience at Warsaw on 3 September 1898, the most impressive films being one of nervous disorders and another of an operation involving removal of part of the skull.

The first medical films taken in Britain were made by a Dr Parchen of London in the spring of 1898 and showed a case of *locomotor ataxia*, in which the patient was unable to stand with the feet together and eyes closed, another of a patient suffering from partial paralysis, with clear views of the wasting of the muscles, and a third of the effects of hip-joint disease. In June of the same year the eminent Parisian surgeon Dr Doyen commissioned Clement Maurice to film his work. By repeated filming of the same operation, Doyen was able to refine his technique by the elimination of all wasteful and unnecessary

PIONEERS
Film can labels from some of the early production
companies, *c.* 1910–14 *(Brian Love Collection)*

Above: *Twist Around the Clock* (US 61) was released just 28 days after producer Sam Katzman decided to make a movie about the new dance craze. It was the shortest production schedule on record for a full-length feature film. (See p. 148)

Below: The serial craze began with *The Adventures of Kathlyn* (US 13). (See p. 257)

Above: *Ben Hur* (US 59) won more Oscars than any other single picture in the history of the Academy Awards – a total of 11. (See p. 234)

Below: Howard Hughes caused the first breach of the Hays Code when he exhibited *The Outlaw* (US 43) without a Seal of Approval. (See p. 192)

movements, thereby reducing the time taken to operate and increasing the patient's chances of survival. Although activated by the highest motives, the distinguished surgeon was not above a little self-advertisement. Some years later Eclipse-Radios-Urban released a film called *The Operations of Dr Doyen* (Fr 08), which showed five amputations in the goriest detail. This movie was shown as entertainment and was hugely successful, especially in Russia, where audiences regularly became hysterical and many fainted.

The first American medical film was *Epileptic Seizures* (US 05), shot at Boston with a Biograph camera by Walter G. Chase.

The first medical talkie was a film about internal urethrectomy made at King's College Hospital, London, by the Kodak Medical Department and premièred before the Royal Society of Medicine on 27 June 1929. The commentary, by Sir John Thomson-Walker FRCS, OBE, Senior Lecturer in Uriology, was on synchronised disc. The first American medical talkie was a film of Dr C.R. Murray setting a broken ankle, made at the College of Physicians and Surgeons, Columbia University in 1930. The commentary was by Dr Murray himself, who explained his technique.

The first three-dimensional medical film was made by Floyd Ramsdell and presented before the American College of Surgeons in March 1953. The subject was a stomach operation and the illusion of depth enabled students to follow the surgeon's technique more effectively than would have been possible in two dimensions.

Microscopic cinematography was first achieved by American scientist Dr Robert L. Watkins, who filmed the action of bacteria through a microscope in 1897.

X-ray cinematography was pioneered by Dr J. Macintyre of Glasgow, who showed a film of the movements of the knee joint of a frog before the Glasgow Philosophical Society in March 1897. Since X-ray motion picture film did not exist, Macintyre had roentgenograms (X-ray stills) taken in sequence and then recorded them on standard cinematographic film. This technique was the earliest application of animation. Direct kinetoentgenography, using X-ray mo-

tion picture film, was first achieved by A.E. Barclay in the USA in 1933.

The first 3-D X-ray films were made by Prof. R. Janker of the University of Bonn with an Askania R camera in 1938.

SERIALS

The first serial was the 12-episode Edison production *What Happened to Mary* (US 12), starring Mary Fuller as a foundling seeking her lost inheritance, of which the first episode was released on 26 July 1912. It has been claimed that the film was not a true serial, but a *series* of episodes each complete in itself. Although it is true that the cliff-hanger element, an essential element of later serials, was missing from *What Happened to Mary*, in fact the *dénouement* was not revealed until the final episode, and the various adventures were all part of a continuing story-line. *The Adventures of Kathlyn* (US 13) added the missing ingredient, leaving audiences in an agony of suspense at the end of each succeeding episode until the final triumph of the heroine.

The first British serial was *Boy Scouts Be Prepared* (GB 17), directed by Percy Nash in eight parts for Transatlantic films and featuring Sir Robert Baden-Powell playing himself. The story was of a squire's son and a miner's son who join the Scouts and foil a gipsy spy who is supplying fuel to U-Boats. Only three other serials were produced in Britain prior to World War II: Hepworth's *The Amazing Quest of Mr Ernest Bliss* (GB 20), starring Chrissie White and Gerald Ames; Torquay & Paignton Photoplays' *The Great London Mystery* (GB 20), starring the celebrated magician David Devant and Lady Doris Stapleton; and a solitary talkie serial, Mutual's *Lloyd of the CID*/US: *Detective Lloyd* aka *The Green Spot Mystery* (GB 31), with Charles Saunders in the title role. Between 1946–69 another 26 serials, all of them designed for children's cinema matinées, were produced in Britain.

Other countries commenced serial production with the following films: *Fantomas* (Fr 13); *Sonka, The Golden Hand* (Rus 14); *Los Misterios* (Sp 15); *Les Habitants de la Lenora* (Arg 17); *Ram Banvas* (India 18); *The Man in the Black Cape* (It 18); *La Belgique martyre* (Belg 19);

End of an era. Columbia's *Blazing the Overland Trail* (US 56) was Hollywood's last serial

---

El Automovil gris (Mex 19); *Die Herrin der Welt* (Ger 20); *El Genio del mal* (Cuba 20); *Sekai no Jo-jo/Queen of the World* (Jap 25). Besides America, France and Spain were the only countries to make a significant number of serials.

The first talkie serial was Mascot Pictures' 10-episode jungle yarn *King of the Kongo* (US 29), starring Jacqueline Logan, Walter Miller and Boris Karloff.

The longest serial was *The Hazards of Helen*, directed in 119 one-reel episodes by J.P. McGowan and James Davis for Kalem, and starring Helen Holmes (episodes 1–26), Elsie McLeod (episodes 27–49) and Helen Gibson (episodes 50–119). The first episode was released on 7 November 1914; the last on 24 February 1917. The complete picture had a running time of over 31 hours.

The last Hollywood serial was Columbia Pictures' unremarkable *Blazing the Overland Trail* (US 56), directed by Spencer Bennet.

Serial output: During the 44-year life of the episode film, American studios put out an estimated 350 silent serials and 231 talkies.

SPORTS FILMS

The first film of a sporting event was taken at the Edison Laboratories, West Orange, NJ, and depicted a six-round boxing match fought between Mike Leonard and Jack Cushing on 14 June 1894. Leonard, the better known fighter, was paid $150 for his services and his opponent $50. The ring was only 12 ft (3·6 m) square, in order that all the action might be followed by the immobile camera. Having knocked Cushing out in the last round, Leonard summed up after the fight: 'I hit him when I liked and where I liked. I'd hit him oftener, only Mr Edison treated me right and I didn't want to be too quick for his machine. I generally hit 'im in the face, because I felt sorry for his family and thought I would select the only place that couldn't be disfigured.' The film was premièred at a Kinetoscope parlour at 83 Nassau Street, New York, probably at the beginning of August 1894. From a commercial point of view it was not a complete success, as each round was shown in a different Kinetoscope peep-show machine for which a separate charge was made. At 10c a round, it cost 60c to see the whole fight, so most patrons opted to pay a single dime to witness the knockout round only.

The first British sports film and the first anywhere in the world of a regularly scheduled sporting contest was made by Birt Acres of the Oxford and Cambridge Boat Race on 30 March 1895. **The first motion picture of a horse race** was also taken by Acres, of the Epsom Derby on 29 May 1895. **The earliest known film of a football match** was made by R.W. Paul at Newcastle upon Tyne, England, in November 1896. **Baseball** was the subject of a dramatic movie, Edison's *Casey at the Bat* (US 99), just before the turn of the century and **the earliest known record of a basketball game** was filmed by American Mutoscope & Biograph at Missouri Valley College (a girls' school) in 1904.

TRAVELOGUE

The first travelogue of sufficient length and variety to warrant the term was R.W. Paul's *Tour in Spain and Portugal* (GB 96), a 600 ft film made by cameraman Henry Short during a five-week tour of the two countries in September 1896. It comprised 14 scenes of Lisbon, Madrid and Seville, including a bullfight, and was premièred at the Alhambra Theatre in London on 22 October 1896. At the end of October,

Paul issued a booklet publicising the film, a forerunner of the exhibitors' campaign book.

The term 'travelogue' was coined by Burton Holmes, who presented his first such movie, a 50ft view of St Peter's, Rome, at Oak Park Presbyterian Church, Chicago, in 1897.

WAR FILM

The first war to be filmed was the Graeco-Turkish War of 1897. Sole cameraman in the field was British war correspondent and pioneer cinematographer Frederick Villiers (1852–1922), who filmed the Battle of Volo in Thessaly, Greece, in April. He wrote in his memoirs: 'Luckily I was well housed during the fighting in front of Volo, for the British consul insisted on my residing at the consulate. To me it was campaigning in luxury. From the balcony of the residence I could always see of a morning when the Turks opened fire up on Valestino Plateau; then I would drive with my camera outfit to the battlefield, taking my bicycle with me in the carriage. After I had secured a few reels of movies, if the Turks pressed too hard on our lines I would throw my camera into the vehicle and send it out of action, and at nightfall, after the fight, I would trundle back down the hill to dinner.' These first historic war films were destined never to be seen by the public. When he finally arrived back in London, Villiers found to his consternation that Star Films of Paris had already flooded the market with dramatised reconstructions of the campaign and there was no demand for the genuine article. He was equally unlucky the following year when he filmed the Battle of Omdurman from a gunboat on the Nile. As the gunboat's battery opened up, the camera tripod collapsed and Villiers' camera hit the deck, the magazine fell out and the film was exposed to the light.

America's first war film was a 30-minute record of events during the Spanish-American War released by Vitagraph under the title *Fighting with our Boys in Cuba* (US 98). It was made by the two young English founders of Vitagraph, J. Stuart Blackton and Albert E. Smith, who embarked for Cuba on the transport carrying Colonel Teddy Roosevelt and his celebrated Rough Riders. Having filmed the landing at Siboney on 17 June 1898, Blackton and Smith spent the next few days covering life in camp and then obtained their first battle scenes when the Rough Riders made their victorious attack on the Spanish position on San Juan Hill. After two Mauser bullets had passed through the camera, Blackton and Smith decided on a strategic withdrawal and took the next transport back to Tampa, Fla. They left just as the American fleet was engaging the Spanish fleet, and were so chagrined at missing this opportunity that on reaching New York they promptly faked the battle in a tank in the Vitagraph offices, using cut-out cardboard models of the ships and miniature charges of gunpowder, and showed the resulting *Battle of Santiago Bay* (US 98) as a supposedly genuine news film together with their actuality footage of the Rough Riders.

Despite the presence of two other war cameramen in Cuba, Billy Bitzer representing the Mutoscope & Biograph Co. and William Paley for Hollaman & Eaves, all footage of the Spanish-American War has been lost; none of Villiers' Graeco-Turkish War films survive, nor does the work of at least two other cameramen besides Villiers who were filming during the Sudan War of 1898. The earliest surviving news film taken during a military campaign consists of scenes of the 5th Northumberland Fusiliers at Orange River, South Africa, during the Boer War of 1899–1902. Made by John Bennett Stanford on 12 November 1899, it is preserved in the National Film Archive.

CHAPTER 17

TELEVISION AND THE MOVIES

TELEVISION

The first film shown on television was British Sound Film Productions' *The Bride* (GB 29), featuring George Robey, which was transmitted experimentally from the Baird Television Studios in Long Acre, London, on 19 August 1929.

The first television station to show films as part of their regular programme service was the De Forest Radio Corporation's W2XCD Passaic, NJ, commencing 1 March 1931. These were mainly documentary and travel shorts, two of the earliest to be aired being *People Who Live in the Desert* (US 30) and *Lumbering in British Columbia* (Can 30). Five days later the Baird Co. followed suit in Britain, starting with a boxing short and airing a Chaplin comedy with the Keystone Cops on 9 March.

The first full-length feature film shown on television was *Police Patrol* (US 25), transmitted in six daily episodes by W2XCD Passaic, NJ, 6–11 April 1931. Directed by Burton King for Gotham Productions, it related the story of a New York policeman (James Kirkwood) who arrests a girl thief (Edna Murphy) the exact double of his sweetheart (also Edna Murphy).

The first feature film shown in scheduled service in Britain was *The Student of Prague* (Ger 35), starring Anton Walbrook and Dorothea Wieck, transmitted by the BBC on 14 August 1938.

 The first film made for television was a short silent comedy titled *Morgenstude hat Gold im Munde/The Early Bird Catches the Worm* (Ger 30), produced by F. Banneitz of Commerz-Film AG, Berlin, on behalf of the German Reichs-Rundfunkgesellschaft. Intended specially for transmission by low-definition television, the actors' movements were exaggerated for visual emphasis and the costumes were designed for greater tonal contrast than in a normal cinema film.

The first film drama made for high definition television was *Wer fuhr IIA 2992?/Who was Driving Car Number IIA 2992?* (Ger 39), a thriller scripted by Gerhart W. Göbel of the Reichspost and produced by UFA in Berlin. Göbel devised the plot after seeing a police announcement on television appealing for help in a murder case. The scenario centred round a hit-and-run driver, since the Nazi Propaganda Ministry would not allow murder as a theme for films to be shown abroad. The film was first shown during television demonstrations in Bucharest and Sofia in 1940 and was also used after the war when the German Post Office resumed experimental transmissions in 1950.

The first British television film drama and **the first TV film aired in scheduled service** was *A Dinner Date with Death* (GB 50), a pilot for a TV series titled *The Man who Walks by Night*, shot at Marylebone Studios by Vizio Films Ltd, 11–14 July 1949, and transmitted by BBC Television on 28 September 1950. Produced by Roy Plomley of *Desert Island Discs* fame, the film was directed by Eric Fawcett, scripted by Duncan Ross, and starred Patricia Jessel and James Cairncross. Designed for a half-hour programme with a break for commercials, it was also **the first British television drama to be televised on network TV in America.**

The first feature-length television film or TVM was *High Tor* (US 56), a whimsical ghost story starring Bing Crosby as an idealist who refuses to sell High Tor, a peak of the Palisades on the Hudson River, to property speculators. The film, networked coast-to-coast on 10 March 1956, was shot in twelve days at a cost of $350 000 and is chiefly notable for the fact that it featured Julie Andrews in her American TV debut. *Films in Review*'s critic commented: 'The commercials were a welcome relief'.

In 1931 *Police Patrol* (US 25), a now forgotten movie, earned the distinction of being the first full-length feature shown on television

The first of the major Hollywood studios to sell television rights to its films was RKO in December 1955. The studio's entire pre-1949 film library of 740 features was purchased from Howard Hughes by Thomas F. O'Neil of General Teleradio Inc. for a package deal price variously reported as $15 million and $25 million. First of the RKO package to reach the small screen was *King Kong* (US 33) early in 1956. New York's WOR-TV was so overwhelmed at its good fortune in having a genuine Hollywood release to play – formerly only foreign product had been aired – that they transmitted it twice every day for a week. Once RKO had breached the big studios' agreement to have no truck with the tube, the others followed suit, Warner Bros selling off their pre-1949 library to Associated Artists Productions for $21 million in February 1956.

The first feature film shown on BBC television – Anton Walbrook *(centre)* in *The Student of Prague* (Ger 35)

The first motion picture based on a television play was a Merton Park 'B' picture directed by Michael McCarthy titled *Assassin for Hire* (GB 51), scripted by Rex Rienits from his own 1950 TV production.

The first American film from a TV play was Delbert Mann's *Marty* (US 55), with Ernest Borgnine, from writer Paddy Chayevsky's acclaimed TV production about a shy New York butcher courting an equally shy schoolteacher. The motion picture version, which won Academy Awards for Best Picture, Best Director, Best Actor and Best Screenplay, was very much in the TV genre of simple narratives about simple people in a familiar setting, and at variance with Hollywood's fantasy world of the rich and successful living in a world of opulent but emotionally wrought make-believe.

The first television series based on a film was the BBC's 20-year long marathon *Dixon of Dock Green* (1955–76), starring Jack Warner in the role of Dixon, who had actually been killed off in *The Blue Lamp* (GB 49). In the USA *Peyton Place* (US 57) gave rise to the 1964–69 TV series of the same name; *Coogan's Bluff* (US 68), about a lawman from Arizona (Clint Eastwood) who goes to New York to extradite a murderer, was the basis of the long-running TV series *McCloud*; *Madigan* (US 68), about a tough New York cop (Richard Widmark), spawned a TV series with the same title; and *Paper Moon* (US 73), which brought Tatum O'Neal to fame as the nine-year-old partner of a small-time con-man,

did the same for the talented Jodie Foster in the TV spin-off. Similarly, Alan Alda established his reputation playing the Hawkeye role in the TV series of *M*A*S*H* that Donald Sutherland had created in the 1970 movie. The sci-fi picture *Logan's Run* (US 76) offered the attractions of the then unknown Farrah Fawcett in a supporting role and the producers of the TV series doubtless regret that they omitted to seek her services before she was offered *Charlie's Angels*.

The first motion picture based on a TV series was *It's a Great Day* (GB 56), with the original cast of Roland and Michael Pertwee's TV series *The Groves*. The adaptation of TV series as feature films appears to be a peculiarly British phenomenon. Others have been: *Johnny, You're Wanted* (GB 56); *I Only Arsked!* (GB 58); *Life in Emergency Ward 10* (GB 59); *Inn for Trouble* (GB 60) – based on *The Larkins; Bottoms Up!* (GB 60) – based on *Whacko!*; *Dr Who and the Daleks* (GB 65); *Daleks – Invasion Earth 2150 AD* (GB 66); *Till Death Do Us Part* (GB 68); *Pufnstuf* (US 70); *On the Buses* (GB 71); *Up Pompeii* (GB 71); *Please Sir* (GB 71); *The Alf Garnet Saga* (GB 72); *Never Mind the Quality, Feel the Width* (GB 72); *Father Dear Father* (GB 72); *The Lovers!* (GB 72); *Doomwatch* (GB 72); *Steptoe and Son* (GB 72); *For the Love of Ada* (GB 72); *Mutiny on the Buses* (GB 72); *Bless This House* (GB 72); *Nearest and Dearest* (GB 72); *Steptoe and Son Ride Again* (GB 73); *Holiday on the Buses* (GB 73); *Man at the Top* (GB 73); *Man About the House* (GB 74); *No. 96* (Aus 74); *The Likely Lads* (GB 76); *Sweeney* (GB 76); *Are You Being Served* (GB 77); *Sweeney 2* (GB 78); *The Muppet Movie* (US 79); *Star Trek – The Motion Picture* (US 79); *Rising Damp* (GB 80); *George and Mildred* (GB 80).

TV versions of theatrical motion pictures: Films shown on television are generally cut to fit the available programme time, but occasionally the reverse takes place. The TV versions of *Requiem for a Heavyweight* (US 62), *Earthquake* (US 74), and *Airport 77* (US 77) were all expanded by the inclusion of footage edited out of the theatrical version. The two *Godfather* movies (US 71 and US 74) were combined in 1978 to make one marathon TVM lasting $7\frac{1}{2}$ hours. Titled *Mario Puzo's The Godfather. The Complete Novel for Television*, the new version was not only resequenced, so that the saga was related chronologically, but also set a record for expansion – some 75 minutes of out-takes, equivalent to a short feature by itself, was added to the film. The material added to *Earthquake* actually introduced a new character (played by Debralie Scott) and in the case of Joseph Losey's *Secret Ceremony* (GB 68), the producers shot additional scenes three years later to enable the film to fit a two-hour slot on American television. The additions, according to Losey, 'exactly reversed the meaning and intention of my film'.

The most popular film ever shown on US television was *Gone with the Wind* (US 39), which scored a Nielsen rating of 47·6 (ie 47·6 per cent of all sets monitored were showing the film) and a 65 share (65 per cent of all sets turned on in monitored homes were tuned to the film) when the first part was aired on 7 November 1976. The second part was transmitted the following day, scoring a Nielsen rating of 47·4 and a 64 share.

The first feature film to be premièred on television was *African Journey* (Fr 47), with Victor Francen and Harry Baur, which was transmitted by WNBT New York on 1 January 1948.

The first feature to be premièred on network television in the USA was *The Constant Husband* (GB 55), with Rex Harrison and Kay Kendall, transmitted by NBC on 6 November 1955.

The highest fee paid for television rights to a movie was $35 million by CBS to MGM in April 1978 to televise *Gone with the Wind* (US 39) 20 times over the following 20 years. The value of the TV rights represented about 6½ times the production cost of the film.

The highest price paid for British TV rights to a movie was an unconfirmed £2 250 000 by the BBC for *The Sound of Music* (US 65) in 1978.

The lowest fees paid for film rights by any national TV network is by Haiti, where US product earns $75–100. **The most profitable market outside the US** is West Germany, where the price range for Hollywood features is generally $50 000–150 000. The two British networks expect to pay within the $40 000–100 000 price range.

In the US home market, new films with star names but only modest box-office potential sell to the networks for figures in the $3·5–4·5 million region.

CHAPTER 18

AMATEUR FILMS

The first home-movie outfit was the 35 mm Motorgraph projector-cum-ciné camera offered for sale at 12 gns (£12·60) by W. Watson & Sons of High Holborn and advertised for sale in the *British Journal of Photography Almanac* in November 1896. Like most early amateur projectors, it was designed to be used in conjunction with a magic lantern as light source. The machine itself was tiny, measuring only $6 \times 4 \times 5\frac{1}{2}$ in ($15 \times 10 \times 14$ cm), and was undoubtedly the first camera small enough to be held in the hand. However, due to the wide arc of the turning handle – the name Motorgraph was a misnomer, as it was not motorised – it would have been unsteady unless mounted on a tripod. Used as a projector, the film ran through the gate into a basket, since there was no take-up spool; for use as a camera, film magazines were fitted to the top and bottom. Watson's also supplied a range of about 100 films available to the home-movie enthusiast.

The first sub-standard gauge home-movie outfit was the Birtac, also a combined camera and projector, which was designed by pioneer film-maker Birt Acres and marketed in Britain in 1898 at a price of 10 gns (£10·50), or 12 gns (£12·60) including a developing and printing outfit. The film used was 17·5 mm gauge, chosen because it could be produced by simply slitting standard 35 mm film down the middle. It was supplied in 20 ft daylight-loading cartridges at 2s 6d (12$\frac{1}{2}$p) a roll. For projection illumination an upright Welsbach mantle fed from the domestic gas supply was used, the gas being pressurised in a bag with weights loaded on

to it. Picture size was claimed to be up to 3×4 ft ($0·9 \times 1·2$ m).

The first commercially produced films on sub-standard stock for home use were 25 ft subjects in 17·5 mm gauge offered by the Warwick Trading Co. in April 1899 at 10s (50p) each. They could be shown on the Birtac or the Warwick Trading Co.'s own Biokam projector.

An astonishing range of home movie outfits was available to the Victorian amateur cinematographer. Besides the Motorgraph (1896), the Birtac (1898) and the Biokam (1899), English enthusiasts had the choice of the Cynnagraph projector, marketed at 5 gns (£5·25) in September 1898, the French-made Pocket Chrono of 1899 at £7, or the La Petite – British made despite its name – offered for £5 10s (£5·50) in 1900. Across the Channel, Oskar Messter of Berlin listed an Amateur-Kinetograph, plus library of films for home viewing, in his October 1897 catalogue. In the same year Reulos & Goudeau of Paris produced the Mirographe and it was they who were to coin the term 'amateur cinematography' for the hobby in 1900. In 1899 Faller's 'cinématographe des familles' was introduced and also **the first motorised amateur cine camera,** the Gaumont Pocket Chrono.

Considering the number of home movie outfits which were available by 1900, it is surprising how little is recorded about the pioneer amateur film-makers themselves. None of their films are known to survive and few of their names have come down to us. **The earliest amateur film that can be positively dated** (though

The world's first home movie outfit. The front part of the 1896 Motorgraph could be detached for use as a cine-camera; in conjunction with the lantern at the rear it was a serviceable projector

no longer extant) was made by Russian enthusiast A.P. Fedetsky, who shot some scenes of Cossack trick riders at Kharkov on 29 September 1896. In Britain, the same year, William George Barker started to make his own films; when he had a sufficient number to make up a programme he began giving free film shows. Barker was the first of many amateurs so smitten with cinematography that he decided to turn professional. In 1901 he founded the Autoscope Co. and became one of Britain's major studio heads of the silent era. The first woman known to have taken up the hobby was a Mrs Main, who received favourable mention in Cecil Hepworth's *Animated Photography: The ABC of the Cinematograph* (London 1900) for her 'animated pictures of snow sports in the Alpine regions' – evidence that the holiday home movie was pioneered in the reign of Queen Victoria.

The first private cinema was installed at Esplanade House, Bombay, by millionaire industrialist Jamshedjee Tata in 1898.

The first royal cinematographer was the Crown Prince of Siam, whose enthusiasm for the hobby was noted in 1914. He also had his own private cinema in the Palace at Bangkok.

The first 16mm camera and projector was the Ciné-Kodak Model A and the Kodascope Model A, respectively, both marketed by the Eastman Kodak Co. of Rochester, NY, on 5 July 1923. The original intention when development of the new gauge began under J.G. Capstaff in 1920 was to introduce a 17·5mm safety film, but this was rejected owing to the

possibility of unscrupulous dealers splitting 35mm nitrate stock and selling it to amateurs. The choice of 16mm was a purely arbitrary one, being close to 17·5mm but obviating this danger. The immediate success of 16mm was mainly due to the fact that the orthochromatic safety film supplied by Kodak served as both negative and positive (the positive print being produced on the exposed film by a reversal process), reducing costs considerably.

The first 8mm camera and projector was introduced by Eastman Kodak in August 1932. The camera used a special 16mm film which was run through twice, once in each direction, then slit down the middle after processing. This almost halved the cost of home-movie making. Super-8mm was introduced in 1965. The perforations were made smaller to allow a 50 per cent larger frame, and consequently much improved definition.

For other sub-standard film sizes *see* GAUGES (p. 141).

The first amateur cine club was Cambridge University Kinema Club, founded by Peter Le Neve Foster and friends on 28 November 1923. The club's first production was *The Witches' Fiddle* (GB 24). The first British club open to general membership was the Amateur Cinematographers' Association, established in May 1926 with studios in Upper Charlton Street, London W1. The first provincial club open to all was Owlpen Pictures of Bowdon, Cheshire, founded in June 1926.

The world's first amateur cine club open to general membership was the Barcelona Kinema Club, established at the end of 1923 with headquarters in disused studios at Horta. The first in the USA was the Motion Picture Club of the Oranges, covering East Orange and West Orange, NJ, founded in the fall of 1924. The club's inaugural production was *Love by Proxy*, a three-reel drama shot with a 16mm Cine-Kodak Model A and premièred in December 1925.

The first amateur film contest was sponsored jointly by *Photoplay* magazine and America's Amateur Cinema League and was for the best 35mm, 16mm and 9·5mm movies submitted by 15 February 1928. Prizes of $500 in each of

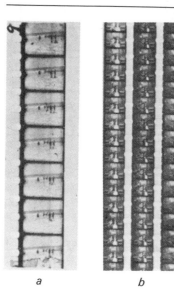

a   b   c   d

LESLIE WOOD and his invention for presenting amateur "talkies."

Above left: Amateur Gauges: (a) 17·5 mm Birtac 1898 – the first substandard gauge; (b) 22 mm Edison Home Kinetoscope 1912; (c) 28 mm Pathé K.O.K. 1912; (d) 9·5 mm Pathé 1922. These were the most popular gauges prior to the introduction of 16 mm in 1923. Home movies only began to achieve widespread popularity with the introduction of (b) and (c), the first non-inflammable film stocks for amateur use

Above right: Leslie Wood with the apparatus used for making the first amateur talkie in 1929

these divisions went respectively to the Motion Picture Club of the Oranges for their comedy *And How!*, Mr B.V. Covert of Lockport, NY for a film about quail hunting, and Clarence Underwood of St Louis for his film about St Louis Zoo. The producer of *And How!*, refrigerator engineer Russell T. Ervin, was awarded a five-year contract with Fox on the strength of the picture.

The first British contest was organised by the committee of the National Ciné Convention for films submitted by 17 October 1929. There were 14 classes of award, including Best Amateur Film Play, Best Travelogue, Best Topical, Best Colour, Best Trick Photography, Best Cartoon and Best Film Illustrating a Gramophone Record. Entries were judged by two directors, the Hon. Anthony Asquith and the Hon. Ivor Montagu, and Danish star Carl Brisson.

The first home talkie projector was the Baker Kinematograph, produced in Canada in 1904. The images of the film were arranged in a spiral on a disc and shown in synchronisation with accompanying sound discs played on a gramophone. The first to use conventional film was the 16 mm De Vry Ciné-Tone, a synchronised record apparatus working on the same principle as Warner's Vitaphone system. It was marketed in the USA at $250 in the spring of 1929 for use with a library of De Vry Ciné-Tone home talkies. The first to use sound-on-film was RCA's 16 mm Model PG-30, introduced in the USA in 1930. In Britain five 16 mm sound projectors appeared on the market in 1931 – the RCA Portable Home Talkie, the Talkiephone, the Gaumont Acoustic Portable, the Reylik and the Animatophone.

The first amateur talkie was *The Opera Singer* (GB 29), made on 9·5 mm stock by Apex Motion Pictures of London by a process called 'Cinephone'. Devised by Leslie Wood, the technique used was not divulged. The members of the group asserted categorically that it was not a synchronised disc system and would only admit to having acquired the equipment needed 'from Caledonian Market on Christmas Eve and a suburban lunatic asylum'. The film was completed by the middle of January 1929.

The first amateur talkie in the USA was the University of Virginia's *The Highest Degree* (US 29), a three-reel comedy directed by Prof.

H.R. Pratt of the School of Dramatics and featuring members of the university dramatic society, The Virginia Players. The 35 mm film was in production in May 1929.

The first colour film for amateur use was Kodacolor, marketed in the USA by Eastman Kodak in July 1928. The two-colour additive process had been developed by French inventor R. Berthon, and Kodak had acquired the rights from the Société du Film en Colours Keller-Dorian in 1925. A special Kodacolor screen was needed ($25), as well as a banded filter for the camera ($15) and another for the projector ($18). The price of Kodacolor film stock was $6 for 50 ft. In Britain, Kodacolor was demonstrated for the first time before the Royal Photographic Society on 18 October 1928 and introduced commercially the following year.

The first three-colour film stock for amateur use was 16 mm Dufaycolor, marketed in Britain by Ilford Ltd in 1934. In the USA the first three-colour stock was 16 mm Kodachrome in 1935; 8 mm Kodachrome followed in 1936.

The first videotape cassette system for home use was Avco Cartavision, marketed at $1600 by Sears, Roebuck in the USA in the spring of 1972. Feature films on cassette were available for hire at $3–6 each and included *Stagecoach, Hamlet, High Noon, The Bridge on the River Kwai, Cactus Flower* and *The Anderson Tapes*. Maximum duration of a single cassette was 112 min.

The first cassette system using Super-8 film was the Kodak VP-1 Super-8 Video Player, launched in 1973 at $1195. Playback was on any standard TV set.

The first videodiscs of movies were launched by Philips/MCA in Atlanta, Ga., on 15 December 1978. The discs played 30 min a side and cost per album was $20 for opera and ballet, $15·95 for recent features, $9·95 for 'oldies', and $5·95 for shorts and interest subjects. A library of 108 features was available. The Magnavision player cost $695. The idea was not a new one – videodiscs of television programmes had been marketed by Major Radiovision Co. of London at 7s (35p) as far back as June 1935.

The first instant home movies were demonstrated by the Polaroid Corporation at Needham, Mass., on 26 April 1977. A cassette film having been exposed in the Polavision Camera, the cassette is then slotted into the top of a projection unit resembling a portable TV set. The film is automatically rewound and processed at the same time, being ready for viewing on the 12 in screen of the projection unit 95 seconds later. Cassettes held 42 ft of Super-8 film, lasting nearly three minutes projection time.

The first film society was the Bungei Katsudo Shashin Kai (Literary Motion-Picture Society), founded in Tokyo, Japan in 1912 with the intention of encouraging the exhibition of foreign films based on works of literary merit.

The first film society in Britain was the Stoll Picture Theatre Club, established on 3 January 1918 with an inaugural programme in which Baroness Orczy presented *The Laughing Cavalier* (GB 17), an adventure movie she had scripted from her own novel. Subscription to the society was one guinea (£1·05) a quarter, which included a season ticket and admission to the club rooms at the Stoll Picture Theatre, Kingsway. Lectures were delivered every month, beginning with popular novelist E. Temple Thurston on 'The Future of the Author for the Film', in which he castigated directors for 'insisting upon constant action to the detriment of the author's idea'. Other early speakers included T.P. O'Connor, Hannen Swaffer, Hillaire Belloc, G.K. Chesterton and St John Ervine, a selection which suggests a pronounced literary bias to the proceedings, though there were occasionally talks of a more general nature, such as 'German Film Propaganda' at the March 1918 meeting.

The first film society in Europe was Le Ciné-Club, founded in June 1920 by Louis Delluc and others at a conference held at La Pépinière cinema in Paris. It had been preceded some ten years earlier in Germany by what might be described as an anti-film society, an institution called the Goethe Society which was established 'to combat the evil influence of the cinema'.

CHAPTER 19

OUT-TAKES

● No actor has been portrayed on screen by *other* actors as often as Charlie Chaplin. It started with Leslie Henson playing Chaplin in a satire by James Barrie called *The Real Thing At Last* (GB 16), which was about an American film producer modernising *Macbeth*. In the same year Fred Evans did a Chaplin role in *Pimple – Himself and Others* (GB 16) and Essany followed with *Chase Me Charlie* (US 17), in which Graham Douglas impersonated Chaplin (who had left Essany for Mutual) in a compilation of genuine Chaplin extracts made into a story with linking footage. The Ming Hsing Film Co. of Shanghai made two 'Chaplin films' in the early 20s – *The King of Comedy Visits China* (China 22) and *Disturbance at a Peculiar Theatre* (China 22) – with British amateur actor Richard Bell taking the part of Charlie. Japan also had a home-grown Chaplin in the person of Katsuo Mikoshiba, who looked almost indistinguishable from the real thing in his baggy pants, bowler and toothbrush moustache, and Germany had her own Charlie Kaplin. The Chaplin impersonation industry seems to have come to an end with a full-scale biopic, an unauthorised *Life Story of Charles Chaplin* (GB 26) starring Chick Wango in the title role, which was suppressed and never shown.

● Six out of ten US films lose money, according to a *Financial Times* report of 5 January 1979.

● One of the most remarkable finds of lost silent films in recent years occurred at the Klondike gold rush town of Dawson City, Yukon, in 1978, where over 500 pictures dating from 1903 to 1929 were literally dug up from a hole in the

Katsuo Mikoshiba, the Nipponese Chaplin

ground. The 35mm nitrate films, many of which have not survived elsewhere, were perfectly preserved by the permafrost.

● World cinema has not always been dominated by American output. In 1908 Pathé Frères of France were selling twice as many films to the USA as the combined output of all the American production companies.

● Emil Jannings' passion for realism was such that he demanded a real derelict's clothes for his role as the aged bum in *The Way of All Flesh* (US 27). Wardrobe man Arnold MacDonald could produce nothing to satisfy him until eventually he encountered an old alcoholic on Skid Row wearing tattered rags that Jannings deemed sufficiently demeaning. When Mac-Donald returned next day to the flop house where the old man slept, he was told that he had died in the night. The clothes were acquired from the morgue in exchange for funeral expenses.

● Few films have attained such a bizarre level of realism as Barbet Schroeder's *Maitresse* (Fr 79), in which the deviants, enjoying the punishing attentions of Bulle Ogier in the title role, are played by real, volunteer masochists. Wearing masks to conceal their identity, a number brought their own instruments of torture with them.

● For the cornfield scene in *Oklahoma!* (US 55) where Gordon Macrae sings that 'the corn is as high as an elephant's eye', the producers engaged an agricultural specialist to grow corn for them to a skyscraping 16 ft (5 m). They need not have bothered. The eye of a full-grown elephant is only 8 ft (2·5 m) from the ground.

● The only British monarch to have acted in films was King Edward VIII when he was Prince of Wales. In March 1919 he performed in two patriotic war dramas – like Indian stars of today he economised on time by playing his scenes for both films at the same time. This was made easier by the fact that he was portraying himself in each and that they had remarkably similar plots. *The Power of Right* (GB 19), directed by F. Martin Thornton for Harma Photoplays, was about a colonel's son who joins the cadets and succeeds in killing an escaped German internee, while *The Warrior Strain* (GB 19) was also about a cadet, this time an Earl's son, who foils a dastardly plot by a German baron to signal the enemy from Brighton. In the latter film the Prince played a scene with Sydney Wood (as the boy's father), and another in which he presents each of the members of the cadet section with a gold watch as a reward for thwarting the wicked baron. Some years later he again played himself in BIP's *Remembrance* (GB 27), a story about disabled war veterans.

● Courtroom dramas were barely practicable on the silent screen for obvious reasons. George Beban overcame the problem, however, when he wrote, directed and starred in *The Greatest Love of All* (US 24). The film was presented at the Rivoli in New York in November 1924 with the courtroom scenes played live on stage.

Emil Jannings wore the clothes of a deceased alcoholic drifter in *The Way of All Flesh* (US 27)

● An Italian dictionary contains the word *Lollobrigidian*. It is defined as 'a landscape with prominent hills'.

● In the days when newsreel reportage was as important a means of communication as television news today, it was not unknown for battles to be delayed pending the arrival of the cameramen. On 3 January 1914 the Mexican bandit general Pancho Villa signed a contract with the Mutual Film Corporation assigning them the rights to all battle coverage in the Civil War he was fighting and undertaking that, whenever possible, battles would be fought in daylight hours and at such times as were convenient to the Mutual cameramen. Villa was as good as his word. He postponed his attack on the city of Ojinaga until the camera operator, engaged elsewhere, arrived to record the victory. In a more savage theatre of war, the Nazi destruction of Gdynia in Poland in 1939 was delayed to allow time for cameramen to move forward and film the German forces from in front as they attacked.

● Famous Players' version of David Belasco's stage hit *A Good Little Devil* (US 13) had the cast miming every line of the play.

● Douglas Fairbanks made a film called *The Habit of Happiness* (US 16) which revolved round the theory of the hero that all human misery could be cured with laughter. One scene showed Fairbanks in a flop-house on Skid Row telling jokes to the derelicts. The extras playing these outcasts were in fact real derelicts whom Fairbanks had bussed up to the studio from the nearest Skid Row and all his attempts to make them laugh with straight humour were failures. Risque stories produced some slight reaction, true blue ones provoked smiles, but only when Fairbanks plumbed the depths of obscenity and profane language was he rewarded with the gales of laughter demanded by the story line. When the letters of complaint started to come in from lip-readers, the shots of Doug as raconteur had to be redone with innocuous dialogue and intercut with the footage of the derelicts' response.

● The first Papal Pronouncement on the cinema was made by Pope Pius X (1835–1914) in 1912 and forbade the showing of films in churches.

● The Gidget series, which opened with Sandra Dee in *Gidget* (US 59), had the curious distinction of a different actress taking the title role in each of the four sequels – Deborah Walley in *Gidget Goes Hawaiian* (US 61), Cindy Carol in *Gidget Goes to Rome* (US 62), Karen Valentine in *Gidget Grows Up* (US 69) and Monie Ellis in *Gidget Gets Married* (US 71).

● When Pudovkin's *The End of St Petersburg* (USSR 27) opened in New York, the Chamber of Commerce of St Petersburg, Fla., complained that it would ruin their tourist business.

● The advent of talkies posed severe problems for developing countries with nascent film industries but no sound studios. When the silent picture *The Call of Duty* (Syria 37) was released in Damascus, its director and star, Ayoub Badri, and some of his friends would speak the dialogue into a microphone in the projection room. The audience believed that they were seeing a genuine talkie.

● MGM disposed of a 45-year accumulation of props and costumes in 1970 by selling them to international auctioneers David Weisz & Co. for $1·5 million, who auctioned the 20000 lots for a total of $9 million. The highest price paid for a costume lot was the $15000 bid by lawyer Richard Wonder for Judy Garland's size 4½ shoes from *The Wizard of Oz* (US 39), which exactly matched the price paid by a gentleman from Kansas for the full-size showboat *Cotton Blossom* from *Showboat* (US 51). (It was afterwards alleged that the genuine *Wizard of Oz* red shoes had been given away as 2nd prize in a movie fan contest in 1939.) Other lots included Tarzan's loin-cloth, Gina Lollabrigida's panties, Garbo's slouch hat, Gable's trench-coat ($1250), a bed-of-nails from *Kim* (US 51), Kim Novak's black lace panties and brassiere ($100) from *The Legend of Lylah Clare* (US 68), a grandfather clock ($8500) from *Raintree County* (US 58), Sophia Loren's bloomers ($50) from *Lady L* (Fr/It/US 65) and Bert Lahr's Cowardy Lion suit ($2400) from *The Wizard of Oz* (US 39). There were 150000 costumes in all, including enough Nazi uniforms to outfit a regiment.

● In Eftee Films' production of *The Sentimental Bloke* (Aus 32), the scene of the two-up school was given authenticity by allowing the participants to play for real money – the company's money. Filmed at the height of the Depression, this caused so much excitement among the out-of-work Aussies hired for the scene that they refused to stop playing when the director commanded 'Cut!'. Eventually police had to be called in to clear the studio.

● Geraldine Farrar's armour in *Joan the Woman* (US 16) was made of pure silver. This was not Hollywood extravagance writ large, but a practical solution to the weight problem – silver was the lightest durable metal prior to the widespread availability of aluminium.

● Von Stroheim's famous neck brace which he wore in the role of the Commandant of the POW camp in *La Grande Illusion* (Fr 37) was purchased from the protesting proprietor of a surgical appliances shop in Colmar. The shopkeeper was unwilling to sell it to von Stroheim without a doctor's prescription, but the actor was eventually able to persuade him that he would be making a contribution to screen art by acceding to the request. This was no exaggeration – the neck brace was von Stroheim's solution to the problem of how to amalgamate the roles of the German flying ace and the camp commandant – separate characters in the scenario – into one. The writer, Charles Spaak, was unwilling to compromise his script with a contrived dialogue explanation of why the flying ace had been posted to the camp, but readily accepted von Stroheim's suggestion that a visible sign of injury, such as the neck brace, provided all the explanation needed.

● In 1916, Danish scriptwriter Jens Locher's *How to Write a Film* advised that 'The plot should be contemporary and should be enacted among the upper classes. Films taking place among poor people or peasants are not accepted. Neither are historical, romantic or national pieces.'

● An item under the heading of 'Road Improvements' in the Bengali government accounts for the financial year 1954–55 marks the emergence of international Indian cinema. Since there was no provision in Bengal's budget for grants to aspiring film-makers, Prime Minister Dr B.C. Roy discreetly charged the government grant

Doug surrounded by real derelicts in *The Habit of Happiness* (US 16) – clean jokes failed to raise a smile

for novice director Satyajit Ray's classic *Pather Panchali* (India 55) to the road fund.

● All the screen tests made for the leading role in *PT 109* (US 63) were viewed at the White House by President John F. Kennedy, who personally selected Cliff Robertson to play the part of himself.

● Still 'movies' might be thought to negate the whole purpose of cinematography, but there have been at least two features consisting entirely of still photographs filmed – Agnes Varda's *Salut des Cubains* (Fr 63) and Alan Sekers' *The Arp Statue* (GB 71), about the relationship of a sculptor (Francois Hugo) with a model girl (Mel Lamb).

Mel Lamb in *The Arp Statue* (GB 71) – the whole film consisted of stills

● During the last war, enemy newsreels were regarded as a valuable intelligence source, but the problem was gaining access to them. The British War Office found a solution in 1942 when they borrowed a TV set from HMV, installed it in a hut on Beachy Head with a high aerial, and assigned two RAF intelligence officers to sit and watch the Nazi-controlled transmissions from the Paris TV station. The German newsreels shown provided valuable evidence of the effects of Allied bombing and British Intelligence was kept informed from this source until the Liberation of Paris in 1944.

● One of the most spectacular unscheduled scenes in a movie was brought to the screen when Allan Dwan hired two of New York's toughest street gangs – the Hudson Dusters and the Gas House Gang – to play themselves in a dance hall scene in *Big Brother* (US 23). Both gang leaders had given a solemn undertaking to follow instructions implicitly, though the New York Police Department still decided to send up their 'hard-arm squad' in case of trouble. When the time came to remove the diffusers ('silks') from the Klieg lights ('broads'), the cameraman called out 'Take the silks off the broads'. In gangland parlance both words had a different meaning ('silks' = clothes; 'broads' = girls). The two gangs proceeded to follow what they believed to be an instruction meant for them, the hard-arm squad waded into them, and a police-gang battle was on. The whole episode was filmed and Dwan went off to rewrite the scenario to include the movies' first rumble.

● In 1907 an exhibitor wrote to *Kinematograph Weekly* saying that it was his practice to cut the titles off the films he showed, because otherwise the audience would realise from the trade marks that they came from a number of different production companies. 'I prefer', he wrote with disarming frankness, 'to foster the harmless deception that all have been made by myself, which adds to the respect paid to the show'.

● Sub-titles do not always render what has been said on screen with the strictest accuracy. The Japanese version of *The Rose Tattoo* (US 55) confused its audiences by translating 'he's mixed up in the numbers game' as 'he plays bingo'.

No special effects were used in the crucifixion scene from *Barabbas* (It/US 62) – the eclipse of the sun was real

● The darkening of the skies that heralded the termination of the agony of the Crucifixion was achieved in *Barabbas* (It/US 62) without resort to artificial lighting. Director Richard Fleischer arranged for the Crucifixion scene to be shot on location near Nice when an eclipse of the sun was due – the only occasion on which a genuine eclipse has been featured in a dramatic film.

● The majority of cinema organs which have survived are now in the hands of collectors or preservation societies. Some, though, have been put to practical use. One of the less probable last resting places of a cinema organ is the Chapel of St Francis in Wormwood Scrubs Prison, where the prisoners are uplifted by the strains of the Ealing ABC's Compton.

● In most countries prior to World War II the scandalously low pay of projectionists was proverbial. Nowhere was it worse than in China in the 1920s, where projectionists employed by the China Theatres Ltd chain received $1·20 Mexican a week. The price of a cinema ticket was $4 Mexican.

● Production of all but the most innocuous movies in the occupied countries of Europe during World War II presented seemingly insurmountable difficulties, though clandestine films were occasionally made. The most celebrated is undoubtedly Rosselini's dramatised documentary *Open City* (It 45), harbinger of Italian neo-realism. Less well-known, though equally remarkable as a feat of daring and defiance, was a studio-made anti-Nazi feature film called *Soldiers without Uniform* (Belg 44), which was made right under the noses of the occupying forces. For two years cast and crew met at the studios in Brussels at night to work on the film, which was about a Belgian resistance group helping Allied airmen to escape. As a precaution against a raid on the studios, false scripts were left about the set. These told a strongly pro-Nazi story and all the actors had to be fluent in their false roles as well as their real ones. The completed picture was released after the liberation of Brussels.

● Home-movie making before the war tended to be a pursuit of the leisured classes. In 1930 William Stull ASC suggested that amateurs wishing to adopt a trademark might consider using their coat of arms.

●The custard pie routine was evolved at the Keystone Studio in Glendale, California, by Mabel Normand, who discharged the first cinematic custard pie in the direction of Fatty Arbuckle in *A Noise from the Deep* (US 13), released on 17 July 1913. It was a true case of the biter bit, because in subsequent pictures Mabel was generally the recipient of Arbuckle's pies. Fatty Arbuckle raised the routine to an art-form. He had an unerring aim and an extraordinary physical dexterity that enabled him to hurl two pies at once in opposite directions. At first the pies, obtained from a neighbouring *pâtisserie* called Greenberg's, were the genuine custard article, but when it was found that these tended to disintegrate in the air Greenberg invented a special ballistic version with a double thickness of pastry and a filling of flour, water and whipped cream. The filling came in two flavours, blackberry if the recipient was a blonde, lemon meringue for a brunette.

●The catch-phrase 'Sex rears its ugly head' was originally coined by James R. Quirk in an editorial about *Hell's Angels* (US 30) in *Photoplay*.

The largest number of pies thrown in a custard pie sequence was 3000 in the Laurel and Hardy two-reeler *The Battle of the Century* (US 27). It undoubtedly was

---

●The ballroom of the Palace of Versailles built by MGM for *Marie Antoinette* (US 38) was larger than the magnificent 17th-century original built by Sun King Louis XIV.

●In 1929 a New York cinema booked Pudovkin's searing revolutionary tract *Mother* (USSR 26) as a special attraction for Mother's Day.

●The reason stated by Walt Disney for ceasing to make Mickey Mouse films in 1953 was that Mickey was 'too sweet tempered for modern tastes'.

●Film appreciation is a compulsory subject in Hungarian secondary schools.

●*Wild Bill Hickock* (US 23) opened with a disarming sub-title in which the star of the film, William S. Hart, apologised to the audience for the fact that he bore no resemblance at all to the historical character he was playing.

●In 1940 a decree was published in Nazi Germany forbidding anyone to enter or leave a cinema during the showing of the newsreel. The decree was enforced without difficulty; the doors of cinemas were locked until the newsreel ended. The following year Iran, struggling to maintain neutrality, introduced a statute obliging exhibitors to show both a British and a German newsreel in every programme.

●The microphones used for the scenes in *Lost Horizon* (US 37) involving the barely audible 200-year-old High Lama were so sensitive that carbonated drinks had to be banned from the set. Early scenes had needed to be reshot because stomach grumblings from the crew had registered on the soundtrack.

●In Spain the cinema has its own patron saint, Saint John Bosco (1815–88), whose 'day' is celebrated on 31 January.

●David O Selznick put out a call for 200 exceptionally thin children to be part of a crowd of starving peasants in *A Tale of Two Cities* (US 35). Because of the US Health Department regulations, Central Casting was only able to supply 35, all the others being rejected as 'undernourished' and therefore unfit for work according to law. Ironically those rejected were those most in need of the $7·50 daily fee that would have temporarily relieved their distress.

●In 1924 Hollywood stars found a new source of revenue in allowing themselves to be sculpted as shop window dummies. They received $12 for each dummy on display.

●Judging by US Department of Labor statistics, the motion picture industry is a comparatively safe one to work in. Latest available figures show an incidence of 3·6 injuries annually per hundred workers, making it considerably less hazardous than working in a museum or art gallery (5·7 per 100), less than half as dangerous as employment in a motel (7·8 per 100), and a positive haven compared to supermarkets (11·6 per 100).

●One of the most neglected subjects in American screen history is the War of Independence. Since the inception of feature films in 1912, there have only been nine US movies relating to the most celebrated episode of the nation's history and none was made for the bicentennial year in 1976. Moreover, no Hollywood studio has attempted a biopic of George Washington.

●Long before the modern terror tactic of aerial hijacking had been invented, there had been a lone instance of cinema hijacking. In 1919 John McDonagh of the Film Co. of Ireland made a clandestine film to promote the illegal Irish Republican Loan, a £250000 issue to support the Irish Republican cause. The film, made at St Edna's School, Dublin, showed the elected deputies – those of them who were not in gaol – signing the prospectus of the loan. McDonagh recalled: 'In those dangerous and exciting times no cinema owner would dare risk exhibiting the Republican loan films so it was planned for a few volunteers in fast cars to visit certain cinemas, rush the operator's box, and, at gun-point, force the operator to take off the film he was showing, and put on the Loan Film. On the appointed night, all went smoothly as arranged, and the volunteers got safely away before the British forces discovered the plot.'

●Looking for new source material, screenwriter Jerry Wald once polled 4300 librarians to ascertain what were the most enduringly popular novels. Heading the list were the works of the late Willa Cather. It transpired that Miss Cather was one of the few novelists who have made a specific provision in their wills that none of their works are ever to be adapted for the screen.

Another author whose will has proved an insuperable barrier to film-makers is Thomas Mann. It contained a clause to the effect that his masterwork *Buddenbrooks* could only be brought to the screen if it was a co-production between East and West Germany.

●Franklin D. Roosevelt had the sermon preached in the final church scene of *Mrs Miniver* (US 42) printed as an aerial propaganda leaflet and dropped over the occupied countries of Europe.

●The first films from the free world admitted into Red China were *Tora! Tora! Tora!* (US/Jap 70), *The Sound of Music* (US 65), *The Go-Between* (GB 70) and *The Tales of Beatrix Potter* (GB 71) in 1972. They were purchased principally for study purposes, but it is believed that the first and last films listed were screened to selected audiences. The first western movie to be released to cinemas was Chaplin's *Modern Times* (US 36) in 1978. The first Red Chinese film released in the USA was the anti-British tract *Lin Tse-hsu/The Opium War* (China 78), which opened at the Guild Theatre, New York, in August 1978.

● Alfred Hitchcock was under surveillance by the FBI for three months following the release of *Notorious* (US 46). Although released after the first atom bomb drop at Hiroshima, it had been made before the world learned about World War II's deadliest secret weapon. The story line of the film was about allied secret agents in Rio attempting to find out what was hidden in the cellars of German underground head-quarters. The actual nature of the secret was subordinate in the storyline to the drama occasioned by its detection so, casting about for something unfamiliar, Hitchcock and script-writer Ben Hecht decided that it might as well be the little known ore uranium that was hidden in the wine cellar. Since no one outside the top secret atomic programme was supposed to know that uranium was vital to the war effort, Hitchcock found that his purely arbitrary choice of secret had aroused alarm and suspicion amongst the authorities.

● 'The last year saw the filmdom experiencing unhappy things. One director and six movie stars were suspended from directing or palying [*sic*] on charges of smoking marijuana cigarettes.' – *Korea Year Book 1976*

● The famed World War II pin-up picture of Betty Grable in a one-piece bathing suit with her head tipped saucily over her shoulder was used officially by the US Army for instruction in aerial map reading, portions of the lady's torso being zoned off in photographic enlarge-ments.

● It was sometimes remarked, in the days before stark realism invaded the screen, that nobody in films ever seemed to feel the call of nature. As early as 1912, though, a Hungarian company called Hunnia had made a film titled *Bitter Love or Hunyadi János* (Hung 12) which was entirely about going to the lavatory – the plot centring round an aperient water called Hunyadi János which had an extraordinarily stimulating effect on the bowels.

● In 1917 Fox child star Catherine Reichert – 'Kittens' to her fans – claimed to be the only six-year-old in the USA with her name in the telephone directory.

● There is at least one attested case of someone being literally 'frightened to death' by a film. In 1956 a small boy in Oak Park, Ill. died of what the coroner described as 'a heart collapse after extraordinary tension while watching a movie'. The film was *The Creeping Unknown* (GB 55) and the scene that precipitated his death was the explosion of a space rocket.

● The Depression closed down 13 130 cinemas in the USA (1929–36).

● *Yawar Mallku/Blood of the Condor* (Bolivia 69) was so complicated that it was screened twice running at each show, the first time round with a story-teller to unravel the plot, and the second time without so that the audience could concentrate on the dialogue, much of which was in the Quecha and Aymara Amerindian dialects.

The German film *Geschichten vom Kübelkind* (W.Ger 70) was also presented in unusual fashion. The story of a wholly uninhibited girl who emerges from a dustbin to confront an imperfect world, it comprised 22 episodes lasting a total of nearly $3\frac{1}{2}$ hours. When the film was first shown at a Munich restaurant, patrons could select any of the 22 episodes and pay to have it screened. To see the whole film involved paying 22 'admissions'.

● The reverence currently accorded to the work of the more prominent pioneer film-makers was certainly not apparent when the movies were 'coming of age'. In the 1920s the negatives of no less than 1200 films by the French trick film-maker Georges Méliès, dating from the 1890s and early 1900s, were sold to a manufacturer of footwear, who melted them down to make composition soles.

● Alfred Hitchcock's famous cameo appearances began with his first suspense film, *The Lodger* (GB 26), in which he appeared *twice*, once in an office scene and the other time as one of the crowd at the arrest. (The only other double role was in *Under Capricorn* (US 49).) His appear-ances in *The Lodger* were occasioned by nothing more significant than a shortage of extras.

Subsequently, he played cameo roles in another 34 of his 54 films, finding it necessary in the later productions to appear within the first five minutes to avoid distracting audiences who were looking out for him. Among the more memorable were his fat and thin man 'before and after' pictures in a slimming advertisement on the back of a newspaper in *Lifeboat* (US 43) – since the entire action of the movie took place in a lifeboat there was no way he could play a live bit part – and his corpulent silhouette reflected onto a glass door inscribed 'Office of Vital Statistics' in *Family Plot* (US 76).

●Blushing is almost impossible to film. The only successful attempt was in *Little Old New York* (US 23), in which Marion Davies flushed prettily.

●William Boyd proposed to Elinor Faire during a take for Cecil B. DeMille's *The Volga Boatman* (US 26). Boyd as Feodor was chained to a gate waiting to be executed when he made his declaration of love to Elinor as Vera – both in and out of the story. Miss Faire was astute enough to realise the proposal was for real and not a gilding of the scenario and accepted him. The only fans privy to the engagement were lip-readers.

●In 1906 Prince Bengesco of Romania, a dashing soldier, sought the hand of the beautiful Mlle Marie Balteano. She, having heard of his reputation as a philanderer, would only agree to marry him if he kept himself free of all other liaisons for a period of two years. At the end of the period the Prince claimed his betrothed and the marriage was set for 27 August 1908. A few days before the wedding Bengesco took Marie to a cinema in Bucharest, where a news film was showing of *Roumanian Army Camp Life in Summer*. When the Prince spotted his own orderly on the screen, and then a view of his own tent, he decided it was time to go. Marie insisted on staying. The camera panned back to Bengesco's tent and with frozen horror the Prince saw the image of himself walking to the tent, then the mischievous face of Mlle Mandrea, a well-known demi-mondaine of Bucharest, emerging from the tent flap and welcoming the warrior with a kiss. Marie stormed from the cinema and the wedding was cancelled.

Garbo laughs in *Ninotchka* (US 39)

●Garbo talking (*Anna Christie* US 30) was not followed by Garbo laughing until *Ninotchka* (US 39). However, those who believed the lady incapable of such a reaction were proved correct – the laughter had to be dubbed after she had failed to produce more than a sombre Swedish chuckle.

●The story that a DeMille cameraman failed to hear the director's order to 'Turn over!' at the commencement of the Parting of the Red Sea sequence in *The Ten Commandments* (US 23) and chirped 'Ready when you are, Mr DeMille!' at the termination of the scene is, regrettably, apocryphal. However, a similar and well authenticated episode did occur during the filming of Universal's *Flirting with Death* (US 26). In a spectacular scene an entire building was dynamited so that it would collapse. As the swirling clouds of dust finally cleared to reveal a vast heap of rubble, it was also revealed that the cameraman had failed to uncover the camera lens.

●The world's first woman Chief of Police silent star Laura Oakley, who assumed office head of Universal City's Police Department on 15 March 1915. As a full municipality, Universal City had its own police and fire services, though law enforcement seldom extended beyond

Harold Lloyd's first appearance with his famous glasses in *Over the Fence* (US 17). In reality he had perfect vision

handing out speeding tickets to those who violated the city's 15mph speed limit. It did, however, on the occasion of Mrs Oakley's first arrest, which resulted in twenty cowboys being fined $5 each for illicit gambling.

● At the end of the thirties, Universal tried a novel but short-lived experiment following demands for encores during the Canadian run of *The Mikado* (US 39). Extra prints of the four most popular song sequences were made and spliced together on a reel. This was wound on a reserve projector at the Palace Theater, New York City, and every time the audience called for an encore, the projectionist stopped the film and switched to the special reel.

● The introduction of sound sent not only the stars into something akin to panic, but caused grave unease among directors, who were faced with the problem of directing a scene without being able to address the actors while they were performing. Lionel Barrymore found a temporary solution when he directed *Madame X* (US 29) by attaching thin wires to various sensitive parts of his players' anatomy and signalling coded instructions in the form of mild electric shocks.

● Among the multitude of inventions about which no more has been heard was the 'Cinematograph for the Blind', demonstrated by Dr Dussaud of the Psychological Institute in February 1901. This consisted of a machine which passed a band of images in relief under the fingers of the blind 'viewer'. Each image being in a position minutely advanced from the previous one, as on an ordinary cinematograph film, the user was supposed to obtain a tactile illusion of movement.

● Bank robber and out-of-work film actor Christian Nohel was captured after holding up the Les Halles branch of the Bank de France in February 1978. He was recognised by under-manager Mme Arlette Dubois, who had seen him playing a bank robber in *The Last Chance* (Swz 46) when it was shown on TV the night before the hold-up.

● Hollywood attempts to simulate the forces of nature were not always successful. Tod Browning transported a number of wind machines to Oxnard Beach, California for the shooting of a desert sandstorm sequence in *Under Two Flags* (US 22). However, the machines were rendered unusable – they were completely buried by a real sandstorm.

● Contrary to popular belief, Buster Keaton did once smile in a film. At the conclusion of *Le Roi des Champs Elysées* (Fr 34), in which he played his penultimate starring role, Keaton embraced the heroine and, before bestowing the final kiss, turned his head and beamed radiantly at the audience.

● Harold Lloyd's famous glasses – they were an on-screen device only – cost 75c in an opticians on Spring Street, Los Angeles. The first film in which he wore them was *Over the Fence* (US 17).

● These boots were made for eating: The shoes eaten by Charlie Chaplin in *The Gold Rush* (US 24) were made of licorice.

● A 74-year-old Copenhagen woman with defective vision had her normal sight restored by seeing the 3-D feature *Bwana Devil* (US 52).

Chaplin's *The Gold Rush* (US 24) – the boots were licorice

She had been suffering from double-vision for eight years, but on donning the Polaroid glasses necessary for 3-D, she found she could see correctly. Thereafter she wore Polaroids all the time.

● Michael Winner, currently Britain's most prolific director, made his directorial debut with an undistinguished travelogue called *This is Belgium* (GB 57). The budget was so tight that much of the film was shot in East Grinstead.

● The only known occasion on which a silent film was presented before an audience of blind people was on 26 December 1924, when a thousand sightless men, women and children attended a Rin-Tin-Tin action drama called *The Lighthouse by the Sea* (US 24) at the Piccadilly Theater, New York. The story was narrated by E.S. Colling, film critic of the *New York Evening Post*, the music being kept deliberately soft so that he could be heard above it.

● The question of whether *Gone with the Wind* (US 39) should have an intermission – no Hollywood movie had ever had one before – was hotly disputed before its release, producer David O Selznick advocating that there should be one, promotion manager Howard Dietz arguing vehemently against. The matter was resolved by having an experimental intermission at a preview and counting the number of people in the audience who went to the lavatory. Dietz had to concede defeat on the overwhelming statistical evidence that calls of nature intervene during a four-hour motion picture.

● *Krakatoa, East of Java* (US 68) wasn't. Krakatoa was 200 miles *west* of Java.

● Film-makers usually exercise caution in selecting names for fictitious characters, but coincidence of nomenclature still occasionally lands a studio in trouble. Retired news-vendor George Standbridge, who had a pitch outside Archway Station in London for 11 years, sued EMI for libel after he had seen screen actor John Laurie portray a news-vendor called George Standbridge with a pitch outside Archway Station in *Hand of Fate* (GB 75). EMI insisted that the choice of name, occupation and locale were entirely fortuitous, but accepting the hand of fate they apologised and paid damages to the real George Standbridge.

INDEX OF NAMES, SUBJECTS AND TITLES

SUBJECT

TITLE